JUNIATA COLLEGE
Huntingdon, Pennsylvania
Founded 1876

TRUTH SETS FREE

Also by Earl C. Kaylor, Jr.:
Notable American Women, 1607-1950 (Contributor)

TRUTH SETS FREE

*Juniata
Independent College in
Pennsylvania
Founded by the Brethren, 1876*

A CENTENNIAL HISTORY

Earl C. Kaylor, Jr.

South Brunswick and New York: A. S. Barnes and Company
London: Thomas Yoseloff Ltd

378.748
K23t

© 1977 by Juniata College, Huntingdon, Pennsylvania

A. S. Barnes and Co., Inc.
Cranbury, New Jersey 08512

Thomas Yoseloff Ltd
Magdalen House
136-148 Tooley Street
London SE1 2TT, England

Library of Congress Cataloging in Publication Data

Kaylor, Earl C
  Truth sets free.

  Bibliography/p.
  1. Juniata College, Huntingdon, Pa. — History.
I. Title.
LD2651.J72K39 1977   378.748'73   76-58588
SIBN 0-498-02101-7

To
Harriet
Sue
Dave
Jon

78- 7179

Contents

Preface

The historian must always try to honor Othello's plea. He must speak of people and institutions as they actually were—"nothing extenuate." That is easy to do when dealing with the distant past. It is much harder, especially in the case of this book, when it comes to the more recent period. Yet, my Hilltop colleagues have given me no quarter. "Tell it like it is," I have been slangily urged in writing of contemporary times. And so while preparing this centennial history, commissioned two years ago, I have not been deaf either to the entreaties of Othello or my friends.

Admittedly, college histories tend to overglorify, to blink dynamic tensions, to make its dramatis personae too much into saints instead of human beings. I have tried to be prudently honest. A college like ours does not survive one hundred years without its internal strains, conflicting ideas, and personality clashes. But Juniata has always been self-critical, and its motto, the title of this book, has come to symbolize a belief worth sacrificing for.

However, there is plenty of glorifying in the pages that follow. I claim the pardon that Jacob Zuck, himself a most reticent man, would surely be willing to grant me were he alive today. When Founders Hall was dedicated in 1879 he said unapologetically: "In view of our small beginning and past history, it [would be]. . .less than human for us not to boast ourselves on an occasion like this."

There were certain things I hoped to do in this book. I wanted it to be built around people as much as possible, to be abundantly anecdotal. I wanted it to be readable, structured much like a narrative, and so I geared my writing style to that end. At the same time, I wanted it to be a more or less definitive work, thorough and detailed. I had hoped to include appendices giving the names of National Alumni Association presidents, all trustees, and all faculty, administrators, and staff. But the book got too long, and this data, which appears anyway in the *Centennial Alumni Directory*, had to be cut out. Lastly, I wanted this history to be richly illustrated.

In a way, my centennial account is a cross between David Emmert's privately published twenty-fifth anniversary *Reminiscences* and the straight, factual, commissioned history by Charles C. Ellis in 1947.

Someone has said that the "potency of college memories lies in the fact that in those years we made the most memorable discoveries of our lives." I hope this book evokes among Juniatians of all ages happy thoughts of days spent on College Hill.

Acknowledgments

This centennial history has, in one sense, been a solo project. There was no staff to coordinate routine work or to provide special services. But many people have gone to great lengths to ease the burden. Dr. Robert Wagoner, assistant dean of the humanities, and Dr. Klaus Kipphan, chairman of the history department, ran interference for me the whole time, keeping academic pressures to a minimum.

In the early stages of research Nancy Swigart Shedd was of invaluable aid.

For two years Harold Brumbaugh gave me free run of the museum and its storehouse of private collections, diaries, and college memorabilia. All along he has been a ministering spirit in helping me track down data.

Equally so Robert Sabin, director of libraries, Denise Blaisdell, and others of the librarians, who dropped everything at a call or visit from me.

Some days I practically lived in the registrar's office. Thomas Nolan and his secretaries, Lois Fluke, Marcia Reynolds, and Hazel Braxton, were always graciously at my service.

Some of my students even played historical detectives in tracking down elusive information. I am especially grateful to Allan Husband '75. Helpful, too, have been Thomas Logue, Deidre Kensinger, Jay Graybeal, Jan Gable, and Cindy Sill.

Betty Kenyon, secretary to the academic dean, put up patiently with all my interruptions, as did Jodee Ruby in the student affairs office and William Alexander when he was director of institutional research. Betty Hartman, receptionist and PBX operator, squeezed time into her hectic daily schedule to lend a hand on countless occasions. Verna Horne and

Debra Lynn, Division I secretaries, gave me much of their time, too.

I owe a multifarious debt to those in the alumni and development offices: Barbara Rowe, Helen Weaver, Ruth Heaton, and Mary Ellen Lloyd. The same goes for Charles Pollock and his public relations staff: Jane Cook, Debra Peterson, and Mary Snyder.

To Barnard Taylor, former college editor who is now with the Geisinger Medical Center, Danville, Pennsylvania, in a similar capacity, I am grateful for technical advice on the format and graphics of the book. Thanks to Ralph Church of the English department, too.

I am particularly indebted to Iralene Jackson, secretary to the president, who typed the manuscript and offered many helpful suggestions.

Financial support for this history was generously provided
by
The Women's League of Juniata College
and
The Friends of the Library

TRUTH SETS FREE

Prologue:
The Founders and the Struggle
for Brethren Schools

James Quinter was in his sixty-third year when tapped to head the Brethren's Normal College. It was the summer of 1879. The Huntingdon school had just suffered a traumatic loss in the sudden death of its young principal and first teacher. The trustees, faced with a crisis, created the new office of president. Quinter was their clear choice to fill that post despite his advanced age. A churchman of singular stature, he had relocated his business in the county seat largely because of the college, and when it was incorporated he became one of its biggest stockholders.

But his fellow trustees turned to him for other reasons, too. Ever since the year 1856 his name had been vitally linked with educational reform in the Church of the Brethren. It was Quinter who initially forced the issue of higher education upon the church, sparking a revolution that culminated in the Huntingdon institution, the first permanent Brethren college. For two decades a tiny band of educationists looked to him for inspiration while carrying on a patient but hard-hitting propaganda crusade. They were stymied on every hand by antagonism, apathy, and failure, until their work took lasting hold on April 17, 1876.

Both Quinter and the cause of Brethren education had come a long way since 1856. When that year turned up on the calendar Quinter was a part-time pastor and backwoods schoolteacher in Southwestern Pennsylvania. He was a man of handsome features, with broad forehead, bushy eyebrows, and full-flowing beard. The forty-year-old preacher-teacher was living on a small, run-down farm provided as a parsonage by the George's Creek congregation in Fayette County. He was never one to quip or make small talk, and he seldom laughed. In later life, though, he always recalled his agrarian days with mirthful laughter, joking how the parishioners soon learned he was not "cut out" for a farmer.

Nobody, however, doubted his competence when behind the pulpit or in the classroom. He was one of Nicholson Township's most respected citizens, the examiner of those seeking teacher certification in the district. He was already known as a first-rate debater — sharp witted, eloquent, forceful, devastatingly logical. Within the next half-decade he would emerge as the premier Brethren polemicist in that age of formal inter-denominational debates.

But now Quinter, who had married at age thirty-four, was about to leave his flock of fourteen years and his pupils at Dogwood Hollow School, which he had organized in 1850 and which met in the local Mennonite meetinghouse. Sometime in midwinter he had announced plans to take up new duties as co-editor of the *Gospel Visitor*, the recently introduced Brethren periodical. After nearly five years this humble paper's pressroom was still a springhouse loft on a farm near Poland, Ohio.

When the *Visitor* had made its debut, Quinter began to contribute doctrinal articles under the nom de plume "Clement." His flair for writing immediately caught the publisher's eye and soon brought him the offer of an editorial post. Little did the middle-aged Quinter, who grew up in poverty in Eastern Pennsylvania, suspect that religious journalism would one day make him a man of some comfort and give his life story a belated Horatio Alger touch.

Affluence he never seemed to covet, but one ambition he had long cherished (some said since his youth): the opportunity to establish a "high school" where adolescent Brethren, surrounded by religious influences, could obtain an education beyond the grade school level. For a Dunker elder at that time such a hankering was tantamount to heresy.

But, then, Quinter was something of an educational maverick among the mid-nineteenth-century Brethren. His own schooling had been necessarily meager, much to his everlasting regret. But he had nourished his hungry mind over the years with the impressive private library he was building up, husbanding every cent he could from a scanty income to buy books. He had been one of only a very few members of the denomination to take up public school teaching after the tax-supported systems became law — the late 1830s in his case. Now, twenty years afterward, there were still but a handful of teaching Dunkers.

BRETHREN LIFE AND THOUGHT

The Brethren of the past century were notorious for their stubborn indifference to higher education, a circumstance directly related to their traditional way of life. They were a simple and "peculiar" people. Their religious heritage — the product of a Pietist-Anabaptist synthesis — derived from German ancestors who migrated to Penn's Province in the 1720s, the victims of persecution. (At first officially called German Baptist Brethren, the denomination changed its name to Church of the Brethren in 1908.)

Later generations of Brethren pioneered and followed the shifting frontier to settle together in little Dunker colonies, neighboring with their kind. ("Dunker," or "Dunkard," was a popular nickname for the Brethren, an English corruption of the German word "to baptize by immersion.") Dunkers, until the late 1800s, stayed on the farm or lived in rural villages, distrustful of the city. Some became storekeepers or learned a trade, but few entered the professions.

Their life-style, typical of kindred sects among the Pennsylvania German, cherished such values as nonconformity, nonresistance, refusal to go to court or take judicial oaths, frugality, and plain speech and dress. The sartorial badge of Brethrenism for men was the straight-collared coat, broad-brimmed hat, and full beard (sans mustache); for women it was the bonnet and prayer covering. In business transactions a Dunker's word was said to be as good as his bond.

From colonial times, therefore, the Brethren, unsophisticated and uneasy with distinctions of rank and title — everybody was either "brother" or "sister" — had manifested a deep-seated prejudice against an educated ministry. Originally, it had been the need of a trained clergy that had spurred the wholesale founding of small denominational colleges during the first half of the nineteenth century. But not so with the sectarian Brethren; they refused to place any confidence in education or in a learned leadership. New Testament literalists, they naively argued that if learning was so important Jesus would have chosen some educated men for disciples and the Apostle Paul would have founded schools along with churches. Hence no intramural pressure whatsoever was generated for educating the Brethren cloth; when the church finally did enter the field of higher education it was for another reason.

Instead, the Brethren in those days operated under a system called the "free ministry" — in which part-time preachers were elected from the ranks of the laity, receiving no salary. The highest ordained office was the eldership, attained by progressing through two lower probationary degrees. But for the bulk of elders and lower-degree ministers, nothing more than a rudimentary schooling answered all their educational needs until long after the Civil War.

Thus "worldly wisdom" came to be viewed with abhorrence by the elders controlling Annual Meeting. Three times between 1831 and 1853 the question of higher education was debated by the ruling elders. Each time they vetoed all schooling beyond the elementary level, condemning academies and colleges alike. For example, to the question in 1853, "Is it right for a brother to go to college, or teach the same?" the church fathers replied, "Considered, that we would deem college a very unsafe place for a simple follower of Christ, inasmuch as they are calculated to lead us astray from the faith and obedience of the Gospel."[1] The same warning had been given two years earlier about academies.

Such, then, was the cultural milieu out of which James Quinter came and against which he would set himself over the next two decades as a champion of liberal education.

BEGINNING OF THE BRETHREN SCHOOL MOVEMENT

Coincidental with his occupational shift in 1856, Quinter discovered a co-heretic in Henry Kurtz, his quirky employer, who had himself been privately mulling over a school project. Kurtz, born and educated in Germany, was a defrocked Lutheran dominie turned Dunker. A hump-backed man addicted to the pipe, he had lost his pastoral license in the 1820s for flirting with communal societies. Soon afterward he joined the Brethren. Their clannish ways seemed to promise supportive human relationships like those professed by communitarianism. Overcoming stiff opposition in 1851 he brought out his monthly *Gospel Visitor*, the first authorized Brethren periodical (now called the *Messenger*) and one of the oldest denominational magazines in America. At that time Kurtz was no doubt the best-educated member of the church.

Acting without delay the new editorial team informed the Brotherhood about their "contemplated school" in a rather novel fashion. Quinter, while on a debating tour back East, wrote Kurtz a letter setting forth ways of implementing their brainchild. Kurtz printed this correspondence in the March issue of the *Visitor* with parenthetical comment.

The chief purpose of the school, the letter revealed, should be "to educate young brethren for school-teachers"; secondarily, it should serve as "an auxiliary for the advancement of Gospel truth."[2] Such an institution, it was pointed out, would ensure that Brethren children would not be "deprived of a vital element of education, namely the moral and religious," an educational element, the editors felt, lacking in the public schools.

But in launching the school, Quinter stressed, there was one important desideratum: the need for "well qualified teachers — teachers possessing both literary and moral qualifications." The assistant editor then proposed a plan for finding teachers of high quality. He wrote, "Send one or two young brethren to school to qualify them for teachers . . .I would prefer poor young men who look for success in life, to their own exertions, and the blessing of heaven." He concluded his letter by outlining alternative scholarship programs interested church members could adopt in helping those persons selected for this training.

The dissenting duo knew their school proposal would horrify the hierarchy of elders, but they sincerely believed that the church needed to come out of its cultural shell if it hoped to survive. As Quinter wrote in the heat of controversy, "Shall we as a denomination throw ourselves into a hostile position against the onward march of intellectual improvement?"[3]

There was ample evidence that more and more Brethren youth had educational aspirations and were kicking over the scholastic traces. Teaching had gained new status and stability under the state public school systems, and to many farm-weary Brethren boys it seemed to offer a ticket for escape.

Some of them were finding their way to academies for their post-common school education. Until the 1870s, it must be noted, the academy and not the high school was the dominant secondary institution. Academies were basically private schools, often with church ties, and dependent upon donations, endowments, and student fees for their support. In addition to serving as surrogate high schools, they performed the popular function of training teachers (state normal schools were just coming into vogue in the 1850s).

A recurrent theme in the Kurtz-Quinter argument was that many Brethren students, especially those who attended sectarian academies, ended up defecting from the church. This attrition in membership alarmed them (Brethren at midcentury numbered about twenty thousand). They were convinced that several good Brethren "high schools" would stop this drain of talented youth.

But as expected, Quinter's letter drew immediate fire from *Visitor* readers. They argued that a church-backed school would do more harm than good. Nevertheless, the two publishers stood their ground, and in the September issue of their paper Quinter contended:

> We think it not only right that the church should encourage such institutions in which our youth may acquire useful knowledge, but we think it is her duty —a duty she owes to her God, to herself, and to the rising generation, to encourage and build up such institutions.[4]

Despite the vocal negative reaction, they expectantly moved their press to nearby Columbiana in April of 1857, giving the following explanation to their reading audience:

> It was not only to increase our facilities to send out our Publication, that we desired a more favorable location, but the idea of establishing a school, a subject heretofore introduced, to meet the want of such of the Brethren who desire better opportunities than are now enjoyed among us for obtaining an intellectual and Christian education for their youth, to prepare them for the useful occupations of life, has not been abandoned by us. The propriety of an institution of the kind contemplated, becomes more apparent. . . .[5]

But when a query on the "propriety" of a school came before Annual Meeting that May, it was put down with the verdict: "It is conforming to the world. The Apostle Paul says, 'Knowledge puffeth up but charity edifieth.' "[6]

In the June *Visitor* Quinter betrayed a hint of annoyance at the haste with which some business items on Annual Meeting's agenda had been decided. He implied that the school matter had received less attention than it deserved so that the delegates could bring the conference to a prompt end and leave for home. For the time being, however, he and Kurtz took refuge in the hope "that if it should meet the approbation of the Lord, the plan would in time be matured, and the various means for its expectations obtained."[7]

Quinter, meanwhile, was distracted by his wife's failing health, and in October her death left him with a motherless daughter. Yet, the burden of personal problems did not remove him altogether from the school struggle; he still drafted trenchant editorials.

His adversaries built their case generally on two main fears. First, education would inevitably make the Brethren proud. No longer would they be willing "to stoop so low as to engage in the common kinds of labor, or mechanical arts, to make a living," wrote one die-hard. Second, a school would lead directly to a paid and professional ministry. Dunker "free ministers," the same writer predicted, would be transformed into "gospel sellers," "making merchandize of the Gospel,. . . [and] selling it to them that will pay them the most money." In response to the alarmists, Quinter restated the purpose of the school more broadly than he had originally. Contended the co-editor:

> The design is no more to qualify young men for the ministry, than it is to qualify them for farmers, or mechanics, or school teachers, or any of the avocations of life. The design is to offer to our youth the facilities for acquiring the various branches of useful knowledge which they may wish to acquire, in order that they may be qualified for whatever calling in life their inclinations may profess. . . .[8]

Patient journalism and effective behind-the-scenes lobbying finally paid off at the 1858 Annual Meeting. The editorial pair got the go-ahead nod for their pet project when the elders announced: "Concerning the school proposed in the 'Gospel Visitor,' we think we have no right to interfere with an individual enterprise so long as there is no departure from gospel principles."[9]

What arguments carried the day were never recorded, only the terse sanctioning statement. It was a momentous decision for the church. A new era of Brethren educational history had dawned. However, as we shall see, the antischool sentiment was far from dead at Dunkerdom's grass roots.

The 1858 statement simply acquiesced in the establishment of secondary schools by church members. In no way did it imply that these schools should be regarded as official Brethren institutions although operated and capitalized by Brethren. As a result, from that time on the Brotherhood adopted a strict hands-off financial policy toward all school ventures, giving them a genuinely independent status. Later, in the 1890s, it is true the Brotherhood did lay claim to certain monitorial powers over Brethren colleges. But there was no way it could effectively coerce or penalize any college whose teachings it deemed doctrinally culpable.

EARLY ABORTIVE SCHOOL VENTURES

Ironically, the honor of starting the first Brethren school did not go to Kurtz and Quinter. In April of 1861, just as cannon were booming at Fort Sumter, Solomon Sharp of Central Pennsylvania opened up a school in Mifflin County's beautiful Big Valley. A Mennonite convert to the Dunker fold, he borrowed money from his farmer-brothers and bought

Kishacoquillas Seminary, a defunct Presbyterian plant located about ten miles from Lewistown (the brick building still stands, in good shape).

Sharp, quite possibly the first Dunker graduate of a state normal school, had earned a Bachelor of Elements degree from Millersville in 1860, and with proper credentials in hand, he made known his ambition of becoming the headmaster of a normal school or academy. At the time of his decision to purchase the bankrupt Big Valley institution the twenty-five-year-old educator was the principal of McVeytown's grade school. While teaching there he had cursorily surveyed Brethren congregations in adjacent counties. He came across a goodly number of aspiring teachers who promised their patronage if he started a secondary school in the area. Thus encouraged, he took over the former Presbyterian facility and renamed it Kishacoquillas Seminary and Normal Institute.

Coeducational, Kishacoquillas aimed to prepare its students either to teach or to qualify for sophomore standing in college. It was the first Brethren-related school to offer a curriculum that included college-level work. The seminary also introduced Dunkers to a liberal education, its course offerings embracing the classics, higher mathematics, advanced sciences, music, oil painting, and foreign languages along with regular English subjects.

Sharp operated his school until 1866, managing to survive the turbulent war years in black ink. But five years of sacrificial toil left him jaded and his wife's health broken, and so he sold it—but to someone outside the Brotherhood.

This pioneering Dunker pedagogue, who later achieved eminence as a geologist and put in stints as president of three Brethren colleges, left his mark on two of Juniata's future genitors. One of them was a farm boy named John Brumbaugh, a prize student of his at Kishacoquillas, whose experience there convinced the teenager of the need for Brethren schools. The other was twenty-year-old Jacob Zuck, whom Sharp took under his pedagogical wing at Millersville State Normal School, where he taught for a time after getting rid of the seminary. In 1868 Sharp moved to Tennessee to assume the principalship of the New Providence Institute at Maryville. When Zuck finished his studies two years later, he was very nearly lured into accepting a position as assistant principal at his former mentor's school.

Meanwhile, six months after Sharp had got his seminary underway, Quinter headed up a school of his own—but not in Columbiana as originally planned. Some friends of education in Southern Ohio bought a brick building in New Vienna and invited Kurtz and Quinter to start an academy there. Because the printing business was down at that time, the editors decided against risking a move to another location. But it was arranged for Quinter, lately remarried, to take charge of the school while still maintaining editorial ties with the *Visitor*.

In the three years New Vienna Academy operated, Quinter had the assistance of five female teachers. His principal was Oliver Miller, then one of only two Brethren with an American college diploma. The New Vienna Academy was forced to close in 1864, the victim of wartime conditions and church opposition..

Despite the church's obscurantism Quinter did not despair, remaining confirmed in his Dunkerism. This was something of a curiosity, because as a progressive he often had to play the rebel, yet he never reflected the rebel's sense of alienation. His unwavering loyalty to the church was illustrated by an incident that took place shortly after the New Vienna Academy folded. An educated minister of another denomination heard the ex-academy head preach. At the close of the service he said to him, "You have too much talent to waste on those slow Dunkards."

Replied Quinter, "You say they are slow; then I'll remain with them to help them."[10]

After the short-lived New Vienna venture, the proschool faction attempted nothing more until 1870 when a few of them in the Midwest tried to start a college at Bourbon, Indiana. Known as Salem College and taking Oberlin for a model, it billed itself as of "equal rank with the best colleges in Europe and America."[11] This latest undertaking had an auspicious beginning and finished its first year with 125 students. But internal discord developed, followed by legal entanglements, and the institution went under in 1874, at great financial loss to its investors.

THE BRUMBAUGHS ENTER THE SCHOOL STRUGGLE

Joining the educationists' cry soon after Salem College opened its doors was a pair of new voices: the Brumbaugh brothers, Henry and John. They hailed from Marklesburg, a village a few miles south of Huntingdon. In 1870 they had entered the publishing field with their paper, the *Pilgrim*. Two other Brethren periodicals were then in existence: the monthly *Visitor* (Quinter was now the editor and part-owner), and a weekly, the *Christian Family Companion*, established in 1864 by Henry Holsinger of nearby Tyrone. Holsinger's *Companion*, however, was stridently progressive and offended many Brethren who demanded another weekly with more temperate editorial policies. The Brumbaughs, tenderfoots in the printing trade, hoped to meet this need in a rival weekly publication. Henry Brumbaugh once characterized the *Pilgrim* in this way: "While it was aggressive and always on the side of liberal views, it did it in a way not to arouse antagonism or to engender strife among the church people. . . ."[12] As reformers, the *Pilgrim* publishers, conciliatory yet plucky, were the psychological doubles of Quinter.

Henry Brumbaugh was his brother's senior by a dozen years and the ascendant member of their business partnership. Born on a farm along the Raystown Branch, he began teaching school at seventeen. During the late 1850s he attended Williamsburg Academy (private) in Blair County and Cassville Seminary (Methodist), on the other side of Terrace Mountain from his home, in Trough Creek Valley. The older Brumbaugh, slight of build, his bearded face accentuated by a large nose, deep-set eyes, and wavy hair, taught nine years in Huntingdon and Blair County schools. Until after the *Pilgrim* came out he lived on the homestead farm, helping to work it while making and peddling brooms as a sideline.

In 1855, when nineteen, he became a diarist and for the next sixty years kept a meticulous record of his private and public activities—even the dates, places, titles, and texts of all the sermons he ever preached (he was called to the ministry by the James Creek congregation in 1864).[13]

A voracious reader, Henry Brumbaugh was a deviant Dunker from his youth—long before he pulled an un-Dunkerlike stunt in 1860 by eloping with his boyhood sweetheart (a Lutheran), counting down the days until the scheduled caper by coded entries in his diary. He read widely, not only in the Bible and theology, but in literature, philosophy, psychology, and history. Music also gave him pleasure, and he learned to play the melodeon in defiance of the Dunker ban on musical instruments of all kinds.

John Brumbaugh, his broad face framed by a neatly trimmed beard, shared his brother's passion for a liberal education. He also attended Cassville Seminary, afterward coming under Sharp's tutelage at Kishacoquillas. After teaching school for a while the quiet, reserved twenty-year-old Penn Township native spent a few months as Holsinger's apprentice at Tyrone before entering into the *Pilgrim* partnership in January of 1870.

Within a year after the *Pilgrim's* maiden appearance, the Brumbaugh brothers emerged as ringleaders of a school movement in Pennsylvania, apparently drawing encouragement from the early successes of Salem College. In league with them was Henry Holsinger, the firebrand *Companion* editor whose radical stance would provoke a major schism within the church in another dozen years. The three of them conferred about the project for the first time on March 4, 1871 in Marklesburg.

This meeting inspired the initial Brumbaugh editorial on higher education and Brethren schools. They insisted that "a good liberal education would be an advantage to us all," lamenting that in the absence of a Brethren school "your unworthy Editors. . .were therefore necessitated to place ourselves under sectarian influences."[14] Such an experience, they observed, made them "no worse or better," but they would have preferred going to a school "taught by our brethren."

A second confabulation by the three men followed several months later, on October 19, this time with some district elders present. Several likely locations for a school were brought up: Berlin in Somerset County and four communities in Central Pennsylvania—McVeytown, Mt. Union, Tyrone, and Martinsburg, all boasting rail service. Holsinger pressed for Berlin, near Meyersdale, where he had since relocated his paper, while the Brumbaughs favored Martinsburg, where they had plans to remove their business and introduce a secular newspaper. The *Pilgrim* editors pointed out that Martinsburg was set in a stronghold of Dunkerism and had available the building and grounds of the Juniata Collegiate Institute, then for sale.

The Pennsylvania school movement fell strangely quiescent after that midfall colloquy, probably because of little general support. Nothing more was heard editorially from the Brumbaughs on the subject for a whole twelvemonth—not until October 1872. John was then off studying at Millersville, and so it was Henry who broke the silence and tried to revive interest. In an October 1 article full of kudos for Salem College, he said emphatically: "We are, and ever were, in favor of having our children educated in Brethren's schools, not in name only, but in substance." Then he turned his attention to the dormant Keystone State project. Apropos of financial backing, he wrote:

> Donations from the world we say never, *never*. They are intended to tie our hands and fetter the truth, and besides, it is a disgrace to a church worth its millions and millions to beg the world for money to build a school.

Equally objectionable, argued Brumbaugh, was "the idea of making it a church institution" for fiscal reasons. Rather, he went on: "Let the school be gotten up as a private enterprise, similar to our periodicals. If one brother is not able, let three or four or a dozen, or even a whole district, join together." The editorial concluded by urging the need for adequate facilities in order to begin on a competitive basis:

> Let the funds be sufficient to put up good and commodious buildings and place everything on a clear and independent basis and then have brethren for officers and teachers and there will soon be plenty of brethren's children for scholars. Anything short of this can not compete with the many good unsectarian schools now in the world. Time and money is too precious to spend at schools short of the modern facilities for teaching.

By now, a close kinsman of the *Pilgrim* owners had entered the school fray, using buttonholing tactics rather than the power of the press. This was the Huntingdon physician, Dr. Andrew B. Brumbaugh, their cousin-german. An erstwhile teacher himself (nine years), the thirty-six-year-old surgeon was the first member of the Church of the Brethren to earn a medical degree (University of Pennsylvania, 1866). Before that, he had attended an academy near Newport, Perry County, and the normal school at Millersville. Born and bred on a Woodcock Valley farm, he was mechanically inclined, training himself to be ambidextrous—a skill that later stood him in good stead at the operating table. For a period of time he supported his family as a carpenter and cabinetmaker, all the while preparing himself for medical studies by poring over anatomy textbooks laid out before him on the workbench. Dr. Brumbaugh even learned tailoring in his youth and made his own wedding suit. He was a man of tremendous drive and wide interests, taking the words of Longfellow literally: "Life is real! Life is earnest!"—a line he liked to quote.[15] Dr. "A.B.," as everybody addressed him, was determined to have a Brethren school in the town where he practiced medicine. He saw the birth of the *Pilgrim* at Marklesburg as a logical step in that direction. Many times he was heard to say, "A paper and an advanced educational institution together at Huntingdon."[16] When discussing the subject, he had a habit of striking the palm of his left hand with his right fist for emphasis.

The good doctor bombarded influential Brethren with letters urging the need of an eastern school and Huntingdon as the place for it. He gladly made his Washington Street home, next to the Catholic rectory, a way-stop for church leaders passing through the area. Inevitably, house guests were treated to a buggy ride over the surrounding hills and farms and a tour of vacant West End lots. All the while they had to listen to his spiel about the town's great virtues. Sometime in the early 1870s he took a five-year lease on two corner lots at 14th and Mifflin streets, which were to be used, his diary reveals, "for a mission school or church."[17]

His first choice of locations, though, was what is now the Blair Hospital knoll. One November day in 1872 he took Henry Holsinger up there, and that feisty descendant of Alexander Mack, father of the Church of the Brethren, fairly raved about the panoramic view it afforded. It was, indeed, a splendid site for a school! That night, in the comfort of the doctor's home, he wrote for his column, "Editor's Diary":

> Before we leave Huntingdon, we must not forget to mention the beautiful site for a College. About one mile west of town, is an elevation which appears to have been especially thrown up for some public institution. The scenery is grand beyond description. At a distance can be seen the mountains and hills, dressed in their coats of many colors, overlooking the tallest steeples that rise from the town at its base. If a Normal School should be wanted in that section of country, that Normal Hill is the finest location in our knowledge.[18]

A couple of months after Dr. A. B. and Holsinger took their buggy tour, John Brumbaugh, writing for the *Pilgrim* from Millersville, made a strong plea of his own for a school in the East. He observed that of the five hundred or so students at Millersville only seven or eight came from Brethren families. These young men did not "feel at home" at secular schools, he alleged, and went on to deplore the absence of Dunkeress classmates. He warned that there were too many "temptations" at nonsectarian institutions. The *Pilgrim's* junior partner minced no words in stating his position: "Since I have been here I am more than ever impressed with the necessity of having a school conducted by the brethren, and situated among the brethren."[19]

Four Pioneers of Juniata, all pictured in old age: James Quinter, Henry B. Brumbaugh and John B. Brumbaugh, Cousin Dr. Andrew B. Brumbaugh.

But antieducationists kept bringing up the stock argument that "colleges lead pride into the church." One important elder in Franklin County about that time went around telling people—in the idiom of the Pennsylvania Dutch—"how higher education would spoil their sons, how they would come home from college dressed in fine broadcloth, wearing a high bee gum hat, swinging a little cane, and acting like dudes."[20]

A forceful *Pilgrim* editorial in April of 1873 dismissed such charges as baseless, begging the question. To those "aged brethren" frightened by innovations, the Brumbaughs countered with a warning of their own:

> Again, it is said to be something new, and therefore some object to schools. Schools among the Brethren may be something new. . . .The subject and discussion of it, however, is nothing new, and indeed it is becoming old enough, if there is any virtue in age, to demand some attention. . . .

> Schools are nothing new. They have existed for centuries, and we as a Church have, to a limited extent, availed ourselves of the advantages to be derived from them. This we may still continue to do, but unless we ourselves take hold of the work of education, the surrounding influence will certainly lead many, that may be bright and shining ornaments in the Church, away from it.

And to those who linked education to a professional ministry, the editorial offered assurances:

> There is an idea extant among part of the Brotherhood at least, that were we to establish schools the design would be to prepare our brethren for the ministry, and that our ministers would finally drift into the same channel with other Churches. . . .We can assure you, brethren, that were this so, we would be among the number that would oppose schools.[21]

This editorial provided the first inkling of the kind of school the Brumbaughs envisioned. It advised against any "high sounding" name like "college" and simply recommended "Brethren's School." The implication was that it should be a grade between common school and college—an academy—and, of course, coeducational, teaching the arts and sciences as well as the "humble principles of the Church."[22]

For some time now Dr. A. B. Brumbaugh had been importuning his *Pilgrim* relatives to relocate their business in Huntingdon instead of Martinsburg. Finally, early in 1873, they opted for the doctor's hometown. Their decision, reached while Henry was engaged in visiting possible school sites, was aided by a dream he once described to David Emmert, Juniata's first art teacher. Emmert wrote in his delightful little book, *Reminiscences of Juniata*: "So favorably impressed was the senior member of the firm by his study of the location that shortly afterwards he had a dream in which he saw a school full-fledged and a large body of students marching down one of the main streets."[23]

Huntingdon was then a bustling town of some three thousand souls and a station for two railroads. It seemed to them to give more promise for business growth than Martinsburg where their newspaper, the *Cove Echo*, had not fared too well. (The *Echo* was published from February to September 1872 under the supervision of an employee, who then bought them out.) And so, on April 1, Henry closed a deal with his cousin, Henry Brumbaugh, a prosperous Woodcock Valley farmer and brother of Dr. A. B., paying $250 for a West Huntingdon lot, at 14th and Washington streets. He made plans to begin building on it at once.

Two days prior to Christmas, Henry Brumbaugh and his family moved into an unfinished three-story brick duplex — half of it designed for living quarters, the other half for business. Eight wagons, supplied by relatives and friends, hauled the household goods and shop equipment the twelve miles to Huntingdon, while Susan, his wife, and three-year-old Harvey came by way of the Huntingdon and Broad Top Railroad. The unmarried John took a room on Penn Street above 14th.

Even though preoccupied with all the urgent problems that go with adjusting to new familial and business conditions, the Brumbaughs did not neglect the school question. Salem College's imminent demise at the turn of the new year, threatening to deprive the Brethren of their only school, fired them to push harder for one in Pennsylvania. Now ready to put their scheme to a test of popular support, they and their ally, Henry Holsinger, called a general meeting of interested members for March 16, 1874 at the Martinsburg Church.

A large gathering was on hand when that day arrived, the majority from the Central Pennsylvania region. Some prominent district elders, like the revered James Sell and Graybill Myers, spoke out persuasively in favor of a Pennsylvania school. But the opposition was represented, too, and a real difference of opinion surfaced. Henry Brumbaugh later told of one Dunker elder at the meeting who cornered him and Holsinger and said in all candor: "Well, brethren, I love *you* but I don't love your cause."[24]

The concensus, however, was to push ahead on the project and capitalize the school on a joint-stock basis. Several potential school sites were nominated, but the list was finally narrowed down to three: Huntingdon, Martinsburg, and Berlin. Brumbaugh support went to Huntingdon, but despite the advantages of railroad services and basic public utilities (waterworks and gaslights), that community had no organized Brethren church. So it was ruled out. Martinsburg was likewise dropped after it was decided to locate the school at the place which pledged the most money. The best the Morrison's Cove people could do on the spur of the moment was to raise only a few thousand dollars.

This left Berlin, sponsored by Holsinger and James Quinter, whose representatives came up with thirty-thousand dollars in pledges. Further deliberation produced a name for the prospective school: the Brethren High School of Berlin. Other action set a subscription goal of one-hundred-thousand dollars, but no payments were to be collectible until the total amount was subscribed. Holsinger was appointed to direct the fund-raising drive. He was assisted by Solomon Sharp, who came up from Tennessee where he was then a professor at Maryville College. Central and Western Pennsylvania were thoroughly canvassed, as were parts of Ohio.

The *Pilgrim* men and Quinter (since the previous year the two other Brethren organs had been consolidated under him and headquartered at Meyersdale) put their papers solidly behind this latest school movement. Henry Brumbaugh made several trips to Somerset County over the succeeding months, consulting with Holsinger, Quinter, and other promoters on campaign strategy and progress.

In April of that same spring, Lewis Kimmel — with no fanfare or advance publicity — began his Plum Creek Normal School near the village of Elderton in Armstrong County. He and Oliver Miller, who had been Quinter's assistant at the New Vienna Academy, were the first two Brethren to earn liberal arts degrees (in 1859). Kimmel's three children were the only students to show up on the morning of Plum Creek's opening.

Plum Creek went ignored by the antieducationists, but "letters to the editor" poured into the *Pilgrim* office protesting the Berlin enterprise. These were scrupulously printed along with the far fewer favorable ones. The negative letters fretted about the "dangerous outgrowths of education," or reminded readers that the scriptures did not "authorize" high schools, or kept up the hue and cry about a professional ministry. All of which drove the Brumbaughs to editorialize a bit testily in early October:

> That a school among the brethren means a paid ministry and a hundred other evil prophesies has no real existence, save in the minds of those who have come to these conclusions. . . .Hence we think it unsafe to think certain things and offer them as real, and as supports to our argument.[25]

JACOB ZUCK AND THE SCHOOL MOVEMENT

Though still forty-thousand dollars short of the projected one-hundred-thousand dollar goal by year's end and in violation of the procedural plan adopted at Martinsburg, the Berlin Brethren decided to move ahead with a school as soon as possible. They intended to utilize the Old Grove Church, one mile north of town. Holsinger got in touch with Jacob Zuck, a normal-school graduate pursuing further studies in Ohio, and tendered him the position of headmaster. Zuck had written a few proeducation articles for the church papers during the past year, quickly emerging as one of the leading apologists for the cause.

He traveled to Berlin early in January of 1875 to explore Holsinger's invitation. His visit almost ended in disaster, from the way he later told it. On the thirty-five-mile sleigh trip south from Johnstown, he and his host ran into a blinding snowstorm. Apparently the sleigh bogged down in a deep drift, and, handicapped by his bad hip, Zuck nearly succumbed to the cold before reaching the safety of a nearby farmhouse.[26]

But the Berlin scheme was destined to miscarry. First of all, Zuck's fragile health prevented him from taking over right away, and there was no one else available or willing. Years afterward, the schismatic Holsinger wistfully remarked that the Berlin movement "would, no doubt, have been successful had not Brother Zuck been attacked by one of his frequent indispositions just at the time when it was desired to open the school."[27] Then, on top of that, the depression of the early 1870s struck with a paralyzing blow, and the ambitious fund-raising campaign began to peter out.

Thus, by the end of 1875, the educationists had little to show for all their industry and promotional activity over the past two decades. Lewis Kimmel's quiet work at Plum Creek, carried on in a remote rural locale and taken seriously by few, represented their only tangible gain to date. And so while the nation busily prepared for its upcoming centennial, Brethren schoolmen faced the future with no particular enthusiasm. But this picture would abruptly change in the months ahead—all because of a fortuitous incident.

On New Year's Day 1876 a young man with a noticeable limp got off the train at Huntingdon early that afternoon. A few minutes later John Brumbaugh and Eleanor, his wife of little over a year, heard a knock on the door of their apartment in the *Pilgrim* building, home for them since setting up housekeeping. The unexpected caller was Jacob Zuck, John's good friend whom he had learned to know while at Millersville a few years back. Zuck, older than Brumbaugh by a year and a half, had returned to Millersville in the spring of 1873 for additional study in the sciences (he had graduated in 1870). But he also taught some classes and acted as a residence hall adviser. The two of them had taken to each other at once and afterward kept in close touch by letter or occasional visit.

Now, here was Zuck in the Brumbaugh home—on an impulse to stop off and pay his respects. John urged his visitor to stay overnight and entrain for home the next day, an offer gladly accepted. While the two comrades reminisced, their talk turned to the plight of education among the Brethren.

The guest said, "I'm sorry, but there's surely a pressing need for a revival of educational work among our people." Then he sighed, "But the revival can only be brought about by hard work and sacrifice on the part of the friends of education."[28]

Both Brumbaugh and Zuck, it developed, thought Holsinger had been unrealistic in his grandiose expectation of raising one-hundred-thousand dollars from within a denomination so bitterly divided on the school issue. At this point in the conversation, John Brumbaugh responded,

"All's quiet now, and no effort's being made to start a school anywhere. Let's quietly start one right here. There are a few vacant rooms in the *Pilgrim* building that could be used for this purpose."

Zuck looked at his younger friend in surprise. He replied that "he had no money and that the income from the students he might get would not pay his boarding." To which demurer, his host retorted,

"Do it on a small scale. You can board at least six months in my home without any charge. We'll not let you suffer."[29]

"I shall not forget how he looked me squarely in the eyes," Brumbaugh later recalled, "and asked, 'Do you mean it?' "

The *Pilgrim* journalist affirmed his sincerity, and that ended their conversation on the subject. "For," said John in looking back after thirty-two years, "I felt the apparent absurdity of such a proposition and supposed he did also."

But in about two months—sometime in March—John Brumbaugh received a letter in which Zuck confessed that the school proposition kept "ringing in his ears." He wrote, "I cannot see through the project financially, but am sure the Lord will supply our need. I feel sure we need a school, and if you brethren go on in sympathy and will stand by my work, I am willing to try it."[30]

Elated, the youngest of the Brumbaugh trio shared the contents of this letter with the others. They talked it over in the *Pilgrim* office.

Analyzing the status of the school movement, all three concurred on writing off the Berlin endowment fund as doomed to failure. They also discussed Plum Creek and the apathetic response of Brethren to Kimmel's current appeal for scholarship aid. On the face of it all—what with an oppositionist church and a deepening nationwide recession—they had to admit that another school effort at that moment seemed a mad idea.

But Dr. A. B. had made up his own mind that they should go ahead, regardless of adverse odds. He proposed, his diary reveals, that *"we start a school here,* and ask for students only, and do such work that the school will commend itself."[31] The others "nobly" seconded the proposal.

John was instructed to write Zuck and assure him of their cooperation. In his letter he reminded his former school chum how all three Brumbaughs had supported the Berlin cause even though they had worked to get Huntingdon selected as the school site. However, Zuck was advised, if he wished further confirmation on the attitude of the other two men, he should write them personally—which he did. The prospective teacher was also told that Henry would provide space in the *Pilgrim* building, John would guarantee free board, and Dr. A. B. would recruit students and furnish basic equipment.

Several letters were exchanged, in the course of which Zuck spelled out the nonsectarian policy that the school should follow while at the same time honoring Brethren customs. By then the month of March had passed, and only a few days remained until the announced date of the school's opening—April 17.

Jacob Zuck
The Man and His Experiment

HIS EARLY LIFE

Jacob Martin Zuck, said Emmert in his *Reminiscences,* was the "dominant spirit" in the formative years of the college. Yet, to present-day Juniatians—familiar with his name but ignorant of his background, his dreams and aspirations, his severe physical disability—their alma mater's founding teacher remains much a man of mystery. Even Emmert, in concentrating on Juniata's genitive period, provides no biographical data and gives few clues to Zuck's character and personality. But from all the material that has come to light, he emerges, in the words of Henry Holsinger, as "an ambitious, energetic young man of push and grit."[1]

Born in a log farmhouse at Claylick, near Mercersburg, Franklin County, Pennsylvania, on October 29, 1846, Zuck was the second in a family of six sons and five daughters. When an infant (age two) he fell and injured his right hip, which lamed him for life. At first he walked with crutches but afterward was able to manage with a cane.

Sickly and crippled, he was spared the drudgery of farm work. This freed him to focus on an education. He attended the Lafayette District School, where an older brother taught, although his frail health kept him home much of the time. He probably never started to school until he was eight or nine. On his first schoolday he was tagged with the nickname "limpy." To one bully whose taunts cut deeply, the maimed boy shouted defiantly,

"I can't lick you, and I wouldn't if I could, but I'll beat you in arithmetic before school is over."

Which, as it turned out, was not an idle boast.[2]

In 1863, at sixteen, he passed the examination that certified him to teach in Franklin County. As a teacher, he popularized interschool spelling bees.

Meanwhile, the quietly devout Zuck joined the Welsh Run Church of the Brethren.

STUDENT DAYS AT MILLERSVILLE

Between 1867 and 1870 Zuck spent four summers and one winter at Millersville State Normal School. He paid his own way for the first three summer terms but borrowed money for the winter and summer terms of 1870, putting himself several hundred dollars in debt when he graduated that year. Originally, he had no intention of obtaining a normal degree. As he wrote in a short journal titled *My Last Term at the Normal*, he had felt in 1867 that one session was all he needed to prepare for teaching, "his highest aim."[3] But one taste of formal education and he was hooked for good.

The twenty-four-year-old student, who roomed in Harmony Hall, did quite well his last year at Millersville, although trigonometry and Greek gave him trouble. In fact, he barely missed out as class valedictorian, so his diary claims. His one, all-absorbing extracurricular interest as a senior was the Normal Literary Society, the campus debating club, which elected him treasurer and critic but spurned him for president.

Usually abed by ten and up at five, he complained often of "headaches" and "feeling tired." "Seems I get too little sleep. Much study is a weariness to the flesh, saith the sacred writer," his diary reads for Wednesday, April 29.

He had spells of depression and self-doubt, too. The previous day he had made the anxious entry: "Wonder if *I* can succeed as a teacher? Feel discouraged sometimes. Oh the future!" Two days later, on the 26th, he wrote, "I am pretty near tired of going to school. At times I feel almost disgusted, but at other times I am contented and love to be here."

Earlier, in January, he had seen himself in print for the first time, having written a piece for Holsinger's *Companion* called "Preach to Save and Sow to Reap." In April he submitted an article to Holsinger's juvenile paper, the *Pious Youth*, on the evil of smoking. It was followed in May by a second antitobacco essay. Thus was born Zuck the journalist, his pen to be put to increasing use with the passing of time.

A nonsmoker and teetotaler, the abstemious student was equally chaste in speech, once risking a bloody nose to censure a bunch of toughs for their profanity. It happened during a vacation break when he was on the train going home. Annoyed by the salty talk of some rowdies behind him in the coach, he scribbled the words "Why do you swear?" on a scrap of paper and threw it back to them. The accused, incensed at his temerity, shouted threatening remarks and challenged him to fisti-cuffs—an invitation, of course, he prudently declined.

Zuck, headed for life-long bachelorhood, was no woman-hater in spite of what he wrote in his senior-year journal: "During my school days at the Normal I succeeded quite well in keeping my mind on my books and off the girls." For once final exams were over in July and "after some deliberation and the advice of my chum," he decided to "go for" a girl named Lucie Stager, whom he knew and liked but never took out. He wrote her a billet-doux, then got cold feet and never sent it, missing, he later lamented, a "golden opportunity."

And so, unable to "muster up enough courage to ask for a date," he would leave Millersville having "made but little progress" as a swain.

Sometime in the spring Zuck had written to Solomon Sharp, his one-time professor, inquiring about school openings in Tennessee. Late in June he received a letter offering him the post of Sharp's assistant at the new Providence Institute in Maryville. But he "desired something better," after learning the job paid only forty-five dollars a month. Influenced by a classmate, he accepted a grade school position in Schuylkill County for twenty dollars a month more.

Then, on July 21—a warm, sunshiny Thursday—twenty-seven graduates received their diplomas (Bachelor of Elements) in a day-long commencement program, each graduate giving an oration. Having earned "complimentary honors," Zuck spoke on the theme "The Spirit Supreme." His declamation, reported the Millersville *Daily Express*, was a "dignified, elevated production, carefully thought out, and delivered in a deliberate, impressive manner."

On the first Sunday after commencement, the new graduate attended services at his home church and visited with some of his "old friends." It was a distressing experience, at once sad and revelatory, dramatically illustrating for him the widening cultural gulf between educated Brethren and the rank and file membership. In his diary that night he was moved to say of his past companions:

> They are more like strangers to me than many of my Normal Acquaintances. Very little sympathy of feeling—or rather community of feeling—seems to exist between us. Mental culture is a strange term to many. Pity.

Recently discovered picture of Jacob Zuck (seated front left), beardless and not in Brethren garb. One of young women standing behind him was said to be his sweetheart. Her death was a cruel blow to him. Photograph taken some time before 1876.

THE CAREER TEACHER

His teaching position that fall was in Donaldson, a mining town of about eight-hundred then squarely situated in the heartland of Molly Maguire terrorism. In fact, James McParlan, the undercover Pinkerton detective who infiltrated the infamous Irish fraternal order and brought about its downfall a few years later, made Donaldson the first stop on his exploratory trip to the eastern coal regions to choose a base of operations. A polyglot "patch" made up of Dutch, Irish, English, and Welsh, it was nestled in a long, narrow valley that sliced diagonally through the Sharp Mountain range on a northwest-southeast line.

Zuck arrived at Donaldson on Saturday, September 3, taking a spur of the Philadelphia and Reading Railroad to Tremont and then hiking a mile or so up the valley to his destination. His first impression of the dirty, rough and tumble coal town left him confused and shaken. The typical house was a duplex, "each side having two rooms down and one up" and "made crudely of hemlock boards, with weather stays over the cracks and no plastering, no ceiling, or wall paper."[4] His diary for that day reads:

I find myself in the mountains and among the sooty miners. As the [men] came from the mines today they looked like Africans of the darkest hue. I hardly know what to think of the "Situation."

The newcomer took room and board at Lornison's Tavern at the going rate of five dollars a week. Before long the sensitive diarist admitted privately: "In one respect this is a very disagreeable place for me to live. My host is a rum-seller and I see spectacles about this bar-room sometimes that make the heart sick." There follows in his diary by a few days a description of a husband-and-wife drunken brawl in the tavern — the entry ending with the exclamation: "Whiskey! Whiskey!! Whiskey!!!"

"Few persons of piety" were to be found in Donaldson, claimed Zuck, and consequently he made no close friendships. There was no church in town, and the only public worship service was a Sunday school, which met in his classroom. Occasionally, he officiated in the absence of the superintendent. He spent most of his time alone in his upstairs room, except when at school. His diary speaks of a mountainside "retreat" that he frequented for private devotions, sometimes twice a day in his loneliness.

The school was only a few steps from his front door. He began with seventeen pupils, but the number increased when some of the "breaker boys," out on strike, came to classes later in the fall. His biggest discipline problem, though, was not created by any of these youth, their raw strength exploited by mine operators for crushing coal, but by the sixteen-year-old daughter of his landlord, a perennial troublemaker. "If Alice Lornison were in Europe," he wrote in mid-October, "my school would be so pleasant."

Yet, insisted the determined schoolmaster in his diary, "I mean to have *my* way," concluding philosophically, "I rather like little things to turn up — gives Experience — that's what I want." A good paddling, however, did the trick. "I think my use of the rod on last Thursday has had a wholesome influence on the school," noted Zuck, who rarely resorted to corporal punishment.

But another member of the fairer sex proved to be much more of a thorn in his side, this one a teaching colleague. The feud started with a halfway facetious article Zuck wrote for the Tremont *News*. Earlier, he had helped to organize a Union Teachers Institute, comprising the faculties at Donaldson and Tremont, and had been elected presiding officer. At the Institute's initial semimonthly meeting, he was irritated by certain "lady teachers" who whispered back and forth the whole evening. He singled them out for a mild rebuke in his write-up of the session for the local paper.

Said Zuck of his article afterward, "It created a frightful sensation among the teachers whose toes I have tramped." As a result, he fell into the bad graces of one of these women, who took umbrage at his audacity. "Of all the young ladies I have ever met," he confessed, "I can not think of one that was more disagreeable to me"—and added, "She and I sometimes quarreled—or rather it was *sometimes* that we did not, when we should be so unlucky as to get together." Their relations, however, improved toward the last, and they parted at school's end with her farewell words, "all is square between us."

To augment his income, Zuck ran a night school for ten weeks in the fall, picking up an extra sixty dollars. This allowed him to buy a new alpaca coat and hat—his only major expenditure—in Tremont. But classes were discontinued when they became too much of a drag for him. By Christmastime he was fed up with the anthracite coal regions and already applying at other places.

The next we hear of him is in the fall of 1871, now a grade-school principal in Mercersburg. But apparently a higher salary plus ambition enticed him back to Molly Maguire territory and a bigger position, even though the school year was almost a month underway. The *Mercersburg Journal* for September 28 reported that the local principal, having found a substitute, had resigned to become "superintendent" of the Tremont Schools in Schuylkill County—at seventy-five dollars a month beginning October 5.

Tremont, its population double that of Donaldson, was a "truly live" community, boasted a hometowner in the *News* that October, with its "nicely graded sidewalks, elegant private residences, cozy cottages and everything about the place evincing a thrift and prosperity which makes one feel as if he could anchor there and feel at home." There were foundry and machine shops, buggy and wagon works in the coal town, and, to give it respectability, six churches: Methodist, Lutheran (English and German), Evangelical, Reformed, and Roman Catholic. Over four-hundred pupils attended the six grades in the three-story brick school building under Zuck's charge.

While at Tremont the twenty-five-year-old administrator pulled a personality switch, turning out to be much less of a recluse than he had been at Donaldson the previous year. He introduced a front-page column in the *News*, a weekly, called "Educational Department." For this special feature, he solicited "brief, pointed and practical essays on literary and educational topics," hoping to convince "the general reader that the teachers, and their friends, are awake, and that they do not mean either to fall asleep or let others do so." Many articles were signed with his own initials, and sometimes he used the column to publish compositions by his best pupils.

Another of his outside activities was the recently formed Everett Literary Society, which met bimonthly on the third floor of his school. He was one of its regular debaters and on the committee that planned the program for its first anniversary the last week of February. On that occasion, he took the affirmative side of the resolution: "That we grow more happy as we become more learned"—not at all the opinion, he knew full well, held by the bulk of Dunker patriarchs.

In early July Tremont's principal left the eastern coal fields for good, after conducting a month-long summer select school in the borough. "Mr. Z.," the *News* gave notice on the Fourth, "will spend his vacation rusticating among the fragrant groves and verdant fields of Franklin County—his native place."

But Zuck did more than rusticate on the home farm. In August he slipped off to the big city—Philadelphia—to attend the four-day nineteenth annual meeting of the Pennsylvania State Teachers' Association. While there he joined a "grand excursion" to the New Jersey shore and took an evening ride past President Grant's cottage at Long Branch.

Once back home he prepared full but separate accounts of the convention and seashore excursion for the *Franklin Repository* and the *Waynesboro Village Record*. He could not keep from putting in a plug for higher teaching salaries.

The fall of 1872 found Zuck back in Dunkerland, teaching grade school at Waynesboro, a town of about fourteen-hundred not far from his birthplace. There was a brand new schoolhouse to greet him, the dedication ceremonies on October 4 covered by him for the *Village Record*.

He shared an apartment that year with David Emmert, the eighteen-year-old son of a Dunker preacher, from Benevola, Maryland. Emmert was then a patternmaker in a shop that manufactured farm implements. Later to be reunited at Huntingdon, the roommates discovered, said Emmert in his *Reminiscences*, "that we both traced our line of ancestry to the same great family tree."[5] But for Zuck there was another discovery of greater moment. In the Frick Manufacturing Co. employee he saw artistic genius of a rare order. And he never forgot about it.

In April 1873 when the school year ended, Zuck decided to go back to Millersville for the spring term. Those were the months when he struck up a second fateful friendship—this one with John Brumbaugh. In a Founder's Day speech long after Zuck's death, Brumbaugh recollected the origin of their close relationship in this way:

> My attention was called to him, and I was led to seek his acquaintance, by a reference made to him at the close of the morning chapel service. The reference made to him by Prof. Brooks [the principal] indicated to me that he might be one of our own people, which he proved to be, and from that time on we were intimate friends. I spent most of my Sundays in his room. . . .[6]

IN QUEST OF MORE DEGREES

While the two were keeping company the veteran schoolteacher suddenly came up with plans for the future that "greatly surprised" his Millersville friend as well as himself. He made this decision known in a letter to the editor, captioned "FAREWELL ADDRESS—To the Pupils of the Grammar School," and published in the *Village Record*. He told his "dear Young Friends": "It is my design to devote a year or two more to hard study, so that I may be able to fill a higher position than any I have yet had." The ambitious teacher then appealed to his recent charges in these words:

> Let me entreat you to aim high. Strive to excel. You don't know how useful and honored you may become if you but improve your time and opportunities to the best advantage. All great men and noble women were once boys and girls like yourselves, and many lacked the advantages that you possess.

On September 1 he entered the National Normal School at Lebanon, Noble County, Ohio, and enrolled in the scientific course.[7] Soon after matriculating he sent off a powerful article to Holsinger's *Christian Family Companion*, published in mid-October and headed, "Educate or Perish." He took a different tack in his line of reasoning from other educationists, whose stand tended to be more defensive and less positive about the impact of learning on piety. Turning the oppositionists' argument around, Zuck asserted:

> Pure mental culture may not bring about religious convictions, yet it is favorable to the comprehension of religious truths and to an intelligent discharge of Christian duties. Hence, though the improvement of the intellect will not, of itself, fit us for heaven; yet the wilful neglect of that improvement may be one of the means of debarring us therefrom. . . .Directly or indirectly we owe to education almost every one of the ten thousand blessings that we enjoy over and above what falls to the lot of what we are wont to call the "poor heathen in distant lands."[8]

He then turned his attention to the "need of having a good educational institution among us." His approach here was also novel. He built his case upon two points, the first one curiously suggestive of subtle proselytism. A school was imperative, argued the writer, "in order that we may hold and develop, not only the intellect that is now in the church and that seeks educational facilities; but also that which we can draw into the church by this agency, and by this alone." The second point, after a brief reference to "hundreds of our young people at other church schools," went on to speak of

> hundreds more not wishing to expose themselves to those influences, and having no where else to go, are allowing their God-given faculties to lie dormant, thus curtailing their power, and placing themselves in the centre of a sphere of usefulness that *might* be a hundred times as large.

Several months after this article appeared in print, Zuck's health broke, obliging him to drop out of school the following May. The concerned John Brumbaugh made a special trip to see his invalid friend at Claylick while he was recuperating. But home study and correspondence work enabled the infirmed Zuck to complete requirements for the Bachelor of Science degree by summer commencement time. He received his diploma on August 14, 1874, his graduating oration titled "Spanish Struggle for Liberty."

He was back at the National Normal in September to pursue the classics course. But because of a shake-up within the faculty, he transferred in November to a Professor Carver's Normal School at Medina, a short distance west of Akron.

Once again, for health reasons, he was forced to leave school — sometime early in 1875 — and return home. This was just after his near-tragic trip to Berlin through a Somerset County blizzard. Perhaps because of that ordeal his delicate health gave out for the second time in as many years, necessitating another prolonged convalescence at home.

In September, though, before departing Lebanon, he had written a long article for the Brumbaughs' *Pilgrim* on "A High School Among the Brethren." It was in answer to the denunciatory letters that had swamped the two Brethren papers once the Berlin High School fund-raising campaign began to build up steam. Deplored Zuck: "Some people are always fretting about the prickle; they never see the rose."[9] He ended his rebuttal by holding up the Quakers as worthy of emulation. Also a "peculiar" fraternity, he noted, "their character (simplicity and plainness included) is known and respected in all parts of the civilized world; their devotion to education and institutions of learning is equally well known."

He contributed another piece that September to Quinter's paper, called "The Idea of Utility."[10] A lover of poetry (his scrapbook, preserved in the College Archives, is pasted full of excerpted verse), he accused the stolid, pragmatic Brethren of a "low, materialistic idea of utility" in their rejection of esthetic values. He charged: "Whatever we cannot eat or wear or hoard, or in some way appropriate to ourselves, is of no use." "Are we not more than mere animals?" asked Zuck in his plea for an appreciation of the fine arts.

BACK TO THE CLASSROOM

His facile pen fell silent after his breakdown, and his career plans were left up in the air. But in late summer the rejuvenated Claylick native wrote John Brumbaugh about his appointment for the coming school year at Mt. Pleasant, Maryland — near Boonsboro and Hagerstown. The letter betrayed a lack of self-confidence almost neurotic for a man of his age and administrative experience. It said:

> I am elected principal of a grammar school. I don't feel big enough for it, but I am going to make myself big enough, if my own personal effort will do it. The man who resigned is my superior. He is a college graduate, and I am told a Christian gentleman, so you see what it will be necessary for me to do in order to be a worthy successor. It was necessary for John the Baptist to decrease in the fulfillment of his mission, but in my case it will be necessary to increase. It is the first position tendered me since my graduation [from National Normal School] and, God being my helper, I mean to measure up to it."[11]

Indeed, the crippled principal, whose reputation "as a writer of ability" had preceded him to Mt. Pleasant, had no trouble measuring up.

He added three subjects to the curriculum—geometry, physiology, and drawing. With respect to the last "branch," the *Boonesboro Odd Fellow* declared: "Prof Zuck has certainly been very successful in drawing, when we consider that none of his pupils ever drew before he came here, and I doubt if his scholars can now be beat in the country, especially in map drawing" (there is a booklet in the College Archives with samples of their work). He also encouraged the children in creative writing and arranged for the *Young Disciple*, a Brumbaugh Sunday school publication, to print an occasional essay of theirs. "As a disciplinarian," said the *Odd Fellow* of him, "he has rare abilities, leading instead of driving, thus gaining the love and respect of all his pupils."[12]

The Mt. Pleasant schoolmaster's performance won him a place on the program of the Teachers' Institute of Washington County, held in Hagerstown, December 20-24. His featured address was on the topic "How Much Geography Ought to Be Taught in County Schools, and How Shall It Be Taught?" The *Hagerstown Herald and Torch Light* described his presentation to eighty-five teachers as "marked by more than usual care; it evinced a thoughtful, exhaustive, and systematized classification of the subject and well digested plan of teaching it."

A week after the Institute came Zuck's New Year's Day surprise call on John Brumbaugh in Huntingdon, thus setting the stage for fast-moving developments over the succeeding three months. That impulsive visit, we saw in the last chapter, led to talk of starting a school in the *Pilgrim* building as soon as possible. This was followed by a flurry of letters between Zuck and the Brumbaughs on the feasibility and nature of the proposed "experiment." Wrote Zuck in his scrapbook: "After a serious but very brief consideration of the matter I concluded to accept the invitation of the Brethren at Huntingdon, and to that end resigned my position as a teacher of the public school at Mt. Pleasant, Maryland, a few days before the regular time of closing." "On bidding farewell to his scholars," the *Odd Fellow* said of his leave-taking, "many of them shed tears."

BEGINNING OF THE EXPERIMENT

So precipitately did the founders act that little advance publicity was given prior to the opening of what they chose to call the Huntingdon Normal Select School—the first in an array of subsequent names. The initial announcement was brief, carried by the *Pilgrim* on March 28, and simply read:

> Brother J. M. Zuck talks of starting a select or Normal School in our town, for the coming Summer. His object will be to give his pupils a good, thorough education, and also to prepare young men and ladies for teaching. Bro. Zuck is a man of fine abilities, being a graduate of the Penn'a State Normal, also of a leading Western school. Any of our brethren's children or any others, contemplating going to school during the coming Summer will do well to make calculations to come here as excellent facilities will be offered.

Fuller information appeared in the April 4th edition, emphasizing the existence of an active church (the Huntingdon Brethren had renovated a room in the *Pilgrim* building as a place for regular worship in June 1875) and indicating that students would room and board with members. "The design of the school," this latest announcement explained, "is not to teach religion but to educate; therefore in principle it will not be sectarian." It further stated:

> The departments of the school will be arranged so as to lead students from the elementary branches to a thorough knowledge of all the higher branches of an English education. Facilities will also be afforded for obtaining as thorough a knowledge of Latin, Greek and German languages as is usually obtained at Academies and Seminaries, and preparing them for teaching, for the active duties of life or for entering college.

Jacob Zuck arrived in Huntingdon four days before classes were scheduled to begin. He settled into a one-room apartment, rented for him by John Brumbaugh, directly across the street from the *Pilgrim* building. Only three students greeted him on Monday, April 17 instead of the expected fifteen or twenty. All were from the local area—two girls, Rebecca Cornelius and Maggie Miller, and one boy, Gaius Brumbaugh, Dr. A. B.'s fourteen-year-old son. The teacher refused to open a book the first morning until after he had led his little troupe to the first-floor chapel where the four of them knelt together in prayer.

The nation's economy was still reeling from the effects of the 1873 "crash" when Zuck, a slender, almost delicate man of average height with brown eyes, dark hair and—at the time—beardless, began teaching that

Pilgrim Building as it looks today. School occupied second story, left side (south) facing picture. A printshop was on floor above and on street level was a church-chapel.

"experimental term."[13] Henry Brumbaugh lamented in the *Pilgrim* that while 1876, as the centennial year, should be a time of celebration, the country was mired "in a financial depression that it has been our lot seldom to experience."

Huntingdon, its population now reaching upwards to five thousand, had not escaped the economic fallout. David Emmert's impression of the town upon his arrival in the fall of 1877 was one of patent depression everywhere:

What a town! *Alba longa* (long white town); better *nigra longa* (long black town). For West Huntingdon stretched for a mile or more over a broad plateau and looked as if it had been in the full swell of a great boom sometime and had been stranded by the subsidence of the tide. Here were vacant lots innumerable, with fences and without, signboards everywhere: "This lot for Sale. Apply to _____"; empty houses many, and boardwalks abominable. The streets were unpaved and muddy. The tall stacks of silent factories told the story of industrial decline. Here and there were a few centers of activity. One of these was the *Pilgrim*, later the *Primitive*

Christian office. The older part of the town was somewhat more improved, but in many places the pavements were laid with flat stones. There was no sewerage system and the streets were lighted, when at all, by coal-oil lamps.[14]

The legendary William Beery, an entering student in 1877, has left another first-hand description. In a letter dated April 11, 1944 and headed "Huntingdon as I Found It (Winter 1877-78)," he wrote in part about the West End:

On all sides were old, black frame houses in which lived people who could afford nothing better, most of whom had been employees of the defunct car works. Some places there were old, dilapidated sidewalks, many boards missing. To mention one spot; on Mifflin Street, where Sammy Clemens and wife lived and kept store in the same little house, there was such a walk. They had a cow which roved around there to get the benefit of the grass that grew in spots. This cow seemed to take special pleasure in walking on the few boards and bare spots where the walk should have been, which resulted in making it perilous for a pedestrian lest he step into a hole in the walk, or something worse.[15]

Little wonder Zuck expressed misgivings the day before his school opened. To John Brumbaugh he confided,

"I must confess I can't see the way to success in this enterprise, but I do believe it's right, and I believe God will show us the way as we go onward."[16]

But on the morrow drooping spirits gave way to fierce determination, despite the poor opening-day enrollment. After the last class John Brumbaugh said to him,

"Only three pupils! It looks small indeed, but I hear others are coming."

Replied the teacher, "I'm not scared, and now since I've started, if I can have these rooms and am spared, I'll continue for one year. And if these pupils leave, I'll go out and compel others to come in."

Then he went on to analogize with a twinkle in his eye:

I feel tonight like my mother's old hen. Before I came up here, she told me of the trouble she had with her old hen. She was bound to hatch, whether she had eggs or not. But I'll do better than the old hen; I am not only bound to hatch, but I am going to have eggs, too. There are eggs that must be hatched![17]

For a hatchery, Henry Brumbaugh gave Zuck the use of a second-story flat—rent free—in the south half of the *Pilgrim* building. There were three rooms, one of which was converted into a parlor ($14'$ x $18'$), another into a classroom ($14'$ x $12'$), and the third into a small principal's office. From Zuck's scrapbook we also learn that Dr. A. B. furnished a table and two blackboards, John Brumbaugh a set of chairs, and the sober-miened teacher a bookcase he himself had made. A further scrapbook entry indicates that John Brumbaugh lived up to his promise to board his friend for whatever he could pay—which was nothing for much of the first year.

The Brumbaughs, persuaded that "our brother. . .is the right man in the right place," put their press at Zuck's disposal.[18] The May 23 issue of the *Pilgrim* introduced a column headed "Educational Department," edited by Zuck. He wrote in that edition: "Having had some experience several years ago in conducting a Department of this kind in a secular paper, I enter this new field with less reluctance than might otherwise be felt." The purpose of the column, he said, was to call the readers' attention "to our work in the educational field, and also what we may consider his duty in relation to the same," as well as present "selected articles as may be deemed wholesome" on "all matters relating to the cause in general."

In addition the *Pilgrim* on the 23rd carried a four-page circular insert on the "Huntingdon Normal School," published gratuitously by the Brumbaugh firm. An opening blurb about the school's location assured parents and prospective students that the "health and morals of the place are as good as can be found anywhere and much better than in most towns of the same size." Tuition was listed at seven dollars for a ten-week term and room and board in a private home at three dollars a week—rates "considerably lower than at most schools of the same grade," it was pointed out. The circular further advised that the curriculum would be modeled after that of "our best State Normal Schools." There was also a bit of long-range forecasting: "It will be our aim to extend the course of study until it shall include all the elements of a liberal education."

According to the little brochure the library, which was housed in a corner of the teacher's office, consisted of *Webster's New Unabridged Dictionary* and two encyclopedia sets: the sixteen-volume *Appleton* and the ten-volume *Chambers*. With a few more acquisitions, it was boasted, this reference library "will compare favorably with those found at some of our State Normal Schools."

In the parlor students could keep abreast of current events in "the fields of science, literature, art, politics or religion" through a collection of newspapers and magazines. Besides dailies, like the *New York Tribune*, the

Witness, and the *Graphic*, there were "excellent weeklies, both secular and religious, pictorial and otherwise." The leading magazines included *Harper's, Lippincott, Scribner's,* and *Popular Science Monthly.*

As for "religious advantages," the circular mentioned "a comfortable church room in the *Pilgrim* Building which will answer for a chapel" and that "Sunday school and Bible classes will be organized." Out-of-town students, especially Brethren, were expected to "frequent" all religious services. Affirmed the school's founders:

> Although no attempt will be made to teach or enforce sectarian dogmas or doctrines in the classroom, yet we have no sympathy with that pernicious system of education which confines itself to the training of the intellect and endeavors not to awaken and call forth the higher and holier impulses of the soul. Hence we shall employ every proper means to lead our pupils to realize in the deepest possible sense that the fear of the Lord is the beginning of wisdom.

By May, when the circular for 1876-77 went out, the enrollment picture began to look brighter. Ten more names had been added to the roster: Ida Black, S. C. Peightal, Jennie Stouffer, Ida Johnston, May Durbarrow, B. F. Mark, Plummer Martin, Laura Madden, Helen McHugh, and John Brumbaugh himself—six females and four males. Like the first-day three, they were all from Huntingdon County.

One evening that spring—probably in early May—Zuck was sitting at John Brumbaugh's dinner table, pensively eating. Suddenly he leaned back and said,

"We must have a literary society. I want the students of this school to be able to get up and speak in public, and a literary society is essential to give drill along this line."[19]

That night he and Brumbaugh made out a program for the first meeting. It took place a day or so later in the chapel, but for some reason the distaff side was excluded. Curious, some of the ladies—Wealthy Clarke, Annie Campbell, and Eleanor Brumbaugh—huddled outside the door and peeped through the keyhole, "not a little amused at the proceedings." Soon, however, someone came out, invited them in, and before the night passed membership was voted for all.

The literary society soon became a powerful intellectual stimulus in the life of the infant school. Its programs, integrated with classroom work, featured declamations, lectures, and readings. Debate was not added to its routine until August, during the Teachers' Institute.

When the first term ended in late June screaming newspaper headlines told of Indian wars and the massacre of Custer's 7th Cavalry at the Little Bighorn River in Montana. But Zuck had problems of his own—money, not scalps. His ten-week income from thirteen students grossed a mere $53.95; his outlay amounted to $81.80.

Nor did the Teachers' Institute that summer help to swell the school coffers. Only one student registered on the first day, and the six-week session closed with but a half-dozen in attendance.

THE EXPERIMENT GAINS SUPPORT

The school founders were hardly ecstatic when only fifteen matriculants reported for the fall opening on September 12. But at least a few were out-of-staters (from Virginia, Maryland, and even Colorado), and the roster now included Pennsylvanians from beyond the Juniata Valley, among them a brother of Zuck. Two more made belated appearances in October.

By then the *Pilgrim* publishers had closed a deal that now brought a familiar personage among Brethren educationists into the inner council of the fledgling school. For most of two years James Quinter had hounded Henry and John to consolidate their printing business with his. Finally, in July of 1876, the Brumbaughs came to terms.

In October the two publishing houses were incorporated under the name of Quinter and Brumbaugh Brothers, with a capital stock of twenty-thousand dollars[20] Quinter, the senior partner, took over as editor-in-chief, and the *Pilgrim* building was made the firm's headquarters. The sheet of this merger was renamed *Primitive Christian*, its first number going out on October 25 to almost ten thousand subscribers. On Halloween day Quinter moved his family from Meyersdale to Huntingdon. Later, he was voted the first presiding elder of the local congregation.

In the first November issue of the *Primitive Christian*, Zuck's column lamented the lack of interest in education among Dunker belles. Bothered that his school was "too exclusively made up of representatives of the male sex," the teacher wrote:

> We prefer to have both sexes, as we think the influence of each upon the other is beneficial. The idea of the co-education of the sexes is endorsed by most of the Normal Schools of the country and is gaining ground in some of the leading colleges and universities. How long will it take our young sisters to catch a little of the educational spirit which characterizes the young women found in many of the schools of the country?[21]

Feminity might have been in short supply among Zuck's band of learners but not enthusiasm—especially for the literary society. Its weekly programs were attracting a nonacademic audience—from the *Primitive Christian* staff, the founders' families, and the town—wanting to take active part. This led to the formation of the Juniata Literary Society on January 13, 1877 with forty-nine charter members.[22] A constitution was adopted calling for annual dues of fifty cents. On February 3 Henry Brumbaugh introduced the *Juniata Literary Record*, the school's first paper, which circulated in manuscript form. A weekly, it was a ribbon-bound collection of prose and poetry submitted by members.

Debate, however, was divorced from the exercises of the society for a time between 1877 and 1879. After then, to foster rivalry, the student body was arbitrarily divided by Zuck into three debate clubs: Bryants, Ebenezers, and Irvings.

Meanwhile, there were other promising signs that the "experiment" seemed to be working out. When the winter term began on November 21 the tiny classroom provided by Henry Brumbaugh was suddenly jammed to the walls with people. There were thirty-two registrants on hand, a one-hundred percent gain over the preceding term. Students soon grew impatient with the overcrowded conditions and complained of being "too thick to thrive." Moreover, inquiries were coming in from Dunker bastions in the Midwest—Ohio, Illinois, Missouri, Iowa, and other states. Zuck now found himself in the painful position of having to discourage applicants for want of space.[23] He was forced to alleviate the situation by the time forty-five students enrolled on February 6, the first day of the spring term.

Fortunately, Zuck was able on short notice to rent the Burchinell place, a large, three-story house, one block away at 1224 Washington Street. It had been the home of Thomas Burchinell, the retired owner of a planning mill and sash factory. (The place was razed in 1971 by the Owens-Corning Fiberglas Corporation for a parking lot.)

In 1877 this spacious building, only ten years old, contained two large rooms 14' x 30' and eight smaller ones, not counting the kitchen. One of the big downstairs rooms was used for classes, the other for a parlor. The upstairs space was utilized as a dormitory, and kitchen facilities enabled students to form boarding clubs, for which there had been a growing demand.

On Thursday, February 9 the school moved into the Burchinell House, the student body thereafter making the one-block trek each morning to the *Primitive Christian* building for chapel services. It was beginning to look as if the "experimental" stage had been safely weathered, and already the founders were making bolder plans.

Burchinell Building, 1224 Washington Street. Now razed, it housed school from 1877 to 1879. Zuck, who lived on the third floor with David Emmert (empty dormer window), is shown here seated in center of doorway.

3

The College On The Hill

PLANS TO INCORPORATE AND BUILD

Even before relocating the school upstreet the four founders and their two new allies, Quinter and Joseph Beer, an editorial assistant, had conferred on several occasions about its future. The first meeting was in the office of the *Primitive Christian* on Monday evening, January 22, 1877. There was talk of building, and Zuck showed his own rough diagram of a structure he thought "would meet the wants of both the school and the church at this place."[1]

Zuck had awaited the evening of the 22nd with prayerful expectation, as John Brumbaugh discovered quite by chance. Only moments before they were scheduled to meet, Brumbaugh needed a magazine the teacher had taken to his room across the street. He walked over and knocked on Zuck's door, but there was no answer. Thinking his neighbor was out, he barged in and found him on his knees, absorbed in prayer.

After a while Zuck rose and said, "This evening the question of the erection of a college building is coming up, and I thought I'd have a private talk with God about it."[2]

A follow-up meeting on Saturday of that week resulted in an open and free exchange about how much support could be expected from the church (which by then claimed a following of seventy-thousand) and whether or not Huntingdon was really the best location for a Brethren school.[3] Quinter, at sixty the Nestor of the school fight, played the devil's advocate throughout the deliberation, leaving the others to plead for the county seat. Dr. A. B. argued for "having the school in close

55

proximity to the leading Church paper" (there were two others). He further contended that Zuck's work "manifests no sign of decay but on the contrary exhibits every evidence of vigorous life and healthy and rapid growth." But Henry Brumbaugh clinched the case for Huntingdon with the observation that "freedom from local opposition and interference is a point of much importance." Nobody could dispute that.

A committee of three—Quinter, Zuck, and the doctor—was appointed to draft resolutions organizing the Huntingdon Normal School as a joint-stock company and authorizing a fund raising drive for a building project. The committee made its report to the Huntingdon Brethren on Thursday evening, February 2. Henry Brumbaugh then took it the next evening to a council meeting of the mother congregation at James Creek (not until 1878 did the local Brethren become an autonomous congregation), which gave unanimous approval.

The resolutions provided for a board of temporary trustees, the three committee members plus the Brumbaugh brothers and Beer. This board was given oversight of the financial campaign and charged with finding a school site. Joseph Beer was appointed "general agent and solicitor." After the first month, during which the trustees would pay his salary, he was to solicit funds on a commission basis—seven percent for him, other agents five percent.

Ultimately, there was also provision for a permanent nine-member board of trustees with staggered three-year terms. All had to be Brethren, and at least five of them had to live in the vicinity of the school. The trustees were to be elected by and from among the stockholders, one vote allotted for each one-hundred-dollar share.

One thing the document made clear: although the school intended to honor Brethren tradition and doctrine, it would not be church owned or controlled. Organizing it on a joint-stock basis, people were told, would ensure its private status. In this connection Zuck was wont to characterize the school—a half century or more before the term "church-related" came into popular usage—as "denominational but not sectarian."

EARLIEST FACULTY ADDITIONS, MERGER, AND CURRICULUM EXPANSION

While the trustees, in a display of wishful thinking, spoke of breaking ground by summer, Zuck faced the more immediate problem of coping with the doubled spring enrollment. To assist him he hired Phoebe Weakley, a member of his graduating class at Millersville, to teach Elocution and Literature. He also made use of a student aide, Emma

Miller, a Bedford County native with a State certificate. (Her father, who had died when only twenty-five, had been a pioneer Dunker educator in the early 1850s.) Miss Weakley, a thin, hollow-eyed, plain-looking woman who wore her hair pulled severely back, was baptized a Brethren soon after her arrival. She replaced Henry Brumbaugh as the sponsor of the *Juniata Literary Record*.

By April 17, when forty-five students, representing six states and eight Pennsylvania counties, reported for classes, the trustees were deep in merger talks with Lewis Kimmel, pressuring him to combine their two schools at Huntingdon. As early as March 5 they had delegated Quinter to approach Kimmel on the matter; he was later joined in the parleying by Dr. A. B. Wrote John Brumbaugh in the *Primitive Christian*: "They found him quite willing to confer with them on the subject, and also willing to make any sacrifice in order to remove anything that might be in the way of making a school among us a success."⁴ Consolidation was effected the last week of April, and on the 26th a circular letter went out under Kimmel's name urging scholarship donors to transfer their support to the Huntingdon enterprise. Another public statment by Kimmel appeared in the June 12 edition of the *Primitive Christian*. Soon after that he donated fifty volumes from the Plum Creek Normal library — mainly reference works — and before long his name was to be found on the list of stockholders.

A month after the merger — on Thursday, June 28 — closing exercises for the first full academic year were held in the Penn Street Opera House, conducted by the Juniata Literary Society. Advertised as "New, Entertaining and Instructive," it was an all-day affair, with morning, afternoon, and evening sessions. The *Local News* reported that in the evening Henry Brumbaugh spoke to a crowded house, giving "full and satisfactory reasons for the future success of the school." It further stated: "He believes the day is not far distant when the roll will contain the names of 600 or 1000 pupils."

The teachers' term opened on July 23 and attracted thirty-six registrants, thirty more than the previous summer. The publicity flier on this session reflected a touch of Madison Avenue hucksterism. It said magniloquently: "Those who are preparing to teach, or who wish to review preparatory to examination, will find it to their advantage to patronize the school that is destined to become the leading Educational Institution in this section of the State."

There came to help Zuck that term twenty-five-year-old Jacob Brumbaugh, Dr. A. B.'s youngest brother and an 1874 Millersville graduate. As yet unmarried, Brumbaugh had spent three years at Millersburg, Dauphin County, where he was lauded by the *Herald* for his "sacrificing work as principal of the High School." He had been induced by his older sibling to give up his monthly principal's salary of $120 to join forces with Zuck, taking the classes in science and teaching methods. There was no promise of a regular income at first, and he roomed with Dr. A. B. until Founders Hall was built. Brumbaugh, who would become Zuck's right-hand man, was paid nothing until the following December. For five months' work he received the grand sum of $55 a few days before Christmas.

Meantime, in midsummer, while railroad strikes bred mob violence in Pittsburgh and other eastern cities, bringing death and property damages in the millions of dollars, Zuck pushed for donations of books and equipment and sent out the circular for 1877-78. It announced a revised calendar of three unequal terms—fall, winter, spring—for the regular academic year and a six-week teachers' term. Tuition was hiked from seventy cents a week to seventy-five cents, but there was no change in boarding costs. Laundry expenses, it was estimated, would range from ten cents to twenty-five cents weekly. The minicatalog also set forth a list of "Rules and Regulations":

1. The use of Tobacco in any form is prohibited in the Building or upon the school premises.

2. All students, unless excused, must remain in their rooms during the evening study hours, and it will be the duty of the parties with whom students board to report promptly all violations of this rule.

3. Students from a distance are required to attend regularly the religious services held in the Chapel, unless there is a mutual agreement to the contrary.

4. All students are expected to join the Literary Society and to discharge faithfully all duties connected therewith.

5. Every case of absence or tardiness, unless promptly excused, will be regarded as a misdemeanor and will subject the delinquent to such discipline as the offence may seem to demand.

6. Students of the two sexes, other than relatives, must not meet privately except on business, and then only by permission of the Principal or some duly authorized Teacher. Lady students from abroad will not receive calls from gentlemen not connected with the school, unless the latter first obtain permission to make such calls.

It was explained: "The above rules and restrictions are deemed prudent and absolutely necessary in order that our school may attain that high standard of moral and intellectual excellence which we aspire to teach."

Out-of-towners were told that the "omnibus" fare from the depot to the Burchinell place would cost ten cents, more if a trunk was thrown in.

A two-page supplement was run off in August, announcing the creation of three new subject areas — drawing, music, and languages (classical and foreign).

David Emmert, the principal's former roommate at Waynesboro, showed up in September to teach drawing and oil painting. He had been approached by Zuck the preceding summer, the two talking while he, grease-covered, repaired a threshing machine. But the death of his father prevented him from joining the "noble band of workers at Huntingdon" until the following year.

Almost at once, Emmert, whose facility in the graphic arts later amazed James Whistler, set to work on what today is a collector's item: the 21″ x 30″ lithograph *View of Huntingdon*. Apparently, he was the one who did the ink drawings for Thomas Hunter, the Philadelphia lithographer. Available in July 1878, the picture gave a view of the town as seen from Shelving Rock, with vignettes of local buildings and dwellings arranged in the corners and along the margins. At three-dollars a copy, plain or tinted (or one of each for five-dollars), the proceeds from its sale went toward the library and "apparatus" fund.

To teach voice Zuck hired John Ewing, called by some the "father of Brethren music." An Ohioan, Ewing traveled among churches promoting congregational singing. The tuning fork was his sole instrument in that day of unaccompanied hymnody. He stayed on two years and had a profound influence on William Beery, who soon eclipsed his mentor as the church's best-known singer and composer.

For the classical and modern languages the principal turned to Hugo G. Olawsky, who had studied at the universities of Berlin and Breslau. He is the unidentified subject of the whimsical chapter "The German Professor" in Emmert's book. Olawsky, whom Zuck learned was temporarily staying with some farmers a few miles out in the country, was invited sight unseen to be interviewed for the language position. Emmert describes the school's first glimpse of the candidate in this way:

On a certain day he came. All horror — a tramp! Hair and beard unkempt, slouch and greasy hat, shabby and dirty clothes, pants tucked into his cowhide boots and a faded carpet-sack grip under his arm. The students stood aghast, and even Professor Zuck looked "sold."[5]

Nevertheless, when it came out that Olawsky was not only a German scholar but trained in the classics as well, he was taken on. Zuck, Emmert, and the students rounded up some clean clothes, prevailed upon him to bathe, trimmed his "shock and bristles," and took "real pride" in his spick-and-span appearance.

But the German professor's tenure was very brief. Deprived of his beer stein he grew cranky after a couple of weeks. Soon his students rebelled, calling him "the old tyrant," and, said Emmert, even worse names. Finally, Zuck had to call him into his office for a man-to-man talk. Here is Emmert's description of the outcome:

What was said in the brief interview none but the two professors ever knew. Then the door suddenly flew open, and out came the German professor like a thunderbolt. The students rushed aside; up the stairs he went, three steps at a bound; I followed to see what would happen. What a scene! The old man was in a rage. He threw off his shoes and banged them into a corner; he threw coat and vest and hat all over the room, and, without taking time to unbutton his shirt, he seized it at the collar band, ripped it up the back, and sent it whirling like a flag of truce across the bed. I got out and hastened down the stairs to warn those below to clear the track for what was coming. In a few minutes he appeared clad in his old duds, and, with a jabber nobody could understand, and gesticulations which sent terror to the hearts of the timid ones, he rushed down the street and disappeared from view forever. Professor Zuck was convulsed with laughter, the boys were hilarious, the girls clapped their hands and hallooed, "Good-bye!"[6]

CHANGE OF NAME: BRETHREN'S NORMAL SCHOOL

Zuck and Emmert found themselves "roomies" once again the fall of 1877. Their apartment was on the third floor of the Burchinell Building, a small dormer window letting in outside light. The bare floor they covered with a "cheap carpet." At first the pair boarded out, but on Zuck's suggestion they joined one of the student clubs for their meals. The standard dish for supper, recalled Emmert, was "a sort of potato soup," invariably scorched. Even though the student body had grown to fifty-seven, Zuck had to scramble to make ends meet. As his roommate observed in his book: "It soon became evident that Professor Zuck was under great financial strain to equip the school, pay his teachers (small as were the salaries), add to the library and supply apparatus as necessity demanded."[7]

At the same time, the hard-pressed principal could write optimistically that the near-future would likely bring some changes, not only in name but in the school's academic thrust. In the *Primitive Christian* for September 4 he served notice with the following statement:

We are especially anxious to have young brethren and sisters and Brethren's children come here. It was for this class that our school was started, and it is from this class that we would like to receive the principal part of our encouragement. We would like to make our school a Brethren's school in fact if not in name, and when that is accomplished we trust there will be no objection to our assuming the name that properly belongs to us. If there should be no valid objections, we propose to call our school the "Brethren's Normal School," and if in due course of events the word "school" should give place to some other word, we trust the fitness of things at that time will justify the change.

By November the new name was fixed, and Zuck spoke of issuing "Certificates of Graduation" at the close of the current school year. He also advised *Primitive Christian* readers of plans to add a "Scientific Course," a more advanced program than the Normal English Course, and "to make some advancement in the Collegiate Department."[8]

THREATS FROM THE MIDWEST

But then came "an ambassador from the land of the setting sun," Emmert wrote, urging consolidation upon the trustees and the relocation of their school in a Midwestern town eager to attract one. Emmert failed to identify the place in telling about this upsetting visit, but it was Ashland, Ohio, where the citizens had pledged ten-thousand dollars toward the purchase of a twenty-eight-acre campus. This "man of enthusiastic spirit, good address, and wonderful persuasive power," said Emmert, told of the great scheme to establish a college of the first rank; of their purposes to equip and endow and professor it, and start it a booming success at once.[9] The Brethren's Normal School authorities were asked, "Why struggle through the long, trying period of experimental development?"

Ever since the Berlin High School fiasco Zuck and the Brumbaughs had been skeptical of "instant success" talk. Their operating motto was "little by little," Zuck once wrote, and this explains why they always referred to their initial efforts as an "experiment." As he said in his *Primitive Christian* column, playing upon words: "A mushroom may develop in a night, but Nature's *Normal plan* is 'First the blade, then the ear, after that the full corn in the ear.' "[10] Nevertheless, when the said "ambassador" left with the threat: "Well, if you do not unite with us you will be swallowed up," Zuck fell into deep depression.[11]

In confidential talks with his roommate Zuck admitted anxiety about competition from another school and his "wavering faith" that enough funds could be raised in the East.[12] This fear was evident as early as the previous May, when the young educator, in reporting the Plum Creek-Huntingdon school merger, went on to plead:

> Let us unite and establish one school. Since we have made the move here at Huntingdon, we hear of other similar projects. Of course it is the privilege of any of our brethren who may feel to do so, to start a school, and is all right, but there can be nothing more detrimental to the cause. We have been laboring for years to establish a school among the Brethren, and hitherto have not been successful, and is it possible that we can start three or four at once! Our brethren should not think of this matter. If our school here were not in successful operation we would at once drop it, but as it is now pretty well established, and is apparently doing well, we feel that we should go forward. We wish all similar projects success, but if we have too many of them at once, it may be that none of them will succeed so well. Our motto would be, one at a time, and then build up others as they are needed.[13]

APPEAL TO THE TOWN FOR LAND

The Ashland visitor may have struck fear in Zuck's heart, but he also planted an idea in his fertile brain. On December 6 the *Local News* carried a long article from the principal's pen under the heading "An Address to the Citizens of Huntingdon in Behalf of the Huntingdon Normal." It was written with the trustees' imprimatur. Taking a cue from Ashland, Zuck wrote, "We now appeal to the citizens of the town to assist us by donating the ground needed for the buildings that we propose to erect next summer."

Shrewdly he informed the local merchants that the trustees foresaw not too far ahead a student body of some three to five hundred. Therefore, he estimated, they would stand to benefit anywhere from $100,000 to $150,000 annually from school and student business. "Can our business men, our merchants, tailors, millers, butchers, bakers, etc., see no advantage in this?" he asked. In fact, argued Zuck, "Our students from a distance have already spent as much in your midst as it would cost you to buy the ground that we need for our proposed building."

He then mentioned that "other towns in this State, and at least one town in another State are bidding for the school," one community ready to put up twenty-thousand dollars. In the last instance, of course, he was referring to Ashland, but the trustees were also discussing a deal with Jacob Oller of Waynesboro, an intimate friend of the three Brumbaughs. Oller was trying to sell them on the idea of buying the Clairmont Hotel, located a short distance east of Monterey, and converting it into a school building.[14] Berlin was another locality making overtures. Having called attention to attractive invitations such as these, Zuck went on to say:

> We reserve our answer to [these] propositions until we hear what Huntingdon is willing to do for us in the way of donating a proper school site. The best interests of the enterprise demand that this matter should be brought to a head without unnecessary delay, and hence we urge you to act promptly if you propose to act at all. We do not ask you for 10 or 15 thousand dollars, but merely for enough suitable ground upon which to erect the buildings, and also enough to permit the future growth and development of the enterprise.

Since spring the temporary trustees had been looking at several possible school sites in the Huntingdon area, one of which lay across the river. But by now, Zuck's article disclosed, they had narrowed it down to two sites, both of which were in West Huntingdon. The first location was identified as the twenty lots between Moore and Oneida streets on the west and east, 17th Street on the south, and extending north to the middle of the block between 18th and 19th streets (which took in two lots owned by Dr. A. B. Brumbaugh). "Site No. 2" consisted of the plot of ground bounded by the two alleys between Washington and Moore streets, and extending northward into the Taylor estate between 19th and 21st streets, including "the hill" (Round Top). The trustees, Zuck said, pulling no punches, would accept the first site "unconditionally," but there had to be proof of adequate water supply before they would agree to the second location.

The decision to ask the townspeople to donate land meant that the trustees had to play down the school's inherent Brethrenism. Thus, in his December 6 article, Zuck stressed that while the Normal was designed to meet denominational need, it was also committed to educating all applicants, "regardless of creed, sex, or social distinctions." Such rhetoric had a ring highly suggestive of today's affirmative action pledge. By way of further commentary he observed:

> We have already had students representing many different religious faiths, and we suspect that all have felt about as well suited as though the school were designed for them. We have thus far tried to respect the rights of all, and we shall continue to act upon the same Christian principle, believing it possible for a school to be denominational and yet not sectarian, in the bad sense of the word.

As for the Teachers' Term, said the principal, "We are not over anxious to have our school considered even denominational, but rather *professional* and *normal* in the highest and best sense of the term."

On Saturday evening, December 8, two days after Zuck's article appeared in the *Local News*, the temporary trustees took their case directly to the town fathers. They met with a number of civic leaders in the office of Col. William Dorris, a resident attorney for the Pennsylvania Railroad. According to the *Local News* a committee of five was appointed that night to ascertain the price for "Location No. 2" and to organize a fund-raising campaign. Why the citizen's group made that site selection, given the reservations of the trustees, was not explained. Two days later the same newspaper reported that "some of the owners have already consented to donate their property," and entreated the others to be as "liberal and public-spirited as they can." Zuck informed *Primitive Christian* readers on December 18 that the ground was appraised at five-thousand dollars and, most significantly, separated by a mile from the downtown area. Thus, he gave assurance, it was a safe distance from "the places where students could come into contact with shows and other evil agencies."

THE SMALLPOX SCARE

All thoughts of school sites and subscription lists, however, were pushed aside before another fortnight. Early in December the borough was plagued by chicken pox, the severity of which, said Emmert in his book, "awakened a suspicion that it might be smallpox in mild form."[15] The first diagnosed case of this dreaded disease was found next door to the Burchinell House. Anxious Normal students tried not to notice the little girl "peering from the window with flushed and pitted face" as they passed by on the street. But with her recovery all fears faded, and on Saturday the 22nd the students left for the holidays.

Then, during Christmas week, a smallpox scare swept the borough, peaking shortly after the turn of the year. A couple of physicians— notably Dr. A. B.—denied in the papers that the town had an actual epidemic on its hands. Still, rumors were rife. Students returning by train for the winter term on January 7 were shaken—miles from town—by the cry: "Smallpox at Huntingdon!" They heard wild stories of death and quarantine.[16] Upon their arrival they were met with the odor of disinfectant (carbolic acid) everywhere. The "Seven Orphans," as members of the Zuck-Emmert boarding club were dubbed, dutifully downed liberal doses of molasses and sulphur three times daily. Every day red quarantine signs went up on all sides of the school.

Less than a week after the vacation break, the "scabby foe" finally struck at Zuck's little band. The wife of Edward Kendig, a young minister from Virginia who had entered in the fall of '76, died of the scourge on January 12. Early the next morning—a damp and chilly Monday—funeral services for Mrs. Kendig were held in the chapel. The grief-stricken husband was confined at home with his only child, a baby. That day classes were suspended in compliance with a ban on all public gathering enacted by Town Council on the 10th.

Students and teachers scattered, most to distant homes, a few girls to emergency quarters locally, and that plucky threesome, as we shall soon see, to their Trough Creek refuge. Before dispersing, the school made tentative plans to resume classes on February 18. Nevertheless, goodbyes were spoken with heavy hearts. Wrote Emmert: "Before us lay the possible abandonment of the school enterprise."[17]

As the students were leaving John Brumbaugh said to Zuck, "Well, if there's no hope at all, I suppose we must stop."

But the doughty educator shot back defiantly, "Stop! No!"

And then, in words soon to prove prophetic, he said, "We commenced this work as an experiment and nothing less than death will stop me, and if I should be stricken and die, I hope others will have the courage to take up the work and continue."[18]

On the following Friday—the 17th—Zuck and Emmert took their own "sorrowful leave."

But not before they had tackled the problem of what to do about three of the "Seven Orphans": William Beery, Benjamin Bowser, and Levi Stoner. This trio, all Ohioans, were afraid that going home would mean never to return. On the evening classes were halted, Zuck, Emmert, and the Ohio "Orphans" were sitting together in the unlit parlor, their mood matching the darkness and gloom.

There was a quick rap on the door and in walked Jacob Brumbaugh. His "breezy spirit" was a timely tonic for the downcast quintet, and one of the boys got up and brought a lamp. Soon the group was bantering and laughing as the fate of the "Orphans" was weighed. The boys wanted to move in with some of the farm families close by and wait out the crisis. But, as Emmert later wrote, farmers were boycotting the town, "and it was not likely that even a dog from Huntingdon would be welcomed in their midst."[19] Then, recalled the art teacher:

More in jest than in earnest some one said, "Boys, let's go to the mountains!" "There!" said Professor Brumbaugh, "that just suggests something." Then he told us of a place far out in a deep mountain gorge—"The Forge"—where there were several old houses in fair condition, one of them lately occupied by the wood-choppers.[20]

Thus began the saga of the "Orphans' Retreat," so memorably told in Emmert's *Reminiscences*. The three boys lived out their six-week "exile" near the main picnic area of what is now Trough Creek State Park. According to William Beery's own account of that experience, the three "refugees" reached the "Forge Country" by train and wagon. Accompanied by Jacob Brumbaugh they took the Huntingdon and Broad-top Railroad as far as the Aitch Station. From there Robert Mason, Brumbaugh's brother-in-law, gave them a jolting lift the rest of the way in his spring wagon.[21] (The route they took from Aitch is now partly covered by the waters of the new Raystown Lake.) Mason was the mailman who passed their ramshackle "hide-away" every day, delivering welcome letters from friends.

Both Emmert and Beery refer to frequent visitors, and so the "Orphans' " sojourn was not spent in utter solitude. One of their regular callers was a fifteen-year-old boy from Marklesburg, Martin Brumbaugh. "His greatest delight," said Beery, "was to take us on hikes up and down the valley and over the mountains to show us the sights." Much of the land was owned by his father, George. By their own admission, they had "a lot of fun."

But their enforced vacation brought hardships, too. Beery, who lived to be 103, wrote that each of them, in turn, came down with "an attack of something like the flue." Severe weather that January further added to the drama of the occasion. As the future Normal School music professor remembered it:

> We had no way of measuring the temperature, but we knew it was biting cold some days and nights. During the day time we had no trouble keeping from freezing, with fire in the "furnace" [a cookstove] and vigorous exercise; some nights, with the weather somewhere below the zero mark and the fire gone out, it was different, but there being three of us in one bed we managed to survive without any serious consequences. Mr. Peightel, a sympathetic friend, spent a few of the coldest nights with us, which made four in the same bed.[22]

BACK TO SCHOOL

Finally word reached them that the school would reopen on February 25, a week later than planned. (The borough ordinance banning public meetings had been rescinded on the 6th.) That announcement, said Beery, "was the most welcome news that came our way in the time of our residence at the 'Forge.' " They hurried back, bringing in tow their mountain guide, the budding "M.G."

Other resident students were notified by Zuck through an open letter published in the *Primitive Christian* on February 19. He himself was still at Claylick, ailing and able to get around only on crutches and with great pain.[23] As a result, he said that his own return would be delayed (he did not come back until March 25). The other instructors, he indicated, would carry on in his absence.

Zuck never disclosed, in the statistics he privately kept, how many returnees finished out the term. But apparently there were enough to reassure him that the school had survived the interruption. Furthermore, applications by early April seemed to augur a bumper crop of students for the spring term.

In anticipation of this surge in enrollment Zuck recruited a fifth faculty member—A. S. M. Anderson, a boyhood chum. Anderson was another Millersville degree-holder with further study at Mt. Union College in Ohio. He and the principal had grown up together on adjoining farms and attended the same country school as deskmates. Emmert wrote that the "very disability of Professor Zuck was an additional motive for the marked affection which Professor Anderson showed for him down to the day of his death."[24] The latter and Jacob Brumbaugh shared a third-floor room at Dr. A. B.'s. They had trouble sleeping in the same bed until they put a plank divider between them.

To accommodate the sixty-nine students that reported for the spring term, Zuck rented a second dwelling for a dormitory and boarding club. On April 4 the school tenanted the George Corbin house at 1204 Washington Street, a few doors south of the Burchinell Building. Curiously, this other rental, which was used until the move to Founders, has gone unmentioned in all previous accounts of the college's embryonic stage. (It was razed in 1960.)[25]

Normal School faculty, 1878. Zuck, cane in hand, grew beard and adopted straight coat after coming to Huntingdon. He is flanked by Phoebe Weakley and John C. Ewing. Standing: Jacob H. Brumbaugh, David Emmert, A. S. M. Anderson.

HUNTINGDON COMES THROUGH

Concurrently with this onrush of students came the good news that townspeople were prepared to donate the asked-for plot of ground in West Huntingdon. For two months after the smallpox scare business and professional men of the borough had done nothing about a building site. Their inaction finally provoked the temporary trustees into calling a mass meeting at the courthouse on Saturday evening, March 2, to bring the issue to a head. This call, which brought a response from fifty-some citizens, not only produced prompt action on donated land, but also gave birth to the Huntingdon Board of Trade (counterpart of today's Huntingdon Business and Industry, Inc.). As the *Globe* put it, "the object of this organization was 'to advance the general business interests of the town, and promote the general prosperity of the citizens of the town and country.' " A twenty-man directorship was formed, to which Henry Brumbaugh was elected.

The directors were authorized to begin a subscription campaign at once for the purpose of securing "Site No. 2." Appointed chairman of the subscription committee was R. Allison Miller, who had sold his broom and brush factory—directly across the street from the *Primitive Christian* building—the year before. The rest of the committee consisted of

Dr. A. B. Brumbaugh, William Woods, James Port, and Frank Isenberg. In a promotional spiel on March 4 the *Globe's* editor and proprietor, Alfred Tyhurst, laid it on the line to the borough businessmen. He urged:

> What is to be done in this direction must be done quickly, as the number of pupils has increased so rapidly that the present rented building is entirely too small, and, more than that, western towns have made very tempting offers to take not only the school but the *Primitive Christian* office away from us. If the school is permitted to go through lack of enterprise and liberality upon the part of our citizens, our town will lose at the least calculation, $90,000 every year. Can we afford to lose the circulation of this sum of money in our midst?

That evening the Board of Directors met as a body for the first time in the grand jury room. The subscription committee reported "Site No. 1" now available—at a price of thirty-four hundred dollars, which included all legal fees. This tract, it was explained, covered sixteen lots, broken down as follows: five lots by the Huntingdon Building and Loan Association; seven lots by the Reverends M. R. Foster and M. L. Smith; two lots by Dr. A. B. Brumbaugh; and two lots by Dr. Homer W. Buchanan.

The board, reversing its earlier recommendation, okayed the purchase of this property instead of "Site No. 2." Said the *Globe*, "The best of feeling prevailed at the meeting, and it was the determination of all present to use every effort to raise the amount." The paper indicated that $2,040 had already been pledged to date.

The committee "worked like beavers," declared the *Globe*, for the rest of March before "their efforts were crowned with success." "They met with much discouragement," the paper acknowledged, "but Spartan like, they persevered." On Saturday, March 20 the solicitors made their final report to the Board of Trade, which then directed its treasurer, Caleb C. North, to collect pledge payments and deliver the deeds to the school trustees. In due time—on Thursday, April 25—these deeds for the three-acre plot were turned over to Henry Brumbaugh, trustee president.

The founders could at last breathe a sigh of relief. For there was no question about their readiness to pull up stakes if the Board of Trade's campaign had fizzled out.

BUILDING ON THE HILL

Earlier, on March 11, once it was pretty evident that the local drive would succeed, the trustees had begun to draw up rough sketches of a main building. On that date *Primitive Christian* employee William Swigart became one of the six temporary trustees. An ex-teacher, he replaced Beer, who had left to join Henry Holsinger in a new publishing venture at Meyersdale. They agreed on a four-story T-shaped structure, the front facing south (not, as now, toward Moore Street), to which wings could be added when needed without marring the original plan. But Henry Brumbaugh and Zuck did not see eye to eye on size. Zuck submitted a diagram with an eighty-foot front and a rear extension one-hundred feet deep, which would include a chapel. Brumbaugh held out for a one-hundred foot front. Dr. A. B. talked up the idea of a tower projection, for a buttress rather than for looks. The publisher had his way until estimates came in, none below eleven-thousand dollars. After that the plans were scaled down closer to Zuck's dimensions (84' x 102') but with a tower entrance (12' x 18'). Zuck said of the building's design: "We aim at plainness, but do not wish to ignore correct taste or architectural skill and beauty."[26] Final plans were prepared by the Philadelphia architect S. D. Button, who charged seventy-five dollars for his services.

On the first day of May the school plot — a potato patch the year before — was surveyed and the building staked off. A simple groundbreaking ceremony brightened Monday morning the 6th, the soil soggy and the day overcast. A half-dozen parties took turns at the shovel: Dr. A. B., Henry and Jacob Brumbaugh, Zuck, Quinter, and the doctor's son, Gaius, representing the students. The excavation bid had gone to "Messrs. Jenkins, Brumbaugh, and Stouffer" at twenty-three cents a cubic yard, and after the brief ceremony their crew of twenty or more men started digging the foundation.[27] Within three weeks' time they had finished the job. As construction supervisor the trustees hired William Wright, an experienced carpenter who lived a stone's throw away. They paid him $1.50 a day.

By month's end John Smith, the mason, was laying the foundation wall. His bid on the stone work had been one dollar a perch (24 3/4 cubic foot) and he was to furnish the lime and sand. Also hard at work was the "Italian well-digger," Joseph Ronkenroney, at a spot in the northeast corner of the T (the angle facing the old gymnasium). To dig the twelve-foot well he was to get one dollar a foot for the first nine feet, a dollar and fifty cents a foot through slate without blasting, and two dollars a foot when dynamiting was necessary. Apparently a pick and shovel was all he needed because his bill came to only twelve dollars. In another couple of years he dug a second well near the first one.

THE ACADEMIC YEAR 1877-78 ENDS WITH HIGH PROMISE

While the new site was all ahum with workmen, townspeople were getting more and more involved in the cultural life of the Normal. The Juniata Literary Society had grown too large for the chapel, and so, in April, it was decided to form two groups. One was exclusively for students with private programs: the Junior Literary Society. The other was made up of "town and gown," renamed Eclectic Literary Society, and held public exercises. Each group kept on file its own *Literary Record*. With one-hundred members, the Eclectic Society adopted the motto "Onward and Upward."

This motto aptly epitomized the way things were going in general for the school as summer 1878 came and went. John Brumbaugh, who had assumed Beer's fund-raising chores, was on the road in Eastern Pennsylvania, enjoying good results in lining up stockholders (almost one hundred by August). And with fifty-some teachers in attendance, Zuck took satisfaction in his biggest summer session yet. Promotional literature now spoke of the "Brethren's Normal School and Collegiate Institute," identifying it as "A HOME, A SCHOOL, AND A CHURCH" — a phrase much-invoked over the next decade.

The school's first full-length catalog, a twenty-four-page brochure, appeared in August, flaunting the words "Collegiate Institute" on its title page. Under "Course of Instruction," it stated: "We aim to provide for a full Collegiate Course, but a shorter course has been arrangd for those who desire to obtain a good practical education at a minimum of expenditure of time and money." The academic program for the four-year liberal arts course was laid out in detail. Every subsequent issue of the catalog carried it, regardless of the fact that nobody would show any interest for another two decades.

The Normal English Course was what the catalog really meant to put across. It set forth a two-year diploma curriculum designed to train teachers. But for "ladies and gentlemen of exemplary deportment," only a year's work might suffice.

As for student supervision, the catalog scorned the "spy and police system" in vogue at many schools. At Huntingdon a "high sense of personal and individual responsibility" obtained. Those lacking this trait, it was suggested, "would do better to go to some College where the Professors have time to watch them." Instructors should be "personal friends" of students, the policy statement preached, and then ended with a word on the school's selective standards:

In the educational problem, quantity and quality are both important factors, but we want it understood that we shall ever keep in view, *not so much the number as the spirit, character and influence of our students.*

While Zuck compiled the first catalog the temporary trustees, on August 2, petitioned the Court of Common Pleas for incorporation under the name Brethren's Normal College. The articles of incorporation differed from the resolution of the previous year only in specifying fifteen trustees instead of nine; otherwise, all the provisions remained the same.

Late summer also saw Principal Zuck replace one faculty member and add another one. William Beery, one of the Ohio "Orphans," took over as music teacher for Ewing, who left for more training. Nicknamed the "sweet singer," he would teach part time while working off his degree, awarded in 1882. Beery went on to give thirty years in all to the college, twenty-one as trustee.

In Daniel Flory, a third-year student at the University of Virginia, the School had its eighth instructor. Hired to teach the classics, German, and literature, Flory was let go the following summer because he was not enough of a "generalist." He proved his worth later, however. In 1880 he founded Spring Creek Normal School in Virginia, which evolved into Bridgewater College, now a sister institution of Juniata.

Every member of the faculty that fall of 1878 — one woman and seven men — had somehow managed to escape matrimony.

THE CHARTER AND A FORMAL ADMINISTRATIVE SETUP

The school's third academic year opened on an expectant note. Zuck welcomed sixty students, and work on the new building pushed ahead rapidly. On Tuesday, November 18, the charter of incorporation cleared its last legal test, and the name Brethren's Normal College was made official. This happy event was almost celebrated under a cloud. Only the day before, John Richardson, a carpenter, fell from the cupola on the tower to the roof of the building, sustaining severe injuries. Fortunately, he caught himself before falling to the ground and certain death.[28]

On December 24 Jacob Zuck took the 7:30 morning train for Ashland College on a goodwill trip. He found their building at about the same stage of construction as the one in Huntingdon. His guide was Solomon Sharp, his erstwhile don, who had been elected Ashland's first president. In writing about this two-day jaunt for the *Primitive Christian*, Zuck admitted to his earlier prejudice against the Ohio venture, fearing that the Brethren might "ignore the work that has been done and yet remains to be done here among the hills of the good old Keystone State."[29] But now, the educator wrote, he desired "to form the acquaintance of some of our western educational brethren in the hope that something may be done to bring about greater unity of aim and effort." In return the *Gospel Preacher*, published by Ashland Brethren, paid Zuck this tribute: "The substantial interest now manifested by our brethren on the subject of the proper education of our youth is greatly owing to his unflinching energy and devotion to the educational cause."[30]

In February the temporary trustees gave attention to the administrative organization of the college now that the charter was official. At their meeting on the 28th John Brumbaugh offered the following motion, which passed unanimously:

The Principal

1. The Principal shall be President of the Faculty.

2. He shall have the general oversight of the School, and its working; direct its classification; administer the discipline, and attend to any special correspondence.

The Secretary

1. The Secretary shall act as assistant to the Principal by attending to the general correspondence of the School, the business transactions with the Students, furnishing their books, and performing such other duties as may be requested by the Principal as directed by the Trustees.

Dr. A. B. nominated Zuck for the position of "Principal and President," while Jacob Brumbaugh got William Swigart's nomination for "Secretary." Both were elected unchallenged.

THE MOVE TO THE HILL

Much of the trustees' time in the succeeding weeks went into ordering furniture and equipment for the building, which was fast nearing completion. Each room was to be furnished with a double bed, table, washstand, bucket, pitcher, basin, and two chairs. It was decided to purchase a piano and organ, to be used jointly by the church and college — a decision that bothered conservative Brethren for years to come. To make the best use of dormitory space the trustees ruled against private quarters for the principal and secretary; each had to share his room — and the double bed — with a student.

When the spring term began on Monday, April 7, seventy-five resident students (out of an enrollment of 102) had moved into the still unfinished building, pressing hard upon the carpenters, plasterers, and painters. "To help matters along," Emmert later recalled, "some of us who knew the use of tools quit the classroom some weeks before the moving day and turned carpenter to help complete the work on time."[31]

On a rainy Thursday afternoon, April 17, dedicatory services were held in the chapel. The local clergy participated and James Quinter preached the sermon. Jacob Zuck was in his glory, and to some well-wishers after the ceremony was over, he allowed for the first time: "The day of success is dawning."[32]

The "Building," its unceremonious name before christened Founders Hall in the mid-1890s, stood out starkly in a bare field of slaty rock on dedication day. Emmert graphically describes the unattractive grounds at that time in *Reminiscences:*

> When the first pick was struck for the foundation of this structure, in the whole area of the campus to be, stood one lone stunted walnut tree. The soil was so thin that not a spear of sward-grass grew therein. Insignificant mosses, lichens, and such plants as endure severe drought, gave a tinge of tawny green to the hilltop. When school opened in the new quarters, we were practically in the middle of a plowed field. Fences were not yet built nor walks laid out, and not a tree had been set.[33]

In design and floor plan, the "Building" was as functional as an apiary — and soon as much abuzz with activity. The basement contained the dining room, kitchen and pantry, the laundry, a storeroom, and three apartment rooms used by the steward and kitchen help. There was an underground cellar in the rear.

On the main floor were found the library, parlor, two classrooms, and the chapel, which could squeeze in about five-hundred bodies.

Zuck had his room and an office on the third floor over the library. The bookroom was across the hall. The women dormed in a dozen rooms over the chapel, their wing screened off with a red muslin curtain.

The top story housed the men. Besides the tower staircase a narrow flight of steps wound down to the second floor just inside the Moore Street doorway. Stairs also ran down the back end, for exclusive use of women.

Missing, though, were bathrooms and inside toilets. An outhouse behind the "Building" answered the latter purpose.[34] And sponge baths deodorized the body politic until tubs came along.

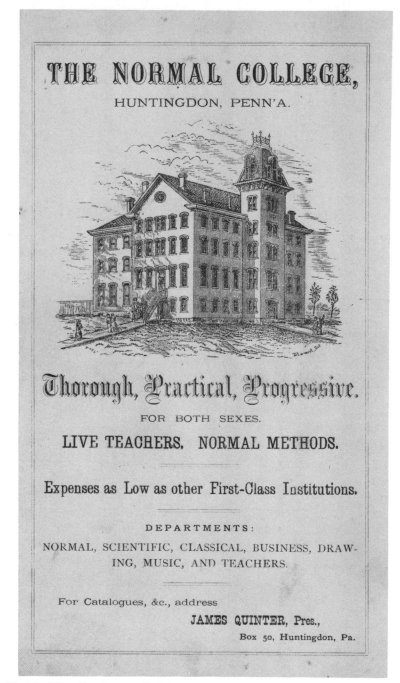

THE NORMAL COLLEGE,

HUNTINGDON, PENN'A.

Thorough, Practical, Progressive.

FOR BOTH SEXES.

LIVE TEACHERS. NORMAL METHODS.

Expenses as Low as other First-Class Institutions.

DEPARTMENTS:

NORMAL, SCIENTIFIC, CLASSICAL, BUSINESS, DRAWING, MUSIC, AND TEACHERS.

For Catalogues, &c., address

JAMES QUINTER, Pres.,

Box 50, Huntingdon, Pa.

The "Building," as it was called for years. Here it is pictured on delightful old advertisement that appeared on back cover of Annual Meeting Report for 1882, printed by Brumbaugh and Quinter. Note fence running north on left, dividing boys' campus from girls' campus.

In the early days a picket fence, running north from the chapel end, divided the "yard" into a "boys' campus" and a "girls' campus." The walk leading from the tower entrance was reserved for coed traffic exclusively. For the fellows, there was the west entrance.

Oil for kerosene lamps was kept outdoors in a barrel. It was strictly rationed. A Normalite could be ousted for disregarding the curfew hour in the use of lamp oil.

Two more bachelors were added to the faculty when the college moved to the Hill. William Cotton, a brilliant orator skilled in shorthand and with striking Oriental features, came to teach Elocution and Rhetoric. The new mathematics instructor was Joseph Saylor, a Millersville graduate—like Cotton—who got to know Zuck there in 1873. Saylor, whom Cupid failed to waylay for another two decades, would spend thirty-two years teaching at the college, seven more than he put in as trustee. Cotton, a non-Brethren, left after two years and later became a federal judge on the West Coast. But he never lost touch with the little school set in the mountain fastness of Central Pennsylvania.

DEATH OF JACOB ZUCK

The euphoria everywhere evident on the Hill those thrilling April days in 1879 lingered on through the spring. Attention now began to turn to another historic event scheduled for July: commencement for the first graduating class. But early in May the college community was dealt a stunning blow by Jacob Zuck's untimely death. Ironically, it was the "Building" that led to his undoing.

The dampness caused by still-drying plaster and the strain from extra stairs aggravated his deformed hip and apparently wore him down. Emmert and others worried about his "feeble state of health" and begged him to put a heater in his room (there was no central heating at first, only hall stoves). But, said Emmert, "He resolutely declined all extra attention on the ground that he would not have what the rest of us had not."[35]

Fatigued, he caught a severe cold that developed into pneumonia in his left lung. On Wednesday, May 7, the dying principal was carried in a chair to John Brumbaugh's house a few blocks away. Four days later, on Sunday the 11th, Jacob Zuck died at 3:30 P.M., dear friend Emmert holding his hand in a deathbed watch.[36] He was seven months past his thirty-second birthday. Quinter preached the funeral sermon the next day, but interment in Riverview Cemetery was delayed until Tuesday morning—after the arrival of Zuck's parents. Long-faced students acted as pallbearers.

On the day Zuck was buried George Phillips, a Virginian, dropped out of school. Reminiscing in 1911, he wrote, "When near the station, I looked back and said to myself, 'What will become of the Normal?' "[37] At first that was the question hanging heavy on everybody's mind. Could the still-struggling school survive the calamity of its founder's death? As David Emmert said, "To take up the thread of his thought and develop the enterprise which he had merely begun was no small task."[38]

But amidst the despair there were also expressions of hope. James Quinter had built his eulogium upon the text, "The Lord will prepare a sacrifice." The grand old man reassured his dismayed audience: "Someone will take up this work where Professor Zuck laid it down. The seed sown in faith and watered with tears cannot fail of harvest."[39]

The evening of Zuck's burial the Huntingdon Brethren gathered on the banks of the Juniata River to observe the rite of baptism. The lone baptismal candidate was the seventeen-year-old Martin Brumbaugh. David Emmert's mother witnessed the scene, the words of Quinter fresh in her memory. As she watched, she turned to Emmert and said,

"That boy may some day fill Professor Zuck's place."

She clung to her intuition til her dying day, shortly before the prophecy was fulfilled.[40]

4

Others Take Up The Work
1879-1888

MEMORIALIZING ZUCK

Dr. A. B. Brumbaugh stood at the lectern-pulpit in the chapel, a prepared speech before him. The members of the Eclectic Literary Society waited for him to begin—on that Thursday evening, June 12. It was to be their memorial service for Jacob Zuck.

The doctor began by characterizing the late principal as an intellectual hermit, "whose brief life was wrapped up in books and study and teaching." Only such self-devotion on Zuck's part and his "determined will," the speaker said, made the Huntingdon school possible. "He pushed forward his work, thinking while others were idle, working while they were sleeping."[1]

No one who heard these words felt that the doctor had overstated his case. For not a single person in that audience could ever remember seeing the no-nonsense educator at play.[2]

Dr. Brumbaugh ended his address on a prophetic note, indulging himself in some predictions about the future greatness of the college. He declared that it was destined to survive as a monument to its founding teacher. But more than that, he promised, "The time will come when the influence of this school movement will be felt from the Atlantic to the Pacific, and from the Lakes to the Gulf."

That climactic sentence, however, never made the copy that afterward went to the newspapers; it was furtively deleted by David Emmert and other confederates. This made Dr. A. B. very unhappy. Emmert wrote of the incident in his *Reminiscences* and explained: "Some of us thought these utterances rather extravagant and felt that such a prophecy con-

78

cerning so small an institution was almost ridiculous. . .[and] would be an injury to the cause at the time."[3] The ringleader, he kept "mum" and let the editorial staff of the *Primitive Christian* bear the blame for "butchering the manuscript." He confessed to suffering twinges of guilt every time the matter came up. Not until the doctor read *Reminiscences* in 1901 did he learn the truth about its author's part in the escapade.

One bright, moonlit night soon after the society's program, a few of the college boys mustered for prayer in the meadow below the Hill. There in a grove of elms, Gaius Brumbaugh, about to graduate, proposed that the students memorialize their deceased principal by some gift to the college. He suggested an oil portrait of Zuck. The prayer band thought it a good idea.

In a matter of days sixty-one Normalites chipped in twenty-five dollars for that purpose. Probably on Emmert's advice they commissioned John Chaplin, a local mulatto artist who barbered for a living, to do the painting (for nineteen dollars). Gilt framed (for six dollars), it hung for years in the "Building's" parlor.

Such a thing was unheard of among the simple, frugal Brethren. The "taking of likenesses" was bad enough, and six times between 1839, when daguerreotype was perfected, and 1879 the church condemned posing for pictures as vainglory. Photography was a still-touchy subject at Annual Meetings as late as 1903.

But to spend so much money on a painted portrait was thought to be sheer prodigality. It could well be that the Zuck canvas was the first one in the Brotherhood.

FIRST COMMENCEMENT

Gradually the trauma of Zuck's death began to ease, although his absence at the first commencement had a tempering effect on all activities. Bouquets were tabooed and there was no applause on orders from the trustees. Held on Thursday, July 10, it was a day-long, all College affair, which started at 8:30 in the morning. The chapel walls fairly resounded to a succession of essays, orations, recitations, declamations, and a variety of musical selections. James Quinter, who only moments earlier had accepted the newly created office of president, addressed the graduates in the evening and gave them their handwritten diplomas. His speech, transcribed by Prof. Cotton, who sat behind a screen near the rostrum, dwelt upon the utilitarian value of a liberal education. In making his perorative point, the hoary-headed president said:

The best and most important thing in an education is not the amount of knowledge acquired, but the training which gives us control of our minds—the power of being able to apply the mind to studies, labor, and duties which the calling we select may require.[4]

Before the historic event wound up, Elder Isaac Price of Chester County, a long-time educationist and then the country's oldest postmaster—in both age and tenure—asked for the floor. (Quinter's first job after leaving school had been in his country store.) The local press reported that the seventy-seven-year-old patron gave a rousing impromptu speech, after which he donated a large Bible that long afterward rested on the chapel pulpit.

Class of 1879. Linnie Bosserman (Grigsby), Gaius Brumbaugh, Phoebe R. Norris.

FIRST THREE GRADUATES

Bachelor of English degrees were conferred on three graduates, only one of whom — Gaius Brumbaugh — had shared with Jacob Zuck the excitement of that memorable April morning in 1876. He and the other two classmates, both women, went on to distinguished careers. Brumbaugh attended several medical schools, earning M. D. degrees from both Howard and Georgetown Universities. Along with his private practice in Washington, D. C., he held a succession of medical posts in the federal government. Dr. Brumbaugh was a man of wide-ranging interests, but he was most notably a history buff. He was also an ardent genealogist and published a monumental study of the Brumbaugh families in 1913. A trustee for forty years, twelve as board chairman, he proved to be an alumnus par excellence.

The other two-thirds of the class of 1879 — Phoebe Norris of Gettysburg, Elder Price's granddaughter, and Linnie Bosserman, a Missourian — left their mark in the world, too. Phoebe Norris taught school for a while and then entered the Postal Department in Washington, D. C. While there she studied medicine at Columbia College (now George Washington University) where she received her degree in 1891. A confirmed spinster and faithful alumna, she was elected vice-president of the Medical Association of the District of Columbia in 1907, one of the first women physicians to be so honored.

Linnie Bosserman (Grigsby), herself an off-and-on medical student, became a schoolteacher out West. Her fields were art and music, and she taught in Colorado and Missouri before going to an Indian school in Oklahoma. There, in the mid-1890s, she became the "happy bride" of the United States Commissioner of Courts.

FIRST PERMANENT BOARD OF TRUSTEES

By the time the Class of '79 departed the campus on their separate ways, important changes had been made in the composition of the board of trustees and in the college's administrative setup. At their May 26th meeting the temporary trustees, in keeping with the charter, acted to elect a permanent board from among the stockholders. They drew up a slate of candidates and sent it out, announcing that the ballots would be counted on June 30. The stockholders elected to the first board were: three-year term — James Quinter (the biggest vote-getter), Henry Brumbaugh, Daniel F. Stouffer (Benevola, Maryland), Jacob F. Oller (Waynesboro), and Dr. A. B. Brumbaugh; two-year term — John Harley (Pottstown), William Swigart, John Brumbaugh, A. W. Mentzer (Ephrata), and

J. W. Beachey (Elk Lick); one-year term—Jacob Connor (East Coventry), Edward Kendig, whose wife was the smallpox victim in 1878 (Fisherville, Virginia), Hiram Musselman (Scalp Level), B. F. Price, son of Isaac Price, and Dr. C. F. Oellig (Woodbury). Nine of the first fifteen board members were church elders.

The day before commencement seven of the trustees-elect were able to be present for organizing the board. They picked Henry Brumbaugh to be chairman, a position he would hold for forty years—until his death in 1919. Daniel F. Stouffer was chosen vice-chairman; Dr. A. B. Brumbaugh, secretary and solicitor for the library; and John Brumbaugh, treasurer and superintendent of grounds and buildings. John Brumbaugh would put in three more years on the board than his brother, while their cousin, the doctor, and Elder Stouffer served twenty-nine and nineteen years respectively. Of the rest of the original members, four put in stints of ten or more years: Oller (eighteen), Harley (thirteen), Quinter (ten), and William Swigart, the Methuselah in terms of service, a phenomenal six decades.

JAMES QUINTER: FIRST PRESIDENT

Having organized, the trustees met again on commencement day, after the afternoon exercises, to name the administrative officers of the college. Jacob Brumbaugh, acting principal since Zuck's death, was elected to that position for another year.

Then, in a surprise move, the trustees created a higher office—that of president. What prompted this step is not at all clear since the minutes for this meeting are typically synoptic. There is no evidence that the idea had ever come under prior review by the Huntingdon men. Probably the decision was dictated in large part by the fact that the other two Brethren colleges—Ashland and Mt. Morris—were headed by presidents.[5] And evidently the holdover trustees, who openly begrudged the rivalry of these western schools, saw in the presidency some kind of status symbol.

Such an interpretation gains more credence when it is noticed that the presidency was essentially a titular position for the next fourteen years—until 1893 when M. G. Brumbaugh assumed the office. The duty of the president during those years was to act officially for the college only on stated occasions, whereas at the two sister institutions he was the chief administrative officer.

Nevertheless, the new post demanded a man of mettle and intellectual stature, a man who could rally the shaken college community by symbolizing the spirit of the founders and the whole cause of Christian education.

He had to be a man who could salve the wounds higher education had inflicted upon the Brethren.

Without hesitation the trustees turned to James Quinter, the sixty-three-year-old sage whose name was synonymous with the rise of Brethren schools. As David Emmert wrote of him: "His high standing in the church, his nobility of character and eminent qualities of mind and heart well fitted him for the position he was so unexpectedly called upon to fill. The influence of his life upon the students who came under his administration cannot be estimated."[6] But Quinter, nearing retirement age, resisted the presidential call. Henry Brumbaugh revealed in the *Primitive Christian* that his business partner acquiesced only with "great reluctance" and at the "urgent request of the Board."[7]

FACULTY

Under the new administrative plan the day-to-day operation of the college remained in the hands of the principal and his assistant, the secretary of the faculty. Except for a two-year hiatus—from 1881 to 1883—the principal's mantle rested on the shoulders of Jacob Brumbaugh from the time of Zuck's death to 1893, when the position was abolished. It was this intense, strong-willed administrator, only twenty-eight when he took over, who was the polar figure in the immediate post-Zuck decade. Short, with dark, piercing eyes, Brumbaugh bore the major responsibility in the Eighties for developing the curriculum, recruiting the faculty, and building up the enrollment. As Emmert said of him and his work:

> When it is remembered that these years covered the most critical period in the history of the educational work of the denomination, a period when the schools were on trial, when favorable sentiment was unorganized and criticism was ranging with loose rein, the difficulties of the position can be imagined. . . .Professor J. H. Brumbaugh's administration covered [Juniata's] youthful period and ended at the point when the young institution attained its majority, made its bow to the world, changed its name, enlarged its equipment and stood up to be counted as a college among the colleges.[8]

The position of faculty secretary was first filled in 1881 by the self-same Jacob Brumbaugh, who, for reasons not given in the trustee minutes, opted to trade administrative chairs for a two-year spell. William Swigart was appointed principal in the interim. Brumbaugh was succeeded as secretary by Joseph Saylor, the first regular college graduate on the faculty (he completed his studies at Ursinus in 1882). He held the office until it, too, was eliminated in 1893 along with the principalship.

Everyone taught for a pittance. In 1882, for example, Saylor was paid $450 a year plus room and board and assigned seven class periods a day. Public school teachers were doing much better than that.

To help make ends meet while principal, Brumbaugh (a bridegroom in 1880) worked on the side as a special agent for the B & O Railroad, representing Western Pennsylvania. In the summers he was on the sales force of E. H. Butler and Company, a publisher of textbooks.[9]

In the early 1880s it was jokingly said that the Brethren's Normal College amounted to a Millersville "annex" because of the number of its graduates on the faculty.

Perhaps so, but because of low salaries—not til World War 1 years did senior professors earn as much as one-thousand dollars—the turnover of instructors was frightfully high. Only Brumbaugh, Saylor, and Swigart gave stability to the faculty during the Quinter years. Phoebe Weakley, a stand-by from the beginning almost, resigned in 1881 because of her rheumatic condition. William Beery was gone from 1885 to 1889, studying and conducting music institutes in the Midwest. And David Emmert took a nine-year leave (1883-92) to oversee and coordinate the work of two orphanages he founded at Huntingdon and Hagerstown, Maryland. The stockholders, however, recognized Emmert's value to the college and in 1884 elected him to the first of nine consecutive three-year terms as trustee. Emmert, always the gentle-spirited humanitarian, was a rare soul, never one to prostitute his artistic gifts for personal gain. John C. Blair, father of the paper tablet, found that out. Theirs was a staunch friendship, an intriguing union of small-town tycoon and good Samaritan.

Long since forgotten, the story of their relationship was first told publicly by Emmert in 1897, upon Blair's premature death at age forty-nine.[10] They first met in the fall of 1877, soon after Emmert's arrival in Huntingdon, when he stopped in Blair's bookstore on the Penn Street diamond. The two young men—only a year's difference in age—struck up a conversation. The storekeeper revealed his ambition to mass produce some line of paper merchandise, at the time thinking it might be wallpaper. Obligingly, the town's newcomer volunteered to make cuts of original designs for Blair's use. Thus began an acquaintanceship fed over the years by mutual admiration.

But as they chatted that fall day in 1877 Emmert occupied himself in fashioning a pad, $5\frac{3}{4}''$ x $8\frac{1}{2}''$, which he intended to use for taking notes while auditing Zuck's rhetoric class. For backing at the top, he scrounged a piece of stiff cardboard. Then he took a stack of papers, trimmed to size, and clamped it together with four large carpet tacks, using an old-fashioned wire clinch borrowed from the bookstore owner.

It was this homemade pad that inspired the "Blair Tablet" and a whole new stationery industry. Emmert's friend had found his "line" and promptly forgot about wallpaper. At first the "modest little tablet of common newspaper" was fastened by ordinary carpet tacks like the ones the art teacher used. Later, Blair employed copper tacks and then followed glue, "a great improvement."

A year or so following, after the tablet had begun to catch on, especially in public schools, Emmert was Johnny-on-the-spot again. As he told it:

> One day as I entered the store [Blair] addressed me in a cheerful mood, "I want to improve these tablets; can you make a design for a cover with a Keystone as a trade mark?" We both seated ourselves on the counter and there on a piece of brown wrapping paper I sketched the design for the "Keystone Pencil Tablet." "That is just what I want, make me a cut at once," he said, without asking cost.

The resourceful ex-patternmaker got hold of a few dental instruments, visited a local blacksmith shop, and forged out most of the tools he needed to make the cut. By 1882 the Keystone trademark, still carried on one Mead Products item today, could be seen on stationery in many European countries and throughout most of the Western Hemisphere. Supposedly Blair was so impressed with Emmert that he offered him half interest in the burgeoning business. But the gifted artist, at the time more excited about building orphanages than about making and marketing tablets, turned the invitation down.

It was a minor setback, then, to lose the services of Emmert and the others so closely identified with the school's origins. But this void was partly filled by a short, boyish-looking individual in his early thirties named William Swigart. As a lad, born in an old cottage along Jacks Mountain, he had led his blind father around Mifflin County selling pins and needles for a living. He attended Kishacoquillas Seminary and from 1868 to 1876 taught public school. A born preacher known for his precise articulation, he next worked in the *Primitive Christian* office before joining the faculty in March 1880. By then he was already on the trustee board.

Swigart, who at first handled a strange combination of subjects— Surveying and Elocution—would come to enjoy a strong and lasting

Above:　Cover and broken backing of tablet Emmert improvised in John C. Blair's Store.
Below:　Trademark Emmert designed for Blair.

friendship with Henry Brumbaugh. Ardent anglers, they whiled away many an hour in each other's company fishing the bass-filled waters of the old Raystown Branch. Between them, they represented a century of yeoman's service on the board of trustees. Swigart's sixty years, however, will likely stand forever as a Juniata College record. As Emmert said of this teacher-trustee midway in his career—a laudation that applied to the very end: "His life has been bound up in the life of the school, and of him, if of any one, it may be said, 'He is wedded to the work.' "[11]

Beginning with 1883 Dr. A. B. Brumbaugh, no less "wedded to the work," got catalog notice as a lecturer in hygiene. At first he made classroom visits only occasionally, but with 1885 one afternoon period every Thursday was set aside for him. A devotee of Dr. Dio Lewis, the famed temperance reformer, he dwelt much, in talking about hygienic living, on the "evils" of tobacco and strong drink.[12] And each year he favored the fellows with a special homily on the "bad effects" of masturbation. The doctor was also available to physiology classes, for whom he sometimes performed vivisections on stray cats captured on campus.

The names of two women appeared with that of Dr. A. B.'s in the faculty listing for 1883. Huntingdon's Ida Pecht, a talented musician, was hired to teach piano and organ while completing her Normal course. (Two female instructors, each for one year, had handled instrumental music before her.) She stayed on for nine years, and when William Beery was gone gave voice lessons as well.

Harriet Wilson, of nearby Alexandria, took charge of the art department for one year. She belonged to a distinguished family of artists and was the sister of Dr. Jerry Wilson, a well-known portrait painter. Jacob Zuck had recruited their sister, Martha, on a part-time basis in the spring of 1877 before Emmert was able to come.

The catalog for 1884-85 names no art instructor, but the following year red-haired Cora Brumbaugh (Silverthorn), Dr. A. B.'s daughter '83, was given the appointment. She taught four years under her uncle-principal in this capacity, taking off the spring of 1886 to attend the Philadelphia Art School for Women.[13]

In 1885 Lizzie Howe (Brubaker), upon her graduation, became the third woman on the nine-member faculty for that year. A farm girl from near Lewistown, she was one of a family of twelve children. Her father, William, was a Dunker elder and served as trustee from 1883 to 1892. Three of her brothers and one sister went on to graduate from the college. She taught English grammar until 1894, and Emmert wrote,

"During these years Miss Howe was a strong factor in the development of the intellectual and moral life of the school."[14]

The staffing of the classics, however, proved most nettlesome. Six different men handled that department during Quinter's nine-year presidency. An octogenarian Baptist minister, J. B. Kidder, former head of the Shirleysburg Seminary, held the position longest—three years, 1880-83.

Not only did low pay discourage non-Brethren members of the teaching staff from long-term commitments. Sometimes the quality of food served in the dining room created morale problems of its own for boarding faculty, to say nothing of students. There was so much grousing about the cuisine by the faculty in the spring of 1880 that the guilty parties were called on the carpet by the trustees. The minutes of that body reveal that the cavillers were "severely admonished concerning table etiquette and discussing victuals at the table."[15]

Then in the fall, hardly before school had even begun, the boarders staged an open protest. This time it was the faculty that asked for a showdown. They presented the trustees with a list of culinary grievances, complaining of such things as "not enough meat," "steak and mush for breakfast but none for supper," "knives too dull," "no sugar in the syrup."[16] The demonstration brought immediate results, and led to the hiring of an additional cook and—as an incentive—raising the wages of each girl in the kitchen to $1.75 a week.

CURRICULUM

The catalogs for this period carried the curricula for three programs: the two-year Normal English and the more advanced Scientific (three years) and Classical (four years). There were no takers, of course, for the Classical and only three completed the Scientific before it was phased out in 1896.

The first to receive a B. S. degree beyond the B. E. was Martin G. Brumbaugh in 1885, a year after his appointment as superintendent of schools for Huntingdon County at the tender age of twenty-two.

Well into the next century it was the custom to confer a Master of English degree on Normal graduates who had taught for two years, "maintained a good moral character," and paid a fee of five dollars.

Virtually all students, therefore, were pursuing Normal English study. Its curriculum was fixed, since the trustees would have nothing to do with the elective reforms of Harvard's Charles Eliot and Michigan's James Angell at this time. Henry Brumbaugh flatly argued that most students were not mature enough to deal with such freedom.

A preparatory year for those needing it—and most did—was developed in 1883. Three years later the trustees imposed a comprehensive examination upon juniors. The seniors, of course, faced a visiting committee of four examiners, one of whom ordinarily was the county superintendent. Indeed, most years county school heads exclusively made up the panel of final examiners. In 1884 the original thesis requirement was dropped.

Normal English students of that time lock-stepped their way through the following curriculum:

PREPARATORY YEAR

FALL TERM—Elocution, Orthography, Penmanship, Political Geography and Map Drawing, Grammar, Arithmetic

WINTER TERM—Elocution, Vocal Music, Drawing, Grammar, Mental Arithmetic, Written Arithmetic

SPRING TERM—Drawing, Physical Geography, Lectures on Teaching, Grammar, Arithmetic, Algebra

JUNIOR YEAR

FALL TERM—Book-keeping, English Literature, History (U. S.), Grammar, Arithmetic, Algebra

WINTER TERM—Physiology, American Literature, History (U. S.), Grammar, Arithmetic, Algebra

SPRING TERM—Etymology, Botany, Rhetoric, Constitution (U. S.), Grammar, Geometry, Mental Arithmetic

SENIOR YEAR

FALL TERM—Mental Philosophy, Natural Philosophy, Latin, Rhetoric, Grammar, Geometry

WINTER TERM—Mental Philosophy, Natural Philosophy, Latin, Grammar, Astronomy, Science of Teaching

SPRING TERM—Mental Philosophy, Latin, Evidences of Christianity, Science of Teaching, Review of Studies

All textbooks had to be cleared through the trustees. American Literature classes, however, had no censorship problems with anthologies of Whittier and Longfellow, two "household poets" of that day. A Whittier-Longfellow symposium was held in the chapel in March 1885, an event of which Whittier was posted by some public-relations-minded Normalite (Longfellow was dead). In response, there came a little note of acknowledgment from the seventy-nine-year-old Quaker bard saying:

Danvers, Mass. 2d Mo. 15, 1885

I shall be glad if the students of the Normal College find something worthy of their interest in my writings. They have my best wishes.

John G. Whittier[17]

Except for the preparatory year, art and music—unlike literature—were offered as electives (this was the only concession on electives made by the trustees). Nevertheless, these areas of the curriculum attracted their share of votaries. The art department provided studio coaching (oils), but its staple offering was drawing and design, especially under Emmert's tutelage. Students of this "born artist," the catalog avouched, "cannot fail to make rapid progress in this highly essential. . .branch of education, giving culture to hand, eye, taste and judgment." Training in visual composition, it was pointed out elsewhere, had practical benefits, too. The experience would prove helpful "not only in the class-room but on the farm and in the workshop," since it involved exercises in mechanical drawing and industrial design.[18]

Elements of Vocal Music and Sight Reading was the music department's counterpart in popularity. In the winter term of 1883 the entire student body of fifty-two took this late afternoon class from William Beery. There were also private lessons in voice, piano, and organ. During the 1887-88 school year sixteen undergraduates—all but five of whom were coeds—received piano and organ instruction, first made available in 1881.

This evidence of keyboard interest was another illustration of changing values among college-going Brethren youth. Church prejudice against playing musical instruments, both in homes and in churches, was still deep-rooted, and their use would remain a vibrant issue as late as the 1920s. In fact, the first catalog in 1878 echoed this provincialism: "We encourage our students to give their attention to Vocal music in preference to Instrumental."

The natural sciences in the 1880s never enjoyed qualified staffing. Subjects were meted out among available faculty. Joseph Saylor, a mathematician, made astronomy his bailiwick, and M. G. Brumbaugh taught all science classes during a one-year appointment (1882-83) while pursuing the Scientific course. Thereafter, a classics scholar might very well end up teaching botany. But nobody tackled chemistry; it was ignored.

Scientific equipment materialized very slowly in those nonlaboratory days. In 1881 the college became the proud possessor of its first microscope, made possible by a fifty-dollar cash gift from a Western Pennsylvania patron. And another piece of scientific apparatus—a "heliotellus" (planetarium)—cost the trustees forty dollars in 1884. The Boston dealer from whom it was bought hawked in business ads: "One of these can be seen at the Normal College, Huntingdon, Pa."[19] Beginning in the fall of 1887 physiology classes scrutinized the latest anatomical charts and had for their use several mannequins with movable and detachable parts.

Charges for a Normal education remained wonderfully stable between 1879 and 1888. Despite the nation's unprecedented industrial and economic boom in that period, tuition for a forty-two-week academic year increased but eight dollars—from $34.00 to $42.00. The cost of room and board reflected even less of an inflationary hike, rising from $115.50 to $121.80, a difference of just six and a half dollars.

Even though the summer teachers' term provided an additional source of income and its enrollment was holding up, the trustees abolished it in 1881. The reason given: "The time is too short to accomplish any effective work in giving culture to the teachers."[20] There was no effort to revive summer study until 1895.

LIBRARY AND SCIENCE MUSEUM

In the decade after Zuck's death Dr. A. B. Brumbaugh took it on himself, among the trustees, to build up the library and develop a science museum. His son, Gaius, had a hand in these projects, too, while establishing his medical practice in Washington, D. C. Dr. A. B. made the catalog his chief organ for sounding the cry of need in these areas.

"The importance of a Library of standard and miscellaneous works in an institution of learning, cannot be over-estimated," so went the catalog appeal—year in, year out—for books and money.

The 1878 lithographic view of Huntingdon—as a premium—went with a donation of two dollars or more. And by way of recognition the names of all donors were printed periodically in the catalog. Even so, by 1888 the library still fell far short of a thousand volumes, much to the disappointment of the Brumbaugh medics, father and son.

In 1885 the Normal College Library was made a repository of all federal publications, thanks to the pull on Capitol Hill of Dr. Gaius and Congressman Louis Atkinson. At the same time Huntingdon County historian, J. Simpson Africa, then State Secretary of Internal Affairs, and Assemblyman J. P. Giles were responsible for placing an up-to-date set of the Pennsylvania Geological Survey in the stacks.

The tiny one-room library was hardly a place of heavy traffic when the "Building" opened for business. For half a decade or more its holdings were kept under lock and key in glass-doored cases.[21] Library hours were limited to Saturday morning—when books could be checked in or out. Each student was allowed to take out only one book every two weeks. Henry Brumbaugh's *Golden Dawn*, a short-lived Christian education journal, noted that just forty-five percent of the students were book-borrowers during the fall term of 1885.[22] Interestingly, the women outnumbered the men three to one in library use.

Later—before the end of the Eighties—library services materially expanded. A reference library was installed in the hall of the main floor, but after a few years it was replaced by separate collections (each of some 160 volumes) for the men and women on their own dormitory floors. The main library itself kept hours each afternoon, a convenience made possible by volunteer student help.

For a quarter of a century after 1879 the care of the library remained in unprofessional hands. Gaius Brumbaugh, while a student, began to inventory the glass-cased holdings. His catalog recorded the call number and title of each book, its value and donor, and its case and shelf location.

The college relied upon student librarians until 1882, when Martin G. Brumbaugh became the first faculty member to take the title of librarian. He was, of course, a part-time assignee, Saturday-morning book checking his major duty.

In 1883 he was succeeded by Joseph Saylor, who over a span of two decades carried a heavy class load along with librarian chores. For many years this lovable, eccentric math prof simply cataloged all works alphabetically in a ledger—by author and by title. There was no card catalog or system of classification; not until the late 1890s did the methods of the American Library Association find acceptance.

During the 1880s the science museum received equal billing with the library in the college catalog. The nucleus of the science "cabinet" was

Jacob Zuck's own collection of a few boxes, which he had displayed on shelves in his cramped office in the old *Pilgrim* building.[23] It contained assorted mineral specimens and some "natural curiosities." Among the very earliest benefactors of the museum was the "Building's" architect, S. D. Button. He contributed a "handsome collection of precious stones."

In 1884 the faculty and trustees anted up forty dollars to buy an assortment of 236 mineral samples from all parts of the continent.[24] That same year the Smithsonian Institution, through the good offices of its head, Prof. Spencer Baird, and Congressman Atkinson, added over one-hundred marine specimens to the museum.[25] Deep-sea dredging by the Federal Fish Commission in the mid-Eighties enabled Prof. Baird to make supplemental donations. As with the library, all museum patrons received public recognition and a lithographic print of Huntingdon.

STUDENTS AND STUDENT LIFE

By modern standards the student mix during the 1880s was far from ideal. Naturally the student body was predominantly Brethren, although Catholics and other Protestants were certainly no strangers to the campus. In 1885 the college took public pride that enrollment figures included members of a half-dozen faiths.[26]

But the school's basic Brethren background and orientation meant that students came almost exclusively from farm families, rural villages, or small towns. Through all the Quinter years only sixteen Normalites claimed residence in a city with a population of ten-thousand or more. Thus neighboring Altoona, where railroad shops were just beginning to lure the Brethren, accounted for but five students.

In an age when most people thought woman's place was in the home, men outnumbered their skirted classmates nearly two to one at the Normal.

And, of course, no blacks at all were evident around the place. The trustees, in 1882, were bemused by that eventuality, however. Dr. A. B. entered the following reminder to himself in the board minutes for January 16:

> The case of our relation to the other Schools of the Church in relation to admitting colored persons in the School. . .[W]rite to Ashland and Mt. Morris asking them whether they would admit them into the building or as day students. Ask official reply.

What lay behind this inquiry, or what came of it, remains a mystery.

Enrollment statistics for this period indicate steady growth except for a slight two-year slump, 1882-84. The fall term always had the lowest enrollment, while the spring had the highest — a trend that would persist until after World War 1 when the college went off the trimester system. In the Eighties, however, the spring figures were usually two and a half times higher than those for the fall. The reason for this variance was that most rural schools closed for the year by April, which allowed teachers to take advantage of the college's third term. Farm boys added to the winter attendance once the fall harvest was in, but then some of them would have to leave in March, at term's end, to help with spring plowing. Thus, for example, the registration figures for 1887-88 went: Fall, 47; Winter, 71; Spring, 141.

Not until December 1886 did the trustees decide to keep fuller records — names, birthdays, home addresses — on all students. And only in 1883 did Joseph Saylor, as secretary of the faculty, begin to keep a registry of final passing grades.

Despite the maturity of many students and contrary to catalog claims of the "personal and individual responsibility" of students, the college adhered closely to the principle of *in loco parentis*. Criticism of the church or an unchaperoned date could bring swift disciplinary action. Levi Brumbaugh, though nineteen and a second-year student, was "sentenced" to Room 52 for a week and not allowed to leave the building because he had been caught strolling with Anna Diehl, his future wife.[27] The trustee minutes for August 19, 1880 reveal that one Johnstown coed was dismissed because of derogatory remarks about the church and keeping downtown company, both equally heinous in the eyes of the trustees.

Earlier in the year, during the winter months, an Altoona damsel had almost fallen into the latter sin but apparently was saved in the nick of time by trustee intervention. She received this letter, a copy of which went to her parents:

Feb. 6, 1880

Dear_____:

It has come to the knowledge of the Board of Trustees of B. N. C., the members of which are your brethren, that you have been invited to go out to-night in a sledding and sleighing party in promiscuous company, the character of which we know nothing, but associations which may lead you into company and places where it would be very improper for you to associate or be as a Christian. We claim the right, as it is our duty, to watch over you and advise you in reference to your conduct and association, and we request you, if any encouragement has been made, to recall the same and remain at your home or place where you will not be led astray, and we ask that in the future you accept no invitation to go away from the Building without consulting Brother Brumbaugh whose duty it is to watch over those under his supervision and who will take counsel of others if he does not know the character of your proposed associates.[28]

The use of tobacco also brought summary suspension. Warned the *Golden Dawn* in 1885: "Tobacco and cards go hand in hand."[29] Tippling, it scarcely need be said, was unthinkable.

In those days, of course, there were no organized sports or supervised games. One early form of exercise was racing around the school block. Football was another favorite pastime of the boys. Among his papers M. G. Brumbaugh has left his personal recollection of pick-up football— before that form of recreation emerged as a mad new college cult about the turn of the century. The game of the Eighties relied more on kicking, rugby style, than its modern-day version. M. G. recalled:

We had no athletic games until 1880 when some of us purchased a round ball and kicked it about on 18th Street east of Moore. Some thought we were headed for perdition. We did not mind. The kicking went on merrily each evening. Lincoln Davis, Howard Keim, Will Livengood, Albert Trent, Samuel McCann and others led in this awful thing.

Later, some improvised gymnastic equipment—a trapeze, a set of iron rings, and a crossbar—was put up behind the "Building."

There was nothing for the girls except jumping rope, and the trustees even frowned on it. Dr. A. B. Brumbaugh condemned the amusement as a "pernicious habit," which sometimes led to fatal brain or spinal disorders. He alleged: "As exercise it is not required among girls of the age indulging in it, and ought to be considered as cruelty to children and therefore prohibited."[30]

Chestnut gathering, however, was legitimate outdoor fun for mixed groups in the fall—but not without faculty escorts. Once snow fell, sledding parties were organized, making good use of bordering streets and surrounding slopes.

The biggest social event of the year was the faculty reception, a very proper occasion, scheduled soon after classes started. Every September for almost ninety years—until the late 1960s—students were expected to handshake their way down a faculty line, the first "How do you do?" said to the president.

Dormitory halls were monitored by single faculty members who lived in the "Building." Roommates had to share a double bed, the fortune of all until single beds were introduced in the 1920s. Dorm life, especially for the men, apparently evoked its share of pranks and horseplay. Even Dunker roughhousing sometimes left destruction in its wake. Hence Dr. A. B. and John Brumbaugh deemed it necessary in March of 1880 to initiate weekly room inspections. At the same time, the trustees directed the principal to charge "liberally" for damage to rooms and furniture.

Formal student evaluation of faculty is a latter-day contrivance, but Normalites had their ways of keeping teachers on their toes or getting rid of them. After the legendary Prof. Olawsky, D. Melvin Long, a graduate of both Millersville and Shippensburg, was the second victim of student wrath.

Hired in the spring of 1882, he survived his first term unscathed, but in October of that fall the seniors rose up in rebellion. They petitioned the trustees for a hearing protesting that the class did not consider Long "a proper teacher" to prepare them for the senior-year final exams. A few days later, on Saturday the 7th, the trustees met with three class spokesmen, Samuel McCann, J. E. Miller, and Galen Royer. They accused Long, who was teaching English grammar, rhetoric, and the natural sciences, of being disorganized and unable to control his classes. Furthermore, they charged, he had difficulty communicating, made lengthy assignments, and had distracting mannerisms.

The standoff dragged on for nearly a week while the trustees conducted an investigation of their own. They gave the beleaguered professor a private audience the following Tuesday, at which time he denied all charges. His accusers, he said, had distorted the facts and, what is more, the three of them were blatantly cutting his classes. That evening, Long called the seniors together in an unsuccessful attempt at reconciliation. Failing, he tendered his resignation on the 13th, effective at once.

A few sparks flew when he delivered his letter in person to the trustees that morning. He argued in parting that he had been victimized because "he took classes that the other members of the faculty *could* not and *would* not take."[31] This brought a challenge from Dr. A. B., who asked,

"They *could* not?"

Long retorted, "Yes, they *could* not!"

Not until a meeting with the faculty later in the day did the trustees act on Long's resignation. Impressed by the "opposition in all his classes," they saw no other alternative but to accept it. The trustees, however, were at pains to make clear that Long's dismissal was not "on account of the Board's opposition to him." He left to head a private school of his own in Maryland and the Normal faculty absorbed his classes for the rest of the term. Even then, student clout was a power to be reckoned with.

A month or so before the Long imbroglio, David Emmert had supervised the erection of the Huntingdon Orphans' Home across 18th Street at the rear of the college grounds. The L-shaped brick and frame building stood in the quadrangle formed today by Beeghly Library, Oller Hall, and Memorial Gymnasium.

Emmert had begun his child rescue work in March 1881 in a small brown, unpainted house in West Huntingdon not far from the school. From the start Normal students proved to be "zealous missionaries" for the home, Emmert said.[32] Some were present at the midweek prayer service when the formal step to establish an orphanage was taken. The first winter students donated three and a half tons of coal to the home. In his book Emmert wrote:

Shall I tell how we found the first matron for the Home? Well, she was a Juniata student. One day as I dismissed a particular class she lingered to tell me how hard the struggle was to prepare for a mission field, toward which she was looking, in South America. I encouraged her all I could and kept in mind her noble purpose. One day, as the movement to establish "The Home" was taking shape, I remembered her words and ventured to ask her if she would like to be a "missionary" at home. I explained the plan, and she cheerfully accepted.

He was referring, of course, to Carrie Miller, the future Mrs. William Swigart. Her successor was Lizzie Howe (Brubaker), who in three years made the jump from matron to professor at the Normal.

In May of 1884 Emmert, who then lived in Hagerstown, came to Huntingdon on one of his periodic visits to the orphanage. He spoke to the Normal students on the general subject of child welfare and urged them to organize an auxiliary to the local home. They bought the idea and promptly brought into existence the Normal Helping Hands Society. The purpose of this auxiliary, its constitution stated, was "to co-operate with the Home at Huntingdon and other associated societies in the work of finding homes for children and to aid worthy poor children in securing an education."[33]

Students were just as ready to pitch in and help landscape the barren campus those maiden years. Each spring until 1882, Henry Brumbaugh's diary reveals, he made trips to the woods in the company of able-bodied collegians to search out sturdy saplings. Elms, oaks, and maples were dug up, hauled in wagons, and transplanted in the Normal yard, tended and watered by a "bucket brigade."[34]

IMPROVEMENTS IN THE PHYSICAL PLANT

In the summer of 1880 the hall stoves were removed and central steam heating installed. College publications played this up for all it was worth: "There is no fire to keep up or ashes to carry away by the students."

In March 1881, almost five years to the day after Alexander Graham Bell's historic summons to Thomas Watson, the trustees contracted for a telephone. The Huntingdon exchange of the Central Pennsylvania Telephone and Supply began operations the next month with thirty-five customers. Even though the number of domestic and commercial phones nearly trebled by 1883, the "Building's" three rings sounded so infrequently that the trustees almost dropped the service in 1887.[35]

In the fall of 1884 the tower got a bell. For years to come the bell served a very practical purpose. It signaled all campus events: meals, chapel, church, and classes. A brick sidewalk was laid and a fence put up on two sides of the campus—along Moore and 17th streets—in the spring of 1886. When the borough waterworks began business that summer the dormitory halls and the kitchen were piped with hot and cold running water. Flush toilets were another convenience that came after 1888 when the Normal building was tapped into the borough sewer line.

The ultimate convenience for that age—electricity—did not come to the Hill until after the turn of the century, even though the Huntingdon Electric Light Company held a charter since March 1887.

PUBLIC RELATIONS AND PUBLICATIONS

Four Brethren schools were in existence by the mid-Eighties, but within the Brotherhood the Huntingdon institution was by far the most suspect. Elder David Frantz of Cerro Gordo, Illinois, alighted on the campus for a passing visit after Annual Meeting in 1885. He explained, "I called to see that which is so much spoken against."[36]

Another visitant the next year was Howard Miller, then a government employee and once Lewis Kimmel's assistant principal at Plum Creek. He wrote in the *Gospel Messenger* (formerly the *Primitive Christian*): "A wide rumor exists to the effect that the Huntingdon church and school are out of line with reference to the peculiarities of the Church." Then he added, in a well-intended but dubious defense of the college: "Such is not the fact, at least not to any considerable extent."[37]

In spite of church resistance, financial support was not lacking, and in March 1884 the trustees announced that the college was debt-free. Unfortunately this good news backfired, bringing a flurry of requests from stockholders for remittals on their investment. To head off this stampede Dr. A. B. Brumbaugh drafted and sent out a form letter which said in part:

> We need, all, to recognize the fact. . .that the great work undertaken is really, merely begun; that a substantial nucleus, only, has been formed, around which we can concentrate our efforts, and where we can bestow of our means that we desire to consecrate to the Master's service, in the direction of the church's great need. No one should seek to withdraw the aid rendered, but each one should rather double, triple or even quadruple the amount already invested, and others, who have so far had no part nor lot in this matter, should come to the rescue, that additional buildings might be erected, and more thorough equipment secured.[38]

Apparently this letter did the trick and kept the stockholders from wholesale defection. For nothing more was said about it after that, and in another year there was even talk of attaching a wing to the "Building," by then badly overcrowded.

If holding on to stockholders was a headache in that generation, enlisting new ones could be just as discomforting. Poetess Adaline Hohf, who co-edited the *Golden Dawn* prior to her marriage to William Beery, commented in 1885: "It required so much labor to procure the funds for the first building that no one feels like undertaking the work again, but the indications are that it must be done in the near future."[39] John Brumbaugh and William Swigart—but mostly Brumbaugh—were the men most on the road for the college at that time. Sometimes they met with outright defiance, but fortunately both of them had a saving sense of humor.

Brumbaugh once told of a trip he made to the southern part of Bedford County in this early period. There in one home he and a native ally had just about talked the husband into buying stock. But the man would sign nothing until he consulted with his wife, who was working in the cellar with her elderly mother. He excused himself, and moments later the men upstairs heard the man's mother-in-law say in a loud voice: "They are good-for-nothing, lazy scamps, and I'd tell them so, too!" The two solicitors were so intimidated by this outburst that they took to their heels, afraid to go back for some personal papers they had left on the kitchen table.[40]

More to the liking of the Huntingdon trustees than money raising was the publishing of their little eight-page paper titled *Advance*. Planned as a monthly, it came out in September 1883, edited by Dr. A. B. It was a chatty news sheet about the people, activities, and alumni of the Normal. Its pages were also larded with articles of general educational interest contributed by faculty and trustees. The *Advance* was the first paper published by the college, but after five issues it appeared irregularly. In all, there were twelve numbers, the last one in August 1890.

Between 1885 and 1887 the college was given extra publicity in the *Golden Dawn*, a Henry Brumbaugh magazine. One of the purposes of this thirty-two-page religious and educational monthly was to promote Brethren colleges. Through it the publisher hoped to recruit students for the four nascent schools in the Brotherhood, and in every edition there was space allotted for news from each of them. Only the Huntingdon Normal, however, took full advantage of this free publicity. To Brumbaugh's regret, the *Dawn*, in many ways a superb periodical, turned out to be a journalistic dud and after two years was jettisoned.

ALUMNI AND THE ALUMNI ASSOCIATION

The ten graduating classes of the Quinter era produced sixty-five alumni, only eighteen of whom were women. A statistical analysis of their postcollege employment, based on class histories, shows they were a competent lot. As would be expected, nearly half of the graduates (thirty) went into teaching, two becoming county superintendents and three of them principals by 1888. Nine Normalites entered the business world and five went into medicine. Another five became ministers, while a few took up farming or studied law. A half dozen continued their education, a similar number became homemakers, and one was lost through death.

Few, if any, of these ante-Juniatians took a greater interest in their alma mater than Gaius Brumbaugh. Not surprisingly, therefore, it was he who proposed the idea of an alumni association in a letter to the *Advance*, printed in its March 1885 issue. He wrote:

Washington, D. C., Dec. 1884

Dear Advance:

Permit me through your columns to urge the formation of an Alumni Association. Such an organization will rekindle the flame of devotion to the highest interests of the Normal; will foster a deeper personal interest among its membership; will form a nucleus for an organized body of active friends and supporters of our *alma mater*; and will afford annual seasons of great enjoyment. Then all will gather, or in thought turn from a distance, to greet each successive class, and to consider methods for furthering the equipment and development of the "B. N. C." I regret that such action was not taken at the last "reunion," of which in the August number you said, "It was indeed the most enjoyable occasion of the day. . . ."

Let each Alumnus at once address Prof. J. H. Brumbaugh, giving his or her desires in the matter. A number have expressed an earnest desire for such an organization, and I believe the sentiment is general. Let us band together and labor more earnestly to aid each other, and to foster the true success of the beloved Normal!

'79'

Animated by this letter, six "Alumnists" and four faculty members met in the library on Saturday evening, June 6, and formed the Alumni Association of the Brethren's Normal College. The graduates were: William Beery '82, Samuel Brumbaugh '82, George Falkenstein '82, John Keeny '82, M. G. Brumbaugh '81 and Cora Brumbaugh '83; representing the faculty were professors Saylor, Brumbaugh, Swigart, and Francis Green. William Beery was elected president and Cora Brumbaugh secretary for that year. In other business the faculty was granted honorary membership, and a committee of five was appointed to draft a constitution. This committee was composed of Beery, Saylor, Falkenstein, Green, and M. G. Brumbaugh.

As stated in the constitution they devised, the object of the association was "the mental, moral, and social culture of its members, and the promotion of the interests of its Alma Mater."[41] The document further provided: "All graduates of the institution may become members of the Association by paying an initiation fee of one (1^{xx}) dollar and signing the Constitution." The bylaws called for a public program by the alumni on commencement eve, to be preceded by an afternoon business meeting.

All organizations then had to have a motto. The alumni chose "On, and Forever Onward."

At first — in 1886 and 1887 — the association sponsored reception dinners in private homes. M. G. Brumbaugh entertained the class at his place (now the Faculty Club) in 1886, and Dr. A. B. made his downtown home available the next year. After this on-campus receptions became the custom.

QUINTER'S DEATH

James Quinter was closing out his ninth year as president when he died under dramatic circumstances at Annual Meeting on May 19, 1888. The seventy-two-year-old elder, who had rarely missed a yearly conference in the fifty years of his ministry, reached North Manchester, Indiana, about noon on Saturday the 19th. He had been ill for several days and almost called the trip off.

Soon after his arrival he went to a three o'clock preaching service in the tabernacle tent, looking pale and tired.[42] He was asked to close the meeting with prayer, and kneeling down began in a trembling voice: "We are glad to meet again. . ." Suddenly he stopped praying and those on their knees beside him noticed with alarm his deathlike pallor. They helped him up, and he stretched out on a table on the stage. Then he gasped a few times and passed away in the presence of three thousand shocked conference-goers.

Few men in the Brotherhood of that day enjoyed the prestige and affection accorded the college's first president. Dr. A. B. once said, "Elder Quinter is the purest man I ever saw."[43] And of his twelve years in Huntingdon, Henry Brumbaugh wrote:

> To both the Church and the school his being with us proved a great blessing, as he was in many ways, a father to both. . . .Indeed, wherever and whenever he came in contact with either teachers or students he was a living model of uprightness and Christian propriety.[44]

Brethren higher education, though still on trial, had made great strides and owed much to this quiet but extraordinary man. It was too bad, on the rainy afternoon of Quinter's burial, that no one thought to quote the words he penned more than thirty years before. They had an epitaphial ring:

> We think it not only right that the church should encourage such institutions in which our youth may acquire useful knowledge, but we think it is her duty—a duty she owes to her God, to herself, and to the rising generation, to encourage and build up such institutions.

5

Rise Of The Brumbaugh Dynasty 1888-1893

ELECTION OF A NEW PRESIDENT

On commencement day, June 28—a Thursday—the trustees met in the afternoon to organize for the coming academic year. Making his first appearance as a trustee was M. G. Brumbaugh, the twenty-six-year-old school superintendent. He was elected the board's vice-chairman.

Two of the fifteen board members were now women—Annie Bechtel of nearby Hesston (1887-90), who never attended the Normal, and Wealthy Clarke Burkholder, then the school's matron (housemother for women). Mrs. Burkholder, a native of the Broad Top area, had little formal education. But in 1870, at the age of twenty-one, she went to live in Henry Brumbaugh's home where she learned to set type in the *Pilgrim* office. From 1876 to 1880 she edited the *Young Disciple*, a Henry Brumbaugh juvenile magazine. She was the first woman to purchase stock in the college and was briefly enrolled as a student in 1883.[1]

Indeed, the stockholders counted among themselves a high percentage of women. Well over one-fifth (thirty-nine) of the 176 shareholders between 1878 and 1888 were females. And as early as 1880 Belinda Stoner of Union Bridge, Maryland, was chosen the first woman trustee. Between her term and Wealthy Burkholder's came two other women: Mary Grubb of Pottstown (1881-84) and Hannah Buck (1883-86), the wife of a New Enterprise farmer and merchant and a benefactress of the college after her husband's death (1916).[2]

After reorganizing on the 28th the trustees then gave their attention to the most important item on the agenda: whether or not to continue the position of president. A long debate ensued, Swigart, Dr. A. B.,

103

Oller, Stouffer, and John Brumbaugh having most to say on the question. Swigart's motion to retain the post was seconded by John Brumbaugh but it failed by a vote of seven to five. The minutes give no clue as to who the seven naysayers were. Presumably the vocal element in favor of the presidency came from among the Huntingdon people and included some—maybe all—of the board officers. At any rate, the issue was not long put to rest by this vote.

Henry Brumbaugh's diary cryptically refers to a couple of short-notice parleys in his office over the next fortnight. Then on Thursday evening, July 16 a third consultation took place, this one minuted. All eight Huntingdon trustees were present and, after a lengthy discussion about the "difference of feeling in the Board," Dr. A. B. moved the election of the board chairman, Henry Brumbaugh, as president. Henry's other cousin, the principal, supported the motion, which carried unanimously, and the college had its second president—the result of a minor but uncontested coup on the part of local trustees.

All of this was entered in Henry's diary in a most matter-of-fact way: "8:30—Had a trustee meeting. Elected J. H. B. principal and self president."

At fifty-two, H. B. (all the founders and some early teachers went by their first two initials) was a man of some means. But though known and respected throughout the Brotherhood, he lacked his predecessor's eloquence and charisma. He would have more time, however, to give to the presidency than Quinter had.

Some five years previously, in 1883, Quinter and Brumbaugh Brothers had merged with a Midwest firm into the Brethren Publishing Company. With this consolidation it was decided to publish only one adult church paper—the *Gospel Messenger*—but operate with two branch offices, at Huntingdon and Mt. Morris, Illinois. Quinter was made editor-in-chief, a position he held until his death, and Brumbaugh was named eastern editor. For a time the *Primitive Christian* building housed the *Messenger's* Huntingdon office. Then in 1885 it was moved downtown across from the Opera House on Washington Street. Finally, in the spring of 1890 the two branch offices were centralized at Mt. Morris.

With the closing of the eastern office, Henry Brumbaugh, though still an editor, found his journalistic duties much less demanding in time and energy. Thus, much more than Quinter, he involved himself in the academic life and planning of the college.

FACULTY AND "TEACHER-TRUSTEES"

Under the second president the faculty was expanded and stabilized. To be sure, classical languages still presented problems. Two instructors were fired, one for "want of religious sentiment" and the other for dereliction of duty.[3] And the sciences continued to suffer from being farmed out among willing but unqualified faculty.

On the more pleasant side, David Emmert returned to the classroom and instructional ranks were swelled by four Brumbaugh kinsmen. Emmert, whose child welfare work had by then earned national recognition as the "Huntingdon Idea," came back in 1892 to teach biology and botany along with art. The Brumbaugh influx began in 1890 when Martin G. Brumbaugh, who had taken a fancy to stogies while school superintendent, was named a permanent member of the faculty in English "on condition he stop smoking absolutely."[4] Two years later Harvey Brumbaugh, the president's son, began teaching Latin and Greek, finally giving those disciplines some rootage. A graduate of the Normal English '86 and Scientific courses '89, he had just received his A. B. degree at Haverford College.

In 1893 Harvey was joined by his Uncle John, the president's brother, who taught in the newly created Bible department. John Brumbaugh gave up editorial work in 1883 after the *Gospel Messenger* merger, taking over as company treasurer and for a few years also ran a haberdashery downtown. In 1888 he was called to the ministry by the Huntingdon congregation (later he was their pastor, 1903-10). He then spent the year 1889-90 in full-time study at Crozier Theological Seminary and the summer of 1893 with Dwight L. Moody, the celebrated evangelist, at his Chicago Bible Institute. Brumbaugh also took courses at Chautauqua, where such noted scholars as William Rainey Harper, president of the University of Chicago, held forth each summer in the company of popular lay leaders like William Jennings Bryan.

Meanwhile, in 1889, the president himself, untrained in biblical studies—except for Chautauqua courses—and self-taught in Greek, assumed professorial duties in the Bible department.

Those years ushered in the heyday of a unique core of men, termed "Teacher-Trustees" by David Emmert. These individuals spent long days in teaching and weary hours at night wrestling with administrative and financial problems.[5] Nothing in the operation of the college escaped their corporate attention—not even the supply of toilet paper on hand.

The men who served in this dual capacity were Jacob Brumbaugh, William Swigart, David Emmert, William Beery, Joseph Saylor, and Martin G. Brumbaugh. This list could also include others who taught part-time: the three Brumbaugh founders, Dr. A. B., Henry, and John.

CURRICULUM DEPARTURES: BIBLE AND BUSINESS

Henry's and John's venture into the classroom came after the Bible department took shape in 1888, four years after Mt. Morris College had started one. The founding fathers had shied away from making the study of religion a part of the academic program because of Brethren fears of a professional ministry. But beginning in 1881 William Swigart, whose glasses always rode on the very tip of his nose, gave a required course called Evidences of Christianity. This course, the catalog said, set forth "proofs that the Bible possesses the authority of God, leading men to believe the doctrine which it teaches, and perform the duties which it enjoins."

Taught "without sectarian peculiarities," it was well-received and seemingly aroused no open antagonism on the part of the church leaders in the district. Among the students it brought a demand for more Bible study. Quinter, mindful that Zuck envisioned a Bible program some day, pushed hard for it in his last years. Encouragement in that direction came from many friends of the college, like the one who wrote: "I have always been a strong advocate of your school, and have tried to secure for it patronage and money; but if you add a Bible department, I will work still harder."[6] Quinter died before realizing this goal, but the first catalog under his successor announced:

BIBLE DEPARTMENT

When this Institution of education was started its founders had two leading designs in view. The first was that our children might have a place to go to be educated where they would be surrounded by the religious influence of our own church and people. And the second was, that our people might have a school where their children could receive, in connection with a literary culture, such religious instruction as is in harmony with our faith and practice.

In accord with these designs, the Normal College, from the beginning, aimed to be strictly religious, both in influence and practice. But of late years we have been impressed with the necessity of making *religious teaching* a part of the *school work*. And to this end we now introduce the Bible Department.

The announcement went on to say that as yet there was no "established course" of study, but the catalog for 1889-90 spoke of two curricula in the field. The Eclectic English Course was intended for students "limited in time and means" and engaged in church work who could spend a term or two on campus. Nobody ever enrolled in the second program, the Diploma Course, since it required two full years of study and, perhaps to many, smacked of professionalism.

Nevertheless, Bible study enjoyed instant popularity, opening the way for liberalizing the elective system. It attracted no less than thirty students the first year, nearly half of whom were women. By 1893 the number of registrants in the department had doubled. Not a few were enrolled in the Eclectic English Course. For decades no other department would outman Bible.

The second president also inaugurated an experimental program of adult religious education for the Brethren by means of annual Bible institutes. These institutes, the inspiration for which came to him while attending one at Chautauqua, were usually month-long and held in midwinter.[7] They were intended to meet the needs, promotional literature said, of "ministers, Sunday-school workers, Bible teachers and all such as wish to pursue a regular course in Bible study and its kindred branches."[8]

The first institute, or "special Bible term" as they were called, took place in the fall of 1890 on short notice and the attendance was small—six counting the two teachers. But by 1893 institutes were bringing to the campus nearly half a hundred from all parts of Pennsylvania and neighboring states. In later years the registration ranged as high as one hundred before the discontinuance of these sessions in 1925.

On the secular side, the most important curricular innovation of H. B.'s administration was the creation of the Juniata Business College. The first step in the direction of business training occurred in 1882 when Joseph Saylor introduced bookkeeping as a required unit in the Normal program. Then, in 1886, the trustee minutes reveal that serious thought was given to some kind of coalition with the Altoona Business College, but the idea was finally rejected. No doubt lack of adequate space was the deciding factor, but in another five years the picture changed. A wing was attached to the "Building," and there was now plenty of extra room.

The next proposition for federating a business school with the college came in the spring of 1890. The instigator was George Snavely of Urbana, Ohio, a stocky, long-bearded man in late middle age. Jacob

Zuck had lived in the Snavely home during his Lebanon Normal School days. His landlord, a Maryland native, was then a high school teacher who later won two diplomas from business schools in the Buckeye State. He also had attended Bethany College and the University of Kentucky.

The trustees gave Snavely's proposal desultory attention until October when a committee—the president, the principal, and William Swigart—was authorized to negotiate with the Ohio educator. On November 7 the committee reported back recommending a salary of seven hundred dollars for Snavely and giving him the use of two classrooms. Further bargaining granted Snavely the right to use the name Juniata Business College and to carry the title of "principal."

But it was to be clearly understood that his work was "under the control of the Normal College."

Also, "clubbing" by commercial students was verboten; they were to take their meals in the dining room, the cost-conscious trustees insisted. Early in September Snavely's family moved into John Brumbaugh's old apartment in what used to be the *Pilgrim* building.

The Juniata Business College opened on September 14, 1891 and the trustees predicted that its debut would "mark an era" in the history of the Normal. During the first year Snavely prepared a fifteen-page brochure promising that "no effort will be spared to make the JUNIATA BUSINESS COLLEGE a useful, practical school." It spelled out the advantages of being associated with the Normal—the benefits of curriculum, library, literary societies, and religious influence. The United States was at the dawn of a new industrial era, the brochure proclaimed, and there was "a growing demand for YOUNG MEN AND WOMEN of sterling good character" to enter the business world.

One page was devoted to the importance of a business education for women as well as men. It called attention to the fact that

> Lady accountants, cashiers, secretaries, clerks, amanuences, type writers. &c., are eagerly sought after, and such positions furnish lucrative employment. In addition to the value a practical education is to a young woman, it renders her more independent and a better member of society; while it protects her against tricks and frauds in business transactions.

"Many a poor widow has had sad financial experience by not understanding business forms of law," readers were warned. "If to her other sorrows, she have added a consciousness that she has no knowledge of business, she is indeed at the mercy of others."

Snavely's promotional pamphlet further stated: "We *aim*, not only to make *good bookkeepers*, but to FIT THE STUDENT FOR ACTUAL BUSINESS LIFE, in the shortest time, at the least expense." Completion of the course, it said, would vary from three to six months, depending on the student's ability and background. The cost, including board, tuition, books, and stationery, was estimated at between $90 to $125. The course covered bookkeeping, business, arithmetic, customs and forms, banking, business writing, business law, and correspondence. Shorthand was also offered (the Benn Pitman System) and "type-writing," both taught the first year by the versatile Cora Brumbaugh of the art department. After that, prize Business College products tutored these skills.

In the fall of 1891 the trustees bought a World typewriter — 15 years after Remington placed the first machine on the market, early in 1874. Typing came of age in Pennsylvania in 1895 when a law was passed giving typewritten documents the same legal force as handwritten ones.

Prof. Snavely trained thirty-four aspiring businesspersons the first year, eight of whom earned diplomas. All were men, although five women took the secretarial courses, stenography and typing. Emma Keeny of Huntingdon and Ida Price of Waynesboro were the first female diploma winners — in 1893. There were fifteen graduates in all that year, the second biggest class ever. Most early alumni of the Juniata Business College worked in the offices of small firms or were self-employed. A few, however, climbed close to the top of a large company — like Richard Blankley '93 of Osceola Mills, Clearfield County. In 1900 he moved up to a main-office post with the Prudential Insurance Company of America, pioneer life insurers of blue collar workers beginning with the 1870s (through small policies with weekly premiums collected by an agent).

In other academic advances under Henry Brumbaugh the catalog for 1889-90 reported that the trustees had authorized a diploma in music. It said: "Diplomas will be awarded by the Trustees of the College to students who have a good English education and have given satisfactory evidence of the requisite attainments in Harmony and Composition, and at least two other branches in this department." The "other branches" were Vocal Music, Vocal Culture, Piano, and Organ. There are no records to show how many diplomas were awarded in what the catalog called the "divine art" during that period.

ORIENTAL AND WAHNEETA LITERARY SOCIETIES
In April 1878, we have already learned, the college formed two

literary societies. One was for Normalites only, known as the Junior Society. The other, called the Eclectic Literary Society, was open to anyone—students, teachers, townfolks. By trustee resolution on September 11, 1879 the all-inclusive society was reorganized under a constitution with bylaws and rules of order. Apparently the Junior Society was dissolved at that time.

Over the next decade, as the student body expanded, the Eclectic Society grew unwieldy in size. Consequently, in January 1892 some of its members mustered the whole school, including trustees, on Friday evening the 15th to discuss reforming into two corrival societies. A committee of four was appointed to work with the faculty and trustees in the choice of appropriate names for the two groups.

The committee reported on January 30 and suggested "Zuck" and "Quinter" to everybody's satisfaction. But within a month this nomenclature was dropped since some students came to feel that competition tended to dishonor "two revered names." The two factions were then denominated Wahneeta Eclectic Society (Zuck) and Oriental Eclectic Society (Quinter). Both daughter guilds adopted elaborate constitutions that were printed and sold in hardback booklets. Each had a multipage section on rules of order. As the preamble of the Oriental Society stated, the object of these literary groups was, in addition to "mental improvement, the entertainment of our friends, and the cultivation of the amenities of social life," to provide "knowledge of parliamentary usages."

It is very hard for us today to appreciate the intellectual ferment and intense intramural rivalry generated by these literary societies. But students then had no intercollegiate athletics, no campus theater, no public events program. The two sodalities, therefore, filled a real cultural void and did much to quicken what at older schools was known as "college spirit." They provided an identity proudly professed; their officers were the BMOCs of that day, the equal of the Phi Beta Kappa key wearer or the varsity letter winner on other campuses.

Edgar Detwiler, who entered Juniata in 1902 and later became a prominent Brethren pastor, found the guilds still going strong when he matriculated.[9] As an entering tyro, he said, "You were soon approached by representatives of the two Literary Societies—the Oriental and the Wahneeta. It was not a difficult decision for me to make for scarcely without exception students from Bedford County belonged to the Oriental Literary Society." Young Edgar, like a good member, penned his share of compositions for the *Oriental Star*, rival manuscript paper of the *Wahneeta River*.

STUDENTS AND STUDENT LIFE

Overcrowded conditions during Henry Brumbaugh's first year in office forced student occupancy of the basement and even the bell tower attic. Despite these less than ideal dormitory accommodations, the *Advance* was pleased to note, the three terms passed without a single disciplinary case. It is a fact that the college never again enjoyed such a saintly spell.

Campus mores nearly took a permissive turn of sorts under the second president. The trustee minutes for September 7, 1891 refer to William Swigart's motion that an area of the "Normal Yard" be open to students from supper to the ringing of the study bell each evening for "association." The motion never came to a vote, alas, although a few benches did get placed in the yard the following summer—for resting, not for flirting.

Nor were the trustees less disposed to relent on off-campus restrictions. College literature never failed to extol Huntingdon's environmental virtues—its healthful climate and its "pure, running, creek water, [which] has never been known to be the cause of any disease whatsoever." Still, it was privately admitted, the town had its dens of iniquity—among them the theater, from which the students had to be shielded. Hence, beginning with the 1887-88 catalog there annually appeared this notice:

> Parents and guardians are requested to grant no permissions to their children and wards to attend operatic and dramatic performances in the Opera House, as the Faculty reserves entire control of such matters.

Even sons and daughters of that Victorian generation must have found campus regulations oppressive. Joseph Saylor, wearer of many hats, was the college postman and watchfully screened all incoming and outgoing mail. As one downtown lad, terribly lovelorn, wrote to Alphia Myers, "A letter addressed to me would certainly draw attention to you. While it is inconvenient to go to the P. O. yet it is much safer. The faculty are naturally suspicious of drop letters and are apt to inquire into their character."[10] Alphia had picked up this missive from its hiding place: an old fence post along the Warm Springs road.

With no apologies, the trustees fully intended to run a "College without temptation," the *Advance* said in December 1889. Where "professors are disposed to have a care for the social and religious welfare of the students," it insisted, "much can be done in the direction of guarding them against the snares and temptations that so often beset the unwary, in places where the mental training only, or with it the physical, receives the attention of the teachers." It is important, therefore, argued the *Advance*, that a "united effort" be made to discourage "the companionship of athletes and pleasure-seekers" if students are to be "guarded" from "dissipation" and "bad habits." In fact, the article concluded:

> Young men who have formed the habit of drinking intoxicating drinks, smoking, chewing, or snuffing tobacco, had better abandon [the scholastic life] before they begin, for their efforts in the direction of high intellectual training will be futile, and all their labors will result in disastrous failures. The best energies of the best minds, and brains, untrammeled by stimulants and narcotics is required to excel in study, and make high attainment; and the sacred precincts where the seat of knowledge is, will never be reached by those who persistently weaken their energies, and dwarf their ability by these things.

Thus the catalog for that period regularly recommended that tobacco-users "who contemplate attending school abandon [the habit] permanently before entering the school."

Even snacking fell within the purview of trustee control, no doubt much to the distress of those plagued with ravenous teenage appetites. Nevertheless, the catalog advised:

> Boxes containing edibles are always injurious to the students receiving them; and, as an abundance of healthful, nutritious food is furnished all boarders at the Normal, we recommend to parents and friends that they do not send boxes containing edibles.

Dr. A. B. Brumbaugh, the most outspoken trustee on sumptuary vices and "clean living" at that time, also became quite a tub-thumper for a gymnasium and for adding physical education to the curriculum. Actually it was his son, in 1884 when in medical school, who first aired the need for a gymnasium. Gaius wrote to the *Advance*: "As a student at the Normal I experienced the need of systematic training." He stressed that "*physical* nature demands attention but little less than the *mental* and *moral*." His letter ended with the challenge:

> In behalf of the students, and in the interests of the Normal, I urge the recognition of this positive need upon its friends and patrons. A separate building could be erected and well supplied with the necessary apparatus at a moderate cost. A gymnasium will render possible a more perfect development of both sexes, and will materially add to the equipment and efficiency of the Normal.[11]

Such talk was a bit premature but the father made the son's cause his own. And when Ladies Hall, the annex to the "Building," was constructed in 1890, he saw to it that one room was designated a gymnasium. A year later he said in an article for the *Juniata Echo* (it supplanted the *Advance* in 1890): "The necessity for a more thorough physical training of the young men and women of this age is becoming more and more pronounced, and the want of it recognized by the thoughtful."[12]

Dr. Brumbaugh deplored the situation in one large city where only one in seven of all applicants, he said, passed the physical examination. He advocated supervised exercise as early as grade school, lamenting the "slovenly physical habits" of most teachers. The trustee-physician went so far as to say: "A correct physical training of a child is far more important to it at the time it enters school, and for some years thereafter, than the mental training it receives during the same time." He concluded his editorializing by saying: "Every grade of the public schools and every place of learning should have its gymnasium and teacher in physical development."

What kinds of exercises took place in the Ladies Hall gymnasium was nowhere mentioned. But it probably included calisthenics and for the men drills with Indian clubs and dumbbells.[13] Though there was no formal or systematic instruction, the trustee minutes for March 3, 1892 do refer to a Miss Phoenix, who was "invited to come and give a talk and exhibition of Physical training." The opposite sexes, of course, under no circumstances made use of the gymnasium at the same time.

PROBLEMS OF WAYS AND MEANS

Steady growth after 1888, nurtured by a more diversified curriculum, brought enrollment figures to 195 by the spring of 1893. Reassuring as these statistics were, the trustees still rankled at a problem no less vexing today: competition between high-cost private education and low-cost public education.

John Brumbaugh vented his frustration through the *Juniata Echo* in 1891 when he wrote: "If. . .our people had a proper appreciation of our schools there would be no necessity for such competition."[14] He went on to observe: "The statement was made recently that in a certain State nearly one hundred of our Brethren's children are attending other schools, and why? Simply because some Normal School nearer home offers lower rates." Trustee Brumbaugh predicted that if "the School at Huntingdon were to put its expenses at $500 per year, or even half that amount, we don't suppose in a year's time it would have a dozen pupils." He cited the example of the Quakers and Baptists, who, he alleged, provided quality education at high costs and succeeded because those denominations were "interested in their own schools, and are jealous of church influence."

Thus, the president's brother repined: "Until our people can appreciate the importance of influence above the dollar, and as long as we must get our patronage by putting our rates below other schools, our work is going to be crippled." He said that even with high charges and the "closest economy, we can barely keep the institution moving," and closed with a tribute to the underpaid teaching staff, some of whom had received offers from other schools double their Normal salaries.

Balancing the books was thus an all but impossible feat for Treasurer William Swigart, when not preparing for classes. Operating expenses for 1889-90 came to $13,117.91, but income from all sources — room and board, tuition, books — totaled only $9,545.39. This represented a $3,000 increase in operating costs over the previous year and a $150 gain in income. Of course, putting up Ladies Hall did nothing to reduce the overhead. Instructional salaries for twelve faculty members, some of whom were part-time or teaching gratuitously, amounted to $3,453.65, a mere $7.27 boost over 1888-89. Student charges, however, remained unchanged from the Quinter administration: $1.00 a week for tuition and $2.90 for room and board.

LADIES HALL ANNEX AND CAMPUS ENLARGEMENT

With the "Building" peopled from bell-tower attic to basement recesses, the trustees took action on February 11, 1889 to begin construction of a four-story annex during the coming summer. Plans were prepared by a Mr. Goodfellow within two months and, by early May, Casper Myers was laying the stone foundation. Meanwhile, a new subscription campaign got going with Henry Brumbaugh's pacesetting pledge of five-hundred dollars, followed by his brother John's two-hundred dollars.

Across the river the Pennsylvania Industrial Reformatory was only weeks away from completion.

In January 1890 William Swigart was relieved of his classes to canvass full-time, assisted by the venerable preacher-poet, Elder James Sell of Morrison's Cove. On March 10 Swigart reported that $3,330 had been raised for building purposes.

As yet — apart from twelve-thousand dollars worth of insurance — little had been done about fire protection. There were still no permanent exterior fire escapes on either of the multistory structures. Back in 1881 William Swigart had been made a "committee of one" to "secure a pole or poles to make ladders for fire security." He did, and these ladders served both buildings until sometime in late 1893 or early 1894 when a set of landings and fixed stairs was attached to the chapel end.

Ladies Hall, as the wing was first dubbed, was ready for occupancy by fall of 1890 and erected at a cost of $12,889.56. By then a little over seven-thousand dollars had been raised in pledges toward this debt. The brick extension, 40' x 100', was connected to the main building by a twenty-foot transept, which stands today as part of Founders' fire stairs.

The entire fourth floor was set aside for the Juniata Business College and the art and music studios. On the two levels below were dormitory rooms with the parlor and rest room located on the second level. Additional classrooms and the gymnasium took up most of the ground floor, which also contained two small apartments. These were occupied by the William Beery and John Brumbaugh families. The Brumbaughs lived in Ladies Hall until moving into a new house in November 1891 on the northwest corner of Mifflin and 17th streets (owned by the college today).

In September of 1890 the trustees altered the entrance to the "Building" and fenced-in grounds by laying a diagonal walk from the tower to the corner of 17th and Moore.[15] The original brick pavement, which ran straight from the tower landing to the street, was taken up. David Emmert was commissioned to make a cut for the catalog showing these alterations and the new arch gateway. As yet there was no walk leading from the west door to Moore Street.

The face of the "Normal Yard" was further transformed in early 1892. This time, though, it was the doings of the Huntingdon church, which shared in the use of the college chapel as its regular meeting place. Supervised by the president, their elder, the congregation put in a baptismal pool along the southeast corner of Ladies Hall. This eliminated the jaunt to the old baptismal site along the Juniata River near the present location of the ice plant. Many a Normalite was ritually immersed three times forward in the "Yard Pool" before Stone Church was built in 1910 with its inside baptistry.

For some time the trustees had been pondering the prudence of buying up land and buildings adjacent to the campus, both as an investment and for future expansion purposes. Though hard-pressed to meet mortgage payments on Ladies Hall, they decided to make the plunge at a March meeting in 1892. Over the next few years they obtained eight lots—all below the 17th Street campus extension, four on Moore and four on Oneida (the present location of Stone Church and the heating plant). In a highly irregular but pragmatic arrangement, considering the financial condition of the college, Jacob Brumbaugh procured the Oneida lots in his name, taking a college note for them.[16] The understanding was, of course, that he would sell them to the trustees at market value at any time in the future. It allowed him to make a profitable investment and yet kept the lots in trustee hands.

THE JUNIATA ECHO

The August 1890 edition of the *Advance* let fall expectantly that it was "about to enter upon an active stage of work, for education among our people, and our fraternity." But these words turned out to be its swan song because shortly after that the trustees changed the paper's name. On October 21 the board agreed that the *Advance* ought to be renamed and settled upon *Juniata Herald*. Then someone remembered that Mifflintown, some forty miles down river, had a newspaper so styled. And so they came up with the "poetic and beautiful" title, *Juniata Echo* — a salute to the "Blue Juniata" and the scenery of its basin, the first edition explained.

Started in November under the editorship of Dr. A. B. Brumbaugh, the *Echo* was issued quarterly until 1896, when it became a monthly. It was a more pretentious publication than the *Advance,* printed on larger sheets with three columns to a page. But the subscription rate — at twenty-five cents a year — was half that of its predecessor. In content and format at first, however, there was little different between the two papers. To encourage good reading, the trustees offered the *Echo* free to all who subscribed to any of the current popular magazines through the college at discount prices.

The *Echo*'s editor preferred to think of it as essentially a literary journal rather than a campus news sheet, and this was reflected in time by the nature and scope of material printed. To gain professional insight and greater competence, Dr. Brumbaugh joined the Pennsylvania Editorial Association, seldom missing its meetings and many times taking part in PEA-sponsored sight-seeing excursions. He also represented the Normal in the Pennsylvania State Educational Association, a college publications body. By summer 1895 Editor Brumbaugh was boasting that the *Juniata Echo*, with more than three thousand subscribers, had the "largest circulation of its kind in the State."[17]

CHURCH ADVISORY BOARD

In 1890, toward the close of H. B.'s second year as helmsman, the church instituted a procedure for keeping closer tabs on Brethren-run schools. It created an advisory board of three district elders for each school, charged with conducting annual visitations. The chief function of the board was to investigate the orthodoxy of textbooks and faculty and file a yearly report with Standing Committee, the ruling body of Annual Meeting.

The 1890 measure stipulated that all Brethren teachers "shall be in full sympathy with the principles and doctrines of the church, and shall conform to the order of the Brotherhood in their appearance."[18] It was further legislated that "at least once a year the doctrines of the church shall be specially held forth in a series of doctrinal sermons." This second requirement was no problem once the Bible institute gained popularity and since the leadership of the local congregation was identical with that of the Normal.

But the dress question did present complications. Already the Huntingdon congregation had been visited by a delegation from Standing Committee in 1888 because of dress code violations. Some of the male members were sporting neckties and shaven chins, while their women were seen in public wearing fashionable hats. Furthermore, senior class pictures provided clear evidence that most Dunker progeny were sartorially liberated. But they were far from being the cane-swinging "dudes" decked out in "bee gum hats" old-order parentage feared colleges would spawn.

Each year the college catalog listed the names of those on the Advisory Board. The first team review took place on Friday, December 18, 1890. Its subsequent report signaled the cordial relations that would always exist between the college and the committee. It read in part:

> Making due allowance for the peculiar circumstances under which an institution of this kind is placed, we have nothing to censure, but much to commend, believing it is doing a good work for the Church. We commend the school to the sympathy and support of the Brotherhood.[19]

For twelve years the chairman of the visitors was James A. Sell, a little-schooled but brainy man who was a live wire almost to the day of his death—at 102. He was widely known in the Brotherhood and throughout Central Pennsylvania as a preacher, author, poet, orchardist, and journalist.

He was the first person in his denomination to publish a book of poems. His writings included the *Lost Children of the Alleghenies*, a true story still regarded as a classic by old-timers of the area. Elder Sell was also blessed with the instincts of an historian. He collected the data for the 1925 history of the Church of the Brethren in Pennsylvania's Middle District and assisted his son, Jesse, in preparing a general history of Blair County, published in 1910.

During this critical period when the college needed a sympathetic interpreter to the church, James Sell was its veritable tutelary saint. He had boomed the institution from the time of its *Pilgrim* building birth and became one of the most popular resource leaders at the Bible institutes. All four of his sons went to Juniata and many of his descendants can be found in the *Alumni Directory*.

Others who served on the Advisory Board were John W. Brumbaugh, John S. Holsinger, William M. Howe, Andrew Bashore, Edward D. Book, Thomas B. Maddock, Walter S. Long, Daniel A. Stayer, Samuel J. Swigart, and Charles L. Buck, husband of benefactress Hannah, the early woman trustee.

ALUMNI AND THE SCHOLARSHIP FUND

By 1893 the B. N. C. had 102 alumni, of whom one hundred were living. Geographically they were scattered in two territories (District of Columbia and Oklahoma), fifteen states, and one foreign country — Mexico. Professionally, the profile of graduates had changed but little in five years. Over fifty percent were in public education, fourteen as administrators. Two were college presidents: Walter Yount '80 at Bridgewater, Virginia and, as of May 1893, Martin Brumbaugh at his alma mater. Only ten were in the ministry and thirty-seven had not yet been led to the altar.[20]

While many of these alumni had to work their way through the Normal with campus jobs, very few had received outright grants. It was not until the Henry Brumbaugh presidency that scholarship help was set up. The trustees, at William Swigart's urging, decided in April 1889 to approve ten scholarships for needy ministers or other "worthy young men" recommended by their church elders. They launched an endowment fund drive, selling stock in one hundred dollar shares. Each certificate had nine coupons attached that could be redeemed in tuition fees. But coming as it did hard on the heels of the Ladies Hall campaign, the fund, as conceived by the trustees, met with general indifference.

Ever since 1886, however, the Alumni Association had wanted to link itself to the college in a more meaningful way than merely by an annual meeting on campus. Thus, soon after the trustee announcement in the spring, some of the resident alumni hatched the idea of a separate association-staked scholarship program. They appointed an ad hoc committee made up of M. G. Brumbaugh, Harvey Brumbaugh, and William Beery to draw up plans for an endowment fund and report at the annual meeting in June.

The scheme as finally adopted provided financial help for "worthy" students—*both* men and women—in their senior year. This aid was actually a loan, to be paid back without interest on a time schedule mutually acceptable to the recipient and the fund trustees. Three trustees, one of whom must belong to the faculty, had charge of investing and disbursing all monies. Grantees were selected by a screening committee made up of the trustees, the president, and the principal.

At the June meeting of the association, with eleven classes represented and twenty-five alumni in attendance, pledges in the amount of $1,870 were raised. At six percent interest, this meant that about $112 was available for the first year—enough for two scholarships. By June 1893, fifty-one contributors had pledged $3,220 to the Alumni Association Endowment Fund. Twelve students over the past five years had benefited from the fund, seven during 1893.

H.B.'S RESIGNATION

Henry Brumbaugh's diary for Friday, May 12, 1893—a clear, warm day—reads simply: "Resigned as President of Normal in favor of MGB." He was fifty-seven then and weighed a wiry 145 pounds. He lived in a new house he had built at 411 17th Street, into which he moved in September 1892. This was less than two months after the Huntingdon militia had been sent to help quell the famous strike at Carnegie's Homestead steel plant, an episode worthy of notice in H. B.'s diary.

For another dozen years after his presidency, Henry continued on as dean of the Bible department. Finally, in 1908 he left the classroom for good, two years into his seventies.

By then his nest had been well-feathered. In 1897 the Brethren Publishing Company was dissolved and its assets transferred to the Brotherhood. At that time its stockholders, chief of whom was Henry, were earning an astonishing twelve percent in dividends.[21] Under liquidation terms H. B. received a cash settlement plus a handsome annuity based on a certain number of shares he had held in the company.

The college's second president was basically a loner, reserved and undemonstrative, and some people thought him cold and distant. Yet he was a man of equanimity. Though a man of principle, he nevertheless tried to avoid controversy. His partnerships—with John and then with Quinter—were remarkably harmonious.

As trustee whip for four decades, he won board esteem for his sound financial judgment. He was a founder of the Union Bank of Huntingdon (1894) and also of the Standing Stone National Bank (1902), in turn a director and officer of each. Over the years, entries in his diary note with pride, he was inevitably—at both banks—the biggest vote-getter in the election of directors.

H. B. enjoyed a long and varied career: preacher, schoolteacher, printer, editor, banker, college professor, trustee, and president. And not only did he help to found and shape the character of a college now a hundred years old, but he resolutely joined forces with those of broad vision struggling to reverse the policies of a denomination benighted by its sectarian past. The history of two institutions, Juniata College and the Church of the Brethren, bear indelible traces of his formative influence and quiet courage.

6

Juniata College Comes of Age 1893-1910 (Part 1)

MARTIN GROVE BRUMBAUGH ELECTED PRESIDENT

"M. G."—he, too, went by his initials on the Hill—had just turned thirty-one when designated president-elect in May 1893.[1] For two months he demurred before making up his mind to accept the office. Already the college's most illustrious son, he had visions of greater glory outside the Brethren fold.

Then there was the problem of his smoking. He was too fond of his pipe and cigars to shake the tobacco habit even for the sake of a college code. But he and the trustees worked out a *modus vivendi* (no smoking in public), whereupon he agreed to take the presidency, secure in his vice. There was no public announcement of his election until the November issue of the *Echo*. In it he was described as one "who brings energy, talent, and ability to take up the work."

One reason his predecessor, cousin Henry, had stepped aside was because the trustees were eager to push the four-year classical course and to move the institution more decidedly in a liberal arts direction. They turned to the youthful Martin, with his splendid credentials, as the person best qualified among Brethren educators to carry out that goal. From the day he turned up in the company of the "Old Forge" refugees the spring of '78, his trustee-kinsmen knew they had a gem of the first water in the

121

Martin Grove Brumbaugh (seated, fifth from left) as he looked upon election as President.

brilliant, winsome fifteen-year-old lad, whose early education had been gleaned for the most part from dime novels — read on the sly.

It was Jacob Zuck, a man he much admired, who steered him toward a career in education. One day the principal said to M. G., his baggy pants stuffed down into hightop boots: "Martin, I believe that if you were to try hard, you could become a teacher."[2]

That fall — 1878 — he began teaching in the Center Union School, north of Huntingdon a few miles, still six months shy of his seventeenth birthday.

His recognition as an educator of promise began with his election as County Superintendent of Schools in 1884. Newly married and at age twenty-two the youngest superintendent ever commissioned in Pennsylvania, he stood six feet tall and square shouldered, a striking figure with leonine head, dark craggy brows, and jutting, double-barreled jaw. He had sprouted a beard by this time to make himself look older. Because of his progressive ideas Brumbaugh soon became a favorite of Dr. E. E. Higbee, State Superintendent of Public Instruction.

It was Dr. Higbee who in 1886 recommended him for summer institute work in the state of Louisiana. Public education in that southern clime was woefully backward. Teachers were ill-prepared, and only three high schools existed in all of its sixty-four parishes. For a half-dozen summers the young Pennsylvanian went south, visiting every part of the Bayou State including the glamorous Crescent City itself, New Orleans. Not surprisingly, Superintendent Brumbaugh was responsible for importing a dozen or more B. N. C. graduates into the Louisiana school system during those years. Some rose to high educational positions there. One of them was John Keeny of Huntingdon. Eventually—in 1907—he became president of Louisiana Polytechnic Institute.

By 1890 institute work alone, both in the South and in his home state, was netting the twenty-eight-year-old M. G. close to five thousand dollars a year.[3]

That year he resigned the superintendency to return briefly to college teaching at his alma mater. The Huntingdon congregation made him a lay preacher shortly afterward. A spellbinder in the pulpit, the new licentiate never hankered for nor was ever elevated to the eldership. He preached his first sermon in the chapel on January 19, 1892, a raw, zero-degree Sunday.[4]

Between 1891 and 1894 he was a full-time graduate student, first at Harvard and then at the University of Pennsylvania. At the time he was named president, M. G. was on the verge of a doctorate at Penn. His dissertation, a study of the post-Elizabethan poet and clergyman John Donne, was in its final stages of completion. Consequently, he delayed nearly a half year—until January 1894—before actively taking over the presidential reins. His Ph.D., granted the following spring, was the first ever awarded to a member of the Church of the Brethren.

The new prexy could not have taken up his duties at a more inauspicious time. The country had been gripped since 1893 by the deepest industrial depression in its history, a depression that was to persist until the beginning of 1897.

AN ABSENTEE PRESIDENT

Just when President M. G. was getting used to his new title the University of Pennsylvania stole him away—at least partially. He was picked to fill a part-time chair of pedagogy created by the Quaker City institution in 1895. It was he who had originally convinced Provost Charles Harrison and Penn's governing board of the need to furnish graduate and undergraduate work in education even if on a limited scale at first. This, on top of his superior academic record as an Ivy League Ph.D. (he made Phi Beta Kappa), placed him among the front-runners for the professorship when it was set up. He himself had touted Dr. Oscar Corson, Ohio's Commissioner of Common Schools, the man given first chance at the chair. But Corson declined and, turning the tables, supported his own nominator. That was as far as it went; Provost Harrison had his man.

This was an awkward turn of events. It raised serious questions about Brumbaugh's commitment to his presidency. He divided his time between two places all the academic year 1895-96. Weekdays he spent in Huntingdon and weekends in Philadelphia for Friday night and Saturday classes.

It took the blithe small-college and university professor no time at all to cut a figure among his Penn colleagues. One of them much impressed with him was Edward Potts Cheyney, a leading historian of that day. Dr. Cheyney later became the university's official chronicler. Telling how the school of education got its start, he spoke of its first chairholder as "a man of great energy and competence" and a teacher of "much influence."[5] In short order, Dr. Cheyney wrote, "women and men alike came trooping to his classes."

Back at the college, however, the question of governance became a bit more ticklish when in June of 1896 the president let it be known he was moving to Philadelphia to live. On Monday the 22nd, according to Henry Brumbaugh's diary, he met with the trustees and "defined his future relations to the College." But nowhere in the records were these "relations" spelled out.

Needless to say, the trustees were in a predicament. To fill the administrative void they contrived the position of vice-president, giving it to H. B.'s son, Harvey. Dr. M. G. was on campus as much as possible over the next fourteen years—for important events, crucial trustee meetings, and to lecture. But not til 1925 did he again call Huntingdon his home.

As might be expected, the idea of their headman off living at one end of the state left everybody on campus wondering and uneasy. To bolster morale Dr. A. B. Brumbaugh stressed in an *Echo* editorial: "The success of the work and the prosperity of the school will not depend on the presence or absence of any one member of the devoted workers as long as there is a united purpose."[6] To some this sounded a bit like whistling in the dark, but time bore out the truth of Dr. A. B.'s words.

The college's third president, it would seem, found routine academic oversight and small-town life a terrible bore in the afterglow of doctoral study in a metropolitan area. Quite likely the fire of his genius, soon to burn bright, would have flickered out had he not been able to escape from what to him seemed a stifling, parochial milieu.

Yet the totality of his devotion to the college and to the denomination that nurtured it was beyond question. In 1897 he dedicated his published Juniata Bible Lectures on the Book of Ruth to "the Church of the Brethren and Juniata College, the Church and School I love"—a sentiment he never tried to hide. In the end he probably did more for his alma mater as a truant chief-executive than he ever could have by on-campus guidance. His name, influence, and contacts, to say nothing of his own generous out-of-pocket giving, enriched the college in countless ways.

PRESIDENT M. G.'S EXTRAMURAL FAME

Upon landing the Penn professorship Dr. Brumbaugh began to keep a hectic pace. None of his contemporaries made any bigger hit on the teacher-institute circuit than he did. Though barely in his thirties, he often shared headlines with the famous. At one state teachers' convention in Ft. Wayne, Indiana, he sat on the platform with G. Stanley Hall, world-renown psychologist and university president. As his reputation spread he was deluged with invitations to speak at high school commencements—some years thirty or more.[7] Religious, historical, and civic groups further crowded his schedule with speaking engagements.

Brumbaugh's way with words soon displayed itself in writing as well as oratory. In 1897 he and Dr. Joseph S. Walton, Chester County's superintendent of schools, prepared a supplementary reader, *Stories of Pennsylvania*, for the American Book Co. of New York City. This volume, one of a series on Eastern states, put him in the company of such literary luminaries as Joel Chandler Harris (Georgia) and William Dean Howells (Ohio).[8] Within five months *Stories of Pennsylvania* had gone into its third edition.

Then in 1899 came the Brumbaugh *Standard Readers*, a set of five graded textbooks. Their adoption, both by public systems and academies, was immediate and widespread. His *Fifth Reader* was especially popular and could be found in use long after World War I.

By 1889 the indefatigable M. G. had become—in his spare time—an authority on the origins of his church. That year he authored yet another book: *A History of the German Baptist Brethren in Europe and America.*

It stamped him the denomination's pioneer historian and was a feat of prodigious scholarship. Some of the material for this monographic work had been gathered in the summer of 1896 while he was in Germany studying at the University of Jena. Most of his information, though, was searched out from a private collection of original manuscripts owned by Abraham H. Cassel of Harleysville, Pennsylvania. M. G. later saw to it that much of this valuable library went to the college.

Brumbaugh's history made the Brethren aware, as never before, of an important aspect of their past: the vigorous literary and intellectual activity of colonial ancestors. It revealed that the greatest cultural force among German-speaking colonists had been the Sauer press (a Dunker-family business), not Franklin's as historians thought. Moreover, it brought to light Dunker involvement in the founding of Germantown Academy and the fact that even much earlier, almost as soon as they had landed in Pennsylvania, the church fathers set up a school of their own, woman-taught.

After his history came out Dr. Brumbaugh's academic and scholarly life was interrupted while he put in two years of government service. The summer of 1900 he was appointed the first United States Commissioner of Education to Puerto Rico. The Caribbean island had been ceded to the United States after the Spanish-American War and placed under military control. Then in May 1900 Congress passed the Foraker Act instituting civil government.

President McKinley turned to Provost Harrison of Penn for help in locating some qualified person to organize a modern school system for the Puerto Ricans. Dr. Harrison immediately thought of his popular pedagogy professor and nominated him, but the hesitant Brumbaugh did not exactly jump at the chance. The insistent provost coaxed him finally into accepting and granted him a leave of absence.

While on insular duty, Commissioner Brumbaugh, for obvious reasons, honored the college with only rare presidential homecomings. He did favor the *Echo*, however, with a succession of informative articles from Puerto Rico. They told of his work there, of the island's geography, its economy, its people and their history.

The Commissioner lived in San Juan, the capital; his comfortable house adjointed the governor's mansion. By virtue of his position he held cabinet rank and was an ex-officio member of the territorial senate.[9]

Dr. Brumbaugh found the isle, which had a population in 1900 of about one million, an educator's nightmare. Approximately eighty-five percent of the people were illiterate and not a single public school building existed anywhere among the islanders. Classes were conducted in rented houses or rooms; most of these facilities were unsuited for the purpose.

Puerto Ricans saw dramatic gains in public education between 1900 and 1902. Brumbaugh's major task as commissioner was to reorganize and expand the elementary school system. Under his direction the enrollment in the grades increased by over one hundred percent. The number of school buildings was all but doubled—from 614 to one thousand.[10] Thirty-seven of these were entirely new structures. In addition a high school was erected in San Juan and a Normal school in Rio Piedras. It was the Commissioner's plan to use the Rio Piedras institution to train native men and women and rely less on foreign teachers (mostly from the United States). When he left the island, Puerto Rican teachers outnumbered their American counterparts by better than seven to one.

His leave over, Dr. Brumbaugh resigned in 1902 despite the pleas of Theodore Roosevelt, whom he greatly admired and would biographize in 1922. The San Juans, grateful for all he had done, named a street for him—Calle Brumbaugh.

He went back to university teaching, and during the decade of his forties authored, co-authored, or edited a variety of works. All the while he traveled around the country lecturing at a punishing clip. He brought out several new readers and edited the Lippincott Educational Series and a history of Puerto Rico. A member of the Pennsylvania German Society, history-buff Brumbaugh wrote a biography of Christopher Dock, "the pious schoolmaster of the Skippack," who prepared the first textbook in America on educational theory. Probably his most influential book was *The Making of a Teacher*, published by Harper and Brothers in 1905. It became a best-seller in educational circles and eventually went through twelve editions.

Then in 1906 scholarly pursuits once again took a back seat to administrative employment. In July of that year the Philadelphia Board of Public Education elected him superintendent of city schools. Brumbaugh's new position at once placed severe strains on his already tenuous college presidency, from which he now began to think of resigning. The superintendency thrust him into the thick of a fight to modernize and upgrade the schools of Philadelphia, and Huntingdon concerns got less and less of his attention.

In 1906 the City of Brotherly Love ranked only behind New York and Chicago in population, but in per capita school outlay stood thirty-fourth among all municipalities.[11] Before he left office in 1914 Superintendent Brumbaugh had built up a school system that rated among the best in the United States. And in his judgment, after a trip abroad in 1913, it could even hold its own with Europe's *crème de la crème*.

Campaigning on the slogan, "A decent seat in a decent school for every child in Philadelphia," he was able to erect, in his first six years, twenty-eight new schools. The state's largest city became a model in vo-tech training, pioneered in special education, led the way in promoting parent-teacher groups, in providing school lunches, in conducting night classes, and in developing playground facilities (a special crusade of the superintendent). Other parts of his progressive program, such as practice teaching and a plan for junior high schools, made slower headway.

M. G. TRIES TO RESIGN AS PRESIDENT

The Philadelphia job began to wear on his nerves and sometimes he reacted testily when there was pressure from back home for a presidential opinion or decision. Except in rare instances, the college authorities refused to act on crucial matters until after consulting him — always by mail since, to protect his privacy, he never installed a phone in his Philadelphia residence.

In time an undercurrent of unrest began to tug at the faculty, and his "no-show" reputation as a trustee irritated some board members. Before long M. G. got wind of this morale problem on campus and decided to make a clean break with the college. In a letter dated June 17, 1907 he resigned as both president and trustee. He said in explanation: "I hear from time to time that my relations to Juniata College, as its nominal president, and as a member of its Board of Trustees interfere with its normal development and its more effective usefulness. . . ."[12] That this might be so, he indicated, was a painful thought. As he saw it, the only solution was for him to sever all official connections with the college.

M. G.'s dual resignation shocked the trustees; no one wanted him to quit. They needed him too much. He had been their one and only link with Andrew Carnegie in getting a new library. On him hinged the hope for more help from that benevolent Scotsman. Moreover, the trustees had talked about using President Brumbaugh to cultivate John D. Rockefeller. Therefore, action on his letter was deferred, and Dr. A. B. wrote him urging that he reconsider. But his reply of July 10 was terse and adamant, insisting that he "meant" what he had said.[13]

Yet, in the end, he did back down, though there are no clues why. He stayed on as president three years more. But for him, apparently, it had been all over once, as superintendent of schools, he had moved into Philadelphia's City Hall. When asked to supply data for a biographical sketch in *Who's Who in America*, he listed the years of his presidency as 1894-1906.

HARVEY BRUMBAUGH: VICE PRESIDENT/ACTING PRESIDENT

The anomaly of an absentee president for a decade and a half could have proved much more disruptive for the college had it not been for Harvey Brumbaugh, the president's second cousin who stoically and ably pinchhit for him all those years (he preferred to be called I. Harvey). Although a de facto president, kindly, self-effacing Harvey knew his place in the batting order. Of the pair of them, it was all too clear who wielded the greater clout with trustees. Unintentionally, M. G. held charismatic sway over the campus and there was no escape from his haunting presence.

From 1876, when his father became identified with Zuck's work, Harvey had been a part of the institution. David Emmert recalled in *Reminiscences*;

> As we used to go in and out of the old Chapel in the publishing house at 1400 Washington street, there frequently peeped at us around the corner a timid little boy whom we called "Harvey." He grew up serenely, a quiet and thoughtful youth, and when he came to mingle with the big boys on the hill the teacher of arithmetic had to stand him upon a chair that he might put his work in proper position on the blackboard.[14]

He was barely sixteen when graduated with a Normal degree in 1886. Staying on, he became in 1889 the second person (after M. G.) to complete the Scientific course. Then he was off to Haverford and a B.A. in 1892. That fall, a slender dark-haired youth of twenty-two, he was added to the Normal College faculty as a teacher of Greek and Latin. A year's leave of absence for study at Harvard bred a second B.A. diploma in 1895. It was the next summer, while at the University of Jena, that he was made vice president when M. G. announced his plans to move to Philadelphia.

Three years later, in June 1899, spouseless Harvey was given the title of acting president.[15] This came at the end of another leave of absence during which he picked up a Harvard master's degree in classics. The year in Cambridge resulted in not only a promotion and a graduate degree but an *affaire d'amour* that led him to the altar. His marriage, however, would have campus-shaking repercussions and involve him in a seriocomic episode, the scenario of which could hardly have been more paradigmatic of Victorian morality.

In looks, Harvey Brumbaugh was anything but a Lothario, what with his long, narrow face and large hawk nose on which usually perched a pair of round black-rimmed glasses. Before his first Harvard leave, the then twenty-four-year-old professor was quoted in the *Echo* as lamenting: "Marriage for me is an unknown, indefinite vanishing factor."[16] His nuptial prospects bettered, however, in 1897 when he, the vice-president, began to court a Somerset County coed. Brethren both, they were soon engaged. But then came the fateful year's interlude at Harvard and his secret romance with Amelia Johnson, the daughter of a highly placed Cambridge family.

Their private wedding on Thursday, April 26, 1900 took the college community by complete surprise.[17] Prof. Brumbaugh had left Huntingdon a few days earlier supposedly to visit his father in a Philadelphia hospital. After a brief stop-over there he sped his way to Boston town. In the meantime a batch of mail came to College Hill bringing the unexpected wedding announcement. Upon their arrival on campus two days after the ceremony, the bridal pair was given a lively welcome that included a roaring bonfire down on the ball field. That October they moved into a new house on the corner of Mifflin and 17th streets.

Two years later Harvey Brumbaugh suffered a great indignity when his former lady-love dragged him into court on a breach-of-promise suit. The trial, which lasted four days, began on Monday, September 11 and engaged the services of no less than eight lawyers. Resorting to the law to settle personal disputes was a violation of Brethren teachings, as everyone knew. Huntingdon fairly buzzed with gossip over the scandal, and crowds shoved their way into the courtroom each day out of curiosity.

The acting president's ex-fiancée, who had been urged to take legal action by her angered brothers, was suing for twenty-five thousand dollars in requital. Defense attorneys argued that the engagement had been dissolved by mutual consent, which the plaintiff's counsel, of course, denied. Both sides submitted *billets-doux* as evidence. "These epistles," so observed the *Semi-Weekly News*, were "dignified in character, yet not lacking in fervor."[18]

They were also damaging to the Brumbaugh case. The trial ended at noon on Thursday the 14th, and the jury deliberated for four hours. By unanimous verdict it found against the defendant but reduced the amount of the claim to $9,250. The judgment gave the *Semi-Weekly News* an opportunity to indulge in a choice bit of moralizing, no matter that it was a slam at the local college executive. The paper advised: "This decision may cause young men to thoroughly know their own minds before they make hasty propositions of marriage, or when such promises are made they may be slow to violate their word."[19]

Higher courts refused to overturn Brumbaugh's conviction, and for decades his suit was a textbook study at many law schools, Harvard's included. He was forced to declare bankruptcy. Never again did he hold property in his own name, his new home no exception. Thus he never paid out a cent to the jilted woman, but her brothers, one of them a Dunker preacher and former Normal student, would get back at her ex-suitor by and by. They would strike at him through a vengeful act against the college. Meanwhile, Mrs. Brumbaugh, a noble, refined woman, was emotionally scarred for life.

And so was Harvey, who was much too fine a man to be treated the way he was. But many Brethren were cruelly unforgiving. Though the Huntington congregation eventually advanced him to the eldership in 1907, he never won a place in the higher councils of the Brotherhood where he properly belonged. As for the college, the trial unfairly hurt his money-raising efforts among the Brethren ever after.

JUNIATA GETS ITS NAME AND BECOMES A LIBERAL ARTS COLLEGE

The name "Juniata College" first appeared in public print in the *Echo* early in 1894. It had been adopted officially at the January board meeting of the trustees, who planned to legalize it later by amending the charter. This action came about in deference to a ruling of Annual Meeting against use of the term "Brethren" in naming a school. Place-names — like that of a town — were recommended.[20] (Of the existing six Brethren-founded colleges today, all are so denominated except Juniata.) Thus were the words "Brethren's Normal College" consigned to oblivion.

The eponym "Juniata," of Indian origin, means "beautiful." Legend has it that the nearby river is the namesake of a comely Redskin lass — "thus showing," Henry Brumbaugh wrote in the *Gospel Messenger*, "that nature's children love and admire that which God has made so "beautiful."[21] And since much of this beauty can be seen from the bell tower, explained the top trustee, it was only natural to rename the college after a river. In September 1896 the rechristening was made legal under a new charter.

The year 1896 was an important milestone in Juniata's history for another reason: that was when it became an accredited liberal arts institution. A state law, passed a year earlier, initiated a certifying board called the College and University Council. It also set minimum standards in terms of assets, facilities, and teaching personnel. There is some question whether Juniata technically qualified for accreditation under certain provisions of the act, but President M. G.'s magical influence with the twelve council members did the trick.

Though far from being any golden-dream college Jacob Zuck might have envisioned, Juniata now had a status of sorts. Its graduates automatically received a permanent state teaching certificate. And, jubilated the *Echo*, a Juniata B.A. meant admittance "without examination into the post-graduate departments of the great universities of this country and of Germany."[22]

CHARTER REFORM AND THE TRUSTEE BOARD

Ever since the late 1880s the trustees had fussed about some way of putting the college in a tax-exempt category. In June 1888 a committee was appointed at the annual stockholders' meeting to study the situation and recommend a plan of action. But nothing came of its work, and eleven years later the stockholders were still fretting about the taxation problem. As long as Juniata remained a joint-stock corporation—at least on paper—there was no legal ground for tax relief. Actually, the total value of college stock by the 1900s amounted to only fifteen thousand dollars.[23]

On February 1, 1904 the stockholders authorized the trustees to "make any legal changes in the charter necessary to further the interests of the College."[24] In another two years the trustees were ready to act and decided that, to dispel a general misconception on the part of stockholders and others, all evidences of private ownership must be abolished.[25] They came up with six points to stress in making their pitch to owners of stock certificates:

1. The money invested in stock was never intended to pay dividends but to be used to promote education.
2. In twenty-nine years no earnings were ever divided among the shareholders.
3. The college is able to go on because of endowment and current gifts.
4. The college is a "public charity" while technically the present charter makes it a business corporation.
5. Abolishing the joint-stock setup would solve the taxation problem.
6. This would also allay the misgivings which some philanthropists might have.

To recharter Juniata as a nonprofit institution meant the cession of every share—271 3/4 in all—before any court action could be taken. This proved to be a somewhat troublesome and dragged-out process. Once the trustees finally agreed to amend the charter, on January 28, 1907, M. G. wrote his cousin Harvey urging that John Brumbaugh

> get into the field at once and visit as rapidly as he can, securing either the complete surrender by endorsement on each stock certificate or secure proxies properly signed and witnessed in each case. As fast as it is discovered that the owner will not surrender in either of the two ways named you should let me know the name and number of the stock. Also in cases where the persons subscribed are dead and legal executors or administrators cannot be found to sign the surrender you should also then let me know the name and number of the stock. Each of those shall have to become a special action and the sooner we get them the better. Please hurry this matter as every minute is precious.[26]

The trustees spent months trying to track down all the certificates, not a few of which had been lost. Some had been sold without anyone's making a transfer on the stock records of the college. In the end most were ceded willingly and readily, but not all. A few persons, whose stock was inherited or bought from someone else, thought it had commercial value and resented being asked to yield it as a gift. And then there were the brothers of the girl Harvey Brumbaugh had jilted. Their chance to get revenge had come to hand at last. They held out for full redemption of their father's single share plus twenty-five years' interest (about two thousand five hundred dollars).[27]

By year's-end all stock was surrendered, and on January 20, 1908 the trustees adopted a set of amendments to the charter. These revisions cleared the court on September 21. Under the amended charter, all stock was canceled and control of the college vested in a self-perpetuating board of trustees, still fifteen in number.

Dr. M. G. had made sure that the revised charter was clean of even the most innocent sectarian allusions. This brought a mild protest from Harvey, who once wondered in a letter to him whether it was "wise or necessary to remove all reference to the church."[28] But the President had George Henderson, the trustees' Philadelphia counsel, on his side.

Because of them two important changes were made in the charter. These made explicit the college's legal, if not actual, independence from the church. The first one expunged the provision that trustees had to be Brethren. In the second case the purpose of the college was restated. The reference in the old charter to preserving "the doctrines" of the Bible as believed and practiced by the Brethren" was amended to read: "The purpose or design is to establish a college or institution of learning which will provide the young with such educational advantages as will fit them for the responsibilities and duties of life."

With reorganization came board-of-trustee bylaws for the first time, adopted December 11, 1908.[29] Honoring the charter, the bylaws eliminated a Brethren test for membership. But a "recognized religious character" remained the prime qualification. Familiarity with the college's history and its ideals was also essential. In addition to fostering the "intellectual life of the college on the highest possible plane of efficiency," it behooved the board to "direct and maintain the morale and religious life of the college in harmony with the principles. . .set forth in the Holy Bible."

This was only window dressing, however, since nobody really intended to go out looking for non-Brethren trustees—and for years never did.

The board of trustees suffered a great loss not long after the bylaws went into effect. In January Dr. A. B. Brumbaugh, its go-getting secretary, passed away after an emergency appendectomy. At the time of his death patients owed the seventy-one-year-old surgeon, a largehearted man, thousands of dollars. As someone said of him: "He is a good doctor, but a poor collector."[30] So overwhelming was the show of community mourning that his funeral had to be held in the Huntingdon Presbyterian Church, the only sanctuary big enough to accommodate the crowd. Dr. Gaius took his father's place on the board.

Another trustee veteran took leave in those years, too, but not because of the Grim Reaper. In 1908 fifty-six-year-old William Beery resigned from the faculty and left for the Midwest. Then in December 1910 he gave up his board position which he had held for upwards of two decades. By resolution the trustees lauded him for helping to "make the life and spirit of Juniata College." The "Forge" hero had half his life yet to live, during which his alma mater was never far from mind.

There had been a five-year hiatus after 1890 when women were absent from the board, but they were well-represented during the crucial years of charter reform. Mrs. Mary Geiger of Philadelphia came on the board in 1895 and served til her death in 1916 at age eighty-eight. She was a godsend in that day when the college needed big money. Her sister trustee for years was alumna Jennie Stouffer (Newcomer), a late-married schoolmarm and daughter of Elder Stouffer from Hagerstown. Elected in 1900, she gave the college thirty-eight continuous years, the longest tenure ever for a woman.

After the charter-reform years fewer trustees hailed from the local area, and faculty-trustees were much less in evidence. The precedent was also set at this time, as specified in the 1908 bylaws, for an annual written presidential report on the state of the college.

DIVERSIFIED CURRICULA: ACADEMY THROUGH COLLEGE

By century's turn there were three degree-granting programs: liberal arts, teacher education, and biblical studies. Three other courses of instruction—music, business, and the academy—conferred diplomas. For a short time, from 1896 to 1900, there was also a seminary course for women who had no interest in the professionally oriented Normal curriculum. Stressing languages, literature, and history, it was designed, the catalog said, "to give young women such liberal culture as will fit them for the varied duties of home and public life." The seminary program was discontinued when the Academy was started.

LIBERAL ARTS

Anticipating accreditation, eight Normal graduates—all men but one—began the liberal arts course in 1894. A select group on campus, they were tagged with the moniker "posts" (postgraduates). One of them, William Howe, a Louisiana principal, had been gone since 1886. Daniel C. Reber was the first "post" to receive the B.A. degree (in 1897), not long before he became the second president of Elizabethtown College. He was followed the next year by Charles C. Ellis, likewise destined for a presidency—of his own alma mater. The B.S. degree, however, was dropped in 1894 (although the Scientific course was continued for another two years) and would not be revived until 1920.

Phasing out the Scientific course and doing away with the B.S. degree in no way meant a downgrading of the sciences, however. President M. G., an old hand with microscopes and other laboratory tools, made sure of that. Ever since becoming a trustee in 1884 he spoke out for strengthening that area of the curriculum. Thus from the start the course in Arts required some work in at least five of the natural sciences. Once the elective system was introduced in 1897 it was only another three years until advanced courses were being offered. Biology and math led the way, with physics and chemistry right behind. Geology, though, remained a one-course field. In 1897 the science laboratories were expanded and moved into part of Students Hall basement shortly after that building was erected. Next year the whole basement was pre-empted.

Among the sciences, astronomy, still the sideline of math-prof Saylor, was the perennial ultrapopular elective. In time there was talk of putting up an observatory on Round Top. John Brashear, the far-famed astronomer and precision lens maker of Pittsburgh, fevered it all while lecturing on campus in the summer of 1907.[31] But the star-gazers never got their observatory although the college did acquire a brand-new five-inch Brashear telescope (for five hundred dollars) in 1909.

The elective system gave no less of a boost to the study of social science than to natural science. By 1910 there were as many as eleven open slots for upperclass students. And so from one course each in psychology and economics the social science curriculum was expanded to include sociology and political science, for a total of seven courses in all.

There were also a few options in the humanities although art and music failed to qualify as credit-bearing electives. But it was the humanities, of course, upon which the arts curriculum was built. A breakdown of required courses in 1910 shows twenty from the humanities, three from the social sciences, and eight from the natural sciences. Language study began in the freshman year with Latin and either Greek or German. All students had to take two years of Latin and at least one year of German and French. There was one Bible requirement, two in history (both European), three in philosophy, and four in English and literature.

In the sixteen years between 1894 and 1910 the population of B.A. degree-seekers had grown from eight to forty-five, of whom nearly half were women. The all-inclusive fee for pre-World War I Juniatians ranged from $209.00 to $218.50, depending on which of three dormitories they were in.

In those early twentieth-century years Juniata was one of about five hundred degree-granting colleges in the United States. Of these, 350 had an enrollment of less than 160.[32] Ivy League colleges, among the nation's oldest, attracted about ten percent of the student pool—some two hundred thousand—at that time.[33] Of the top ten in size as the 1900s dawned, Harvard headed the list with well over five thousand students, while tenth-ranked Johns Hopkins enrolled a few more than six hundred.[34] Only one out of every four hundred teenage Americans then sought a college education.[35]

THE SCHOOL OF EDUCATION

The new century saw most state normal schools switch to a four-year curriculum, the better to prepare teachers for the multiplying numbers of high school positions. Somewhat belatedly Juniata joined the parade, and in 1910 announced that the Teachers School had been reorganized under the name School of Education. Charles C. Ellis, with his recent Penn Ph.D., was made its dean.[36] In compliance with the state school code, aspiring high school teachers and principals now had to take a fourth year of study.

The old three-year normal course was retained only one year more. The Bachelor of English degree was withdrawn and replaced by a diploma.

Between 1911 and 1924 all teacher training, elementary and secondary, was a four-year program.

Reflective of student backgrounds and teaching ambitions, the curriculum was built largely around the needs of the rural school.

As an alternative to teaching, the catalog promised, School of Education graduates could enter any college in this country. And when M. G. stepped aside the school had 159 on its rolls. It remained Juniata's very life-blood during this time when liberal arts students came to the Hill in nothing more than a trickle.

THE BIBLE SCHOOL

That era's Juniata was a pace-setter among Brethren colleges in furthering theological education (as opposed to biblical), against which there was a church ban dating back to 1882.[37] The college's leadership came out openly for a trained clergy, expanded the curriculum in biblical studies, and added two degree programs. Juniata was the second of the sister colleges to engage a seminary-trained theologian and the only one ever to endow chairs in religion.

In 1897 the college introduced a three-year course that led to the degree Bachelor of Sacred Literature. At first there were no entrance requirements. By 1900, however, applicants were expected to have the equivalent of a high school education. Involving the study of Greek and Hebrew, homiletics and hermeneutics, the Sacred Literature Course provided basic pastoral training, the first of its kind in the Brotherhood.

There were twelve B.S.L. graduates, including three women, before the degree—but not the course—was discontinued in 1911. The B.S.L. was replaced by a diploma, after which interest dropped to practically nothing.

Meanwhile, in 1908 the catalog outlined a new four-year program offering the Bachelor of Divinity degree. It amounted to a bona fide seminary curriculum, much more professionally oriented than B.S.L. work, and admitted to study only those with at least two years of college. The B.D. program attracted no attention, however, for another decade.

For one thing it was a bit ill-timed. Granted, by then many Brethren were finding a professional ministry more to their liking. But the old bugbear of an educated, salaried pastorate still frightened a goodly number of conservative churchmen, the most of them Pennsylvanians.

Then, too, there was the rivalry of Bethany Bible School (later renamed Bethany Theological Seminary and today the church's only graduate divinity school). Founded in Chicago in 1905 it had, because of its geographic location, a decided advantage in competing for Far- and Midwest Brethren. Later on, in the 1920s, when fundamentalism found a hotbed on the Hill, Juniata's B.D. program would take on life. Some came to see it as the church's answer to the modernism allegedly then taking sprout at Bethany.

But however dormant its theological programs might have been, the Bible department was centric to the total curriculum, and as the years crept up on Henry and John Brumbaugh, M. G. and Harvey brought in new blood. In 1897 Amos Haines, a graduate of Rugers and the Yale Divinity School, began his twenty-year stay at Juniata. He was the church's second seminary graduate.[38] Haines was joined on the Bible staff in 1907 by Tobias Myers, the fourth Brethren seminarian.[39] Holding degrees from Temple and Crozier Theological Seminary, "T. T." Myers enjoyed two distinctions as a clergyman-educator. Beginning in 1891 he was the first regularly salaried full-time Brethren pastor—at First Church, Philadelphia. Twenty-three years a Bible prof, he was also named the first occupant of the college's oldest endowed chair.

This chair—in New Testament Literature and Exegesis—was made possible in 1907 by a twenty-two thousand dollar gift from Mrs. Mary S. Geiger.[40] "Mother" Geiger, as she was affectionately called, was a wealthy widow widely honored for her charitable, reform, and church activities. President M. G. had known and admired her ever since his doctoral days at Penn. It was he who cultivated her friendship for Juniata over the ensuing years.

THE SCHOOL OF MUSIC

Since first issuing diplomas in 1890, the music department made steady progress in upgrading its instruction. It was designated a "school" in 1906, along with Bible, education, and business, but this did not alter its status as mainly a service discipline. Like art, the extent of its academic offerings was one basic course for the Academy and one for the School of Education.

In 1904 the college hired its first conservatory-trained musician and five years after, when William Beery retired, the second. Both were women. With their appointments the school became increasingly involved with extracurricular music groups and performances. By 1910 the music staff was handling as many as eighty-eight students through private voice and instrument lessons.

THE BUSINESS SCHOOL

When the college was rechartered in 1896 the trustees did away with the name Juniata Business College. For a while it was called a "department" until made a "school"in 1906.

A year or two earlier the future of business education on campus had hung in the balance. In November 1904 the trustees began to raise questions about the legitimacy of such a program, even in an adjunct relationship, within a liberal arts setting.[41] The following March they seriously considered wiping out the department at the end of the spring term.[42] But backing off, perhaps out of mercy for George Snavely, then dying of cancer, they decided to wait another year before making up their minds.

Snavely died in September, at age sixty-three, the first to pass away while teaching since Zuck, more than a quarter-century before. (In all of Juniata's one hundred years there have been but six deaths among full-time faculty under sixty-five.) Homer Sanger, a twenty-five-year-old Snavely protégé and college freshman, took over the department in January.

The next summer the trustees ruled against scrapping the business program. Sanger stayed on as its head until 1916. Business graduates took part in commencement exercises for the first time in 1907. Prior to then the principal had distributed diplomas in private. June of 1907 also gave rise to the Business Alumni Association. It was disbanded in 1919 when all graduates of degree or diploma programs were made eligible for membership in the parent body.

The Business School flourished in the two decades after 1891, and by 1910 it could list 248 living alumni. Of this breed of Juniatians, over a third were office workers of some sort. Nearly as many were self-employed and a surprising number—about ten percent—had entered one of the professions. Sales, banking, and civil service attracted another thirteen percent.

THE ACADEMY

Schooling beyond the grades was still a rarity for most *fin de siècle* Americans, and only as late as 1895 were second class cities in Pennsylvania ordered to have at least one high school. Moreover, current state compulsory attendance laws applied to few teenagers. Youngsters in rural areas were virtually denied a high school education.

This posed a real problem once Juniata was accredited. Most of its students came from the country, and at first some of them hoped to use the Normal English Course to get admitted to the college. But that meant dragging out their precollege training for five years in order to meet entrance standards. Many youth were discouraged by this prospect.

The faculty and trustees acted to remedy the situation at once. They introduced a three-year College Preparatory Course in the fall of 1899. In announcing this move the *Echo* said: "It is the purpose of Juniata College to prepare students, not only for the classical course. . . , but to train them that if they desire to go elsewhere they may have an equipment equal to that given by the best schools of the time."[43] Thirteen college-bound boys and girls appeared on campus in September to enroll in this latest program.

The Preparatory Course was institutionalized as the "Academy" in 1901, when its curriculum was expanded to a full four years. There were no separate buildings for the Academy and no separate faculty. Nor was there any discrimination at first in the dormitory assignments. Beginning in 1907, however, all college men were housed in Students Hall. Academy pupils got few breaks in costs; except for tuition fees, which were fifty cents a week less, they were charged the same as collegians.

By 1907 the Academy had an enrollment of 109, second only to that of the School of Education by a few students and triple the number in the college. The trustees began to think hard about divorcing the Academy from the rest of the operations in every way—facilities, instructional staff, administration. On July 9, 1908 they met with the faculty to debate both the wisdom and feasibility of such a step.[44]

A strong consensus emerged on this occasion for developing two different campuses. It was proposed to relocate the college on Round Top, leaving the old property for the use of the Academy. This proposal called for annexing the suggested site and the erection of two new buildings. The trustees were actively exploring such a plan when M. G.'s resignation in 1910 brought all talk of expansion to a halt.

SUMMER SCHOOL

For many years after the teachers' institute was dropped in 1879, there was no interest on the part of the college to conduct a summer program on its own. But in 1896 M. G. pulled strings to bring to campus an outside organization, the Pennsylvania Summer School, which was based at Juniata each July for three straight years. Its two-week sessions exposed school teachers to a faculty of top-notch educators from all over the state. In essence, though, the school was only a glorified version of the old-time county institute and, as such, gave no academic credit.

In 1902 a pair of young professors, Perry Hoover and Charles Hodges, went to bat for a summer term that offered credit-bearing courses.[45] This was a novel idea in higher education then, although some places—like Chicago and Ursinus—had already taken the step. The trustees were hesitant at first, and both Hoover and Hodges had gone by 1909 when Juniata finally fell in line.

The 1909 session enrolled thirty-eight students and course offerings came from the college, the Academy, and the School of Education. But summer work never drew very well and would be dropped in 1914 for a brief spell.

HOLDING A CORE FACULTY

The old teaching mainstays, Jacob Brumbaugh, William Swigart, and Joseph Saylor, were still around when M. G. called it quits as president. But gone were David Emmert (1905) and William Beery (1908).

With M. G.'s presidency a new crop of loyal Juniatians took over the classrooms. Amos Haines and Tobias Myers anchored the Bible Department for more than two decades. Charles Ellis returned in 1907, after an absence of six years (he previously taught 1894-1901), with a Penn doctorate. (An earlier one from Illinois Wesleyan in 1904 made him the fourth Brethren to earn that degree.) His was the only Ph.D. among the fixed faculty until Alphaeus Dupler and Charles Shively joined the ranks after World War I. "C. C.," trained in education, would wear a variety of hats on the way to becoming president in 1930.

From Mt. Morris College came Oscar Myers in 1905, his B.A. and M.A. from the University of Michigan, to teach English and modern languages. This Lewistown native, a future church elder, spent thirty-seven years with the college. The last eighteen he put in as treasurer and business manager. In 1905 the *Echo* dubbed "O. R.," with his ready smile, the "Sunny Professor."[46] Students liked the "cheerio, man to man atmosphere" of his classes, the paper said.

Three other worthies were Allan Myers, Martha Shontz, and Frank Holsopple. Elder Myers, farm born and bred near McVeytown and an 1887 Normal graduate, brought stability to the sciences between 1893 and 1909. Afterward he replaced Dr. A. B. as trustee secretary, serving nineteen years on the board. Mrs. Shontz, who came in 1906, stepped into Emmert's shoes, and for the next fifteen years held a dual appoint-

All with beards take front row! Faculty 1907-08.
Row 1:   F. F. Holsopple, W. J. Swigart, J. B. Brumbaugh, H. B. Brumbaugh, J. H.
         Brumbaugh, A. H. Haines, T. T. Myers, J. E. Saylor, J. A. Myers.
Row 2:   M. Shontz, S. M. Kanagy, C. C. Johnson, Mrs. J. Scholl, J. Martin, I. H. Brum-
         baugh, C. C. Wardlow, L. Shuss, H. F. Sanger, C. C. Ellis, M. Shenck, S. P.
         Uhler, O. R. Myers.

ment as art instructor and matron. Frank Holsopple '91 taught English
from 1901 to 1914 before leaving for other fields of endeavor.

Though doctorates were in short measure in that day, the faculty did
their graduate work at some of the best universities in America and
Europe. In 1904 the catalog began to list faculty credentials and where

degrees were earned. From then on it carried names of schools like Harvard, Yale, Penn, Chicago, Michigan, Rutgers, Vermont, Berlin, Leipsic, and Marburg.

NEW BUILDINGS

Despite the severe economic recession of the mid-Nineties and the lesser one of 1907, M. G.'s first presidency produced a major transformation of the campus. Its bounds were expanded sevenfold — to more than twenty-three acres. And by 1910 the campus complex consisted of seven buildings.

STUDENTS HALL

By 1894 the college had outgrown its classroom space. That October work began on a four-story brick building, 40' x 80', at the southeast corner of Moore and 18th streets. To drum up support M. G. penned a general letter for the *Echo* outlining a fund-raising gimmick. He wrote:

> It is our belief that this building should be regarded as STUDENTS' HALL; and we desire to have all students of the College from its beginning, together with their friends, erect this Hall. To further this end we make to you this personal appeal to subscribe, for as many bricks, at one cent each, as you may feel able and willing to contribute. . . .Surely we can contribute 300,000 bricks to this project.[47]

How well this plan paid off is not known, but it brought at least one enthusiastic response. From Chicago Lizzie Howe, now a social worker, wrote the *Echo* editor that the kids of her mission hoped to subscribe a good-size pile of bricks.[48]

Students Hall, designed by David Emmert and built under his eye, was completed by July of 1895. The basement housed the science laboratories and a gym room. The library occupied the west side of the main floor; the east side was divided into two classrooms. There were four classrooms on the third story. Office space for instructors was provided by the two-floor projections at either end. The top level became a men's dormitory, fitted up for some twenty roomers.

In 1897 a stack room for the library, 16' x 26', was added to the rear of Students Hall. The two structures were joined by a fireproof transept, 8' x 16'. M. G. and H. B. Brumbaugh picked up the tab between them ($350 each) for this addition. When Carnegie Library was built the annex was converted into the biology laboratory. Then, following the erection of Science Hall in 1916, the two rooms were put to use for classes. Not til

1928, when the fourth-floor men were moved out, was all of Students Hall given over to instruction.

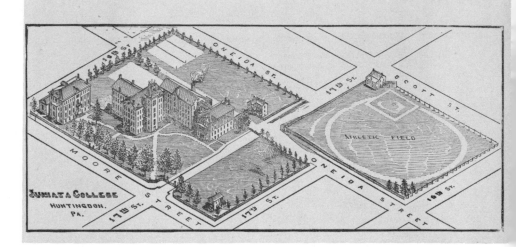

The Campus in 1900.

ONEIDA HALL

Oneida Hall, almost to a foot the same size as Students, was built in the spring of 1898. Fronting the campus, it was attached to the south end of Ladies Hall, connected by an eighteen-foot transept that also served as the main stairway. (The south foundation wall encroached upon the outdoor baptistry, which was now moved to a spot directly east of the chapel.)

The college had long outgrown the old basement dining hall in the "Building." Oneida was built chiefly to solve that problem. The new refectory, high-ceilinged with large windows and an open fireplace, was bright and airy. Occupying all the main floor, its thirty-two tables could seat 260 boarders. On the evening of May 11, moving day, Henry Brumbaugh joined a jolly crowd for the first meal served there.[49] David Emmert remembered: "It was like coming from a dark cave into the open light of day."[50]

The kitchen and pantries were in the basement, from which food was sent up to the dining room on a large dumb-waiter. The upper two floors were made into a women's dormitory, which relieved another over-crowded situation. A veranda off the third level overlooked the main campus.

William Swigart was the one who came up with the name Oneida Hall. According to the *Echo*, "It received the appellation partly in honor of a neighborhood township and valley by that name, and partly because the street on which it stands is called Oneida street; but most of all, it was named in honor of a famous tribe of Indians that long ago hunted over these hills and valleys."[51]

INFIRMARY

In the early days the sick were cared for in their own rooms. Bunk-mates carried in meals and dosed out the medicine. Then, for a few years, a college infirmary was located in a suite of rooms on the first floor of Ladies Hall. But there was too much noise and, late in 1899, a three-room cottage was remodeled back of Ladies Hall. It contained four single iron beds and a kitchen but lacked a bathroom. A trained nurse was on call at all hours, answerable, of course, to Dr. A. B.

THE GYMNASIUM

Erected in 1901, the old gymnasium stands as a salute to student gumption and enthusiasm. For years there was grumbling at the lack of space for indoor team sports and vigorous gymnastic exercises. The low, cramped basement room in Students Hall hardly sufficed even for simple calisthentics.

In December 1900 the students, with the blessing of sports-minded profs, formed a committee to plan and push for a gymnasium building. At first they thought in terms of a simple frame structure resting on locust posts. Then someone, dreaming bigger, suggested a dual-purpose facility: auditorium and gymnasium. This idea intrigued the trustees and by early next year they had caught gym fever, too. The *Echo* reported: "Mr. J. J. Oller of Waynesboro started the financial ball rolling by volunteering one-tenth of the entire cost of the structure."[52] The students "backed up their talk" by coughing up well over one-thousand dollars in pledges and cash.[53] Nor did the alumni shirk in their generosity.

Constructed and equipped for under nine-thousand dollars, the brick building, with its steep, hip-shaped roof broken by gables, was designed by an Altoona architect. The rostrum, created by the fifteen-foot extension on the east side, made it an ideal place for receptions, lectures, concerts, and commencement as well as athletic events. When used as an auditorium it could comfortably seat on folding chairs, by the *Echo*'s estimate, a few less than one-thousand persons.

Sweaty athletes, though, had to wait until 1908 before the basement got a shower stall and dressing room.

CARNEGIE LIBRARY

From the moment M. G. took office the library became the academic apple of his eye. In 1895 the erstwhile student librarian donated 315 volumes to the college. He saw to it that Mary Quinter, the late president's daughter, was made Joseph Saylor's assistant that year and urged her to introduce a card catalog and a system of classification. Her seven years in that position (she left for the mission field in 1903) gave the library a modern trend.

In 1897 he helped foot the bill for the stacks-addition to Students Hall. At his entreaty, that year was also when Mrs. E. C. Summers, widow of a local historian, turned over to the library on "loan exhibit" a fragment of the second Standing Stone.[54] (This historic relic, later donated to the college, is now on display in the museum.)

It was President Brumbaugh, two years later, who brought to College Hill part of the famous Cassel collection. Abraham Cassel was the Dunker antiquarian from Eastern Pennsylvania whom M. G. got to know while researching original sources for his study of Brethren origins. A stock-holder, he had been a Juniata booster from the start; his daughter, Hannah, had put in a year of study back in 1877-78. Cassel's was one of the largest private libraries in the country—over fifty-thousand items, dwarfing many public and college libraries. Juniata got about a third of this collection—some eleven-thousand books and four-thousand pamphlets.[55] The bulk of it comprised existing manuscripts, letters, and diaries relating to the early Brethren. There was also a stock of rare foreign works, valuable colonial imprints, and almanacs galore. Thrown in as a bonus was the Cassel correspondence—three boxes full, in themselves a treasure-trove for Brethren historians.

Getting his hands on this coveted miscellany cost M. G. a small fortune. Cassel decided to sell off his library in 1898. At once the president began bombarding his septuagenarian friend with urgent letters.[56] He pled that the Brethren materials be kept intact and argued that Juniata was the place for them. The fireproof Students Hall transept, he contended, would ensure safekeeping.

Cassel agreed but there followed months of haggling before they finally settled on a selling price of $2,500. The college, with its Oneida

Hall mortgage, was in no position to bear the expense. And so M. G. had no choice but to go it alone on a demand note, on which he made good in less than two years. The date of purchase was February 1, 1899. Later the Harleysville bibliophile kicked back five-hundred dollars of the purchase price to the college.

Building upon the Cassel collection, President Brumbaugh hoped to make Juniata the chief respository for Brethren publications, past and future. In 1900 he sent out circulars to one-thousand ministers in the eastern part of the United States asking for old books, magazines, newspapers, almanacs, and anything else that might have been published by members of the denomination.[57] His project never panned out, but the Cassel library, preserved in the college Archives and the Treasure Room, remains to this day a veritable gold mine for church and social historians.

In 1904 the college came into possession of another collection: the Quinter library, donated by his heirs. It included about one-thousand volumes, most of which dealt with theology.

The year 1904 was also when the college hired its first trained librarian.[58] In the spring of 1904 Dr. M. G. offered to pick up the tab for someone — a professional — to come in during the summer months and begin putting the library in order. He made this overture on condition the trustees continue the work. In June Sarah Bogle, a Drexel graduate in library science, was appointed librarian. Along with her came classmate Mary Wilde, with the title of cataloguer.

The team of Bogle and Wilde, with student help, put in long hours cataloguing — by the Dewey Decimal System — and setting up open stacks. In two years time they had compiled Library of Congress cards for all books copyrighted since 1898. By 1907 Juniata had a "well-cataloged and easily accessible Library," the acting president could say in his annual report. At that time there were over twenty-eight thousand volumes on the shelves.

Miss Wilde left in 1906 and Sarah Bogle the next year. They were followed by a brace of librarians also from the Drexel sisterhood: Jean Martin (1907-08) and Mary Hershberger (Miller), an Academy alumna (1909-11). Ella Sheeley, a Juniata student, filled in between them, getting the title herself — along with a diploma — in 1911 (she was librarian until 1918).

Meanwhile, Carnegie Library had gone up in 1907, the proud show-piece of M. G.'s first presidency. It was the gift of dwarfish steelmaster, Andrew Carnegie, then the world's greatest philanthropist, retired since

1901. Believing that a man who dies rich dies "disgraced," the "Napoleon of the Smokestacks" dedicated the remaining years of his life to giving away his wealth for public libraries, pensions for professors, and other humanitarian purposes — in all disposing of about $350,000,000.

Curiously, the canny Scotsman was almost a soft touch, for it took M. G. less than half a year to sell Carnegie on Juniata's need for a new library. And even more remarkable, the money did not come from the Carnegie Foundation but from the ex-steel baron's personal bank account.

The good news came to the trustees via an M. G. letter on March 22, 1905.[59] They were told that Carnegie agreed to a grant of fifteen-thousand dollars for a library but on a matching-fund basis, a policy in American philanthropy he originated. The college-raised money was to be used for maintaining the proposed structure.

The college acted posthaste. Within weeks Edward Tilton of New York City had been commissioned the architect. The designer of most Carnegie-financed buildings, he had made a minor splash on the world scene in the restoration of the Heraeum at Argos in Greece. Also, all summer and spring everybody on campus, it seemed, took it upon himself to go out and beat money-bushes. The yield was worth it; by early winter $20,500 had been raised in cash and pledges. Most of the credit for this successful canvass, though, properly belongs to John Brumbaugh and Allan Myers; they did the lion's share of legwork.

A needs study, however, dictated a bigger library than originally planned. And so on September 26 M. G. wrote Carnegie at Skibo Castle, Scotland, his retirement estate, explaining the situation and asking him to jack up his pledge. Carnegie wasted no time replying. On October 13 M. G. received a cablegram from his secretary that read:

> Mr. Carnegie. . .wants me to say that he will be glad to increase his allowance for [a] Library Building for Juniata College from Fifteen Thousand to Twenty-eight Thousand Dollars, as requested, in recognition of the progress you are making.[60]

The site of the library, the trustees agreed in June, should not be on the already crowded campus. They wanted a proper setting, one that would permit the building to face toward town. After much thought they chose the northwest corner of Moore and 17th streets.

But there was one problem: Jacob Brumbaugh's brick home stood on that lot. The board vice president did not take too kindly to giving up his domicile, it was soon learned. He dragged his feet for months, causing some bad feelings, before he came to terms. For a neat profit he sold all his property across the street — three houses and six-and-a-half lots — to the college. This plus the purchase of David Emmert's property gave it ownership of the whole Moore Street block.

The cost of the library site added up to sixty-five hundred dollars. Once again, as in 1878, the college turned to townspeople for help. On November 2 David Emmert huddled with concerned citizens in the courthouse and outlined a trustee request. This time, though, there was no appeal for outright charity. The trustees proposed a seven-thousand dollar ten-year loan, interest free. The cash was to come from burghers and businesses through personal advances. But there was a slight catch. Should the trustees find themselves able to amortize this loan before it fell due, then the college was to get a five percent rebate on each note.

The citizens group endorsed the plan and Emmert masterminded the canvass that followed. As an incentive President M. G. spread word that if the town responded he would give an equal sum toward campus expansion. In the spirit of '78 the people of Huntingdon met the challenge, handing over the wherewithal in time enough.

Work on the library — architecturally a combination of Doric and Ionic — began in March 1906. Dedication ceremonies took place on Founders Day of the next year, a bevy of state dignitaries in attendance. The cost of construction came to slightly less than twenty-eight thousand dollars, leaving a small balance on the Carnegie grant.

It was M. G. who sparked the idea of memorial library windows in honor of Zuck and Quinter. Alumni and older students of the college made possible the Zuck window in the east wing. Church leaders were solicited for the Quinter window. Costing about $250 each, these memorials were installed in late spring 1908.

CAMPUS EXPANSION

Beginning with 1899, when land along Oneida Street was bought for an athletic field, the main campus grew from four to nine acres in the next decade. For the bulk of this ground the college laid out better than twenty-two thousand dollars in all.

But a parcel of it was a gift from President M. G. in 1907. True to his word, given when Huntingdon was solicited for Carnegie Library, he turned over to the college a tract of land valued at seven-thousand dollars. This block-size plot north of Students Hall contained three buildings and extended east to the Orphans Home.

Then, through a series of real estate transfers early in 1909, the college—to the tune of $11,500—got possession of the Round Top terrain. It included the area between Washington and Moore streets and from 19th Street north to the foot of what is now Taylor Highland. This brought college-owned acreage to more than twenty-four.

Impetus for this ground-grabbing on the Round Top side of Moore Street came from the faculty-trustee conclave of July 1908, which had recommended separating the college and Academy. Then, too, there was a year-old commitment from the alumni to build a dormitory for forty or fifty college men.[61] Alumni Hall, its proposed name, and a combined administration-academic building would become the nucleus of an across-the-street campus.

Before long, however, the trustees began backtracking on the idea. Obviously a two-branch operation would prove too costly. Moreover, the growing popularity of public high schools raised real questions about the Academy's viability. Thus the matter was let die.

But the Round Top plot, treeless and slaty, was not ignored. The spring of 1909 alumnus George Wirt, then director of the State Forestry School at Mount Alto, volunteered his time to landscape the knoll and its slopes. He planted two-thousand white pine seedlings on the west hill and fifteen-hundred oak seedlings, both red and white, on the east hill. Along the Washington Street curb line, the length of the property, he placed a row of elm saplings. On either side of the Mifflin Street extension more elms were planted, and a double row was run the whole way up to the crest of the knoll, forming a lane.[62] So it was that Round Top got its arboreal cover.

Long before Round Top belonged to the college, however, it had become a mecca for JC students every commencement week—the sacred site of a special vesper service. It was Carman Johnson who conceived the custom of a sunset prayer service for graduating seniors—in 1894. But it was a gratuitous remark by M. G. Brumbaugh's mother that sent seniors from the foot of the hill to its crown.

The hillock was named for Little Round Top, the rise back of Dwight L. Moody's home in Northfield, Massachusetts. Here the famous evangelist conducted vespers for college students attending his "life work" conferences. Campus delegates brought the name back and Juniata's "Round Top" was dedicated in June 1902.

Prior by a year or so to annexing Round Top the college got Pulpit Rocks, located along the old Alexandria Pike (near the Huntingdon Correctional Institution). These rocks, on an acre and a half of ground, were the gift of J. Murray Africa in 1907.[63] In an earlier day they were considered one of the East's natural wonders. Charles Dickens, who passed through Huntingdon in the 1840s, mentions the sandstone formations in *Notes on American Travels*.

CAMPUS FACE LIFTING

After nearly two decades, sometime in 1896 or 1897, the "Building" picked up a name: Founders Hall. Originally Founders was not only nameless but porchless. But a fire law, requiring exterior doors to swing out, forced the trustees in 1905 to put a porch at the west entrance for protection against the weather.

A cosmetic—and romantic—touch was added to Juniata's oldest building by Dr. Charles Ellis in 1908. He planted ivy stalks, which still wind their way up the south side, from a slip he brought from the campus of Antioch College. The original stem had come from Sir Walter Scott's home at Abbottsford, Scotland.[64]

In October 1899 a borough ordinance closed all alleys and streets— Oneida and 17th—that cut across the campus. The trustees then moved some buildings, including the soon-to-be infirmary cottage, on to the Oneida Street right of way. The 17th Street stretch was torn up, regraded, and that part of the grounds terraced.

When Carnegie Library was on the drawing boards the trustees proposed—and Borough Council tentatively okayed—blocking off Moore Street between 17th and 18th. But the trustees had second thoughts and nothing came of the idea.

As the college domain enlarged sidewalks became a necessity. The stretch between Students Hall and Founders was brick-paved in 1903 and linked with a walk to the gym in 1905. The Diagonal, not yet a frosh taboo, remained a gravel path. In 1907 the west side of the main grounds was paved, as was the north side to the gym. An $8' \times 10'$-wide pavement across muddy Moore Street was laid in 1907 between the main entrance at 17th Street and the library. Another crossing was put down the next summer farther up the block, directly out from the Founders-porch walk. Meanwhile, the old picket fence along Moore Street came down in 1906.

At the beginning of this century Juniatians still studied at night by light of kerosene lamps. Electrifying the campus was a prolonged, step-by-step process. Normal student George Wirt, the future pioneering Keystone State forester, noted in his diary for January 27, 1898: "Today they commenced putting wires in the buildings for electric lights."[65] The first wiring lighted the halls only, but the new gym in 1901 had electricity from the start. In the spring of 1901 Founders Hall office got a light bulb. The coeds then set up a clamor for an electric globe in the parlor. They got their way that summer. By early fall 1907 all dorms and classrooms had incandescent lighting, and oil lamps were shelved for good. Wilson Light and Power Co., at Raystown Dam, provided the electrical service.

In 1910 the Huntingdon Brethren built Stone Church on the south edge of the campus. (Founder John Brumbaugh was their pastor.) The congregation took a ninety-nine-year lease on the site, a small annual rent involved (long since forgotten). Originally Stone Church and the college were not divorced; the same relationship existed as when the Brethren worshipped in the chapel. For years the minister at Stone Church was called the College Pastor.

The new place of worship was patterned after a countryside church in England that had once caught the eye of Mrs. Harvey Brumbaugh. Edward Tilton, the architect for Carnegie Library, drew the plans.

TWENTY-FIFTH ANNIVERSARY AND EMMERT'S LITTLE BOOK

Latinist that he was, Harvey Brumbaugh should have known better. Nevertheless, promotional literature kept referring to 1901 as Juniata's Quadri-Centennial (the word means four-hundredth anniversary, not quarter-century). To make the most of the festal year, all celebrating took place during commencement week in June. Souvenirs abounded, among them the school's first wall calendar — a miniature — on which there was printed in bold letters, "Juniata: A College of High Standard."

But without question the choicest memento of the anniversary year was David Emmert's *Reminiscences of Juniata College: Quarter Century, 1876-1901*. While convalescing from a serious illness in 1900, he began to put on paper his personal memories of the college's early days. He started this little narrative with the idea of passing it on to his sons as a keepsake. Friends paying him sick calls were treated to chapters as they were finished. Soon everybody was urging him to put his "story-like history," the *Echo*'s apt description of it, into book form.

And so he did, underwriting the printing costs himself and filling the pages with over one-hundred wood cuts and photographs. He wrote that if *Reminiscences*, a "record of incidents and experiences grave and comical, joyful and sad, shall lead anyone to understand better the motives and principles upon which Juniata, as it stands to-day, was founded, and the spirit in which it had gone forward," then the book had been worth his while.

Juniata College Comes Of Age 1893-1910 (Part 2)

STUDENT LIFE IN GENERAL

Today's late-rising Juniatians would hardly long for the "good ole days" of the Nineties when their ancestors had to roll out of bed for seven o'clock classes. Nor would they find it any better to start the day at 7:45 A.M., the schedule imposed in 1904.

In loco parentis was still very much the code of the day. "Jakie" Brumbaugh—a student-inflicted nickname he very much resented—was tagged as the campus snoop; he had an uncanny ability of catching miscreants red-handed on his prowls. And at mail call in the chapel Joseph Saylor, who expertly sailed letters into waiting hands, could sniff out envelopes addressed with fingers nicotine-stained. In 1902 the trustees reaffirmed, with his backing, the long-standing rule that tobacco users would be subject to dismissal or denied degrees.

But, of course, for most students then, as now, a special thrill derived from breaking campus canon. George Wirt's diary for 1897 tells of boys taking girls up to their rooms, worry-free of tattlers. And in those days before the LCB card, callow Hilltoppers now and then slipped downtown for a sneaky snort or two at the Washington House.[1] Illicit

Room of Harry Sieber (left) and Lloyd Harman, future trustee, Founders Hall. Note double bed, lower right corner, furnished in all rooms until 1922. For some reason no kerosene lamp is in evidence.

drinking would persist as a problem despite the threat of tough penalties and the wrath of student prohibitionists.

Likewise vandalism, nowadays the woe of student deans, was not unknown in those less permissive times either. One of the worst cases of wanton destruction at Juniata occurred in 1908, making local front-page news.[2] For some reason the biology professor, Frederick Burt, got on the wrong side of a few students. One evening, during a Lyceum lecture, four of them broke into Burt's room. They destroyed many of his books and valued manuscripts, including his priceless collection of insects, the result of years of work. The books were smeared with ink and many of the pages pasted shut. They were then placed on a pile and the mischief-makers dumped molasses and "slops" over them. Curtains were ripped from the windows and, along with the professor's clothes, soaked in the dirty water. With some sleuthing the scamps were identified and shown to the station.

According to George Wirt's diary, chapel in 1898 was still a time to moralize on the impropriety of mixed couples walking up and down the street together. But things began to loosen up a bit in 1903 when men and women were allowed to fraternize for two hours every weekday (4 to 6 P.M.) and three on Sunday (3 to 6 P.M.).

Another change toward "social amelioration" came with Saturday-evening partying, an innovation in January 1899. Held at first in the chapel and then in the new gym, these get-togethers ranged from hunting peanuts to pulling taffy to intellectual games. But the favorite pastime, Edgar Detwiler remembered from his turn-of-the-century student days, was the Virginia Reel. Sometimes, reveals Wirt's diary, the fun on Saturday nights ended with devotions. . .levity had to be tempered with piety.

The social as well as the intellectual life of students further improved with the creation of the College Lecture Bureau in the fall of 1897. This was a faculty committee of one — Amos Haines at first — which brought in two or three outside speakers. In time professional musical groups gave variety to these public events programs.

For quick trips downtown after June 1907 Juniatians had the use of the "Toonerville Trolley." The electric streetcar line, however, only ran as far as 17th Street in West Huntingdon.

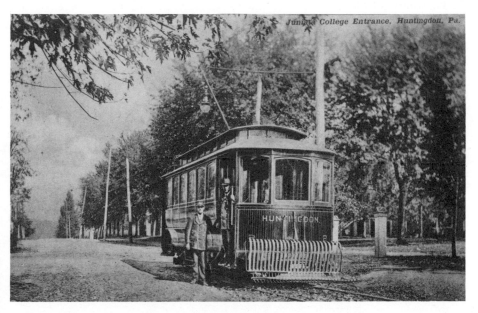

"Toonerville Trolley." Parked at 17th Street in 1919.

The new century bred the early tradition of Mountain Day. The first all-college outing was to the "Forge" in May 1896.[3] Everybody that day, reported the *Echo*, "arose very early, ate a hasty breakfast, walked to the station, boarded a special train, crossed the Juniata River, rumbled southward over the Huntingdon and Broad Top, arrived at Marklesburg, climbed into big farm wagons, [and] jolted over four miles of indifferent country road" to get to the creekside refuge of the smallpox exiles of '78. By 1900 getting "away to the woods" had become a fall instead of a spring event.

Henry Brumbaugh coined the phrase "Mountain Day," a Thursday, October 22 entry in his 1903 diary. Terrace Mountain soon rivaled Trough Creek Forge as the favorite alfresco locale. In 1906 the caravan bound for Terrace Mountain consisted of 110 students in seven farm wagons, a buggy, a carriage, and a victuals-ladened dray.

On March 2, 1906 the trustees officially decreed another Juniata tradition. Beginning that spring April 17 was to be celebrated each year as Founders Day. For decades this event marked a high point in the college calendar.

Up to 1898 Juniata had no common visible symbols upon which to build "college spirit." Each class chose its own colors and motto, thus inspiring peer rather than institutional loyalty. The breakthrough came in 1898 when Dr. George Lyon composed the first alma mater.

Then that June the college got its colors. This, trumpeted the *Echo*, "marks another step forward" in Juniata's progress. "Blue and Gold. . . What does it mean?" the nameless writer asked rhetorically. He answered in gung-ho fashion:

> . . .[it means] that we recognized true devotion in the respect which students ofttimes pay to their college colors, that we now have an emblem which shall represent our own Juniata when we assemble in reunions and when we mingle with schoolmen from sister institutions. . .in short, it means animation, without which the scholar soon becomes a nonentity.

A quatrain followed this commentary, telling what the colors stand for:

> True as the blue
>   And pure as the gold,
> Thus may our lives
>   To their fullness unfold!

Another big day for insignia-minded Juniatians came in the fall of 1902. On October 25 Harvey Brumbaugh announced at a reception in the gym that the faculty had officially adopted a motto, a seal, and a new college pin.[4] The seal and the motto were of the speaker's own devising. He explained that around the seal would appear the Latin words, "Sigillum Collegii Juniatienses." In the center would lie an open book. Above and below the book would be one word of the motto, "Veritas Liberat"— "the truth sets free." This motto was based on the words of Jesus in the Gospel of John: "You shall know the truth, and the truth will set you free" (8:32). The "open book," the acting president said in his announcement, "has always been and ever shall be the only fountain and guardian of true knowledge, of truth."

As early as December 1899 the *Echo* makes passing reference to "the popular Juniata College pin" but gives no description of it. Apparently, then, one was in circulation before 1902, when it was redesigned. It now had a triangular shape with an old English "J" in bas-relief. In each of the two lower corners appeared one of the motto's initials.

All this ado about signets, colors, and mottos indicated a breaking down of Brethren bias against regalia. Perhaps the most obvious symbol of this liberation was the college flag, another 1902 novelty. The *Echo* took pleasure in how it waved "gayly," beneath Old Glory, on the flagpole outside Founders.

Other innovations soon followed. College seniors, disappointed in 1900 by a trustee order to show up at commencement, as before, in "citizen's clothes," paraded begowned across the gym stage in 1904 to get their diplomas. Female diploma-awardees in other departments wore white dresses for a special touch. Honorary doctorates were next—D.D.s (doctor of divinity) conferred on Tobias Myers and Amos Haines in 1905.

The faculty, though, went slow on pomp for itself. Because of a strong difference of opinion—oldsters vs. upstarts—they went without academic trappings at commencement until the late Twenties.

RELIGIOUS GROUPS

By the close of Juniata's first quarter-century, religious life, once the business of the local church, had come to rest largely in student hands. There were still college constraints, of course: compulsory Sunday worship—somewhere in town—and daily chapel. But the Brethren mid-week service had given way by 1890 to a student prayer group.

The first student religious organization was the Young Peoples' Missionary Society, started by the women of the church (Sisters' Missionary Circle) in May 1893.[5] The object of this group was "to educate young people to mission work, to encourage a living, active missionary spirit among them, by the reading and study of missionary literature and by contributing means in support of the work." Practically the whole school joined and under Harvey Brumbaugh, its first president, Lizzie Howe's Chicago mission was made the group's main project.

It was Carman Johnson, next year's prexy, who changed its name to Young Peoples' Missionary and Temperance Society. Teetotalism preempted the society's interest during the great prohibition fight, spearheaded by the Anti-Saloon League, that culminated with the 18th Amendment and the "Noble Experiment." But by that time the society had died out (1917).

Foreign-mission emphasis, in the meantime, was taken over by the Volunteer Mission Band, which allied itself with an intercollegiate organization, the Student Volunteer Movement.[6] The impact of the Volunteer Movement on idealistic American youth has no parallel in history, except perhaps the Peace Corps of the 1960s. It was a dramatic outgrowth of the late nineteenth-century foreign-missions thrust. As Uncle Sam's commercial and political influence spread abroad after the Civil War, the attention of Protestant churches was drawn to needy people beyond the seas. Soon they were out to evangelize the heathen peoples of the whole world.

Student enthusiasm for the "White Man's burden" was sparked in 1886 at Dwight L. Moody's conference center in Northfield, Massachusetts. There one-hundred collegians volunteered for foreign-mission service, and the delegates carried their enthusiasm back to local campuses. In 1888 this zeal was channeled into a permanent organization, the Student Volunteer Movement, which adopted as its slogan "The evangelization of the world in this generation." For the next three decades SVM was to enlist the very ablest men and women on the nation's college campuses and to send them to the far corners of the earth. Possibly the most outstanding product of the student missionary movement was Huntingdon's own Robert E. Speer, a Princeton graduate and Presbyterian layman.

Juniata's Volunteer Mission Band was organized in March 1899.[7] The previous year three Juniatians—Jesse Emmert, Lewis Keim, and Acting President Brumbaugh—had represented the college at an SVM convention in Cleveland. Then Robert Speer visited the campus and built up further interest. Dedicated to the Brethren mission field, all volunteers took the pledge: "It is my purpose, if God permit, to become a missionary. As to whether it will be in the home field or abroad, I await the further guidance of the Spirit."

Robert Speer once said that the great need for the world was "to be saved from want and disease, injustice, inequality, impurity, lust, hopelessness and fear."[8] The college solidly put its stamp of approval on this goal of all-out world salvation, a goal that Juniata, it was felt, had a duty to advance. The moral and educational call of the times, President M. G. told the stockholders in 1900, was to "meet the mission need."[9] Echoed William Swigart on the same occasion: "The mission work is a product of the schools. We need the men, the women properly educated."

Five volunteers kept their pledges and answered the missionary call—all to India—within the next few years. They were: Jesse and Gertrude Rowland Emmert (1902); Jacob Blough (1903); Mary Quinter (1903); John and Florence Baker Pittenger (1904); Joseph Swigart (1904), who died a few weeks before sailing.

By March 1919 when the Band presented to the college a missionary-service flag—to hang in the chapel—twenty-six Juniatians had dedicated themselves to being foreign missionaries.

The early 1900s also gave rise to active Student YMCA and YWCA chapters. But at first church and college officials offered resistance. The Brethren had long gone on record against local community Ys because they provided their membership with amusements. On campus the Y's forerunner was the Boys' Christian Band, started by Charles Ellis, then a student, in March 1897. Its members vowed to do "at *least one* good act for Christ each week."[10] A Girls' Christian Band was organized in the spring of 1898.

In December 1901 a faculty-student committee petitioned the local church elders and the trustees for permission to begin a student Y chapter.[11] They argued that the "college movement" was "distinct" from community Ys since it operated under a different kind of constitution. But, reported the October 1902 *Echo*: "Juniata did not yet consider it wise being identified with the YMCA."

By 1904, however, the trustees and elders had changed their minds and sometime that fall a campus chapter sprang up. "Almost all boys and girls have joined," the *Echo* noted. Then in February 1907 Juniata women chartered themselves as the YWCA.

It was the two Y groups that later introduced the custom of holding student-led worship services in the county jail. They also pioneered in Sunday-afternoon deputation services at outlying rural schoolhouses.

PHYSICAL EDUCATION AND THE RISE OF
INTERCOLLEGIATE SPORTS

In 1897, when the gym was still in Students Hall, English Prof. Samuel Heckman voluntarily began to hold daily workouts for students, using dumbbells, Indian clubs, and wands. Such drills continued under Amos Haines and Fayette McKenzie, who supervised the men, while Mrs. George Lyon and Nellie McVey directed the women. After Oneida Hall was ready for use in 1898 the gym was moved to the old dining room in Founders basement. Dinner hour by then had been changed from five to six o'clock to allow more time for exercising. The new gym in 1901, of course, made possible a vastly expanded program.

Thus in that year Joseph Yoder, a sports-minded Amish freshman, became the first paid "physical director." In 1904 he was succeeded by Elmer Shriner N. E. '01, who had studied physical education at Harvard and was now in Juniata's B.A. program. He was let go in 1906 and after a year's lapse Chester Wardlow, himself a student, held the position until 1912.

In 1904 there was some form of organized physical training at 270 American college and universities. At seventy-two of them it was required and another twenty-four gave credit. Shriner (it was his Harvard mentor — Dr. Dudley Sargent — who transformed Teddy Roosevelt from a ninety-pound weakling into a physical-fitness crank) crusaded for gym credit while he was physical director. He failed at that, but in 1905 phys ed did become a requirement (credit was not granted until 1923). Some enthusiasts imagined that they detected an "immediate" improvement in student health.

Outdoor sports got a big boost in the spring of 1899 when the site of the Huntingdon Bookbindery on Oneida Street was bought and made into an athletic field. At that time, though, the field extended east only as far as Scott Street. A partial fence went up in the summer and the whole field was enclosed in 1905. Bleachers, seating a couple hundred, added spectator comfort in 1909.

For several years there had been both a Boys' and Girls' Athletic Association that looked after intramural events and an occasional town-gown baseball game. But in September 1900 the two groups were integrated into the Juniata Athletic Association. Dues were set at fifty-cents a year, and each sport — tennis, baseball, football, basketball, lacrosse — named a manager. The person in charge of keeping up the field and the tennis courts and purchasing equipment was the field manager. The first student elected to this position was Ewing Newcomer, inventor one day of the glass-lined thermos bottle.[12] JAA's big event of the year was "Field day," an all-afternoon, all-sports affair. Even profs got a chance to show off their athletic prowess. It was JAA, egged on by the Rev. Haines, that set in motion the drive for the new gymnasium.

In 1902 supervision of the athletic program fell into the hands of a faculty committee. Haines, Oliver Hoover, Carman Johnson, and Frank Holsopple (chairman) were the first ones to serve. Through these men intercollegiate athletics came to Juniata.

They hounded the trustees until permission was given in 1903 to compete in four sports: baseball, track, tennis, and basketball. (Football, banned as too dangerous even for intramural play in 1902, did not get its turn until after World War I.) But, it was stipulated, "all arrangements shall be made in accordance with the spirit of Juniata College" and "with schools who are responsible for the conduct of their students." Initially the physical director did all the coaching.

Juniata's first intercollegiate sports event was a home track-and-field meet with Susquehanna University on June 5, 1903. The Blue and Gold, taking but three first places, lost 60 to 41—all because, the *Echo*, rationalized, Susquehanna was "bigger and better trained." Whatever the final score, the person reporting was happy to say that no one, neither athlete nor fan, had spoiled the day by poor sportsmanship. Before long JC trackmen were winning more than their share of meets.

In 1909 the Juniata Athletic Association began to keep an official book on track-and-field records, including those set in previous years. Against Lock Haven in 1906 senior Norman Brumbaugh, son of "Jakie," ran the 100-yard dash in ten seconds flat—which was not broken for sixty-six years. The other marks of that time, not nearly so formidable, were eventually eclipsed.

Baseball is the oldest organized sport at Juniata, three games having been played in 1899 against local sandlotters. The June *Echo* issue that year carried a picture of the team posing on the steps of Students Hall, a big "J" on the shirt worn by each person.

The Hilltop-nine was also the first college team to play out of town— in May 1903. On that occasion the J-men crossed bats with Rockview Academy at Shirleysburg. It was a two-hour trip by train and wagon, and the Hilltoppers, decked out in new uniforms, won 16 to 3. The Rockview Academy catcher had trouble, the *Echo* explained, holding his pitcher's tosses. In 1904 there was a seven-game schedule involving three different opponents on a home-to-home basis: Rockview, Susquehanna, and Bellefonte Academy.

The 1905 season was a disaster. The winless season (with scores as bad as 18 to 2) provoked a front-page *Echo* editorial suggesting that more practice might work wonders. Taking the cue, the trustees saw to it that the batters got a preseason jump thereafter. They okayed the purchase of an eighty-foot net batting cage that could be used in the gym until spring practice moved out to the diamond.

Basketball, invented by Dr. James Naismith in 1891, was just a rising new team sport in the early 1900s. At Juniata the earliest roundball games — beginning in 1904 — were against area high schools on a home-to-home basis. Two first-stringers that initial season were Caribbeans: a Cuban, and a Puerto Rican. Urging the team on at home contests was the "Rooting Club." Their favorite yell was the "rocket cheer — with all the sound effects: s-s-s-s-ses and booms."

Baseball Team, 1899. Pictured on steps of Students Hall. Harry Sieber, catcher in lower right-hand corner, claimed he started sport at Juniata.

Juniata moved up to the college ranks in the 1906 season and was mauled. The *Echo* lamented in February:

> What is the trouble with basketball this year? There seems to be some missing links in the chain. If we are to have basketball, let us enter into it heartily, let us put up the best team that is possible. . . .It is no disgrace to lose sometimes, but certainly some games should be won.

Perhaps one problem was the gym's chilled interior. It went unheated until 1910, when it got a furnace of its own. (It was connected to the central heating plant in 1915.)

Basketball disrupted evening quietude and this gave the trustees some concern. At their January 27, 1908 board meeting they decided that the postgame meal for players should be "a lunch only, instead of a feast." The team was to eat as soon as possible after games so that dorms could get "quieted down" all the earlier.

In those early days "moral victories" were the usual fate of JC hoopsters. Not til World War I years did college quintets begin to enjoy an occasional winning season.

Tennis, a British petticoat import in 1874, was pretty much a pattycake affair seventy years ago compared to the vigor of play today. But it was the rage of the campus among both sexes, the ladies demurely returning service in toe-length skirts. In 1902 tennis courts had to be reserved a week in advance. Two years later students were up and swinging rackets at five in the morning if they hoped to squeeze in a few sets. And in 1908 the Tennis Association of Juniata College, with its 135 dues-paying members, imposed a one-hour limitation on court use per couple or foursome.

In 1896 the college put in its first court, a dirt one, on the part of the campus where Stone Church now stands, then a corner lot. Two more courts were built the next year on the upper campus, behind where the gym would go. And in 1903 another pair popped up at the foot of Round Top. Norman Brumbaugh's private court, just next door, got plenty of college use, too, as did the one near William Beery's place in the 1700 block of Moore Street.

Never, though, did students dare a mixed match; tennis then was a sex-segregated sport on the Hill.

College-level tennis competition at Juniata began in 1907 but only casually—a couple of matches with Lock Haven. The JC netmen that year included two profs, which understandably made Lock Haven unhappy.

But the baseball team had filched their best players and this left the tennis squad short-handed. The sport got into full swing in 1910 with a five-match schedule, including three across-state schools: Swarthmore, Lafayette, and Lehigh. All three schools were played on their courts.

The first athletic letters were awarded by the JAA at a special chapel exercise on March 25, 1908. They were given in baseball, basketball, and track. Eight-inch block "Js" went to five college men: Joel Flora, John Gaunt, Brown Miller, John Landis, and Joseph Carroll. Five Academy athletes who made varsity teams each received a smaller "JC" monogram.

Already on the American intercollegiate scene unwholesome influences were at work. And the *Echo* in 1905, referring to a June article in *McClure's Magazine* on "The College Athlete," blistered the "win-at-any-cost" philosophy of college coaches and the recruiting pressure this created. In 1908 Yale helped set the pace in commercializing sports by putting up its thirty-thousand-seat football bowl. Said the *Echo* commonsensically of Juniata, "Let us keep college athletics on a high level."

INTERCOLLEGIATE DEBATE AND PUBLIC SPEECH

Intersociety debate had long been an integral part of campus intellectual life. For a number of years the keen but polite rivalry of the Oriental and Wahneeta Literary Societies involved both college and Academy students. But the faculty came to feel that it would be better to have one society exclusively for collegians. And so the Juniata Lyceum was begot in September 1899.[13]

Thanks to the Lyceum, intercollegiate debate got the green light in 1902. At once it took the campus by storm. At the invitation of Susquehanna University the two schools tangled in the Selingsgrove Opera House on April 25. The subject debated was: "Resolved, That the United States should hold permanent control of the Philippines." The JC debaters — Joseph Johnson of Uniontown, Joseph Yoder of Belleville, and alternate Jacob Blough of Johnstown — took the negative side and won handily.

Susquehanna lost out two more times to Juniata in that period. After one triumphant return from Selingsgrove — in 1904 — the debaters were met at the train station by Charles Vuille, the local auto dealer, and a gang of students. He brought the victors up to campus in his "Tried and True" Cadillac (there were five motorcars in Huntingdon then), with horn honking all the way. Juniata colors were draped all over the automobile, which was trailed by the entourage of "rooters," singing college songs and giving college yells. A bonfire, the usual victory salute to JC disputants, soon blazed high on the athletic field.

In nine years Juniata won eleven consecutive debates before suffering its first loss, a close decision (2-1) in 1912, to the University of Pennsylvania.[14] Besides Susquehanna, other defeated colleges included Penn State, Bridgewater, Waynesburg, Swarthmore, and Westminster. All intercollegiate debates at that time were arranged by the Lyceum. Among the early debaters were Harry Wagner, Daniel Kurtz, Arthur Culler, Edmund Lashley, Will Judy, Brown Miller, Quincy Holsopple, Leonard Gaunt, Jacob Blough, Cletus Fisher, Edgar Detwiler, and Harry Roher.

Ever since 1877, when Phoebe Weakley came to teach Elocution, public speech had been an academic requirement. And orations, moreso than debate, had been the very lifeblood of all the literary societies. With the early 1900s oratorical contests became major events, attracting a large share of out-of-class time and interest.

Debate victors over State College, 1910.

Their popularity was fostered by cash prize awards. For its members the campus Intercollegiate Prohibition Association began to hold annual oratorical contests soon after its founding in 1904. The winner got twenty-five dollars and represented Juniata at a state talkfest hosted by "drys." Eugene Carney '00, a North Dakota district judge, put up prize money for a contest each year between 1909 and 1924. Competition was open to all students on the Hill. Only collegians, however, qualified for the John M. Bailey prize, established by his wife and son in 1909 as a memorial to the distinguished jurist. (Still on the books, it has not been awarded in a long time.)

MUSIC AND PERFORMING GROUPS

Extracurricular music, vocal and instrumental, began to sound forth on the Hilltop with unprecedented vigor as the "Gay Nineties" passed into history. The two literary societies — Oriental and Wahneeta — each had choristers, and singing was a regular feature of their weekly programs. Ordinarily there were special numbers, from solos to choruses. And William Beery for several years had readied a choir at commencement time, recruiting Oriental and Wahneeta singers, many of whom took voice lessons from him.

But, apparently, the first major noncommencement choral performance took place at Christmastime 1897. A Beery-directed choir gave the cantata *King of Kings* to a "delighted audience" in the packed chapel. From then on it became the practice for college choirs to present several musicals each year. The Beery songsters had grown to fifty voices by April 30, 1903, when they sang Mendelssohn's oratorio *Hymn of Praise*. In 1908 the choir was going under the name Juniata Choral Society.

With the arrival of Latinist Dr. George Lyon in 1896 college songs began to fill the campus air. This amiable scholar, with a University of Cincinnati M.D., set everybody to singing in his brief three-year stay. He composed many "local hits" himself, making good use of the college quartet whose existence he inspired in 1898. His minstrel four were: Bruce Book, Edgar Ninninger, Horace Wells, and Lloyd Hartman.

In the spring of 1900 the quartet became the nucleus of a men's glee club. That summer the fellows published a booklet, *Campus Songs of Juniata*, dedicated to "Those who never sing, but die with all their music in them."[15] Most songs were Lyon compositions, some a mite maudlin by today's lyrical tastes. There was no music printed with the words, the songs set to familiar tunes. *Hail to Juniata!*, the original alma mater — written by Lyon probably in 1898 — rated page one. There appeared old favorites like, *Bring Back My Bonnie, Old Black Joe, The Watch on the Rhine*, and *Rig-A-Jig*. Curiously the booklet, which sold for fifteen-cents a copy, included the drinking song *There Is a Tavern in the Town*. In 1904 the songbook was revised and enlarged, regarded by everybody as an indispensable article at any social occasion.

The Juniata Glee Club, twenty-four harmonizers strong by 1904, soon took to the road as ambassadors of the college. But this mission hit a sour note in 1908 when the trustees and the singers fell out over the "dress suit" question. Apparently reacting to outside criticism the trustees that spring forbade the group from wearing "dress suits (tuxedos) where this will be objectionable to our church people." Fred Good and Seymour Ruthrouff, representing the club, went to see some of the trustees. They protested, arguing that formal clothes added "class" to their concerts, but the trustees stood their ground. "Tuxes," so it was, had to wait til a later day.

Instrumental music also enjoyed some gains in that age. Piano students shared firsts with the choir on the evening of the *King of Kings* in 1897. Several keyboard solos had preceded the cantata; never before had student pianists performed publicly.

The first piano recital as such, however, was given in June 1898 by seniors who had studied under Miss Nellie McVey. Graduation recitals now became a tradition, enhanced in May 1905 by the purchase of a Steinway Grand piano (for thirteen-hundred dollars). All-faculty concerts, however, were still a thing of the future.

A small orchestra formed in the fall of 1902 under Miss Rose Clark, who succeeded Miss McVey as the music department's instrumentalist. She was followed by Mabel Snavely, daughter of the Business School principal, who carried on the work with stringed groups. The first time an orchestra (nine pieces) gave a public performance was in the fall of 1904. Next year a five-member group, calling itself the Juniata Concert Company, scheduled a couple of out-of-town engagements—at Defiance and Saxton. A full-fledged college orchestra, however, did not materialize until 1913.

Beginning in 1902 outside musical groups—like the Boston Concert Company—regularly added professional entertainment to the public events calendar.

EARLIEST FOREIGN STUDENTS

Juniata's first overseas student was Richard Arno Dassdorf, an army deserter from Saxony, Germany. Between 1897 and 1900 he earned a Bible

School diploma. Dassdorf, then in his mid-twenties and disowned by his family, had lived with Abraham Cassel for a time after fleeing to America. A Lutheran, he joined the Church of the Brethren his first year on the Hill. He later told about his conversion in a published pamphlet titled *How I Found the Church of the Brethren at Juniata College.*[16] The "Flying Dutchman"—a nickname he good-naturedly accepted—paid his way at Juniata by doing odd jobs and teaching German. He also borrowed money from Cassel and Mary Geiger. In 1918 Dassdorf, a husband and father, died in a tragic elevator accident in the Pittsburgh office building where he worked as a custodian.

From Puerto Rico came two students in 1900, sent at government expense by President M. G. Brumbaugh, in his first year there as United States Commissioner of Education. In all, Juniata hosted ten islanders before they stopped coming in 1911. The most enrolled in any one year was eight—in 1902, when the Caribs organized a Puerto Rican Club. Two died while away from home, one of whom, James Laza, was buried in Huntingdon. Most took business courses or enrolled in the Academy; only one graduated with a B.A. degree. That was Juan Miranda in 1908, who then studied law at the University of Pennsylvania and became a successful Philadelphia attorney.

Two other nationalities were represented in the early 1900s. From Cuba came six students and from Guatemala, three.

A THRIVING ECHO AND OTHER PUBLICATIONS

In January 1896 the Juniata *Echo*, still a pacemaker among campus papers in the state, became a monthly (except August and September), was enlarged to sixteen pages and repriced at five cents a copy. Dr. A. B. Brumbaugh, ailing and seventy-one, stepped down—after seventeen years—as editor-in-chief in October 1907. For the next half-dozen years or so the faculty manned the editorial post. Carman Johnson, a historian who had worked on the paper as a student, took Dr. Brumbaugh's place until he left in 1910. Then Frank Holsopple, an English instructor, took over for two years. After that editorial duties passed wholly into student hands.

There would be no pictorial yearbook until the *Alfarata*'s debut in 1915, but an annual souvenir was not entirely unknown on the Hill. Three senior classes in the late Nineties put out little hardback books with inspirational titles: *Leaves of Industry* (1897); *Blossoms of Life* (1898); *Fruits of Virtue* (1899). Each of these, however, was largely made up of class-day orations by Normal students, B.A.ers just then coming on the scene (four in the three years). The "classbooks" for 1898 and 1899 contained a group picture of all seniors (Normal and college) and a shot of the campus. The one for 1897 was illustrated with charming miniature woodcuts, probably the handiwork of David Emmert. No explanation was ever given why other classes failed to follow suit, but cost certainly had a lot to do with it.

In January 1904 the trustees inaugurated the *Juniata College Bulletin*, a quarterly publication. Explained the October 1905 issue: "The bulletin was begun as a definite and dignified means by which to present information about the college and its work to the public, and it is the purpose to make the different members expressive of the varied interests and activities of the institution." This new periodical gave the annual reports of the president and treasurer and carried faculty-authored articles on all sorts of academic topics. One of its quarterly issues was made the college catalog. Decades later the *Bulletin* would be taken over by the alumni office and made its official newsletter.

ALUMNI AND EARLY REUNIONS

An item under "Notes and Personals" in the *Echo* for July 1897 disclosed: "For several years the Ohio students of Juniata have been in the custom of holding a meeting to pledge anew their loyalty to their college and to strengthen the old ties of friendship with one another." Thus the first off-campus alumni reunion was held in the Buckeye State — in 1894. But these gatherings of the Ohio "tribe" got no *Echo* notice until 1896. That year, of the sixty in attendance, it was reported, twenty-one were alumni. The reunionists assembled in a grove on the Mikesell farm, a half-mile north of Covington, on Saturday afternoon, August 22. A picnic dinner and a formal program highlighted the day. Two of the speakers were Juniata professors — Charles Ellis and Samuel Heckman.

Other alumni-studded areas soon followed with their own summer rendezvous. In 1899 Annie Brumbaugh, M. G.'s wife, planned to open their Philadelphia home for a day to Juniata friends. But she soon found that there was not enough room to accommodate the guest list and so she got the bright idea of entertaining them at the Belmont Mansion, in Fairmount Park. The sixty-four who showed up on the afternoon of June 22 were treated to a meal of croquettes, deviled crabs, soft shelled crabs, lobster salad, potato salad, chicken salad, and other tasty fare. This epicurean repast was topped off with a fun-filled program, after which the Philadelphia Alumni Association organized, to be headed by M. G. The Philadelphians met again in 1900, but there was a lapse of two years while M. G. was in Puerto Rico.

The *Echo* recorded other summer reunions in 1899 and the creation of alumni branches. There was one in Juniata County, and about eighty persons from Bedford and Huntingdon counties convened at Bedford Springs (called "the Carlsbad of America" by the *Echo*) on July 29. One week later Juniatians of Mifflin County were reminiscing in Granville.

Later in the summer Bessie Rohrer and May Oller hosted a cluster of alumni at Waynesboro. George Cashman, who had been a student in 1879, was there and told of the early history of the school. He said that he had a cane that belonged to Jacob Zuck when he was principal (it is now in the college museum, a gift from Cashman). From this impromptu fellowship sprang the Pen Mar reunions, which by 1904 were attracting over three-hundred alumni and friends from Southern Pennsylvania and Maryland. The park by that name near Waynesboro was their favorite gathering place as long as outdoor reunions lasted.

The early 1900s spawned several more alumni clans. One was formed in Somerset County in 1903, meeting at Meyersdale. Cambria County was added to the list in 1905. Lakemont Park, in Altoona, became the retreat of Blair County alumni in 1906. Meanwhile, Juniatians attending the Brethren yearly meeting took to socializing on one of the days as early as 1902.

At all of the reunions, of course, someone from the college staff was there to bring greetings. These gatherings were quite independent of the annual alumni meetings held at commencement time. David Emmert at the time was trying to promote area reunions through what he unimaginatively called the "Old Students Association." But the name never caught on and later, during the war, some of the reunions died out.

John Wertz, a Johnstown schoolteacher, was sire of a remarkable alumni family of that period. He sent nine of his children—four daughters and five sons—to Juniata, and the name Wertz was for years familiar in the dorms. The father and his wife were themselves perennial attenders at Bible sessions—making eleven Wertz-family alumni in all. The head of the household must have been a wizard at managing money on a teacher's income because never once did he ask for cut rates. No doubt, though, his offspring held campus jobs.

So did other Juniatians. And some had to rely on the Alumni Endowment Fund. About five students each year were on alumni scholarships. A little over one-hundred loans had been made since 1889, but the acting president's report for 1910 noted that thirty-eight were still outstanding, many long overdue. The Sisters' Missionary Circle of the

Brethren congregation set up the Women's Aid Fund for needy coeds around 1902, its assets amounting to more than two-thousand dollars by 1910.

In 1902 a constitutional revision admitted Academy graduates into full Alumni Association membership. But Harvey Brumbaugh's proposal in 1908 for a permanent resident alumni secretary would go unheeded for another dozen years.

During the M. G.-I. Harvey era, Robert Zentmyer '82 was four times the association's prexy (with another term yet to come). Zentmyer was a civil engineer by profession and then one of Tyrone's leading citizens. No one at Juniata has ever come close to equaling the amount of presidential time he gave to alumni affairs.

PRESIDENT M. G. BOWS OUT

Artic weather settled like a great frozen shroud over Huntingdon the early months of 1910. William Swigart said that he could not remember a winter like it. Ice was six inches thick on some streets. The cold hindered last-minute work on J. C. Blair Memorial Hospital, scheduled for a Memorial Day dedication. In April Harvey Brumbaugh took abed with a severe case of pneumonia. And before the summer was gone his father, as trustee kingpin, would get more bad news.

Under Harvey and his cousin M. G. the college had indeed come of age in the last seventeen years. Accredited in liberal arts, it had survived two hard depressions and grown to nearly 350 students (spring term). Its costs were but a fraction (less than a quarter) of those at Ivy League schools. Running the place had become far more complex, and in the fall of 1906 the acting president was given a private office, just inside Founders entrance. There, behind a big roll-top desk in one corner, he looked after college business.

A strong Brethren constituency continued to give Juniata its identity. The local elders appeared annually on inspection visits until 1908. Then Annual Conference created a central Educational Board to care for the religious atmosphere of the existing ten Brethren colleges. Now the examining committee came out of this national board, and one area of campus life it scrutinized carefully was intercollegiate sports. Outsiders, it was feared, might infect the moral health of Juniata athletes.

Yet under the Brumbaugh cousins the college was no less mindful of other constituencies. The Juniata Valley, once vowed the acting president in 1905, would never be ignored as a prime recruiting area.[17]

For many of its youth, he pointed out, the Huntingdon institution represented their only chance for a better education.

But as the new century wore on faculty morale took a nose dive. President M. G. found more and more bad-humored letters in his mail, griping mostly about low salaries. In one letter to Harvey on the pay problem, he wrote:

> But I wish you would lay before them the spirit of this letter, if not its words, saying that it seems to me that if they have the same devotion to the Church and to the work of the College for the Church as their predecessors have had, they will be ready to write the word "sacrifice" deep in their lives, for the sake of the cause that is eminently just. And if they protest against this advice on the ground that it comes from one who himself was not willing to make the sacrifice, let them remember that I made the sacrifice for ten years, and that ever since I have been away I have sent back into the treasury of the College more money than I could possibly have earned had I remained in the Faculty.[18]

He ended by saying, not unkindly but sincerely: "There is the further fact that a man may be very successful in Juniata College who might not be equally successful somewhere else."

Meanwhile, M. G. had been given his pick of several college presidencies. This bit of information he left to posterity in a confidential memorandum among his private papers, dated February 28, 1910. The memorandum said nothing, however, about his refusal to be a candidate for chancellor of the University of Nebraska, despite strong pressure from influential friends. He spurned that invitation, so the *Echo* said, because he was "wedded to Pennsylvania."

Between 1907 and 1909, according to M. G.'s memo, three schools went after him, all of which he turned down. One was Girard College in Philadelphia, whose overseers blinked the fact he was an active churchman and a preacher (Girard's charter banned clergymen from office-holding). But, confessed M. G., "the 'pent-up' character of the place depressed me." In 1907 Penn State put in its bid with no better luck. His friend, the historian Edwin Sparks, got the job. Franklin and Marshall wanted him in 1909, but, wrote M. G.: "I declined in loyalty to Juniata and in justice to my family. My present work, though more arduous, is more remunerative. I can give more to Juniata."

By 1910 M. G. was beginning to pay the penalty for years of overwork. He was worn down, and before the year was out he would have to take a leave from his Philadelphia post to rejuvenate. That spring, therefore, he decided to unburden himself of his alma mater's presidency which, though nominal, was not without its demands on his time and energy. Moreover, with all the talk about a new science building and an endowment push, he was afraid the pressure on him to get more involved would only mount. Quietly he let Harvey know of his intentions and that this time he would not back down — no matter what!

Together — in July — the two of them submitted letters of resignation. The trustees, knowing what M. G.'s name meant to college prestige, tried to head him off again by reshaping the administration. In August they voted him the title of chancellor, while naming Harvey president. But both men turned thumbs down on such an arrangement. Harvey was then asked — and agreed — to continue as acting president for the time being.

Toward A Greater Juniata
1910-1924

HARVEY BRUMBAUGH: DE JURE PRESIDENT
Harvey Brumbaugh had put up with a lot in his eleven years as acting
president, running the college in M. G.'s shadow. But he was far from
egoless. In October he let the trustees know that they had better resolve
the presidency in double-quick time or he was through. And so on March 6,
1911 forty-one-year-old Harvey was elected Juniata's fourth president,
Curiously, not a hint of this election leaked out until William Swigart made
it known at the first chapel service in September. In fact, M. G.'s
resignation itself had been kept an absolute secret for a whole year.
Hence, Swigart's chapel announcement caught everybody off guard.

To the students he would always be "Professor Harvey," for he had
been a popular teacher. On the basis of his stint as acting president, the
faculty viewed him as "naturally conservative" but a man of "genial
affability," "approachable."[1] The news of his election drew "hearty
applause" from the chapel audience.

CHARLES ELLIS MADE VICE-PRESIDENT
Back in 1890 the *Echo* said of a sixteen-year-old Normal grad from
Baltimore: "Mr. Ellis is not very large in stature, but he makes up for this
in intellectual ability." Juniata's second B. A. winner in 1898, Ellis was
cast much in the mold of M. G. Brumbaugh. An Illinois Wesleyan Ph.D.
(1904) and another one from Penn (1907) had put him in select
Brethren company. Like M. G. he took to the lecture platform, billed
as the "Boy Orator." At first he made pedagogy his academic specialty,
but with time developed a strong interest in religion as a disciplinary
field.

Having taught at Juniata a few years before, Dr. Ellis came back in 1907, at age thirty-three, with no intention of staying. Soon other schools began to seek him out with attractive offers. Penn State, for one, came after him in 1917 with a twenty-five hundred dollar contract, almost twice his salary at Juniata.[2] It was this across-the-mountain overture that prompted the trustees that June to make Dr. Ellis vice-president. With the promotion went a raise — all of one-hundred dollars, but his income still fell short of fifteen-hundred. For all practical purposes, however, Ellis's title was only honorific. Keeping an eye on Academyites was his main administrative duty.

Outsiders continued to look upon the vice-president as fair game over the next few years. Moody Bible Institute gave him a hard chase in 1919. The trustees wrote the Chicago school asking it politely, but pointedly, to stay away from Dr. Ellis since Juniata "could not afford" to let him go. Then in 1921 the trustees learned that more than one college was after him for their top position. The board promptly passed a resolution begging him to stay — which he did, having by then come to terms with his life at Juniata.

PLANS FOR A "GREATER JUNIATA"

As president, Harvey Brumbaugh liked to say that he was running "A right little, tight little college."[3] By "right" he meant Christian, by "tight" he meant friendly, close. He gave fuller expression to this image of Juniata in a 1913 chapel talk:

> The small college with high ideals of training and character, but with moderate ambition in material equipment, led by scholarly and consecrated teachers, maintaining simple standards of living — the small college, with all the affection which the term implies because of the intimate association of its daily life, has yet a mission to the church and a message for the present-day world.[4]

In many respects a "moderate ambition" nicely characterized Harvey Brumbaugh's thirteen-year presidency. But it did produce the first major concerted endowment fund campaign. Ever since 1903 there had been a long-range two-hundred thousand dollar endownment plan on the books — to strengthen certain departments, put up new buildings, buy additional land, pad faculty salaries. The Mary Geiger endowed chair was part of this low-key effort, as was a ten-thousand dollar gift in 1912 from the Jacob Oller family of Waynesboro, honoring their deceased parents. But the trustees had gone about this plan in piecemeal fashion, first Carnegie

Library and then, beginning in 1910, Allan Myers's canvass for a science building. It was one of Juniata's most liberal benefactors, the genial business executive, Joseph Oller, who prodded the trustees into an all-out endowment thrust.

At a board conclave in January 1916 Oller proposed an immediate one-hundred thousand dollar drive and the formation of a special group, wider than the board, to carry it out. His suggestion won quick acceptance. A few days later President Brumbaugh "tore aside the veil that shrouds the future of Juniata" in a chapel talk, whipping up enthusiasm for the endowment goal. The *Echo* jumped on the bandwagon and in April put out a "Boost Juniata Number." It was this issue that coined the slogan for the campaign: "A Greater Juniata."

Echo student-editor John Baker (one day to become #1 trustee) asked representative Juniatians—a trustee (M. G.), a professor (Charles Ellis), two alumni (Carman Johnson '01 and Roland Howe '94), and a student (Ethel Trostle)—to submit articles forecasting "What kind of a greater Juniata" they saw in the distance. They were to look ahead forty years, to 1956, and dream. Most shared Dr. Ellis's vision to a certain extent:

> So if I might be permitted the magic wand for a day I would hasten to crown Round Top with an artistic and well-arranged group of college buildings sufficient to care for three hundred students and twenty-five professors and assistants. The value of this plant would be at least five hundred thousand dollars backed by an endowment of twice as much. Supplementing this of course would be the present plant caring for two hundred preparatory students.

Carman Johnson's musing, though, focused on the "genius" of a liberal arts college, zeroing in on an issue that still keeps educators at odds. The Pittsburgh social science teacher wrote:

> . . .we realize that this age is demanding the "scientific," the "engineering," the "vocational," the "practical," in short the materialistic result from the educator; but it becomes the duty of some of us, it becomes the God-given burden of some choice small colleges in America to stand true to the wholesome traditions of the "humanities."

He was not denying the need for "technical" and "applied" education in the modern world, he said. But neither was he admitting that "there is nothing practical, useful, or applicable in the liberal or classical cultural courses." Juniata's "valuable" contribution to society, Johnson contended, should continue to be that of sending out "a class of men and women who because of their rich training can hold key positions as teachers, preachers, missionaries, social workers, principals, superintendents, presidents, commercial masters, secretaries, reformers, and the like."

Out of the interest thus engendered came the group Oller had in mind: the Juniata College Extension Association for a Greater Juniata, formed on March 21, 1918. The organizational meeting was held in the Executive Mansion in Harrisburg, hosted by M. G., then the governor. The constitution and bylaws of the association were adopted and an Executive Committee of twelve members was elected from the college's constituency at large. Governor Brumbaugh was named president of the association and Joseph Oller its vice-president. Harry Cassady, then the college pastor, became the campaign director. His coworker was Galen Royer, who had just left the General Mission Board in Elgin, Illinois, to teach in the School of Theology.

At Harvey Brumbaugh's prompting the association called its proposed one-hundred thousand dollar fund the James Quinter Memorial Endowment, in honor of the college's first president. Its main campaign booklet was unapologetically pitched at a Brethren public. In fact, all the denomination's colleges were similarly engaged at the time in promotional work as part of a general Brotherhood program called "Church of the Brethren Forward Movement." The booklet presented a list of twelve "FACTS," showing what the college had done for the church. The first eight gave a particularly impressive picture of Juniata's vital contributions to Brethren life and work:

FACT (a)

Of the missionaries who have been and are on the foreign field, Juniata has furnished 22.

FACT (b)

The presidents of six of our 10 colleges of the Church of the Brethren are Juniata Graduates.

FACT (c)

In the Middle, Western, and Southeastern Districts of Pennsylvania there are 36 fully supported pastors who are giving their entire time to the church; of these 28 are from Juniata.

FACT (d)

Of the 1,160 graduates from Juniata, 135 are ministers and missionaries of our church.

FACT (e)

Ninety-five young men have received the A.B. degree from the College. Of these, 44 are ministers in the church.

FACT (f)

Eighty-five per cent of our College graduates are members of the Church of the Brethren.

FACT (g)

Over 1,500 people have been received into the Church of the Brethren in the College Church.

FACT (h)

More than 50 young men have been elected to the ministry in the College Church.

Despite the war and then the flu epidemic, progress toward the one-hundred thousand dollar goal was so encouraging that in April 1919 the trustees raised their sights to two-hundred thousand dollars. The one-hundred thousand dollar mark was passed in 1920, and in April of the following year the second phase got rolling.

The purpose of the 1921 campaign, it had now developed, was to meet the endowment requirements of the Middle States Association, whose accreditation the college was seeking. A representative of Middle States and one from the Carnegie Foundation visited the campus in February, and though finding things better than expected they had serious questions about the adequacy of the less than four-hundred thousand dollar endowment. The association's minimum for accreditation was set at five-hundred thousand dollars.

Cassady and Royer were no longer available for phase two, and so the trustees engaged a professional fund-raising organization, the Hockenbury Co. of Harrisburg, to direct the drive. The campaign was to be confined almost wholly to the Juniata Valley.

It kicked off in Huntingdon during the week of May 31 to June 7. The local chairman was Chester Langdon, a graduate of Lehigh University and prosperous coal mine operator. "Chet," soon everywhere to be known as "Mr. Rotarian," now began his long friendship with Juniata. More than 170 workers, many of them women, took part in the seven-day canvass. Once again the people of Huntingdon proved "true and generous," as the *Echo* put it, and by week's end over sixty-five thousand dollars had been subscribed.[5]

The appeal was then extended up and down the Valley with equally good success, although it took more time. A chart hanging in the chapel plotted the progress. By the end of the fiscal year 1923 President Brumbaugh could report going "over the top" in the "Greater Juniata" crusade. This put all endowment funds at more than $507,000.

Some of the trustees had responded very generously. Joseph Oller, contributor to the gym, to Stone Church, and to campus expansion, turned over a batch of securities valued at better than twenty-four thousand dollars. The governor himself came through with a bundle of bonds worth ten thousand dollars. From John Fogelsanger, a non-Juniata businessman from Philadelphia, the College got five thousand dollars for scholarship aid.

One other substantial contribution came in during the campaign, unsolicited. This was a five thousand dollar unrestricted bequest in 1919 from the estate of Elmer Africa, president of J. C. Blair Co. when he died. Though Africa had been a Juniata patron, no one at the college knew beforehand of such a provision in his will.

BOARD OF TRUSTEES: CHANGING PERSONNEL AND CHARTER REVISION

Some familiar faces disappeared from the trustee scene over the course of Harvey Brumbaugh's presidency. H. B. Brumbaugh, the board's only chairman for forty years, died on June 28, 1919, just past his eighty-third birthday. The death of his seventy-four-year-old brother, John, on June 11, 1922 marked the passing of the last of the founders. David Emmert had already taken his earthly leave in 1911. And another old faculty-trustee, Joseph Saylor, became a retiree in 1913. Only William Swigart and Jacob Brumbaugh were left from the early days. Mary Geiger's death occurred in September 1919, ending her twenty-two-year tenure on the Board. Elder Jacob Myers of Oaks, Pennsylvania, died in 1915, having served twenty-five years as trustee.

After three decades of almost no change in board officers there now was a period of rapid shift. Jacob Brumbaugh had become vice-president upon Dr. A. B.'s death in 1908. Then with Henry's passing, M. G. served as trustee head for the duration of Harvey Brumbaugh's administration. When Joseph Saylor retired from the faculty and left the area in 1911,

Allan Myers, Juniata's natural science instructor, joined the board as secretary in his place.

In October 1920 William Swigart, who had not taught in the last year, resigned as college treasurer, then a trustee post. The highest salary the veteran of forty-two years had ever received as teacher-treasurer was eight-hundred dollars. His long letter of resignation included a reccommendation for some sort of pension plan and other fringe benefits for the faculty.[6] He ended with the hope that Juniata might "steadily" continue to provide an "education free from the influence of extravagance and the contaminating evils so dominant in the world." Swigart stayed on as trustee, however, until 1939 when he died at age eighty-eight.

After Swigart the position of treasurer was no longer filled by someone on the board. From 1920 to 1924 it was combined with the office of alumni director. Adie Ressler, who succeeded Swigart, and then Stoler Good held this dual appointment in those years.

In terms of years of service the only trustee old-timers left in 1924 were Jennie Newcomer and Joseph Oller, whose appointments dated back to the century's turn. But some of the new blood showed remarkable staying power, too. Newton Long of Hagerstown, Maryland, served forty-eight years (1923-71) and Altoona's Ardie Wilt, two less (1913-59). Bessie Rohrer, a Normal alumna from Waynesboro, was a board member for thirty-six years (1922-59). Waynesboro's John Fike, who moved to Somerset, Pennsylvania, became a thirty-four-year veteran (1923-57). John Fogelsanger would be a twenty-two-year member (1914-36), while Allan Myers's trusteeship (1911-30) ended at his death after a nineteen-year hitch.

Most of the others elected at that time put in at least ten years. Those who fell into this category were: Perry Blough of Hooversville, Pennsylvania (1910-20); Henry Gibbel of Lititz, Pennsylvania (1911-27); Frank Foster of Philadelphia (1917-35); Lewis Knepper of Berlin, Pennsylvania (1919-33); Harvey Replogle of Oaks, Pennsylvania (1920-33); William Gahagen of Windber, Pennsylvania (1922-36).

Rounding out the list of inductees during the Harvey Brumbaugh era were: Harry Sieber of Philadelphia (1919-27); W. Emmert Swigart of Huntingdon (1922-26); Jay Ross of Huntington, West Virginia (1923-30).

Death cut short the tenure of two men elected just prior to Harvey's presidency: William Howe of Johnstown (1908-17) and Huntingdon's David Swayne, a two-termer (1889-98; 1908-11).

Apparently not all of these board newcomers were happy about what had been done to the college charter in 1908. One source of displeasure resulted from the deletion of Brethrenism as a condition for becoming a trustee. Consequently, the board's bylaws were amended in 1918 to reinstate this criterion.[7] Furthermore, it was stipulated that in the event of dissolution the college would convey all its property to the Church of the Brethren.

Through these changes the reactionary element on the board sought to reaffirm Juniata's historic ties with the church. It was also responding to pressure from the denomination's General Education Board. At the time the Board was investigating the charter to determine if it "safe-guarded fully the interests of the church."[8]

The Board got upset when the charter was not made to comply with the bylaws on the transferral of property. This led to a real hassle among the trustees. M. G. opposed inserting such a clause in the charter; he was bucked by William Swigart.[9] The M. G. faction won, but the controversy did lead in 1923 to another reworking of that section of the charter on the college's purpose. The phrasing of President Harvey, it was made to state:

> The founders of the Commonwealth provided for religious freedom and the extension of learning. The fathers in the Church of the Brethren were the first in this Commonwealth to print the word of God and thus lay the foundation for education imbued with Christian purpose. Believing that the principles of Christianity should be and can be taught, that the Christian motive should be the animating force in all teaching, the Trustees of Juniata College associate themselves to perpetuate good and sound learning distinguished by Christian principles that the youth of the Church and the State may be trained for such service as an enlightened mind and a quickened conscience may lead them to render to God and to man.

It has not been tampered with since.

The charter was also altered to increase the number on the board to twenty-one.

THE FACULTY: PASSING OF THE OLD GUARD

Four classroom greybeards laid down the chalk in those years, all teacher-trustees. After a long, painful illness David Emmert — artist, teacher, philanthropist — died in the summer of 1911. When he fell at his post the fifty-seven-year-old father of three sons was still active in child-welfare work. His monument as a humanitarian was the nationally acclaimed "Huntingdon Idea." An orphanage, Emmert always said, must only be a temporary home for a child until placed with a permanent family. He strongly believed in rearing orphans in a normal home environment. He measured his success, observed his *Echo* necrology, "not by the number of children he could gather together into an institution but by the number he could place out in well-selected families."[10]

Joseph Saylor was the next to leave, in 1911, at age fifty-eight. The alumni raised a cash retirement gift for him—for his son's education—and he spent the final eleven years of his life on a farm near Schwenksville, Pennsylvania. William Swigart was the third early-day survivor to hang it up. The last one was Jacob Brumbaugh—in 1923—who had been relegated solely to Academy-level teaching toward the end.

But Juniata did not want for equally dedicated teachers. Still around were Charles Ellis and the two Myerses, Tobias and Oscar. And under Harvey, the president, this nucleus of regulars grew larger. They were joined by Clyde Stayer (thirty-five years) and Charles Shively (twenty-three years) in mathematics, librarian Lillian Evans (thirty-four years), musician Charles Rowland (thirty-one years), and Bunn Van Ormer in philosophy (twenty-four years). Others of lesser years of service who gave stability to the faculty were Alphaeus Dupler (biology), Perry Hoover (classics), Galen Royer (missions), Katharine Roberts (English), and Luella Fogelsanger (business).

Two supposedly established staffers, who expected to be around for a long time, got their walking papers in that period. Rum-foe Frank Holsopple, married to Grace Quinter, daughter of the first president, made the mistake of backing the wrong gubernatorial candidate in 1914. He openly campaigned for M. G.'s Democratic opponent, Vance Mc-Cormick, who was endorsed by the Anti-Saloon League. This was an unforgivable act of institutional disloyalty in the eyes of the trustees and they quietly fired the English teacher of thirteen years. He then worked for the Anti-Saloon League for a couple of years, after which he became president of Blue Ridge College in Maryland.[11]

Amos Haines, Juniata's first full-time teacher in Bible, got cashiered after nineteen years. He was purged in 1916 because his theology had taken a liberal turn. Students were pumped by local trustees about what he was teaching in his Old Testament classes in building their case against him.

By 1924 the combined college-Academy faculty numbered twenty-eight. Six held earned doctorates, and there were eleven women teachers. One of the Ph.D.s was Robert Mehl (1923-25), a chemist who later discovered the gamma ray.

Another of the Ph.D.s was Alphaeus Dupler, whose suicide in 1928 cut short a most promising academic career. This biologist not only brought scholarship to his discipline for the first time at Juniata, but gave vital administrative leadership. An elder and only forty-four at his death, the tall, dark alumnus was asked to set up a registrar's office in 1911. Under him, in those academic deanless days, it became a position second only to the presidency in importance.

Then in 1921 he was put in charge of the summer program that had been dropped in 1914 for lack of support. For in the meantime the Department of Public Instruction had raised its standards for teacher certification, setting 1927 as the deadline for meeting the new requirements. And so in the expectation of a great rush by public school teachers the trustees authorized a revival of summer study. With Dr. Dupler's guidance, the summer session enjoyed the largest enrollment in its history— 1927 being the banner year with 485.

Dedicated though most of the faculty were, they were far from indifferent about their standard of living. Tobias Myers, because of his endowed chair, was the first to break the one-thousand-dollars-a-year salary barrier in 1911, some while before most. A salary schedule, based on academic rank, went into effect in 1920—to which exceptions were made at once. Over the next few years two men in the chemistry department, both transients and with doctorates, were paid above the maximum level for their rank. Somehow the word got out and a quintet of stalwarts—Dupler, Shively, Van Ormer, and the two Myerses—accused the trustees in writing of outright injustice, if not deception.[12] The board severely reprimanded the petitioners for questioning its integrity and refused to listen further.

As yet no pension plan existed, although the trustees did have hopes of participating in a retirement program funded by the Carnegie Foundation. In 1916 a sick-leave policy was adopted. It allowed full salary for the first eight weeks, half salary the second eight weeks, and nothing after that.[13]

The democratic character of the college had always discouraged any distinctions of rank and title. But the catalog in 1920 began to identify faculty by the three grades of professor, assistant professor, and instructor. The salary schedule introduced that year was correlated with these three ranks. But old-timers still successfully fought off the use of academic regalia on high occasions as calling too much attention to differences of station.

In those days the faculty—as it would to 1938—chambered weekly. Its first set of extant minutes are dated September 23, 1915. The academic progress of problem students occupied most of the faculty time, a reading of early minutes reveals. Disciplinary action—for social infractions as well as low grades — was ordinarily a matter of corporate decision. A structure of standing committees, however, did exist to carry out faculty-set policies.

There were signs, meanwhile, that the technological age had reached the Hill. Staid Jacob Brumbaugh was the first to turn his back on horse-and-buggy travel. The spring of 1912 he put "Doc" out to pasture and could now be seen "going to and fro in his Buick."[14] Two years later Oscar Myers was sporting a horseless carriage (make unknown) of his own. And Ben Wampler, the music prof, was hammering away on a garage, also bitten by the "auto bug."

JUNIATA MAKES THE GRADE:
MIDDLE STATES ACCREDITATION

Harvey Brumbaugh was elected secretary of the College Presidents Association of Pennsylvania in 1918. As a member of the Executive Committee, he was well-informed about new standards being set by emerging regional accreditation agencies. Though of late nineteenth-century origin, these agencies only began to exert their influence after World War I. Thus by the time the Middle States Association of Colleges and Secondary Schools (it was formed in 1885) initiated evaluation visits within its region, the "Greater Juniata" campaign was in high gear.

Juniata's visit, we saw earlier, came in February 1921. The evaluators had some strong reservations, particularly about the endowment. They left without giving any guarantees. Middle States' first approved list came out the following November, but Juniata did not make it. The association also issued a supplementary register called the "gray list" — colleges that did not fully meet accepted standards but were making good progress toward accreditation. Juniata was on this one.

To keep the pressure on, college authorities warned that Juniata was "at the crossroads of her history." And President Brumbaugh impressed upon the trustees in February 1922 that "Juniata College cannot go independent of standards set by outside organizations if its graduates are to be accepted in professional fields."[15] The conditions for accreditation, advised Middle States, were fourfold: (1) physical separation of the Academy and college; (2) endowment of at least five-hundred thousand dollars producing an income from twenty-thousand dollars to twenty-five-thousand dollars; (3) higher salaries; (4) better-degreed faculty.

Steps had already been taken to meet the last three of these criteria. And at a trustee sitting in April a deadline was set for complying with the first one — within two years. Administratively even this move had been anticipated a year and a half earlier. In October 1920 Clyde Stayer assumed charge of the Academy as principal. The two faculties still overlapped, though each met separately for its own business, joining in a once-a-month congress.

In late May 1922 President Brumbaugh, armed with the April trustee action and an up-to-date "Greater Juniata" report, ran down the appropriate Middle States commission in New York.[16] Impressed with this latest evidence, the commission now took the college off the "gray list." "Juniata Ranks As First Class College" shouted the highly colored caption for the *Echo* article telling of the coveted promotion.

As a "first-class college," Juniata automatically qualified for recognition by the the American Medical Association. The official word from the AMA came sometime in 1923. Alumnus Dr. Irvin Metzger '94, president of the Pennsylvania Bureau of Education and Licensure, wrote a congratulatory public letter, printed in the *Echo*. He closed by saying: "The Juniata spirit, enforced by an adequate medical education, should make an ideal doctor. I should like to welcome more from my beloved Alma Mater."[17]

REORGANIZING THE CURRICULUM AND NEW PROGRAMS

A major regrouping and consolidation of academic divisions took place in 1918. They were reduced to four: College of Arts and Sciences; School of Theology; School of Music; Academy.

COLLEGE OF ARTS AND SCIENCES

Still basic to the college was the B.A. degree, although this would gradually change after the B.S. degree reemerged in 1920. To keep up with the times the humanities added Spanish to the new department of foreign languages in 1916. Explained the *Echo*, this was done "in accordance with the trend of educational sentiment, which emphasizes subjects of commercial value as well as those of cultural training."

An overall curriculum built upon major-minor fields went into effect in 1922. Under this now-familiar scheme both B.A. and B.S. students had to declare one major (eighteen to thirty hours) and two minors (twelve hours each). In 1924 the catalog listed seventeen major fields: Bible, biology, chemistry, commerce and finance, education, English, French, German, Greek, history, home economics, Latin, mathematics, music, philosophy, physics, social science.

The college began operating in 1916 on the credit-hour system (120 hours total), but not until 1921 did it adopt a two-semester calendar (eighteen weeks to a semester). Upperclassmen of the early Twenties thought they had gotten a raw deal: the minimum passing grade for juniors and seniors was eighty (lowered to seventy-five in 1926). For all students, however, debarment from the final exam in a course was the penalty for excessive cutting (more than one-tenth of the classes).

Meanwhile, the study of science got a boost with the establishment of the A. B. Brumbaugh Science Prize (then ten dollars) in 1916 for "proficiency" in physics, chemistry, or zoology. Then with the inception of a General Science program in 1918, the B.S. degree made a reappearance. Francis Byers of Bellwood, Pennsylvania, was the lone B.S. graduate in 1920. But in another four years there were ten (all males), which represented about a quarter of the class.

Earlier, in 1916, the college inaugurated a two-year premedical program that met standards set by the Pennsylvania Board of Professional Education. But after 1918 the college urged aspiring medics to earn a four-year bachelor's degree. Finally, in 1926 the premed curriculum was phased out and incorporated under general science studies.

One of the rising stars in the firmament of college curricula as the 1900s set in was "domestic science" (the American Home Economics Association organized in 1908). Harvey Brumbaugh felt that such a program could serve Juniata's purposes, telling the trustees so in 1913. But until the projected science hall was more than talk, he advised against full-blown work—just a general summer course, like the one taught by Cora Myers in 1912.

With Science Hall a reality, a home economics department got going in 1915. At first it offered a two-year diploma course, designed to prepare secondary teachers. Sloe-eyed Isabel Cook, Toronto University trained with further study at Wisconsin and Columbia, came to set the department up. Sixteen coeds enrolled the first year, picking up more recruits as time went on.

With the fall of 1920 home economics blossomed into a four-year program leading to a B.S. degree. Its curriculum was now broadened to train graduates for institutional jobs as well as to teach. By 1924 there were nineteen home ec majors.

Another of the period's departmental births was that of commerce and finance. With the divisional regrouping of 1918, the Business School had been absorbed by the Academy. Its offerings were drastically reduced; eliminated were all banking and accounting courses. But in 1923 these reappeared as part of the college curriculum in economics. Herman Hettinger, a Wharton School graduate, played midwife to the department but left the next year. Harold Conner then became the resident economist—

until 1937—outlasting a whole cavalcade of departmental colleagues. But within the first two years twenty-four majors were lured into the field of commerce and finance, seeking the B.S. degree.

Like business, teacher-training had also been demoted in 1918 to Academy-level rank. It still continued, though, as a four-year program. Then in 1923 education became a B.S.-degree option and given full departmental status. Though there were only ten education majors in 1924, this statistic would soon take an upward leap. Practice teaching, first tried out in 1917 with the Academy, now became an annual ritual, administered in cooperation with the public schools.

SCHOOL OF THEOLOGY: SEEDBED OF FUNDAMENTALISM

During the years 1916 and 1917 the Bible School retrenched its B.D. program, but then, with the reorganization of 1918, brought it back. At the same time it took a more pretentious name: The School of Theology. Besides a B.A. Bible major and B.D. work, the school offered a three-year curriculum in Christian Worker's Training for Brethren laypersons that drew quite well. However, its three-year Bachelor of Religious Education program, instituted in 1920, was an absolute bust.

Deaned by T. T. Myers, the School of Theology—whose staff some years numbered as many as nine—emerged in the postwar years as the most articulate forum of fundamentalism among the Brethren. Over the period 1918-31 the men of its faculty showed a zealous interest in preserving the basic doctrines of Christianity that went beyond distinctive Brethren tenets.[18]

The early 1920s marked the heyday of fundamentalistic thought and influence in American Protestantism. Harry Emerson Fosdick's heresy trial brought the issue of orthodoxy to a head and branded him the despised symbol of undisguised modernism. Schisms rocked all but a few denominations. Antievolution laws swept the South, keeping Darwin out of the public schools. The climactic event of the modernist-fundamentalist battle was the sensational Scopes trial of 1925, when William Jennings Bryan and Clarence Darrow locked horns at Dayton, Tennessee. It became one of the most publicized legal cases in modern American history.

A distinction needs to be drawn, however, between fundamentalistic theology, which conservatives of all denominational genera could accept, and the fundamentalistic spirit, which is self-righteous, vituperative, intolerant, ill-mannered. The men at Huntingdon were anything but disaffected Brethren insurgents. They were not the least guilty of rancor and dissidence. Nevertheless, they did take a dogmatic stance, feeling some uneasiness with the church's historic noncreedal position and the silence of its leaders on the scientific and doctrinal issues of the day. The School of Theology was their answer to the alleged liberal learning of rival Bethany Bible School in Chicago.

Of the Juniata theologians, Charles Ellis alone came to enjoy wide recognition in the larger, non-Brethren, fundamentalist camp. And it was he who nudged the college into taking a sympathetic stand. His biblicism had its roots in his two-year residency (1902-04) at Zion City, Illinois, forty-two miles north of Chicago. At that theocratic community, founded in 1901 by John Alexander Dowie from the down-under continent, Ellis was principal of both the preparatory school and the college.

Dowie headed a sect called the Christian Catholic Apostolic Church and regulated Zion City by a series of strict "blue laws" that included the prohibition to eat pork or to use tobacco, liquor, drugs, or medicine. Dowie's writings (banned from the Juniata library by the trustees in 1900) argued that the earth is flat and held to an expectation of the immediate second coming of Jesus Christ. This latter doctrine, known as premillenialism, now began to shape Dr. Ellis's schematized view of the future.

He was not exactly welcomed with open arms when he left Dowie's utopia and returned to Juniata the fall of 1907 — which was one of the reasons he made no long-range plans involving the college. If some trustees had had their way Ellis need not have come back, but M. G. stood up for him and won a reprieve. The passing years vindicated the wisdom of giving C. C. a second chance.

As time went on Dr. Ellis's interest in theology took an academic bent. For a year and two summers (1919-20) he studied at Princeton Seminary and Temple University. From the Philadelphia school he received in 1920 the B.D. degree in religious education. But this sojourn in theological study only confirmed him in his biblicism.

Beginning at this time he became a regular contributor to the *Sunday School Times* and the *Bible Champion*, two influential fundamentalist organs. His book, *The Religion of Religious Psychology*, was published in 1922 by the Sunday School Times Co., located in Philadelphia. It was later revised and reprinted (1928) by the Los Angeles Bible Institute, the West Coast sister of Moody Bible Institute — then the two educational strongholds of fundamentalism. Dr. Ellis taught at Moody in the summer of 1923, and even gave serious thought to locating at the Chicago institution.

Private religion "is the plain biblical truth," insisted Ellis, the premillennialist and social gospel foe, one of whose heroes was the famed American evangelist, Dwight L. Moody. The social gospel theology, which

Moody had deplored, equated the Kingdom of God with the progressive transformation of society. But for Moody—and Juniata's evangelical vice-president—all human history was a struggle between Satan and Christ. In their view of last things social ills will never be cured until Christ comes to judge the world, destroy Satan, and set up his reign. Indeed, Dr. Ellis once felt constrained to say that actually the Bible contradicts the idea of God's fatherhood and man's universal brotherhood, the central belief of social gospelers.[19]

Thus it was Dr. Ellis's firm conviction that Brethren colleges should become citadels of the "Fundamentals." In 1920 he wrote an article for the denomination's *Gospel Messenger* titled "A College Entrance Examination."[20] In it he raised the question: "Does the college with all its individual instructors hold and teach the following:"

1. The unique and infallible inspiration of the Bible. . .
2. The lost condition of all men by nature since the fall of Adam.
3. Redemption for men only through the death of Christ. . ., receiving in himself the penalty of man's sins and the necessary and holy wrath of God against sin.
4. The deity of Christ, different not in degree, but in kind from any so-called "divinity" that man has.
5. The virgin birth of Christ.
6. The resurrection of the body of Christ and of all men.

These points—plus the second coming, curiously omitted in the article—were the *sina quo non* of fundamentalism. Dr. Ellis concluded: "It is not always easy to answer for other individuals, but for the college and those who are its leaders it ought not to be difficult to answer."

For Juniata there was certainly no difficulty; the vice-president saw to that. From the time the School of Theology got its name, its watchword was "Loyalty to the Word." And in the section of the catalog that listed the religion courses there appeared a ten-point doctrinal preamble that touched every orthodox base. Juniata College, readers were assured, "firmly believes in these fundamentals and emphasizes them in her teaching."

A lot of people wanted to hear this, Harry Cassady told his fellow trustees one time in 1919. The college pastor was then out drumming up support for a "Greater Juniata," coming across a good many Brethren who had "gained favorable opinion" of the college because of the credal statement.[21]

And the response to the statement outside the Brotherhood was no less favorable. From the editorial rooms of the *Sunday School Times* came a little note to Dr. Ellis in August 1924 saying: "We are constantly being asked to recommend a safe Christian college and it is a pleasure to speak a good word for Juniata whenever possible." Included was a brief testimonial from Miriam Dugan (Bryngelson) of Long Island:

> I must say that I find Juniata the most excellent little college in the world, and am most grateful to the Sunday School Times for recommending it a few years ago.[22]

Four Dugan sisters and a brother ended up on the Juniata rolls. Scores of Hilltoppers would peddle bread — as a summer job — for their father's multi-million dollar bakery business during the Twenties and early Thirties.

Over its seven-year life span the School of Theology graduated thirteen divinity students, the last one in January 1925. But its days were numbered. As early as 1923 sentiment began building in the Brotherhood to make Bethany Bible School the church's official seminary. M. G., Juniata's trustee chairman, led the fight against this maneuver in a losing cause. The general feeling at Annual Conference was that the Brethren should only have one seminary, and in 1925 Bethany was officially taken over by the church.

The School of Theology then became the department of Bible and theology, and the nonliberal arts programs were all dropped. Its credal affirmation, however, was retained in the catalog for another decade.

SCHOOL OF MUSIC

For a time after the 1918 changes the School of Music still continued as an ancillary discipline. But in 1920 it gained departmental status as part of the liberal arts curriculum. Then with the introduction of the major-minor system in 1922, it qualified as an area of concentration. But departmental majors got the Bachelor of Music degree, not the B.A.

Even before the Twenties music had not been a second-rate operation. Its staff had enough stature in 1918 to attract a two-hundred dollar annual scholarship from the Presser Foundation of Philadelphia — to train music teachers.

Between 1913 and 1917 the School of Music sponsored a "May Festival" each year. These festivals, the *Echo* said in 1915, are "an established event in nearly all Colleges and schools where music has a place." Prof. Herbert Harroun of Oberlin Conservatory was guest vocalist the first three years. As long as Peter Buys was around in those years

(1912-19), the college had an orchestra of some merit. Trained at the Amsterdam Conservatory of Music and the Hague's Royal Conservatory, Dutch-born Buys, who had spent three years with John Philip Sousa, was Mt. Union's bandmaster when discovered by Juniata. Buys would later win many honorary degrees and decorations and head the American Bandmasters Association. After his departure the orchestra had a checkered career until 1925, when it took a fresh lease on life.

Choral music fared much better. In 1917 the Choral Society gave way to separate glee clubs for men and women. Then in 1920, with the coming of Virginian Charles Rowland, Juniata singers were put on the map. He introduced the annual concert tour his first year, one for each club (not til the 1930s would a mixed choir travel together). The bushy-haired director, ever the wit, took each group—the men in formal attire at last—to churches of constituent Brethren districts throughout the state. The Men's Glee Club went on the air waves for the first time in March 1924 over radio station WFBG in Altoona.

THE ACADEMY AND ITS DEMISE

Along with education and business after 1918, the Academy also housed what was called the Expression Department (speech). Introduced in 1913, speech became a subdivision of the college's English department in 1924 when the Academy closed.

It was the Middle States' evaluation in 1921 that sealed the doom of the Academy. The trustees came to see that their two-campus dream was unrealistic. To erect a whole new complex of buildings on Round Top and still hoist the endowment to where Middle States said it should be would require some monetary miracles. But the Academy was the only one the Brethren then had and the trustees—as well as many alumni—sincerely felt that somewhere within the Brotherhood there ought to be a good church-related preparatory school.

Beginning in 1920 the board made overtures to Blue Ridge College, then on its last legs, about working out a merger. They had in mind making the Maryland school, whose enrollment was barely half a hundred, the Brethren academy. Juniata would swap its one-hundred or so preparatory students for Blue Ridge collegians. A series of conferences took place—in Baltimore and Hagerstown—but in 1922 Blue Ridge decided to limp along on its own. That same spring Morrison's Cove Vocational High School, a private institution, got a visit from merger-minded college officials. These talks also fell through.

And so on February 22, 1924 the trustees voted the Academy out of existence with the end of the current academic year. There were nineteen in the valedictory graduating class. Most of the other forty-three "preps" joined the growing ranks of high schoolers in their home areas.

ERECTION OF SCIENCE HALL

Once Carnegie Library and Stone Church were out of the way, the trustees set their sights on a science building. It became the baby of Allan Myers, who, elected to the board in 1911, gave four travel-filled years to it, raising thirty-two thousand dollars. Two gifts in January of 1913 made his job easier: Joseph Oller's five-thousand dollars, topped by Mary Geiger's seventy-five hundred dollars (Oller threw in an additional five-thousand dollars in 1915).

In the fall of 1913 a site was chosen—the upper end of the library block opposite Students Hall. Edward Tilton, by now a campus habitué, started working on designs the following spring. Excavation began in the summer, and, on Founders Day 1916 (Juniata's fortieth anniversary) Science Hall was dedicated. One of the dignitaries there—from a large university—was greatly impressed by what he saw. He said to Harvey Brumbaugh: "I am convinced that a dollar goes farther at Juniata than at any other college of which I know."[23]

A half-century later the structure would be renovated and enlarged into Good Hall. But as originally laid out, the first floor belonged to physics, with the dynamo and electric room in the basement. Biology and geology shared the second floor. Topmost were the chemists, whose laboratory stenches clashed with the kitchen odors of the home-ec girls.

SOCIAL REGULATIONS—AND FREUDIAN FEARS

By 1924 more than two-thirds of the student body was non-Brethren. Over forty percent of the Hilltoppers came from the Keystone State.

Since 1920 "Joe" Yoder had taken to the road recruiting students on a part-time basis as High School Visitor (his job for another twenty years).

Forty-six Juniatians were on outright scholarships the academic year 1923-24, and scores more depended on loans and on-campus jobs.

Calvin Coolidge was in the White House now, giving the Harding regime a badly-needed moral fumigation. The Coolidge Twenties were delirious years, a paradoxical, bizarre decade. It was an era of technological revolution—the radio, the movies, the automobile gaining a mass market. It was the age of Prohibition and KKK terrorism—when the "business of America," as "Silent Cal" once said, was "business."

It was also a time when American manners and morals went into convulsion. Victorianism was on its way out.

The "Roaring Twenties" swept with less fury over College Hill than over many other campuses. But the breakaway trend in fashions and values after the war was clearly evident. *Alfarata* photography documents rising hemlines, though not to "flapper" girl heights. Bobbed hair was common, lipstick less so. Every now and then the college pastor sermonized about "extravagant" coed dress. "Timely," was the faculty's stock response to these preachments.

For America's "flaming youth" the automobile was hailed as the symbol of freedom from restrictive nineteenth-century values. Guardians of public morals, however, decried Henry Ford's invention as "houses of prostitution on wheels." Obviously, the college powers-that-be felt the same way. The Students' Guide for 1921-22 stated: "Women students are not permitted to go automobiling in the evening and not during the day except by permission and with approved chaperon." And pity the poor fellow behind the wheel if a couple got caught joy-riding.

"Lights out" was 11:00 P.M. One freshman wrote for the 1922 *Alfarata*: "We soon learned that there is nothing to do after sundown but to go to bed; nothing stays out after the retiring bell, except the trees on the campus." No doubt he knew better by the time he was a senior. After-hours trysting behind Ladies Hall was a common sport, no matter that the trustees tried to thwart it with better outside lighting.

The Victrola made its appearance when a hang-out for men—the Boys' Club in Founders basement—was set up in April of 1916. The parlor got one later, for the women's listening pleasure.

But dancing to Victrola music was a campus sin. Nobody could do the Charleston, though, like the president's new secretary in 1921. Her name was Anna Groninger (Smith). As much a whiz in the office as on the dance floor, she would work for four presidents over the next forty-three years.

Cards were perforce another underground pastime. The basketball team was hit by a poker-playing scandal in 1923 that cost the coach his job and three starters their positions. Cardsharps who played for stakes received no mercy; instant suspension was their lot when snatched by the long arm of campus law.

The dating game, as Freudian ideas swept America, was all the more an object of Comstockery. Car rides, as already noted, were out unless chaperoned. Women had to head for the dorm with their dates as soon as a campus function was over. Senior coeds were allowed to go out once a week, juniors once in two weeks, and sophomores once in three weeks. Freshmen girls had a one-a-month quota—always with a chaperon. All women were locked in at 9:45 P.M.

During weekdays dating couples of the early Twenties were restricted to the campus. On Saturday afternoon they could go downtown. Sunday walks—between 3:00 and 5:00 P.M.—took couples beyond the eyes of campus watchdogs. But the territorial limits were strictly set: from 10th Street to the Hospital to the south side of Round Top, an area more or less dally-proof.

The president was, in effect, the dean of students. He enforced all penalties. Until the time of student government (1922), resident faculty still supervised men's dorms as live-in monitors. Mrs. Katharine Roberts, who came in 1922, was the first to be called dean of women (the original title of matron had been changed to preceptress in 1912). This pleasant, white-haired teacher of English was dean eleven years. It was she who made the office as much one of counseling and guidance as of administration.

Faculty-student relationships were kept stiffly formal. Students were almost always addressed as "Mr." or "Miss," rarely by their given names (and certainly not by nicknames, President Brumbaugh warned in 1919). The faculty never hesitated to correct a student—on any occasion—for a gaffe in speech or manners, so hard was it for the professoriate of that time to let their hair down outside the classroom.

NEW YOUTH MOVEMENT: STUDENT SELF-GOVERNMENT

A Council of Cooperation (sometimes called Student Council) came into existence in February 1919 in an attempt to improve faculty-student communications. It grew out of student unrest over the daily schedule. Normally, a student had six forty-five-minute classes or four classes and a lab. This load, it was argued, was overly heavy and academically counter-productive. Students wanted the faculty to adopt the system in operation at most colleges: three sixty-minute classes a day per person with two hours of outside preparation for each class.

The faculty stood firm, but a proposal from the juniors did result in the creation of the Council. It consisted of five students—two seniors and one from each of the other classes. The Council was so constituted as to guarantee at least one woman representative. For the first time the student body could speak with one voice and expect to be heard.

In turn, the faculty established a three-man liaison committee. Good faith was presupposed on both sides.

The *Echo* trumpeted: "This marks the beginning of a new era in the student life at Juniata. And why not? Co-operation is the advance-word of progress; and the spirit of democracy dominates in the new order of things following the war."[24]

In 1922 student leaders began to agitate for greater autonomy in regulating dorm and campus life. Guided by Dean Katharine Roberts, they drafted a constitution that eventually gained faculty and trustee consent. The constitution called for two self-governing bodies, one for men and one for women. Both had eleven representatives: five seniors, three juniors, two sophomores, one freshman. Each body drew up its own set of bylaws and social code.

What this meant was that the students were now empowered to regulate themselves, administering penalties by a system of demerits. They were not at liberty, however, to fix rules without faculty censorship. Nor could they enforce penalties imposed by the councils without prior approval. In point of fact, therefore, social restrictions remained as tight as ever.

Installation day was October 26, 1922—at the morning chapel service. President Brumbaugh, a hearty advocate of student government, did the honors. Witty, popular Donald Brumbaugh headed the Men's Student Council. For the other ruling arm it was Madolin Boorse (Taylor), the "Pottstown prodigy" and "all-round athlete."

What was heralded as the "New Youth" movement had at last brought democracy in full measure to Juniata, the *Echo* exulted, overstating the situation. Miles Murphy, Windber, Pennsylvania's "silver voiced" debater, praised the college for this "expression of faith in the essential goodness of student nature."

Ironically, however, the New Youth movement would help to hasten the resignation of the very person who backed it most—President Brumbaugh himself.

A RESTRICTED CAMPUS BUT NOT A DEAD ONE

Social life was practically defunct during the war years, 1917-18. A general exodus of men—into military service or back to the farm—depopulated the campus. The deadly end-of-the-war flu epidemic closed the school for three weeks the fall of 1918. Because of the man-power shortage intercollegiate athletics were all but suspended.

But up to America's entry into the war social outlets on the Hill were far from nonexistent.

Drama hit the campus for the first time in the spring of 1911—scenes from Greek plays put on by the Lyceum with Prof. Holsopple's help. But not with costumes, thanks to a trustee decree. Shakespeare's "King Lear" and "Merchant of Venice" followed in 1913, now with props and period dress. Reluctantly, the trustees let the junior class stage a full-length play in the spring of 1916. It was a current hit-comedy, "The Private Secretary." Thereafter annual class plays—excepting the freshmen—took on the nature of intramural rivalry. This form of interclass competition ended after a drama club got started in 1926.

In 1914 the Lyceum took to sponsoring an annual "Ausflug." This was an off-campus banquet held in a neighboring community—usually in a church basement—to celebrate the end of midyear examinations. With 1926 the "Ausflug" became an on-campus affair, soon thereafter passing away as a tradition.

These junkets, as close as Juniatians then ever came to after-finals bacchanals, took their rise after "blue books" and an end-of-the-semester exam period were introduced in 1912.

After Prof. Holsopple gave up the editorial care of the *Echo* in 1912 there was no faculty editor-in-chief except for a few months in 1914.[25] In the interval a student committee edited the paper. But in October 1914 Holmes "Falky" Falkenstein, a transfer from Elizabethtown College, took charge of the *Echo*. Ever since then a campus news sheet has been a student body responsibility, but always with faculty advice.

Historically, however, most colleges like Juniata have treated their student-run newspapers more as house organs than as full-fledged members of the press. Student journalists have been free to report and comment as long as they did not dishonor or disgrace the school. To be sure, after 1912 and until only recently the Hilltop press functioned under a heavy presidential thumb. More than one editor down through the years has been summoned to Founders Hall to face a very unhappy president.

The year 1915 fetched the *Alfarata*, the yearbook named for the "Indian maid" of ancient lore. A senior project, it was dedicated to President Brumbaugh, "who has helped us to translate 'Veritas Liberat' in terms of life and character." M. G., then governor, got a special page as "Almus Pater Juniatiensis," which was loosely translated, "Our Intellectual Daddy." Math-wonder Harry Baer, Beau Brummel of the campus, edited this natal issue. There was no *Alfarata* in 1916, nor for the three years 1918-20. After 1921 the yearbook became a junior class commission.

A May Pole materialized on the lawn in front of the gym in 1916.

Around it—in a climactic dance—forty girls in "flowing Grecian gowns" weaved blue and gold streamers. But alas! the first queen and her attendants remain unidentified beauties. Next year's Queen of May, though, was the lovely Ruth Williams (Replogle) a senior from Royersford, Pennsylvania. (Consort Prince Charming did not become part of the festivities until later.)

The spring of 1916 was a time when many students made their first visit to the cinema. With trustee permission they saw David W. Griffith's classic film, *The Birth of a Nation*, an exciting but bigoted story of the Civil War and Reconstruction. Not til 1922, though, did the trustees purchase a movie projector for college entertainment.

Student activism was evident on the Hill long before the 1960s. After 1907 national prohibition became the social reform issue of the day. And Juniata could boast its share of do-gooders in the cause against "demon rum." They engaged in numerous local "no-license" campaigns, dedicated to the Anti-Saloon League goal: "America Dry in 1920." As for woman's suffrage, also well on its way to constitutional redress, it was long "the rule at Juniata," said the *Echo*. JC suffragettes were no strangers at the downtown "Votes for Women" headquarters.

The General Information Test, brainchild of a nameless patron, was initiated in the spring of 1917. For decades campus eggheads made it a prestigious challenge (yet it only paid fifteen dollars to the winner, ten dollars to the runner-up). Paul Moyer, a sophomore from Chicago and a drop-out the next year, topped thirty contestants the first time around.

After World War I the campus quickly revived, the New Youthers in command.

JC debaters continued their winning ways. In 1919 they began to receive academic credit for their out-of-class efforts. The overall debate record through 1924 came to twenty-three victories in twenty-nine contests.

Women took to the forum in 1920, contending against Grove City in a dual meet. The team of Captain Esther Funk, Harvey's daughter Barbara (Reed), Betty Lockington, and Gladys Lashley (Hoover) argued the affirmative on the "closed shop" question. They lost on a split vote. In 1924 women polemicists went undefeated in six encounters.

Club life flourished. In 1920 departmental clubs made their appearances as subgroups of the Lyceum: English; history and social science; music (in addition to the glee singers); science; modern languages. Still going strong were the on-campus debate club, the Lyceum, the Volunteer Band, the two Ys, and the Oriental Society. The Wahneeta Society, however, was not around (it folded in 1912). Gone also was the Intercollegiate Prohibition Society and its oratorical contest, now that the 18th Amendment had supposedly made America "dry."

The Press Club took its rise in 1923, the inspiration of Prof. Herman Hettinger, on-the-side director of publicity. In the interest of a "Greater Juniata" its motto was: "Publicity Above All Things." A bevy of some seventy reporters, writers, and typists prepared and sent out regular news releases to over fifty papers in Pennsylvania, Ohio, and Maryland. Monthly, the hometown newspaper of every student received the latest write-up of college happenings.

Soon after the war dorm-dwellers gained an added measure of privacy. Bunkmates literally split up in the fall of 1922, "roomies" no longer forced to sleep together. The men's halls got double-deck beds while the women were furnished with single "couch" beds.

"Carding" at Sunday evening Stone Church services remained mandatory. But New Youth students rebelled against compulsory attendance at Sabbath morning Bible classes. This trend was deplored at faculty meetings. The administration tried to crack down, inviting parental pressure—but to no avail. It was this minor rebellion that caused the faculty, in 1922, to lengthen the daily chapel period to a half-hour.

As extracurricular activities abounded as never before, "all around leaders" now came in for special recognition. Dr. Fred Hutchinson of Huntingdon established two annual prizes of twenty-five dollars in the summer of 1922. The winners were to be a senior man and a senior woman, chosen by popular vote, who "contributed the most to the life of the College" in their four years on the Hill. The criteria were the same as those for the Rhodes Scholarship. These included force of character and leadership, literary ability, and participation in athletics. The first Hutchinson Award winners were announced at the 1923 commencement. They were Madolin Boorse (Taylor), she of Women's Student Council glory, and class president Harold Engle. ("When it comes to supporting the little world of Juniata," said the *Alfarata* of Engle, "Hardy has it all over Atlas.")

Campus "brains" also made the limelight at graduation ceremonies in 1923. Before then the college had never given academic honors. But that year seniors with an average of ninety or higher graduated "cum honoribus." Out of a class of twenty-nine, four made the grade: Melvin Horst, Mrs. Nettie Howe, Miles Murphy, and John Thompson. However, beginning in 1925 "laude" was conferred in three Latin parts—cum, magna, summa—as tradition would have it.

Not only were the seniors of 1923 the first to graduate comrades "cum honoribus," but they introduced the "Torch Lighting" custom. At the conclusion of their Class Day exercises the Saturday before commencement they marched past President I. Harvey, seated on a pedestal. In his hand he held a large lighted candle that kindled a smaller one carried by each senior. This was to symbolize the "light which they would carry from Juniata to their life work." The name "Candlelighting" was soon substituted for "Torch Lighting."

About this time the "Mantle Ceremony" was introduced—when the outgoing senior president placed the mantle of authority on the shoulders of the incoming one. The Candlelighting and Mantle ceremonies remained traditions to the end of the Calvert Ellis presidency.

ATHLETICS AND THE BIRTH OF FOOTBALL

Athletic facilities expanded to meet the demands of a growing intercollegiate program after 1911. The gym gained added space with a rear addition in 1913.

A grandstand, seating over one-thousand, went up on the northwest corner of the athletic field the summer of 1914. Bought for seventy-five dollars, it came from the County fairground. The baseball diamond, which originally faced west, was now reversed and given a professional look. It boasted a grass infield with skinned base paths. Around the fenced-in area ran the regraded cinder track.

The rearranged athletic field sufficed until the coming of football, when more space was needed. With alumni help additional ground was acquired east of Scott Street in 1923. The borough then closed Scott between 16th and 17th streets.

It became the policy after 1911 to schedule only schools of college and university ranks, although exceptions were made at first. America's entry into World War I, of course, put a crimp in the athletic program. In the spring of 1917 the college reaffirmed the policy of using second-year Academy boys on varsity teams, a practice other colleges of the state were trying to discourage. For the duration, however, intercollegiate competition was drastically curtailed.

Postwar Juniata athletes gained a new sense of camaraderie through the varsity "J" Club. It organized on January 13, 1920 "to foster and create interest in College Athletics." Also, it jealously sought "to govern the promiscuous wearing of letters" by setting up rigid standards of eligibility. Baseballer William Flory, "an Apollo in physique," became the "J" Club's first president.[26]

Athletics had become so much a part of campus life with the early

Twenties that "Clean Sports" was named first in a list of college ideals the catalog began to feature in 1921. "Juniata," the catalog affirmed, "believes in the Roosevelt motto, 'Play the game, don't foul, hit the line hard.' " "In all contests," the statement went on, "Juniata will play hard to win" but not "to gain any honor unfairly."

Winning teams need good coaching, and in 1915 student "bench coaches" became a thing of the past. Ivan Bigler, an Academy alumnus, coached basketball and baseball that year. In 1916 the college brought in a "Pro" for these two sports—Ward Putt, an ex-Hilltopper and player in the New York Eastern and South Atlantic baseball leagues. Ronald Kichline followed in 1922, turning out one of Juniata's finest baseball teams ever. It finished with a 13-6 record, amassing 196 runs to the opposition's ninety-six. A trio of fireballers made up the mound corps: Richard Snyder, John Donelson, and the freshman sensation, Joe Shaute from Packville, Pennsylvania. The team, loaded with long-ball hitters, blasted twenty roundtrippers on the home field alone.

That July "Lefty" Shaute broke into the major leagues with the Cleveland Indians.[27] He threw his first pitch—as a seventh-inning reliever—against Babe Ruth in the second game of a double-header with the Yankees. Before the afternoon was over the rookie had calmly fanned the "King of Swat" not once, but twice.

The six-foot, 190-pound Shaute spent thirteen years in big-league baseball, with three different teams. He was a twenty-game winner in 1924 and ended his career with ninety-nine victories and an ERA of 4.15.

Shaute was not the first Juniatian to go "big time" in baseball, though he was the first to jump directly from campus. Two others, also pitchers, had earlier made the grade. William "Wild Bill" Ritter of McCoysville, Pennsylvania, a student in 1910, went up in 1912 for a four-year stay. Allen Sothoron of Bradford, Ohio, who pitched for the 1912 JC team while enrolled in the Academy, began an eleven-year major league career in 1914. Another pitcher, Perce "Pat" Malone of Altoona, played on Juniata's 1921 team, and seven years later was a moundsman for the Chicago Cubs. For thirteen years he was a major leaguer, part of that time with the Yankees and managed by Joe McCarthy.

On the hardwood court, Juniata quintets, playing a schedule of as many as twenty games some seasons, were no pushovers. But there were more defeats than victories.

Several hoopsters of that era later became trustees. Two are current board members: John "Slats" Baker and Jack Oller. Both played more than one sport—Baker (three), Oller (four).

Women's basketball came into its own in the winter of 1922 (it had been given a try earlier, in 1915). A six-game intercollegiate schedule was played the next year—Drexel, Temple, Indiana Normal, Gettysburg (two). The Marian Dill (Hurlock)-captained sextet produced the first coed varsity letter winners. And in 1924 women roundballers were assigned a training table of their very own.

Before the Twenties the track schedule never amounted to much despite good material. A relay team of Clyde Stayer, John Baker, Galen Horner, and Harry Manbeck competed at the Penn Relay Race Carnival in 1916. They finished fourth in a field of eight. Stayer, then the record-holder in the 220-hurdles, became track coach when he returned to teach in 1919. Stayer-coached cindermen entered twice more in the Penn Relays and with 1921 took part each spring in the Middle Pennsylvania Intercollegiate track-and-field meets. Out of the war years came a spikeshoe mark still supreme: Jefford Oller's 21.6-seconds time for the 220 yard dash in 1918.

As for Juniata netmen, they competed against college squads for the first time in 1917. But not until 1921 was tennis promoted to a varsity sport. The 1923 racket wielders, self-coached, were almost unbeatable, logging one of the best records in tennis history on the Hill. They won nine, lost two, and tied once. The team's captain was a skinny senior named Calvert Ellis.

With the 1920s there came another varsity sport—one for the fall. Students had been pestering the trustees since before the war to give the green light to football. In 1919 they symbolized their feelings by making a campus fetish of a football bought with student funds. A determined lobby went to work as soon as school began the next September. For days the faculty and trustees were besieged by gridiron enthusiasts before giving in. It was the advocacy of two top scholars that turned the scales: John Montgomery and George Griffith—both destined for distinguished medical careers.

The student body raised over six-hundred dollars for new equipment practically overnight. Roy "Pee Wee" Wolfgang, who would become a four-sport, twelve-letter man, then set out for New York City by train to make the necessary purchases, two empty trunks in tow. He was sent on the mission because he could ride free on his father's railroad pass.

But who would be the coach? The question was answered in the person of Dr. Vernon Cecil, the chemistry professor, who had coached football for fifteen years at St. Johns College in Baltimore.

A holiday was declared to level part of the baseball outfield, which was steeply banked, into a playing surface. Students pitched in with shovels, barrows, and wagons to make the dirt fly.

Then there was the matter of a schedule. Jesse "Shark" Miller, student manager, went feverishly to work and in a few weeks lined up five games: Bellefonte Academy, Lebanon Valley (two), Albright, Shippensburg. The season opened on October 23. The blue-togged gridders, captained by quarterback Edwin Donelson, were victors but once that first season — over Shippensburg, 28-0. A speedy Albright eleven wrought disaster the very next Saturday, however, running up a score of 77-0.

Lop-sided scores were not unusual in football's nascent years. But there was no denying its mystique; from the very first kickoff it has been the reigning Juniata sport.

Coaches of the 1920s, though, never stayed around very long. Six of them came and went in that decade.

WORLD WAR I: OBJECTORS AND SERVICEMEN

The peace position has been the historic trademark of the Brethren. And from 1900 onward, as a militaristic spirit was increasingly displayed in the domestic life and foreign policy of the United States, the college took a strong stand in favor of pacifism and disarmament. M. G. actively participated in the Annual Lake Mohonk Conferences on International Arbitration. And in 1904 the *Echo* envisioned him one day on the Hague Tribunal where he could work "to make the principles of our Brotherhood a powerful factor in world peace."

W. J. Swigart was no less a diligent peace partisan. He represented the college in 1905 at a peace conference on the Goshen College campus where he read a major paper. In 1911 Annual Conference appointed a Peace Committee to educate the Brethren on the "sinfulness and folly of resorting to arms." The chairmanship of this committee went to Swigart. After Congress declared war on Good Friday, April 6, 1917, the church created the Central Service Committee to represent it in all matters pertaining to the draft. Its chairmanship also went to Swigart. The Central Service Committee worked closely with the other historic peace churches — Mennonite and Quaker — in gaining recognition for conscientious objectors. There was no provision in the draft law for pacifists, and it took months of mediation before they were allowed to perform noncombatant duties. Meanwhile, Swigart and others on the Juniata staff visited army camps, counseling with resisters kept under detention.

Some Juniatians were among the hundreds of those placed in guardhouses as war resisters. But the actual number is unknown.

1920 Football Squad in Front of Old Grandstand.
Row 1: P. Hanawalt, D. Snyder, E. Donelson, G. Griffith, R. Wolfgang.
Row 2: R. Snyder, G. Nolan, K. Kephart, P. Stein, J. Montgomery, J. Smucker, J. Oller, H. Engle.
Row 3: J. Miller, R. Conrad, C. George, R. Brumbaugh, L. Howe, W. Myers, R. Baker, R. Mattern, Unknown, G. Cunningham, J. Weimer, F. Bechtel, R. Mackey, B. V. Cecil.

Because of their peace heritage, college authorities refused to participate in a War Department program called the Students' Army Training Corps. This plan, announced in May 1918, made cooperating institutions a place for combined military and collegiate training. The purpose was not to interrupt the education of draft-age youth in technical and professional fields until necessary.

But it meant the involvement of military personnel as instructors, and the presence of uniformed men — the symbol of war — was unthinkable to the trustees. Turning down the SATC program, they knew full well, would be costly in terms of male students.

The college did cooperate, however, with another national wartime measure introduced in late April 1917. The faculty rationalized it as a "moral equivalent of war." This was the effort to meet the food shortage, both at home and abroad, by mobilizing a temporary "Agricultural Army" in each state. Under this program undrafted young men could drop out of college with impunity by volunteering several months of farm work wherever assigned. They would receive full academic credit for the disrupted spring term. Any number of Hilltoppers answered this patriotic call. Because this worked havoc with the academic program, all final exams were canceled in June.

For most draft-age Juniatians, of course, patriotism meant military duty. A service flag with seventy-nine stars was placed in the chapel by the YWCA on April 16, 1918. But other stars were affixed later, one of them represented Walter Eshelman. He was the first Juniatian to die in uniform, a flu victim, on October 2, 1918, at Camp Dix, New Jersey.

The one Juniatian to fall in battle was Cloyd Davis, a marine from neighboring Petersburg. He was killed on the Blanc Mont Front in France on October 4, 1918. His sergeant found him lying at the base of a tree, a Bible clasped to his chest.

FURTHER CAMPUS GROWTH AND CHANGES

While work on Science Hall pushed ahead the summer of 1915, a new central heating plant, with a towering steel stack, went up next to Stone Church. The old boiler house behind the dorms, its chimney toppled, was converted into the college laundry.

Earlier, in 1912, M. G. sold the college a 50' x 150' corner lot (Moore and 19th streets) at the foot of Round Top. Then in 1921 the town council vacated all streets and alleys cutting across the Round Top tract. Next year the purchase of five lots (each 50' x 150') below the Orphans Home further enlarged the campus grounds.

By then the college owned fifteen dwellings and a four-family apartment house east of the gym. Included in its property holdings was Henry Brumbaugh's house, next to Carnegie Library, which the Oller relatives deeded over in 1921. The home economics department now had a ready-made "Practice House."

In the fall of 1922 the campus got a long-needed post office — in the basement of Students Hall — complete with 300 lock boxes. The narrow front stairway in Founders Hall was torn out in 1922. This alteration gave more space to the treasurer's office and added three dorm rooms. But it took away the fun of rolling objects down the steps, to crash against the door of the president's office with a resounding thud.

Ladies Hall, by petition of the women in 1922, was renamed Brumbaugh Hall in honor of the Brumbaugh group of founding figures.

And with Coolidge prosperity came the paving of Moore Street between 17th and 18th — in summer 1924.

NEW TWISTS TO ALUMNI RELATIONS

In 1911 the alumni transferred their twenty-eight thousand dollar scholarship fund to the college as part of its endowment, still to be used for student aid.

The idea of quinquennial class reunions, or multiples thereof, at commencement time was first broached in 1912. The class of '98 set the example in 1913, on its fifteenth anniversary.

Prior to 1914 an index of graduates by classes and schools, with current addresses and occupations, appeared in every catalog. A separate *Alumni Register* came out the next three years, but there was a hiatus between 1917 and 1925.

Back in 1908 the corresponding secretary of the Alumni Association had been delegated special responsibility for building up the interest and support of ex-Juniatians. The job went to W. Emmert Swigart of Huntingdon, son of "W. J." and an up-and-coming businessman (insurance and real estate). For the next dozen years he did what he could in his spare time to keep alumni interest alive.

Then in 1920 the Alumni Association finally took Harvey Brumbaugh's advice and appointed a Field Secretary who, though part-time, would be paid. The position went to Allan Myers, and he began to put out the "Juniatagram," a mimeographed newsletter on college activities. He devoted some of his time to reviving local organizations that had fallen inactive during the war years.

Then in 1922 Stoler Good '18, a Waynesboro, Pennsylvania, banker, was appointed to the dual position of college treasurer and alumni director. Within a year there were several active big-city alumni clubs:

Chicago, Cleveland, Pittsburgh, Johnstown, Philadelphia, Reading, Washington, D. C.

It was Stoler Good who planned the first Homecoming Day, November 3, 1923. The big event of the afternoon was the football game against Susquehanna, a battle royal. But the Blue and Gold came out on the short end of a 5-0 score. At halftime the alumni paraded around the field, cheered on by the more than five-hundred spectators.

The "old grads" came from all walks of life. But, due to Brethren dislike of litigation, law had never been a popular profession for Juniatians. This slowly began to change after the war, Juniata setting the example for its kin colleges. Of the eleven known law-schooled Brethren attorneys in 1923, seven were JC alums.[28]

By then nine alumni had gone on to earn Ph.Ds. Two were women who took their doctorates at the University of Pennsylvania: Florence Fogelsanger (Murphy) in English (1917) and Frances Holsopple (Parsons) in psychology (1919). Both, top-ranking scholars, were denied a Phi Beta Kappa key because of their sex.

HARVEY BRUMBAUGH RESIGNS PRESIDENCY

From 1920 on some of the trustees became increasingly upset about campus discipline, which they felt was "far below what it should be." They saw Juniata as an "institution of the church" whose purpose should be to teach "true Christian piety."[29] The rise of student government particularly distressed them because of their fear that behavior might deteriorate completely. Troubled trustees began to put pressure on faculty members and the president, demanding that they show "more concern."

The president, because of three high-spirited daughters, tended to be quite lenient on the matter of campus mores. But the hullabaloo finally got the best of him and in February he asked for a year's leave, to be spent at Columbia University in study. The trustees honored his request unhesitatingly. But C. C. Ellis balked when told he would be the interim deputy while Harvey was gone.

For one thing, the vice-president did not take kindly to giving up his institute work. But more than that, he protested, it was an "unfortunate time" for President Brumbaugh to go away. There was the paramount problem — at least in C. C.'s opinion — of student government and the need for someone to lower the boom. And just beyond the horizon — in 1926 — loomed Juniata's semicentennial and all the dollar signs it conjured up.

Harvey was a tired administrator — twenty-eight years he had run the school in one capacity or another. He needed to get away, and when

Dr. C. C. threw up a roadblock he saw no out except to resign. The trustees received his letter on June 2, 1924. His future relationship with the college was a matter to be determined later.

Bringing In The New Era
1924-1930

MARTIN GROVE BRUMBAUGH REDIVIVUS
On more than one occasion after 1922, complaints about the quality of student life besetting him from all sides, I. Harvey had suggested bringing M. G. back to straighten things out. Perhaps the ex-governor could awe the students into more respect for authority. And then when there seemed to be no solution for an administrative stand-in during his leave, he pressed the idea on the trustees all the harder. At the same time he indicated a willingness to resign, thus opening the way.

In anticipation of the upcoming board meeting on commencement day in June, the trustees went to work on their chairman. They swamped him with mail, beseeching him to come to the "rescue of Juniata College," as Jennie Stouffer (Newcomer) put it.[1] She further exhorted, "You surely cannot close your mind to the fact that you are the man for the crisis." Frank Foster told M. G.: "You are the one man that can bring harmony out of discord, order out of the confusion that exists at the college."[2]

To this chorus of epistolary appeals Dr. C. C. Ellis, to whom New Youth gains were something of a scandal, added a refrain of his own. He informed M. G. of a recent crack-down on the social code intended to leave student leaders "under no misapprehension as to the fact that all their authority is delegated to them from the trustees through the faculty."[3] He mentioned the need of a "capable watchman" and of "more campus light." It was important to him that the music rooms be moved out of Brumbaugh Hall to keep men from "ever being on that side," and he "wished" that the women's dorm was "absolutely separated." "The

208

only opportunity I can see for permanence in the things we have started," Dr. C. C. stressed in closing, "is your acceptance of the presidency."

At the time — and ever since leaving the governor's office — M.G., then sixty-two, made his living as a lecturer. He spent the years 1919-24 criss-crossing the country in behalf of educational reforms.[4] He spoke out for required physical education in public schools and championed the cause of vocational training. He also stumped for the National Recreation Association of New York City, booming public playgrounds. And until its defeat he used the platform to campaign against universal military conscription, which had strong postwar support.

The summer of the college crisis, however, he was scheduled to teach at Bates College in Maine, near his vacation home (Wayne).

His was a pro-forma election when the trustees convened on commencement morning. But there remained the matter of compensation. The college could not hope to meet his current income of seventy-five hundred dollars, and it was proposed that he supplement his president's salary with lecture fees. But M. G. nixed that expedient, with a knowing second from his wife. He finally agreed to five-thousand dollars a year.

For the first time the salary differential between the highest paid professors (twenty-five hundred dollars) and the president amounted to more than a nominal figure.

In late June M. G. sold his forty-thousand dollar Germantown home. His plan was to honor his summer commitment at Bates and his speaking engagements in the fall. He would then take office the first of December, making his Huntingdon residence a second-floor apartment in the new Mission Home.

He importuned Charles Ellis to continue as vice-president, expecting to give more responsibilities to that office. And he made it understood that there would be a place for Harvey Brumbaugh after his year at Columbia was up.

M. G. THE GOVERNOR

Ex-governors, because of political debts owing from many different sectors, can expect to collect on them for a good while after leaving office. And that, of course, was what the trustees were banking on, with the Jubilee Year all but at hand. For M. G. had done honor to himself as occupant of the governor's chair, and was still a man of far-flung influence. While historians today do not assess his administration as outstanding, they do rate it as successful.[5] And none fail to laud him for his character and high sense of public calling.

M. G. had never thought of getting involved in politics until William Vare, Republican city boss of Philadelphia, put the notion in his head. Politically astute, Vare had the ability to read the "sign of the times" — the trend of the country after 1910 to place educators in public office.[6] Woodrow Wilson, Princeton's president who went from the governorship of New Jersey to the White House, was the classic example.

As 1914 approached, the senatorship and gubernatorial office were both to be filled in Pennsylvania. Boies Penrose, head of the State Republican machine, declared his candidacy for the United States Senate. But he was opposed to Vare and the Vare organization. The Philadelphia boss, however, foresaw the reelection fight Penrose would have on his hands. This would be the first election of senators by the direct vote of the people. Furthermore, Progressivism was in its heyday, and Teddy Roosevelt had personally widened the breach between his followers and Penrose. But Penrose intended to call the shots, as he had since 1904, on the Republican candidates for key state posts — among them, of course, the governorship.

A year or so before the election Vare decided to push an opposition gubernatorial candidate in the Republican primaries. If successful, this would be a telling blow in breaking Penrose's grip on the party. One day he asked his brother, Ed, what was the "most prominent school name" in Pennsylvania.

"Brumbaugh," came the immediate reply.

Vare said, "He's the man for us." His brother agreed.[7]

Six months before the fight started, Vare resorted to a clever ruse. He had M. G. speak before school and other civic groups that later passed resolutions for him. The cagey Quaker City politico rightly intuited that the State's thirty-thousand teachers would constitute a solid Brumbaugh bloc and help attract thousands of independents who had left the Taft ticket two years before.[8] M. G.'s well-placed educator-friends played up the fact that he had been the leading member of the commission that drafted the School Code of 1911. This measure repealed every school law that had been passed since the beginning of free education in Pennsylvania. It substituted the new Code covering all phases of public schooling.

M. G.'s strength developed overnight, and within ten days Vare had forced the Philadelphia school superintendent upon Penrose. Penrose yielded to the coup because he wanted to avoid a "costly and uncertain fight." But he would have nothing to do with M. G. during the whole campaign. Yet the two men refrained from public vituperation against each other. This refusal to deny he was tied to Penrose's bandwagon hurt M. G. with not a few independents.

Almost everyone on College Hill hailed with pleasure his entrance into politics. Some saw the White House at the end of the road for him. To them it was destiny-certain that he was the Republican Party's answer to Wilson.

But others had misgivings, among them Charles Ellis. C. C. tried to talk him out of running for governor for fear he would get "mixed-up" in "gang" politics.[9] M. G. gave assurance, however, that there were no "entangling alliances." He spoke of himself as an "Independent Republican."

He refused to do any preprimary campaigning. And he made it clear that he would reject the nomination unless it came as "the call of the common people, the people who work with their hands."[10] That call came in May when M. G. garnered four-fifths of the Republican vote (253,788), the largest ever recorded for a state candidate before woman's suffrage. He received more than twice the votes polled by Vance McCormick, the victor of the Democratic primary.

On the campaign trail M. G. spelled out a thoroughly progressive platform, which included the ballot for women. He hit hard on the theme that as governor he would be "unfettered" and "unbossed in every way." Some three thousand voters in Philadelphia's Town Hall heard him one October night make his most caustic utterance against machine politics. He said, "I hate a boss as much as you hate a boss, and if ever a slimy thing throws itself in my path I will scotch it."[11]

For M. G. the wet-dry question was no less of a political hot potato than bossism. The ties between the Republican Party and the liquor traffic had long been close. Thus the Anti-Saloon League, skeptical that Brumbaugh was his own man, threw its support to McCormick. But M. G. defied the state party, which counseled silence on the alcohol issue. He promised the drys: "I will do everything I honorably can to support local option." "No license" rather than blanket prohibition, he sincerely believed, was the "practical solution to a vital problem facing the people and legislature."[12]

A number of minor parties were also in the field, and M. G. found himself caught up in a spirited campaign. But he won handily in November despite diverse opposition. His nearly 489,000 votes represented a solid majority.

College Hill went wild the day after the election. The tower bell pealed the glad news. The faculty and students sent the governor-elect a congratulatory telegram. Classes dismissed. Parades marched all day. Speechifying filled in between parades. At night a huge bonfire, fueled by rubbish hauled in from all over town, lit up the sky from down on the Athletic Field.

For M. G. victory was tempered with sadness. In July his wife of twenty years, the former Anna Konigmacher, had died unexpectedly.

In several respects his election was unique. No other Brethren has ever held a gubernatorial office, and he was the second and last clergyman in the Commonwealth to do so. Moreover, he was the only college president as well as the only Ph.D. holder to become Pennsylvania's chief executive.

Though a Progressive at heart, M. G. decried, in his inaugural address, the tendency to make too many laws. Additional statutes did little for social and political reform, he felt, unless they had distinctive merit. Therefore, he vetoed 409 bills as governor.[13]

Nevertheless, new laws of social significance readily got his signature. These included a Child Labor Law, the Workman's Compensation Law, and the act establishing the Direct Inheritance Tax. Legislation during his administration also created a Bureau of Vocational Education as a subdivision of the Department of Public Instruction and a Commission of Agriculture. Acreage by the thousands were set aside for conservation purposes. However, local option — his answer to the liquor problem — failed of acceptance in the legislature.

Ironically, Governor M. G., the peace-loving Dunker, was called upon to preside over the Commonwealth in wartime. Many Brethren criticized him when he mobilized the Pennsylvania National Guard, which went to France as the 28th Division and took part in some of the chief campaigns in the last months of the war. They felt that he had breached the peace stand of the church. But for him signing the order had been an act of duty. (He had, in fact, sent an antiwar telegram to Senator Walker after Congress had made its declaration.)[14] At any rate, the war and its demands overshadowed the second half of his administration.

For awhile it looked as though M. G. might not finish out his term. The Vare faction pushed him into the race for the United States presidency in March 1916. Penrose bitterly fought this maneuver and tried to coerce him into quitting. He made public accusations about irregularities in financing M. G.'s gubernatorial campaign. His tactics failed, and Governor Brumbaugh became one of eleven candidates nominated at the Republican convention in Chicago. He received twenty-nine votes on the first ballot, although in the meantime he had pledged his support to

Theodore Roosevelt. Charles Hughes became the party's banner-bearer, but he lost out to Wilson, who was reelected.

Boies Penrose had been out to discredit the governor from the start, and M. G. did not leave the state capital unscathed by scandal. After his first wife died he bore the brunt of vicious gossip about his relationship with Flora Belle Parks. The Brumbaugh family had taken her, as a ward, into their home while M. G. was still County Superintendent of Schools, more than twenty years before. A distant relative of his, she was a girl in her midteens when he became her guardian.

Attractive and socially refined, she made a perfect substitute First Lady for Pennsylvania's widowed governor. But M. G.'s political enemies could see nothing innocent in his sharing the Executive Mansion with so comely a woman, almost young enough to be his daughter. Scandalmongers were silenced for the time being when they were married in February 1916, a month before he entered the presidential race.

Then in 1917 the Penrose crowd attempted to impeach Governor Brumbaugh by more mud-slinging. They publicized extracts from state records allegedly revealing extravagant personal expenses paid for out of public funds. The most sensational charge was that the people of Pennsylvania bore the cost of his 1916 bridal tour with Flora Belle Parks. Penrose, however, came out a loser with his impeachment ploy.

M. G.'s PROSPECTUS OF A "GREATER JUNIATA"

On the whole, the student body had felt a genuine affection for Harvey Brumbaugh. When he returned for M. G.'s inaugural he met with a rousing welcome at an evening chapel get-together. On behalf of the seniors Stanley Stroup, their prexy, presented him with a watch-chain charm "as a token of the high esteem in which he is held by Juniatians everywhere." And three days later he was the guest of honor at their class dinner held in the Leister House (across the street from the railroad station).

Nevertheless, toward the end of his administration students had begun to complain about "screws being put on." And after his resignation an editorial in the campus paper predicted "more order and better organization" under the incoming president. Its scribe went on to voice the expectation that someone with M. G.'s background would "not long entertain some of the characteristic medieval narrowmindedness which has long been present."[15] This was not meant to be so much an indictment of the ex-president as of the trustees and certain faculty members. Still it must have cut the sensitive Harvey.

But the new president, himself not fully sold on student government, as a matter of fact saw his alma mater quite like his predecessor had: as a "tight little, right little college." His inaugural speech in January served notice on rambunctious New Youthers. In identifying "salient objectives" for the Juniata of his presidency, he said of the school:

> It is a Christian College dedicated to the advancement of right living here and teaching that there is a hereafter of tremendous significance. It accepts the Bible and teaches that it is the key to the hope of immortal life. From this ideal, it should never depart. In this respect, the College is not only conservative but immoveable. The College wants not only to teach right but to do right. "Knowledge that is not refined into conduct is a curse, not a blessing."

He recognized the fact that the student generation of the Twenties embodied a vastly changed set of moral and cultural values. Spiritual ideals, he lamented, lay "shattered" and "broken" in the wake of war, the American home and the schools in a state of moral decay. This gave rise, in his view of things, to a set of problems more complex than college administrators had ever before faced. But the values of Juniata have not changed, he asserted, and therefore the college "dedicates itself to a spiritual revival." During his presidency he hoped that it would be "counted among those agencies that stand in crisis for law, for country, and for righteousness."

Here in this last statement he preveniently sounded the theme that he would later choose for the Jubilee Year: "Law and Law Observance."

M. G. made much of the point that Juniata "must remain small," a community in "close personal touch." He was, of course, taking over a now Academyless campus, its population sizably reduced. "Small" he translated into an enrollment of five-hundred. By 1928 this mark, up a couple of hundred over his inaugural year, had been reached and even slightly surpassed.

For reasons of his own, he did not see fit, in limning the "Juniata of tomorrow," to say anything specifically about the college's Brethren heritage, or its obligations as such. But never once during his second term did M. G. betray the slightest desire to lead Juniata out of the denominational fold. Indeed, in a 1929 letter to a Brotherhood dignitary he made no bones about "trying here to build a school of the Church of the

Brethren." He further stated: "We are certainly as loyal to its principles as I know how to make the school."[16]

Even so, he could rankle at what to him looked like signs of undue church interference. In 1929, the doom of Blue Ridge College past dispute, the church's General Education Board sought to keep Juniata and Elizabethtown from recruiting south of the Mason and Dixon line. Territorially, Maryland was reserved for two smaller schools in Virginia. But M. G. wanted Maryland declared "open territory." He argued that Juniata had already been forced to reach out into "other fields" for students because it had grown faster than the church. In strong words he let the people in Elgin know that he did not want the church "through any of its Boards or actions to cripple us in any way."

Postinaugurally, President Brumbaugh's scenario for a "Greater Juniata" came to include membership in the Association of American Colleges. Founded in 1915, the AAC had become the patron saint of liberal arts institutions. Its benediction was bestowed on Juniata in January 1927.

THE NOT SO GOLDEN JUBILEE

In 1925, at the close of its first half century, Juniata College owned a physical plant worth a half million dollars. Its endowment fund amounted to a few thousand more. Thanks to thrifty management, the school was solvent, not a cent of mortgage indebtedness owing on its grounds and buildings.

But to accommodate the five-hundred students optimally projected, there was need for added facilities and greater endowment income. M. G. and the trustees expected, of course, to exploit the college's semicentennial to the hilt. And so they came up with a dream campus for the future, the drawings made by M. G.'s son, Edwin, a Philadelphia architect. The plans included a men's dormitory, a social center, another women's dormitory, a new gymnasium, a music and arts building, a home economics building, an ample dining room, an administration wing, and additions to Science Hall and Carnegie Library. At the center of the campus was to stand a natatorium, flanked on one side by formal gardens.

To complete the first units in this expansion program and—most critically—to lift the total endowment to the million-dollar figure, meant a seven-hundred and fifty thousand dollar Jubilee Year campaign. In October 1925 the trustees engaged Ward, Wills, Dreshman, and Gates and Co., then the oldest professional fund-raising firm in the country, to direct the drive. The canvass proper began in mid-May and lasted two weeks.

Off campus, the campaign concentrated on three constituencies: the alumni, the church, and the community. The "community," however, embraced more than the immediate river basin. It took in the whole two-hundred-mile stretch between Lancaster and Pittsburgh. Declared canvass publicity: "Juniata College is the only general college on the main line of the Pennsylvania Railroad."

On campus—among trustees, faculty, and students—there had been a precampaign solicitation. Nineteen trustees subscribed one-hundred thousand dollars, J. J. Oller the pacemaker with his twenty-five thousand dollars. The student body canvass, headed by Clarence Pentz, a senior BMOC, netted some thirty-three thousand dollars, an average of almost one-hundred dollars per student. Pentz' class of fifty-five members, which playfully labeled themselves "M. G.'s Sunbeams," whipped up contagious enthusiasm among undergraduate peers. From the twenty-eight faculty members came subscriptions in excess of fifteen thousand dollars. Amazingly, not a single person in any of these three groups refused to sign a pledge card.

Overall, however, the Jubilee Campaign turned out something less than a howling success. It fell far short of its goal, by nearly three-hundred and fifty thousand dollars.

M. G. had done his best to prevent failure. To set the stage for the May drive he had gone all out the previous month to make a grand occasion of Juniata's fiftieth anniversary. He built the events of Founders Day weekend around the theme of "Law and Law Observance." Robert von Moschzisker, Chief Justice of the Pennsylvania Supreme Court, was the featured speaker. In his own welcoming address the president spoke of constitutional law, of the responsibility of free citizens to state government. He hailed "education as the means and safeguard of American Democracy." From "Jubilee to Jubilee," he adjured, the college must always honor "in an enlightened way the values of our country."

Why this emphasis? Not because M. G. purposed to turn Jubilee Day into one of theatric flag-waving. Patently, he was out to contrive a fresh image of Juniata. He intended to show the larger world that his was not a backwoods institution, that in vision and commitment it was attuned to the times. Particularly, he hoped to make the college more visible to Pennsylvanians, to "firmly entrench" it, as he once said, in the "heart of the Commonwealth."

He brought to campus for the Golden Jubilee, not only jurists and legislators, but two "names" in state business and industry. Howard Heinz of "57 Varieties," a close friend of his in ecumenical Sunday school work, got an honorary degree. So did M. G.'s boyhood acquaintance, Charles Schwab, then board chairman of Bethlehem Steel.

But the payoff was practically nil. Heinz did make a modest gift, but Schwab proved closefisted, insulted by someone's lack of tact in explaining Juniata's hopes for his philanthropic help.

It soon became apparent—to M. G.'s great disappointment—that he lacked a Midas-touch in cultivating big-money men. He could get them to campus—nabobs of Schwab-Heinz opulence: Bruce Barton, Josephus Daniels, Owen Roberts, William Woodin—but never with their checkbooks.

In the case of Woodin, the railroad-banking magnate and later FDR's Secretary of the Treasury, the antics of silly students probably jinxed his 1929 Hilltop visit. Everyone knew why he was getting an honorary degree on Founders Day. Yet a gang of fellows stood outside M. G.'s office, stupidly chanting: "We want Woodin nickles." "We want Woodin nickles."

No doubt Dr. Claude Flory has put his finger on why the president's well-to-do friends gave him the financial go-by. As a Juniatian in the late Twenties, debonair Flory fell into M. G.'s favor and was taken into the family circle. He recently wrote, "I now realize that while the campus of those days looked all right to most of us country students it must have looked terribly unsophisticated—a hopeless educational investment—to men of national and international experience."[17]

But, at the time, optimism ran unchecked. The yearbook for 1927 was called the *New Era Alfarata*. The Jubilee Year, it proclaimed, heralded the dawn of a glorious epoch for Juniata. M. G. wrote a page-long piece for this issue captioned "The Outlook in the New Era." One paragraph read:

> Accepting the challenge of the times and the demands of every prophecy concerning the years ahead we shall enter upon a New Era of service to God and society, resolved to keep close the first things of the Soul and adjust ourselves as fully as may be to the needs of the age. We shall not give up God, the church, the Christocentral life. But we shall adjust our offerings to cover the needs of right ordered living in the years to be.

The sole brick-and-mortar return from Jubilee dreaming and campaigning, as we shall see, was the Cloister, erected in 1928.

ADMINISTRATIVE ADVANCES

M. G. was not a vindictive man by nature, as his gubernatorial feud with Penrose had plainly illustrated. Theodore Roosevelt called him the "wooly little lamb" because of his noncombative spirit.

But soon after returning to College Hill M. G. found himself carping privately about a few of the gerontic but powerful members of the trustee board. He looked upon them as obstructionists, holding him back. One day—in a weak moment—he remarked to his golf partner while playing the Huntingdon links: "What we need is a few deaths on campus."

He once heard from someone who knew about his feelings toward these men. In a letter this person derided them and their alter egos on the faculty as the self-appointed "official Juniata Company." What more his friend had to say did nothing to put down M. G.'s own resentment. The writer confided:

> I know how they howl like hyenas when you go fishing or golfing. They try to know how many cigars you smoke and it makes THEM sick. They consider themselves saints and everybody else a sinner. I wonder how you hold them to an even semi-modern program in the administration of affairs.[18]

Fortunately these tensions remained latent. The majority of trustees, if less vocal, gave M. G. no problems. In 1927 the death of Henry Gibbel put Joseph Oller into the chairmanship. There came onto the board during M. G.'s second term another contingent destined for long tenure. They were: Lewis Knepper, who in 1926 had joined the administration as field secretary (1927-39); Mrs. Florence Gibbel, wife of Henry (1927-56); Lloyd Hartman of Mifflintown, Pennsylvania (1928-51); Albert Horner of Pittsburgh (1927-55); Ross Murphy of Shippensburg, Pennsylvania (1926-60).

In 1925 President M. G. introduced the trustees to the niceties of a budget.

The next year he brought in a business manager. Prior to 1919 it had been the steward who looked after the physical plant and the food service. But when Otis Brumbaugh left, his duties fell upon the bursar's office. With the New Era spurt, however, Oscar Myers, the English professor who in 1924 inherited the ledgers from Stoler Good, called for help. This came in the person of Clarence Pentz, who took the title of business manager and did the job for two years before leaving for medical school. Ralph Berkey followed him and gave the college fourteen years.

Another administrative innovation came in 1927 when Dr. Fayette McKenzie was made dean of men. Ever since 1925 M. G. had been talking about the need for a "moral and religious counselor" who, though an academician, would seek to promote himself as the *fidus Achates* of male students. The women, of course, had Dean Roberts. Dr. McKenzie, a sociologist, had returned to Juniata upon leaving the presidency of Fisk University, a black college in Nashville, Tennessee. All things taken into account, the wirily built Scotsman, known for his wry smile and athletic interests, was a natural choice for the deanship.

As for an academic dean, however, M. G. could see no purpose. He and C. C. Ellis, who now had more administrative say, teamed up to oversee the curriculum and the faculty. But not everybody could accept this, and personal tragedy befell the campus.

Dr. Alphaeus Dupler had been dean of Bridgewater College before rejoining his alma mater in 1919. At Juniata, as registrar and director of summer sessions under I. Harvey, he did the work of an academic dean, if lacking the title. To M. G., after he took office, Dupler on many occasions confided his ambition to have that title of dean. For some reason his wish was never granted, on top of which he lost his summer sessions post to Harvey Brumbaugh. The blow was too much for the forty-four-year-old father of four. Crushed and utterly frustrated, he took his life in a backyard shed in June of 1928. His suicide was something those on the Hill could not quickly put out of mind.

ACADEMICS

By the late 1920s high schools, of which there were then about fifteen thousand in the nation, had become an accepted part of the public education system. But little had been done about investigating how well high schoolers were prepared for college. Nor had there been much study made of curriculum development at the postsecondary level. This task the Carnegie Foundation for the Advancement of Teaching took upon itself in the spring of 1928. It administered an achievement test to seniors at all Pennsylvania colleges and universities. Juniata's group, the result showed, ranked well up the list, slightly above average (Haverford came out on top).[19]

Hilltoppers were pleased by this performance. They interpreted it as an indication that the quality of education at Juniata had not degenerated despite a tripled enrollment in the last decade. This was four times the average growth for colleges of Pennsylvania. Even so, President M. G. expressed the desire in 1929, now that the school had attained its goal in numbers, to concentrate on raising standards of admissions.

From statistics on grade distribution it would appear that the New

Youth were not overly coddled by their profs. A change in policy in 1926 set up six grades, A through F, with E being conditional. Report cards still went out at six-week intervals. The statistical picture at the end of the first marking period the fall of 1929 looked like this: A (7.3%); B (30.3%); C (39%); D (16.3%); E (3%); F (1.8%); Inc. (23%).

The higher minimum passing grade for juniors and seniors went by the board in 1929. In February 1930 the faculty adopted the quality point system, effective in the fall.

Dean Katherine Roberts and Harvey Brumbaugh plugged a dean's list. They cited Yale, Harvard, Radcliffe, and Haverford as places where the practice had found favor. At Juniata, with no academic dean, such a scroll became the "honor roll" in March 1928. Fourteen students — but only one frosh — had attained an overall first semester average of A- or better.

The ex-president also got — in the fall of 1929 — the faculty amen for "honors" courses (independent research projects).

Academic cheating scandalized College Hill. New Youth leaders shed copious editorial tears over this student frailty in the campus paper. To them the honor system, their fond hope, seemed an ever remote possibility.

There was essentially little tampering with the main lineaments of the curriculum. Areas of concentration, though, did undergo a bit of juggling. Philosophy was dropped (1927), and sociology replaced social science (1928). Speech was listed as a major for two years (1927-29). So that science students could take four laboratory courses, the number of hours in a major field was increased from thirty to thirty-two.

In 1928 a B.S. degree in music became available. Approved by the State Council of Education, it took its place beside the B.Mus., which never got Harrisburg's official stamp. The music department's growth plus the need for more dormitory space necessitated removing the music studio and practice rooms from Brumbaugh Hall. Two houses were eventually put to the department's use, one at 1821 Moore Street in 1924 and another up the block (1908) in 1929.

Home economics barely escaped the axe in 1924, its doom seemingly sealed by presidential-trustee concurrence that spring. I. Harvey had been disappointed at the discipline's retarded growth on campus and so called for cutting it out as soon as practicable, to which the board took no exception. But M. G., once in office, raised the yellow flag on axing. Dorothy Saylor (Pentz), a Penn State graduate, came along in the fall and quickly turned the situation around, winning departmental deliverance.

In September 1927 the Oller-purchased H. B. Brumbaugh dwelling became the home ec Practice House. By then the department's staff had grown to three.

The Practice House shift released space in Science Hall, and the chemistry department at once usurped it, adding physical and quantitative laboratories.

In May 1927 America had gone almost mad with joyful pride over the feat of a homespun, modest aviator named Charles Lindbergh, hero-conqueror of the Atlantic. The "Flying Colonel's" exploit was still the talk of Huntingdon when President M. G. went looking for someone to supervise JC seniors in their practice teaching. This search had been dictated by the Edmonds Act of 1921, which, as one provision for raising professional standards, prescribed an apprenticeship for all aspiring high school teachers. Before it closed in 1924 the Academy had afforded Juniatians convenient intern opportunities. But the placing of student teachers in the public system proved something of an administrative care. This was remedied in 1927 when Charles Smith, head of Mt. Union schools, accepted the responsibility. Supervision finally reverted to the education department once and for all in 1933.

But Pennsylvania's teacher training program put the private college at a decided disadvantage. In 1926 the state purchased all the normal schools and transformed them into teachers' colleges. As such, they received appropriations that covered the costs of engaging "critic" teachers as stipendiaries. Some independent colleges did not provide compensation, and it soon became evident that their students often got indifferent supervision as a result. For those institutions, like Juniata, which made recompense, students were penalized with an extra fee.

This whole matter became a great worry of the Association of College Presidents of Pennsylvania. For obvious reasons the Association turned to M. G., a member of its Legislative Committee, for a solution. He drafted a bill in the spring of 1929 that, if enacted, would have subsidized apprentice teaching for schools receiving no state aid. Backed by the Society of College Teachers of Education, it passed both houses of the General Assembly. But Gov. John Fisher's veto signed the bill's death warrant, putting the issue permanently to rest.

Not until 1958, when the all-inclusive fee went into effect, would Juniatians get exonerated from the student-teaching surcharge.*

*However, it was revived in 1976.

It was a future educator, working his way through Juniata, whose own experience at his downtown job led him to challenge the college to broaden its educational outreach. Hilltoppers knew Gordon Drake, a Huntingdonian who wore stylish, black-framed glasses, as a friendly but argumentative "show me" kind of person. A junior in 1927, he conducted a community survey and uncovered appreciable local interest in a "night school."[20] He reported his findings to the faculty and recommended a move in that direction. Drake had in mind the teaching of practical subjects like "commerce and finance."

Out of this idea sprang the Extension Department in 1928—"Juniata's New Door of Opportunity," so advance billing heralded. Actually, continuing education, to use the current lingo, had been given a try back before World War I. In 1910 Prof. Holsopple began holding evening classes in Modern English Poetry—for teachers—in the Altoona High School.[21] His hope was to expand the course offerings, but for some reason the experiment was short-lived.

And, of course, there had been the on-campus annual Bible terms, the last one of which was held in 1925. Then, too, ever since 1919 the college had been sponsoring Bible institutes in local congregations of the three constituent Brethren districts. For a brief time (1923-25) the Religion Extension Service, directed by Prof. Galen Royer, offered correspondence work with reasonably good results.

The Drake-inspired Extension Department was headed by Dr. McKenzie and went into operation in February 1929, with the start of the second semester. Classes met on campus two nights a week for hour-and-a-half sessions. Ordinarily, a course earned one and a half credits. The tuition for each course amounted to fifteen dollars a semester, the going rate for all Juniatians.

Dr. McKenzie promised eventual extramural instruction at outlying places within a fifty-mile radius where the demand might warrant it. Within another year this was happening—at East Freedom and New Enterprise in Blair County. By then adult education enrolled fifty-seven persons—thirty-eight women and nineteen men.

Any course in the whole curriculum could be brought into service if a minimum of six students petitioned for it. But business subjects, as Drake anticipated, came off the most popular, at least initially. They carried titles such as Fundamentals of Economics, Bookkeeping and Accounting, Retailing Methods, The Stock Market and Its Work, and Business Ethics.

Sustenance for much of this New Era academic vigor flowed from a library in remarkable fettle. Since 1918 it had been the beat of alumna Lillian Evans '10, a further trainee of Drexel and Chicago. This gentle woman of quiet proficiency had practically doubled the number of holdings—to forty-six thousand volumes—within a septennate after her appointment. Among colleges and universities of the Commonwealth in the mid-Twenties, Juniata's library had risen to eleventh rank—"quite beyond," crowed President M. G., "what might be expected."[22]

Meanwhile, the new men's dorm released all of third floor Students Hall for academic use. This space was remodeled into four large classrooms.

NEW ERA FACULTY

Death laid a heavy hand on President M. G.'s faculty. Tobias Myers died in 1926, followed by "Uncle" Perry Hoover and Alphaeus Dupler in 1928. These would be the last mortalities among sub-sixty-five-year-old professors until the recent passing (1972) of Dr. John Comerford.

By fall 1929, when the stockmarket went disastrously haywire, the faculty had grown to forty. Earned doctorates still numbered barely more than a half dozen. There were fourteen women, none of professorial rank. All but three were lowly instructors.

I. Harvey Brumbaugh came back from his leave to teach Latin and education. His course, History and Trends of Education, became a perennial favorite with Juniata's future teachers.

Clyde Stayer, after the Academy closed, joined the mathematics department. Known for his hearty laugh and a Brethren minister, he won the reputation for taking the mystery out of math. His ability to relate to students eventually led to his appointment as dean of men.

Not a few New Era recruits evidenced a liking for the Hill. Eleven of them put in full-time stays of a decade or more. A half-dozen taught between ten and sixteen years: Fayette McKenzie (sociology, 1925-41); Harold Conner (economics, 1924-37); May Keirns (Greek, 1929-41); Elmer Craik (history and government, 1924-36); Miriam Fackler (English, 1928-39); Harold Engle (biology, 1923-35).

The other five averaged a whopping thirty-one years each. Kansan Paul Yoder (1926-64) came to Juniata from the faculty of Blue Ridge College. A physicist, this dulcet-voiced Dunker preacher ran a one-man show for the most of his tenure. From 1937 to 1944 he was also director of summer sessions.

Jack Oller (1928-65), son of trustee chairman Joseph, returned to his old haunts to teach French (and later Spanish). Easy-going and ever-mustachioed, he became a European traveler and, among the faculty, the most ardent aficionado of varsity sports.

From the neighboring dominion of Canada came Margaret Mc-Crimmon (1925-53), a Toronto native, to her first and only college teaching position. Another JC habitué of Europe, she developed a strong curriculum in modern languages. "I always felt at home in the United States," the tiny, unpretentious linguist once said, "but if I hadn't been so fond of Juniata I never would've stayed."

Earl Dubbel (1926-54) was Ivy League all the way (Harvard and Princeton), a two-degree seminarian. He became the Shakespearean of the English department. Of ministature, Prof. Dubbel, barely a five-footer, could joke at his own expense. He was sometimes heard to say, in his high-pitched voice: "I might be pitifully short, but thank God I'm symmetrical!"

Son of Jacob, Norman Brumbaugh (1925-49) flunked out of his doctoral program at Harvard. But the sworn bachelor finally redeemed himself at Penn, in 1922 at the age of thirty-eight. Dr. "N. J." was a sports lover and an amateur oboist. In the twenty-four years he was its head, the department of chemistry at Juniata rose to national prominence. N. J. had an inordinately proud father. Jacob Brumbaugh loftily referred to him in public as "my son, Norman."

As yet, the faculty received no term contracts, only annual appointments. N. J.'s reelection letter for 1930-31, stating a salary of $2,850, further read:

It is understood that the faculty members are, in addition to the class work attendant upon election, to hold themselves ready at all times:

First, to perform such services on Sunday in the Bible Classes as may be requested or assigned;

Second, to assist the management in inculcating proper religious as well as educational standards in the College;

Third, not to be absent from class duties of the College without the knowledge and consent of the President;

Fourth, to attend all Faculty meetings unless excused for good reasons.[23]

Nor were sabbatical leaves then customary, though by 1929 President M. G. had pretty much wheedled the trustees into granting them. But his death and the deepening depression squelched any follow through. Nothing would be done about such a policy for another three decades or so.

LIFE AND DOINGS OF NEW ERA STUDENTS

"Huntingdon, Seat of Juniata College" — so two large signs, at either end of town, greeted tourists passing through on the William Penn Highway. Henry Gibbel had them put up in the fall of 1924.

Countians still made up about one-fifth of the enrollment, most of them — as many as eighty in 1929 — hailing from the county seat itself. But only a dozen or so out-of-staters set foot on campus each year. There was one overseas student, the first since before World War I, during the academic year 1925-26. He was Gisuke Kumada, a Japanese Christian. His wife died in March and he did not return the next fall.

In 1929 a year at Juniata cost, apart from lab fees, about $560. By then three local fraternal groups — Civic, Rotary, Elks — had swelled the number of loan funds available to deserving students. That of the Civicists was the largest of its kind in the Pennsylvania Federation of Clubs.

Commuting New Erans had it better than they could ever know, seen retrospectively from the rail-cursed 1970s. Fourteen mainline PRR trains, eastbound, made daily stops at Huntingdon. This was two more than westbound ones. In addition the Huntingdon-Broadtop Railroad and the Petersburg branch of the "Pennsy" each provided passenger service twice a day.

Resident students, however, found their mobility somewhat checked. Nightwatchman John McCracken, "Mac" to decades of Juniatians, began his Cimmerian patrols in November 1924. The student government, taking alarm at "undesirable characters lurking around the dormitories," had asked for after-dark protection. The trustees complied, though as much concerned about enforcing campus regulations as ensuring campus safety. And so began the cat-and-mouse game — to last as long as a curfew obtained — between "Mac" and JC men.

"Who is it?" he would call out of the darkness. At first he got in response all sorts of aliases, exploiting his naiveté. Early in the job he stopped William Shakespeare eight different times trying to sneak in late the same evening.[24] "Mac" was a much wiser night watchman after that. Thanks to him, few curfew breakers or other violators missed a next-morning presidential audience.

But M. G., it soon became clear, was by nature no more of a

nemesis than his cousin. He told the trustees in 1925: "I would much rather be an advisor to young men and women than the disciplinarian of defaulting students."[25] His letters to erring students were unfailingly tender, reflecting personal anguish over their misdeeds. They were liberally sprinkled with phrases like "pained me greatly"; "heartbroken"; "worried about it nearly all night."

He wanted to be as open as possible with Juniatians. His initial months in office he held a series of give-and-take "chats" with sundry sectors of the student body. These presidential causeries sent campus morale skyrocketing.

Still, he had honest doubts about the effectiveness of student government. He said in 1927: "I am not sure yet whether it is the best method of disciplinary procedure." Sometimes, he feared, "this governing group fails to function wisely or even impartially."[26] But he was far from ready to write it off, admitting: "Those governed by the Councils of the student body are for the most part amenable to their own government."

The councils were still bound by a Puritan-strict social code. Any open display of affection, no matter how innocent, rarely escaped an official reproof. M. G. wrote to one father in 1928: "Your daughter, throwing her arms around this boy in the public hall, was resented by every right thinking student." But New Erans won one concession: more room by several blocks for rambling off-campus. Now the ambulatory limits for daters stretched from the foot of Round Top over to the railroad, then down to Penn Street, and from there to Third, with Flag Pole Hill and the hospital the east-most bounds.

Should they run into the president on their off-campus strolls, all students, the code specified, had to salute him by "tipping the hat."

To help orient Hilltop newcomers, the two Ys began to put out, in the fall of 1924, a pamphlet guide called the "Students Handbook." Two years later it was dubbed the "Scout" and, fabrikoid-covered, expanded to 152 pages. It was the bounden duty of freshmen to carry the "Scout" with them at all times.

So stated "frosh regs," a New Era innovation. In the winter of 1925 the Men's Council formed a Tribunal of six seniors and five juniors. Their task was to cook up "customs" to impose upon first-year men. That February the "dink"—black with a green button on top—made its stigmatic appearance on the Hill.

How the Tribunal and upperclassmen lorded it over dink-pated frosh! Freshmen became the campus lackeys, at the beck and call of their superiors. They ushered, they worked on the athletic field, they raised and lowered the flag, they ran errands, they answered the telephone. They had to learn all college songs and yells, performing on the spot at the whim of any upperclassman. They had to attend all home athletic events and all mass meetings of the students, subject to roll call. No off-the-walk short cuts across campus for them. Freezing weather notwithstanding, they could not be seen in public with hands pocketed. They came last in all things — through doors, at the dining hall, at a table, in organizing as a class.

The naive fairly trembled at solemn-feigned Tribunal hearings. Punishment came in funny forms, though some felt humiliated by them. Men in skirts, glaring signs, and peanut rolling episodes became familiar scenes of Tribunal justice at work.

Coed neophytes answered to the Women's Senior-Junior Court, a creature of 1926. Their badge of status was a green band worn on the left arm. They, however, escaped the vassalage borne by men — except for reception room duty. But the keep-off-the-grass ban applied to them, as did memorizing songs and yells and compulsory attendance at certain functions.

Unlike their opposite sex, first-year women got a helping hand, too. In 1926 the YMCA began assigning a "big sister" to each incoming freshman girl. The next year the administration pitched in to help with freshmen orientation days, the importance of which grew with the years.

Frosh customs, beginning with 1927, were removed each spring on Move-Up Day — the time for changing of the guard. This tradition (now defunct), the brainstorm of Telford Blough's editorial cronies, issued from a March 1927 article of theirs in the campus paper. They noted that "heretofore the transition from the old to the new has been uneventful" and called for much more "impressive" procedure. The paper's staff proposed a "brilliant occasion," about a month before commencement, "featuring installation ceremonies, public addresses, an athletic contest in the afternoon, an entertainment in the evening, and a general displaying of class banners, insignia, colors, and regalia."

The plan got immediate support from students and faculty, cheered as "one more big step forward in Juniata's New Era program." Glee Club pianist and science major Silas Shoemaker of Ambler, Pennsylvania, chaired JC's earliest Move-Up Day on Thursday, May 12. One of its highlights was the ground-breaking ceremony for the new men's dorm, in which each class had a hand.

New Erans also pioneered the fall retreats, which in time developed into the student leadership conferences of today. In 1927 the two Y's, at the suggestion of the Stone Church pastor, Foster Statler, sponsored a student retreat a few days prior to the opening of college. It was held at Camp Myler, a Baptist-owned conference site near the breast of the Raystown Dam, where for a number of years the fall retreaters regularly gathered. Originally the emphasis of these "Camp Myler" conferences, as they were called, was religious. But in the 1930s they became two- or three-day diets when student leaders and faculty consultants, under Senate auspices, spent their time goal-setting for the year ahead.

With the New Era came a weekly campus paper: the *Juniatian*. The Press Club had begun to plump for a weekly in the fall of 1923 and circulated a questionnaire among alumni and students. The results gave proof of near-unanimous favor. But the administration expressed its fear that anything less than a monthly could not survive on a subscription basis. Student opinion finally prevailed.

The curtain number of the *Juniata Echo*, which had held sway for thirty-four years, came out in October 1924. The maiden issue of the *Juniatian* appeared on November 6th under the editorship of Stanley Stroup, "campus Romeo" and "man of infinite variety" said his *Alfarata* vignette. In its first year the *Juniatian*, which by May 1925 merited membership in the Intercollegiate Newspaper Association of the Mid-Atlantic States, claimed a circulation of about 550. Then, beginning in 1926, it was included as part of the incidental fees, which gave it financial stability. In another couple of years the *Juniatian* would build up a readership of over 1,225.

A humor column, "The Tommyhawk", cropped up front page of the *Juniatian* on April 7, 1927. "Tommy Hawk" himself always remained anonymous until staff turnover on Move Up Day. Nothing was too sacrosanct for his barbed banter.

Only in 1926 did the fourth estate acquire its own much-needed inner sanctum on campus. It set up editorial offices in one of the basement rooms of Students Hall. There staffers of the *Juniatian* and *Alfarata* mingled with Press Club reporters.

Clubbism, meanwhile, as organized under the Lyceum, fell apart during the New Era generation. Of the five original interest groups, only two were still active the fall of 1926. And even the parent organization itself bit the dust that September.

The *Juniatian* spoke out for recasting the decadent Lyceum system, which was purely literary in purpose, into one more conducive to relaxed sociality. It outlined a scheme that dissolved the old clubs and had the new ones take Greek letter or Indian names. There was the suggestion to keep each coterie small and intimate (twenty-five to thirty members).

The *Juniatian's* ten-point reform plan won quick approbation as "another new Era project." Over the next three years it gave rise to the Alpha Club, Arts Club, Sigma Delta Club, Tapitawe Club, Le Cercle Français, Chemical Colloquium, Home Economics Club, X Club (feminine fencing), Classical Club, Beta Tau Kappa, Ministerium, and Freshman Club. The two Ys and the Volunteer Group remained solidly entrenched, as did the dual glee clubs.

Another spawn of the "new Era project" was the Dramatic Club, redenominated the Masquers in 1927. It debuted early in the Jubilee Year with James Barrie's "Quality of Life." JC thespians in 1927 began to compete in the Pennsylvania State Intercollegiate Dramatic Association contests, besides staging two or three plays on campus each year.

In December 1928 the Press Club renamed itself the Juniata College Press Association, to distinguish it—as a news organization—from the social clubs. Its reportage now fell under the journalistic eye of the director of publicity—Telford Bough '27 the first year and Claude Flory '29 the next four. More than a hundred papers in four states and the District of Columbia received news releases. The JCPA was then the sole avenue to the *Juniatian* staff.

New Era debate, editorialized the campus weekly in 1927, was still "big time." Its status as a major sport on the Hill was enhanced the Jubilee Year when it, like the *Juniatian*, was budgeted under incidental fees. In May 1927 Juniata got a chapter of Tau Kappa Alpha, the national honorary forensic society, then with some sixty active locals. The charter group consisted of Telford Blough, Rufus Reber, Swirles Himes, Samuel King, Raymond Morris, and Claude Flory. As for coeds, Ruth Culbert (Longenecker), Naomi Trostle (Jones), and Marion Commons (Hayes) were subsequent chapter inductees. TKA thereafter assumed sponsorship of Juniata debate and oratory.

The 1927-28 men's team, coached by Dr. Elmer Craik and co-captained by Flory and Morris, argued its way to an impressive 12-3 record. The women sat it out that year, but they were back come the next debating season.

Oratory, debate's sidekick, enjoyed a kind of "varsity" status, too. Hilltop Ciceros, after persistent efforts, made the Eastern Pennsylvania Intercollegiate Oratorical Union in January 1927. Seven colleges, among them Penn, competed in the Union's annual tilt of words. There were also Blue and Gold entries in the National Contest on the Constitution each year. Likewise, JC orators participated annually in the "World Peace" Contest conducted by the Brethren colleges, the finals an Annual Conference event.

Intramurally, the John M. Bailey oratorical contest was joined in 1926 by one in extemporary speaking. Edgar Diehm '17 established it as a prize-bearing memorial to his mother, Emma.

Music was no less "big time" for New Erans, about one-fourth of whom were by 1928 involved in it in some extracurricular way. The orchestra, which had died out after Peter Buys's leave-taking back in 1919, revived under Mrs. Mary Douthett-Desky, the lovely feminist (witness her hyphenated married name) pupil of Leopold Godowsky and Philippe, in 1924.* Dr. N. J. Brumbaugh became the orchestra's oboist and "sugar daddy" upon his 1925 Hilltop return. (He invested over $1,540 of his own money in the orchestra by 1928.)

Instruments were privately owned or donated until N.J. put the bite on President M. G. in 1928 for college funds. M. G. came up with $900, justifying this outlay to the trustees by pointing out that the orchestra "directs the interests of all students to the right kind of music." Then came the punch line: "By the same token it discourages a liking for trashy jazz and dance music." In 1930 Conductor Karl Gilbert's (1927-37) orchestral group numbered in the forties—where it stood for some time to come.

"Trashy jazz," however, suffered little student neglect. A band in 1929, tagged Kappa Phi Psi, specialized in jazz music, and "Klarinet" Tom Knepp '31, JC's answer to Rudy Vallee, led another oft-scheduled troupe of jazzists.

The Men's Glee Club entered the New Era by joining—in 1917—the Pennsylvania Intercollegiate Glee Club Association, which sponsored annual contests for member schools. Prof. Rowland's singers won third place the first time, their best New Era showing.

For many years the gleemen had featured a quartet. But the 1925 quaternity struck out on its own as the "Varsity Four," giving independent programs and making special appearances. They were Cleo Detrick, tenor; Daniel Ziegler, second tenor; George Detweiler, baritone; Robert Cassady, bass.

---

*Her husband, Donald Desky, taught art at Juniata for two years (1923-25) and later made quite a name for himself as an interior decorator. He designed John D. Rockefeller, Jr.'s home and New York City's Radio City Music Hall.

Not to be outdone, the Girl's Glee Club delivered its skirted version of a foursome the next year: Esther Zook (Grove), first soprano; Edith Clark (Shoemaker), second soprano; Mildred Cassady (Clair), first contralto; Mary Grove (Fouse), second contralto.

Quartets—his and hers—were permanent fixtures on campus long after the 1920s.

Spiritual Emphasis Week was another New Era phenomenon. After three decades the special Bible session, which had once exerted a strong stimulus to campus religious life, gave its death rattle in December 1925. Its original prime purpose, an exercise in adult education, was now being served by the college in other off-campus ways. Moreover, its relevance had been lost on most students of the "Roaring 20s."

The Bible session's reincarnation as a more student-oriented spiritual experience—with messages on timely topics and opportunity for personal counseling—came about through a five thousand dollar gift by Mrs. May Oller Wertz of Waynesboro. It funded bringing in "recognized" clergymen and scholars able to relate to college youth. Dr. Andrew Mutch, M. G.'s Scottish friend and pastor of the Bryn Mawr Presbyterian Church, inaugurated the new approach, which, as Spiritual Emphasis Week, remained a regular campus event for the next forty years.

Men of the public press provided New Era "brains" with out-of-class sport befitting their interest and abilities. Joseph Biddle, publisher of Huntingdon County's first daily newspaper, rescued the General Information Test in 1928 when the death of its previous patron threatened its cancellation. And President M. G.'s friend Edward Stackpole, owner of the *Harrisburg Telegraph*, set up an annual prize for the best student essay on the history and development of the Juniata Valley. Thomas Knepp of Yeagerstown, Pennsylvania, the woodwind jazzist, was the lead-off winner in 1929, as well as the two succeeding years. Essayists locked pens for the twenty-five dollar prize until the early 1960s.

All the while, the "Gin and Jazz Age" confirmed college authorities in their desire to turn out a different brand of American. "Chivalrous Manhood, Womanly Deportment and Public Decorum"—these were Juniata's ideals of character and conduct, the catalog gave tongue in bold print. Certain prizes sought to uphold these qualities among Hilltop denizens. One of them, in memory of Justina Marstellar Langdon, was established in 1927, awarding fifty dollars to "that girl in the College who best exemplified the spirit of helpfulness to others, gentleness of character and loyal devotion to the College." Another one, a 1928 memorial to Huntingdon's George Warfel, carried the same monetary reward for two students each — a coed and a fellow — who "give the best expression of the grace of obedience as a fundamental virtue in religion, social life and business activities."*

And, of course, for New Era conviviality there was always the College Inn a few doors downstreet — "Skip's" to all generations of Juniatians who crowded its compact interior. The first "Skipper" was Edward Gutshall, whose "just off campus" combination grocery store and snack shop had a mid-1920 opening. He had once been a conductor of the "Toonerville Trolley," hence his nickname and that of his cafe.

Among the male habitués of Skip's Inn, Greta Garbo was by actual poll their favorite Hollywood pin-up actress.

Juniata New Era women, much less idolatrous, learned in November 1926 that they qualified for associate membership in the American Association of University Women after college.

JC seniors in 1928 introduced a College ring. The next-year seniors ordered what became the standard design for some while — blue cut stone with a Roman gold shank, an Indian head on one side and class numerals on the other.

NEW ERA ATHLETICS AND THE JUNIATA "INDIANS"

It was the Alumni Association that called for an Athletic Board of Control representing the various Juniata constituencies interested in its sports program.** This idea was adopted in the fall of 1928. The first seven-member board consisted of the president; Oscar Myers and Jack Oller (faculty); Ronald Siersema (head coach); Lewis Knepper (trustee); Chester Langdon (alumni); and George Beery (student body). These men passed on the intercollegiate schedule (student managers still did the scheduling for each sport) and directed athletic policies in general.

Chet Langdon was, of course, an honorary alumnus, but all Hilltoppers knew of his rabid interest in Juniata's sports program. The 1930 *Alfarata* was dedicated to him, "in truth, a loyal Juniatian." For many he symbolized the progressive ideal set for New Era athletics.

His father, John, left the college ten thousand dollars for a new athletic field in late 1928. M. G. had gone on record the previous year for redeveloping the old site into a park and a residential area for college families. Langdon Field he visioned located on the north campus in the little hollow back of the new dorm.

*The Langdon prize, still awarded, first went to Ruth Culbert (Longenecker) and Zola Meyers (Detweiler), both of the Class of '27.
**The Athletic Board of Control dissolved soon after World War II.

Chet put a Philadelphia architect to work at once. The plan was to fill in the hollow, which was started, and allow it to settle for several years. But then the depression came along and the project was abandoned. The Langdon money, however, was kept on the books as a segregated fund. The original sum would grow sevenfold by the time Langdon Baseball Field materialized some thirty years later.

"Athletics for all" became the New Era slogan of the revitalized physical education department. The first full-time woman in the department was Miss Florence Bain, hired in 1927 (there had been part-time female directors since 1924). Another addition to the gym in 1928, for coaching staff offices, brought the structure to its present size.

An extensive intramural program, both for men and women, now went into operation, built upon class rivalry. Through interclass sports — softball, basketball, hockey, soccer, track, volleyball — coeds had a chance to win their "J." A Women's "J" Club had organized in the spring of 1926 when basketball and hiking were the only athletic outlets for the campus belles. (Six hundred miles a year of hiking, a club sport beginning in 1925, earned a coed her Old English "J.")

Pre-New Era varsity teams had no "fighting" nickname. They were simply the "Blue and Gold." Then in the spring of 1925 the *Juniatian* stumbled on the sobriquet "Indian." It was headlined in an article (April 9) about the opening game of the baseball season with Penn State. The JC nine were "Indians" the rest of the schedule. The name stuck in the fall in the paper's coverage of pigskin play, and no one has come up with a better one since.

In football New Era Indians were not always the most fearsome. They were victoryless from October 11, 1924 to November 5, 1927 (though two ties). Who could blame the trustees for wailing that football, "with all its disasters, losses, and problems. . ., is. . .most perplexing for the small college?"[27]

However, the New Era's 1929 grid squad, captained by Bernard "Fuzzy" Andrews, the high-scoring quarterback, went down in Juniata's sports annals for more illustrious reasons. Its 5-3 record stood out as the most successful on a won-lost percentage for the next ten years. And it was the only Indian eleven until 1948 to rack up four straight wins in a single season.

From the start footballers had been honored each year by a YMCA-sponsored banquet for them. But the Jubilee Year brought recognition to the sport in a very special way, M. G. the instigator. He got Dr. and Mrs. Thaddeus Hyatt of Brooklyn, New York, "two very dear friends" of his, to furnish a trophy—a silver cup—to go each year to the student who excelled in three areas: "football, scholarship and character." Thus presidentially favored, this award never lacked for prestige among the nonathletic ones. Clarence Pentz, a four-year end, was the 1926 recipient of the Hyatt Cup —along with the A. B. Brumbaugh Science Prize (Pentz also set several track marks, since broken).

In retrospect, the New Era shines forth as a golden age in Hilltop track. Spiked shoe artists twenty-five times eclipsed standing college marks and bettered conference records in five events. The Elmira, New York, flash and strongman, Alden "Holsie" Holsinger (high hurdles, javelin, discus, shotput), was a four-time conference record-setter. His exploits in the 1928 Central Pennsylvania Intercollegiate Meet at Bucknell had all the glamor of a Frank Merriwell performance. The "Bulldog," thrice team captain, reset three CPIM records and one JC record, winning four first places and two thirds. (Holsinger also played football and captained the 1930 baseball team.)

The undefeated 1927 trackmen did their part to fill the trophy case Chet Langdon had recently donated. They were winners at the Penn Relays in April, not the last time JC spikemen would break the tape first in the City of Brotherly Love. In a downpour and ankle-deep mud, Juniata's "four horsemen"—Captain Harry Trout, Edward Apel, Ralph Leiter, Harry Bower—trotted to a sloggy victory. The college got a handsome bronze trophy, the fellows each a gold wristwatch. Two weeks later at Muhlenburg the team won the CPIM Class B trophy for the third consecutive year, which made the Blue and Gold its owners.

On a seasonal basis, New Era basketball broke even—three winners (1924-27) and three losers (1927-30). The 1924-25 team was the winningest, with a 9-6 log under Captain Walter Grove. "Big, fast, smart and well-coached," was the *Pittsburgh Post*'s description of the Indians that year. The paper said further: "Few college teams have played in Pittsburgh this year that are better than Juniata." A guard on that quintet was Philip "Mike" Snider, "J"-man in four sports and soon to begin his long association with the college as coach and athletic director.

Indian maidens, meanwhile, compiled a 12-19 six-year roundball won-loss mark. The winning teams were in 1928 (4-2) and 1929 (3-2), captained by Center Geraldine "Gerry" Laing and guard Marion "Patsy" Neff (Baker) respectively. For a couple of years coed hardcourters were treated to a training table. But, alas, the New Era faculty was no respecter of sex, and more than one lady tosser ran afoul of academic probation.

New Era baseball enjoyed only two winning seasons, 1926 and 1930. The worst won-lost record was in 1927 (4-10) , the year Babe Ruth hit sixty homeruns for the New York Yankees. But the 1930 Indians went 13 and 4, making them, by the *Alfarata*'s rating system, "undisputed champions of the colleges of the Keystone State." Each player on the 1930 team, led by first baseman "Fuzzy" Andrews, wore a black band on the left sleeve of his uniform, mourning the preseason death of Dr. M. G.

Tennis, lamented the 1925 *Alfarata*, "is one sport which is on the decline at Juniata." Yet its overall six year tally of fourteen wins and twenty-one losses was creditable enough. Curiously, thirteen ties were registered by New Era netmen. The captains were John Ellis, 1925; Tobias "Toby" Henry, 1926; none in 1927; Claude Flory, 1928 and 1929; and Alvin "Undy" Underkoffler, 1930. For varsity and general Hilltop use, eight tennis courts served the campus by 1929.

Few New Era fans sat mute at athletic events after the Kat Klub began bellowing cheers in 1928. The golden-sweatered Kats, who replaced the old Pep Club, were recruited by Huntingdon's Marlin Stewart. Though undersize, the "Monk" was a human dynamo, magnetic in personality.

NEW ERA CAMPUS LOOK

New Era dreams produced few direct physical changes on the Hill. Some alterations were minor but frought with sentiment. A clock replaced the circular window on front of Founders Hall—a gift from the Class of '25. John Steen '31 gave the money for a new flagpole on the north campus, its present site. In the Thirties each academic year began with a formal flag-raising, led by the president. The Orphanage, an eyesore and standing less than a stone's throw from the Cloister arch, came down the fall of 1929.

But other advances were of greater moment. Foresightedly, the trustees snapped up more land. The purchase of three large tracts of ground netted seventeen acres, pushing Juniata real estate northward to Cold Spring Road and eastward to Warm Springs Avenue. This created an entire campus of slightly more than forty acres by 1926. It was necessary for the borough to close and cede to the college certain streets and alleys on these undeveloped properties.

Also, there was some college-related construction: a triad of buildings. But only one had a main-campus setting. Two were independently financed, and one of these had strings attached.

First in order was the Mission Home, erected in 1925. It was trustee Ardie Wilt, an Altoona businessman, who popularized the idea of making Juniata a rent-free habitation for missionaries on furlough. He got the Brethren Sunday schools of Central Pennsylvania to raise twenty thousand dollars for that purpose. They built a two-story, brick-veneered, forty-eight-foot structure, which was then turned over to the college, owner of its corner site at Washington and 18th streets. When not occupied by mission-field returnees, the four-room apartments, two on each floor, were rented out to married students or faculty families. The president himself lived in the Mission Home before he built a place of his own.

The Cloister was next, in 1928—the lone monument, as we have noted, to New Era money-grubbing. At a cost of just over \$140,000, it was designed to take care of 102 students. The architect was Edwin Brumbaugh, who enjoyed great success with his original interpretations of the German colonial style. M. G. said of his son's campus masterpiece: "There is nothing like it in college architecture in America. It will be distinctive of Juniata."[28] Until 1933, however, the Cloister, projected as part of a quadrangle in a new complex of buildings, had no name. It was simply "The Men's Dormitory" to everybody.

A President's House came last, but not for total college use until very recently. M. G., as a Mission Home occupant, was greatly handicapped in entertaining big-money prospects, a fact he brought to trustee attention as early as December 1924. The board, sympathetic, commissioned Edwin Brumbaugh to prepare plans. But when estimates of construction costs proved excessive (over thirty thousand dollars), nobody, including M. G., voted to go ahead.

Other alternatives came under consideration over the next several years. One was to buy trustee Harry Cassady's home (now Swigart Hall), whose owner began in 1925 to lay out the Taylor Highland of today. Another was to remodel the H. B. Brumbaugh place. A third possibility was to build a two-story income-producing apartment house on campus. A fourth option was to donate a plot of ground on which M. G. could build a residence of his own, to be bought by the collge when he vacated it.

However, the limited success of the Jubilee Fund ruled out the first three options, and so M. G. decided to take matters into his own hands. He put up twenty-eight thousand dollars and Joseph Oller twelve thousand, both gifts in the form of low-interest annuities. The college, which then assumed the mortgage for the house, donated three lots on the corner of Mifflin and 18th streets. Edwin Brumbaugh drew the plans, modeling them after the architecture of the Cloister. Finished the spring of 1930, the forty-seven thousand dollar duplex was planned with two separate entrances, one for each street. Dr. and Mrs. Brumbaugh, as renters, were to live upstairs, a faculty family below. The house, however, was to revert to the college after he and his wife were both gone.

ALUMNI AND THE NEW ERA

At long last the alumni got a full-time secretary: Telford Blough of Johnstown, in 1927. "Tel," a fresh grad, had been a two-time debate captain and student journalist *extraordinaire*. His successor in 1929 was Lewis Knepper, who combined the position with college fund-raising.

In other developments, a 1928 constitutional amendment made all nongrad Juniatians eligible for association membership. And by 1930 two more cities were hosting alumni chapters: Harrisburg and New York. Several new countywide groups had New Era origins: Bedford, Blair, Cambria, and Huntingdon.

Out of the New Era came the Women's League of Juniata College, initially a quasialumnae organization. Mrs. Bunn Van Ormer, who had been president of a similar college sorority, sparked its rise. The first League formed in Bessie Rohrer's Waynesboro, Pennsylvania, home on April 14, 1928. Others would spring up at similarly strong alumni centers, all in Pennsyvlania. But these leagues, generous in College support, were products of the next decade. A Central Women's League was still twenty years away.

M. G.'s DEATH

Juniata's New Era president was going full-gallop at the time of his death, outside honors falling into his lap despite senescence. He was state chairman of the Christmas Seal Campaign in 1928 and 1929. The latter year fellow presidents of Pennsylvania colleges elected him head of their association. When he died he had his heart set — even at age sixty-seven — on becoming State Superintendent of Public Instruction. He thought the next governor would be his friend Francis Brown, who, the loser to Gifford Pinchot in the Republican primaries, had promised him the post.[29]

The first week of March 1930, M. G., after a thorough physical checkup, left for a vacation at Pinehurst, North Carolina, a mecca for golf enthusiasts, where he was a familiar figure. On Friday afternoon the 14th he collapsed on the Country Club links just after playing the eighth tee. His partner in a foursome was John Kunz of Huntingdon. He was taken to the clubhouse and then to the Carolina Hotel where he died at

1:30 P.M. His burial on the original Brumbaugh homestead near Marklesburg took place the following Tuesday.

M. G.'s end came before he had a chance to move into the new
President's Home.

10

Surviving the Depression 1930-1943 (Part I)

CHARLES CALVERT ELLIS: JUNIATA'S "ARNOLD OF RUGBY"

On Founders Day 1930 Deems Taylor, internationally famed composer whose father had once taught at Juniata (1880-81), was to have spoken and received an honorary degree. But M. G.'s sudden death so close to the event caused the trustees to cancel all arrangements. They met instead that day to name the next president.

Theirs was an obvious choice: Juniata's own veep. Dr. Ellis had been associated with the college almost uninterruptedly for forty-two years, ever since he first came as a student in 1888. Thirteen years vice-president, he was at the time probably peerless in Brethren higher education. But as an educator, writer, and speaker his reputation ranged far beyond the Brotherhood. He was "long ripe for a presidency" declared Dr. Frank Graves, New York State Commissioner of Education, at inaugural ceremonies in October.

With Dr. C. C.'s promotion the thirty-seven-year-long Brumbaugh dynasty came to an end. Over the thirty-eight ensuing years the Ellises— father and son—would make their family name equally respected in Juniata's annals of presidential succession. It was the father's lot, however, to steer the college through thirteen difficult years not only in *its* history, but in that of the nation.

At fifty-five, Dr. C. C., trim and distinguished-looking, was an unassuming man, though somewhat stern, who wore pinch-nose eyeglasses and high celluloid shirt collars. Only Anna Groninger (Smith), it was joked, could read his handwriting, which he readily admitted was all but indecipherable. Husky-voiced, he had a throaty, infectious chuckle and,

239

as a platform orator, was a master storyteller. The Chautauqua circuit and teacher institutes, where he had been a sought-after name, would now occupy less of his time. Initially, though, his four thousand dollar president's salary meant a reduction in personal income, which before had been padded by lecture fees.

Juniata's fifth president, like a true heir of classical Protestantism, believed in Luther's doctrine of vocation—that God "calls" Christians to particular tasks. Accordingly, he put a theological interpretation upon the honor paid him by the trustees. In a letter to them upon his preferment he wrote: "I accept it as a call of duty to a service for our common Lord."[1] This notion of his presidency as one of divine trust came out again when he was formally inducted. He said, in the course of his brief remarks: "I accept this position as a God-given responsibility for which I shall expect to answer to Him in the coming Day, and with the hope that in His Providence I may find at the end of the way also a bit of reward for a duty at least faithfully undertaken."

On his desk, the new incumbent told inaugural-day well-wishers, he had placed the picture of Thomas Arnold, the mid-nineteenth-century headmaster of Rugby School in England. Dr. Ellis liked to identify the English educator, whom he had made the subject of one of his most popular Chautauqua lectures, as his "pedagogical patron saint." On Arnold's picture there was an inscription, which C. C. publicly vowed, would constitute his presidential motto. It read: "God grant that I labor with entire confidence in Him and none in myself without Him."

C. C.'s DESIGN FOR JUNIATA

In a real sense, then, Dr. Ellis conceived the presidency—for himself at least—as inherently a divine commission. There was about his regime, as a result, always a certain note of urgency. He once said, "The consistent aim of this administration has been to justify to our friends and to all who learn of Juniata the term 'Christian College,' a designation for which we make no apology."[2] Upon becoming president he inserted a strong catalog statement that affirmed: "The College is distinctively Christian in spirit and teaching, emphasizing the beliefs and the ideals of character and conduct which are presented in the Bible." And to the trustees he gave the assurance early on that "the College is making a wider appeal to Christian people than [ever] before." The faculty continued to be selectively recruited from "Evangelical denominations," to use C. C.'s terminology, and from among candidates who were "active Christians" committed to the "fundamentals." Indeed, Juniata had the "right to expect. . .by virtue of her history as by the inevitable logic of events," the preacher-president declared one time, a teaching force of this character.[3]

As a "Christian College," Juniata justified its existence, Dr. C. C. was wont to say, only when engaged in shaping the character of students. Scholarship, though important, was not enough. Paraphrasing the Harvard naturalist Louis Agassiz, another of his teacher-models, he wrote while a novice president: "Laboratory and library, dormitory and dining hall, must not be strangers to the wholesale happiness of life that is unashamed to acknowledge God."[4] And when retired he said retrospectively of his hegemonic years: "May I make emphatic the fact that, whatever her shortcomings or the failures of individuals, Juniata has not been guilty of the impossible divorcement of Christian morality from the Christian religion."[5]

The all-vital factor in character building, ran the Ellis refrain, was the teacher. In a 1937 article for the journal *Christian Education*, President C. C. declaimed: "To conserve the permanent values we need more than scientific procedures and more than social goals; we need teachers whose faces are toward the light and whose feet are moving toward the goals of God."[6] At Juniata he wanted professors to be an Agassiz, seeing God in the laboratory, or a Thomas Arnold, seeing Him in history. As one faculty member, a refugee from Hitlerian Germany, learned when called on the presidential carpet, even mild expletives like "damn" or "hell" were not then a public part of Hilltop vocabulary.

Free inquiry as an academic exercise and right was thus no more countenanced under Charles Ellis than it had been before. In Bible courses, for example, the methodology and theories of "higher criticism" — the scientific analysis of vocabulary, style, and historical allusions as a means of determining the authorship and composition of biblical books — were anathema. Any book or article questioning the uniqueness of Christ was banned from reading lists. A student in one of Dr. Ellis's own Bible courses who might raise a touchy, unorthodox point would get a piercing look from the man and this stock reproof: "Doesn't the love of Christ constrain you?" It was a shattering retort for most unsure JC skeptics.

Yet among the science faculty Dr. Ellis, a creationist by persuasion, made little attempt to clip the wings of evolutionists. As a conservative-fundamentalist theologian he resisted, of course, the conclusions and implications of Darwinian biology because they seemed to strike at the very root of a biblically grounded faith. And as president he took a proprietary interest in what students were assigned to read on the subject of evolution. Thus when asked for an official statement from an irate alumnus or elder, he would always insist Juniata stood for creationism.

But C. C. was not ignorant of efforts on the part of evolutionists since long before the Thirties to harmonize their doctrine with the tenets of Christianity. Some of them were Bible scholars he respected who saw no reason why creation as described in Genesis should be regarded as inconsistent with developmental theories. The *Sunday School Times*, in a necrological notice on his death in 1950, stated well his position on the historic tensions between science and religion. The paper said: "[He] sought never to compromise on the fundamentals of the faith, holding that although theories of science and religion may sometimes conflict, true science is in accord with the Bible, which is the unshakable and unchangeable Word of God."[7]

For JC scientists, then, the classroom was preserved more or less as an open forum. Still, campus Darwinists kept a low profile, much to C. C.'s satisfaction.

Though Dr. C. C. wanted the term "Christian College" to be Juniata's trademark, he never meant to disavow or play down the college's Brethren ties. In fact, no Hilltop *duce* up to his time was more honored in the Brotherhood or gave greater service to the church than he. He was three times moderator of Annual Conference—1935, 1944, and 1950; only a handful of twentieth-century Brethren have been as often elected to that office. For several years he was a director of Bethany Biblical Seminary.

Most importantly, though, all through the Thirties decade he was chairman of the denomination's General Education Board. During that time he did much to help unify the work of the then seven Brethren colleges. The Education Board under his chairmanship authorized an in-depth survey of these colleges by the executive secretary of the Association of American Colleges, Dr. Robert Kelly. The Kelly report, published in 1933, "became a distinct stimulus to college improvement in the whole brotherhood," wrote Dr. Ellis in his 1947 Juniata history.[8] JC's raison d'être, its president was quoted in the Kelly report, was "service to the Brethren Church" and "middle class folk."

On the strictly academic side Dr. Ellis's proudest moment as president came in November 1940. At the chapel program on Wednesday, the 27th, he said, "I am about to make the most important announcement I have ever made to any student body of Juniata College."[9] He then revealed that he had just received word of the school's recognition by the Association of American Universities, the highest accrediting agency in the United States. (The AAU discontinued its evaluation of undergraduate institutions in 1948).

This had been his professed presidential goal since taking office. The decade-long dream, in unfolding, produced a fresh, imaginative curriculum, the strongest Hilltop faculty up til then, and sent more students off to graduate and professional schools than ever before. Juniata was the only Brethren college to be approved by the AAU. In 1940 less than one-third of Pennsylvania colleges had yet made its accepted list.

Then in 1942 the chemistry program brought the sanction of the American Chemical Society, adding another feather to Juniata's academic cap. JC was one of the first small colleges in the nation to make the society's list and as late as 1949 there were only sixteen of seventy Pennsylvania colleges and universities on it. By the time the elder Ellis made way for the younger the college had become well certificated. Besides having the approbation of the AAU and the ACS and being accredited by Middle States, the Juniata Valley's only college was recognized by the Pennsylvania State Council of Education, the Pennsylvania Board of Law Examiners, the Board of Regents of the University of the State of New York, and the American Medical Association. Since the 1920s it also held membership in the American Association of Colleges. And in 1940 Juniata linked up with the American Council on Education, the principal coordinating organization for higher education in this country.

Juniata and the Church of the Brethren were not the only concerns of Dr. Ellis while president. He also wrestled with education problems facing the state of Pennsylvania. In 1931 Dr. James Rule, Superintendent of Public Instruction, named him to a commission charged with the responsibility of developing a ten-year program for public education. This appointment lasted until 1935. From 1939 to 1943 he served on another Department of Public Instruction task force, this time the appointee of Superintendent Luther Ade. His committee work over those years was largely devoted to the study of ways to improve the professional training and standing of Keystone State teachers. One noteworthy gain in this area as a result was a Teachers' Tenure Law in 1937 (amended in 1939), which assured a teacher, after a two-year probationary period, of a continuing position from which there could be removal only for cause.

For the year 1936-37 Dr. Ellis was elected head of the College Presidents Association of Pennsylvania, the organization of liberal arts colleges. This office thrust him right into the thick of the fight to guarantee a place for such colleges in the educational picture of the state. At that time there were fifty-seven accredited colleges and universities in Pennsylvania with approximately fifty-eight thousand students enrolled. Slightly less than ten thousand of these students were to be found at state teachers' colleges, of which there were fourteen. Lobbyists for this segment of higher education began to make ominous noises in the legislature, pushing to restrict teacher preparation in Pennsylvania to the fourteen tax-supported institutions.

Liberal arts colleges took alarm. Such an eventuality would deprive them of an educational enterprise intrinsically a part of their historical baggage. Their distinctive contribution in schooling teachers, it was argued, had always been one of a broad, cultural nature. By contrast, the state teachers' colleges were perceived as being avowedly professional schools. Liberal arts colleges, the argument went, have given the prospective teacher an opportunity to wait, to weigh, to measure, to form a ripened judgment before deciding upon a profession.

Moreover, there was real fear, with a worsening depression, that eliminating their education programs would kill off or seriously cripple not a few struggling private colleges. To meet the competition and the threat posed by the erstwhile normal schools, heads of thirty-two privately supported institutions banded together in the Association of Liberal Arts Colleges of Pennsylvania for the Advancement of Teaching. The association took the stand that preparation of secondary teachers should be left to their people, conceding the training of grade teachers to the state colleges. It further held that teacher programs in special fields, like music, home economics, commercial education, industrial arts, physical education, and art should be given in institutions especially qualified for that work, as authorized by the State Council of Education.

The outcome of this particular public-vs.-private college spat was more or less a draw. Stiffer standards for teacher training programs in all fields—elementary, secondary, and special—were established, and any institution meeting these standards had the right to prepare teachers. That has been the law of the Commonwealth ever since.

Juniata College, thanks to its president and to Harvey Brumbaugh, was no bystander to the solutions forged out at the state level on the teacher-training issue. Dr. Brumbaugh chaired the Association of Liberal Arts Colleges' important Committee on Code and Legislation. And Dr. Ellis, as the agent of more than one educational interest in the hassle, was uniquely able to bring a broad, conciliatory perspective to the search for answers.

All the while, an urgent presidential plea went out to the JC faculty at the start of each academic year. The call was for one hundred percent membership in the Pennsylvania State Education Association, which boasted on the Hill an active chapter.

C.C.'s "BRAIN TRUST" AND FACULTY

The office of vice-president was abolished when C. C. moved up in 1930. It was offered to I. Harvey at the time, but he turned it down, questioning the usefulness of a double-headed command at a school of Juniata's size. The trustees came to see it his way, though they hoped to keep him axial to the operation of the college. And so, upon giving him an honorary degree (L.H.D.) they made him secretary of the board, to replace the retiring Allan Myers.

Dr. Ellis, for guidance in presidential decision-making, created an Administrative Council. At first there was, besides himself, Dr. I. Harvey and Treasurer Oscar Myers. Campus insiders whimsically referred to them as the "Unholy Three." Later, upon Harvey Brumbaugh's death in 1937, Dr. Calvert Ellis, who succeeded to the board secretaryship, joined the administrative troika. There still was no dean of the college, though Ellis the son virtually functioned as one by the end of his father's presidency.

Juniata came through the depression fiscally battered, but intact, no paycheck having been so much as a day late, largely because of the purse-strings wizardry of brain-truster O. R. Myers. He was an exceptional man. The ex-English prof, a bow tie his sartorial signature, never wanted to become treasurer back in 1924. He gave in to the trustees only out of a sense of duty. The 1930s brought him the ungrateful task of *not* spending money, and his tight control of finances helped save the college to serve another day. He developed an amazing capacity for stretching a dollar. He guaranteed college solvency by iron-handedly denying credit to fund-less students. "Nickle Snatcher" some churlishly called the Brethren elder and State Sabbath School worker behind his back. Those in the know, however, were well aware of his countless good-samaritan bursary acts. Many a time he salvaged a semester—or a degree—for someone by personally interceding for a bank loan or arranging for an on-campus job. Myers-bossed assistant treasurers over the years were Myrtle Walker to 1935 (she began in 1913), Edward Weber (1935-39), and Fred Livingston (1939-42).

"Professor O. R.," as he was commonly addressed, died at age sixty-eight in 1942 while still in office. His treasurer-council position was filled by William Price, an alumnus '84 and trustee. Earlier, as chairman of the board's finance committee from 1936 on, the Royersford, Pennsylvania, native had helped Oscar Myers institute a modern accounting system on the Hill. It was he who put the deeding of college real estate into order and developed for trustee use a more complete auditing method. In improving Hilltop accountancy he drew upon the expertise of Charles Rice, then a teacher in the department of economics and business administration and today a trustee from Altoona.

When Mr. Price took O. R. Myers' post he was nearly eighty years old and long since retired as treasurer of the *Philadelphia Evening Ledger.* Remarkably energetic, the Brethren churchman would adroitly balance the books all through the leaner-than-the-depression war years. His able office aide was Rhoda Metz, from Big Valley, wife-to-be of Melvin Rhodes, who became dean of students in 1947.

In 1936 alumnus Harold B. Brumbaugh '33 appeared on the administrative scene titled Assistant to the President. A nonbrain truster, the ex-math teacher and high school principal was put in charge of public relations. As such he was a fund-raiser, taking the place of the field secretary. His job also included student admissions, an operation that then pretty much resided in the president's office. This meant following up on contacts made by Joe Yoder in his high school visits.

Harold, a distant kin to the founding Brumbaughs, would practically make Juniata his whole life for the next forty years — to the day of his retirement. "Brummy," his pre-"H. B." nickname stayed spouseless, living in dormitory apartments. For many years it was the Cloister Arch; after 1966 he would billet in an elegant Tussey-Terrace suite, designed specially for him. Tall and slender, with wavy hair, he built up a tailor-crafted wardrobe that over the years earned him the eclat of best-dressed man on campus.

However, it was as alumni secretary — from 1939 to 1962 — that H. B. won his way into the hearts of untold Juniatians. *Mister Juniata* has been the way generations of grads have come to think of him, born with ambassadorial instincts. One day the American Alumni Council would find it fit to salute, because of Harold Brumbaugh's work, the filial loyalty of his alma mater's scholastic family.

There was among other noncouncil Ellis administrators — as with the faculty — a high degree of stability despite the hard times. But, of course, higher education then, like most sectors of the national economy, afforded little or no mobility.

The biggest turnover of administrative personnel occurred with student deans. In 1930 Fayette McKenzie's deanship went to Warren Bowman, a Brethren elder with a Chicago Ph.D. in psychology. He left in

1935, later to become president of Bridgewater College, and was followed by Clyde Stayer. A gifted math teacher, "Prof" Stayer built the reputation during his twelve years as dean of being a "fair dealer" with the men on campus.

As dean of women there succeeded Katharine Roberts in quick order Liberty McClelland (1933-34) and Kathleen Gillard (1934-36). Then in 1936 came New Yorker Edith Spencer, artist and weaver. Dean for the next sixteen years she was a veritable virtuoso in whistling, the star entertainer at many a social event. It was she and Clyde Stayer who began in 1939 to keep an accumulative record file on every student.

Until 1939 the student deans, besides their counseling and disciplinary duties, taught nine hours each semester. After that the teaching load of Miss Spencer was lightened by a couple of courses.

As for the depression-years professoriate, Dr. Ellis has assessed his own administration as one "characterized by a strengthening of the faculty."[10] Aspirations for AAU sanction made this imperative. His goal was a Ph.D. head for every department, which never quite worked out. Nevertheless, by 1937 there were seventeen doctorates scattered throughout a faculty of fifty (this figure dropped to nine out of thirty in 1943).

C. C.'s was the first faculty on the Hill to include women Ph.D.s — four of them during his presidency. Under him three of these ladies, linguists all, unprecedentedly made the rank of full professor. They were: May Keirns, a Chicago-trained classicist (in 1930); Emma Bach, a Johns Hopkins Germanist (in 1931); and Ida Kubitz, another Germanist from the University of Illinois (in 1936). The fourth doctoral holder was historian Bertha Leaman, with a Chicago degree. Professors Keirns and Kubitz put in classroom stints of some while at JC, twelve and ten years respectively. The other two chose to move on after short stays each.

To the cadre of perdurable faculty members it inherited, the Ellis administration superadded, as time would prove, a sizable group of its own. Nine C. C. recruits — all but one appointed during the first half of his presidency — were destined to Hilltop tenures ranging between twenty-two and forty years.

Two perennials were taken on in 1930: Harry Nye and Philip Snider. Prof. Nye was a widely respected Brethren elder who came to Juniata from Elizabethtown College, where he had just put in a year as acting president. Trained as a historian (Penn and Columbia), he taught on the Hill for twenty-three years. Jowly and stately, blessed with a deep, rich voice, the faculty's oft-elected secretary ministered to many of the area's Brethren churches.

P. M. "Mike" Snider was one of Juniata's best known athletes of the middle Twenties. The four-sport letterman came back to coach after four years of high school teaching and working as a surveying engineer. Later trained in physical education, he settled at his alma mater for thirty-eight years, with time out for a Pacific tour as a World War II naval officer.

Another pair of long-termers were 1931 recruits Calvert Ellis and Homer Will. Calvert Ellis had studied at Princeton and Yale after graduating from Juniata in 1923. He took over the Mary S. Geiger Chair of Biblical Studies, later inheriting, after Dr. Van Ormer's retirement in 1939, all philosophy courses as well. Thirty-seven years in all he would give to the college as professor and, in time, president.

Homer Will, a gentle, soft-spoken Virginian, was a Pitt Ph.D. in biology (he had previously taught at Juniata for two years, 1927-29). A naturalist and entomologist, he made his mark on College Hill as a teacher, researcher, and scholar. He became an authority on sawflies, once headed the Academy of Science, and was elected a Fellow of the American Association for the Advancement of Science. For fifteen years he was editor of the *Pennsylvania Science News Letter*. The student body of the early 1960s voted him Juniata's "most popular professor," captivated by his enthusiasm for biology. Long before Homer Will's thirty-two years on the Hill passed by, his affirmative word on a student meant almost certain admission to any medical school in Pennsylvania.

In 1933 came Donald Rockwell, son of the granite state of Vermont, his Ph.D. in chemistry from Yale. A low-key, large-hearted man, he complemented his department head, the incomparable N. J., whose single ambition was to prepare students for graduate school. Dr. Rockwell understood the person who wished to study chemistry as an elective and not as a major subject. He would wear many academic hats during his forty JC years, among them department chairman, division chairman, and dean of the college. Like a good Yankee, with jack-of-all-trades ability, he loved the outdoors. He was the first faculty member to move out of town—to a run-down farmhouse, which his family rebuilt, along the Cold Spring Road. A hoedown devotee, he became the campus' official square dance caller. Ten generations of Hilltoppers learned "allemande left" and "allemande right" under his patient instruction.

The English department in 1933 gained Harold Binkley, a Canadian (Alberta) and Harvard Ph.D. He came to Juniata from the faculty of the University of Michigan. Dr. Binkley, a very short man sporting a bushy mustache, was a self-ordained cynic who affected a gruff manner. But students soon learned that his bark was worse than his bite. Nevertheless,

Picture of some post-World War II faculty members and administrators a few years after Calvert Ellis (front row, center) became president. However, it includes most of long-termers mentioned in this chapter and recruited by his father, also shown.

Row 1: F. McKenzie, G. Butler, L. Evans, A. Groninger (Smith), M. McCrimmon, E. Spencer, F. Mathias, H. Binkley.

Row 2: C. Rowland, H. Nye, P. Yoder, H. Will, C. C. Ellis, D. Rockwell, H. Kiracofe, J. C. Stayer.

Row 3: H. Brumbaugh, P. Crummy, P. M. Snider, C. Shively, J. Oller.

Inserts: N.J. Brumbaugh (left), E. Dubbel.

he was a scholar with high academic standards, and in his classes there was no room for the slothful or the mawkish. They were doomed to feel the whiplash of his scorn. One of his favorite reprimands was: "Piety is no substitute for learning." During his twenty-nine years at Juniata, Dr. Binkley served as department and division chairman. Among his colleagues, who often found his mordant wit a catalyst to action, he was thought of as an "astute academician and pundit professor."

For the thirty-four years after 1935 home economist Gertrude Butler could be seen flitting here and there across campus in headlong, mincing stride. A native Keystoner, she had received the B.S. degree from both Keuka College (1926) and Juniata (1931), and in 1938 would earn her M.A. at Columbia. Her retirement in 1969 would coincide with the phasing out of the home ec department. But in the interval after 1935 she would shepherd 330 of her "wonderful girls" through their degree programs.

Sandy-haired, forty-two-year-old Edgar Kiracofe joined the faculty in 1937, coming from Elizabethtown College, where he headed the department of psychology and education. The easy-going Old Dominion native took Harvey Brumbaugh's place, vacated by death. His doctorate from the University of Virginia, he made the eighth Brethren minister on the faculty and administration. Destined to become another long-time department and divisional chairman, Dr. Kiracofe was named—in 1939 —the Martin G. Brumbaugh Professor in Education, a title made possible by memorial funds in honor of its namesake. With time, Kiracofe recommendations came to carry the same weight with public school officials as did those of Homer Will with medical schools. His tenure at Juniata lasted twenty-three years.

Accordionist George Clemens, a top JC grad of 1936, came back the next year to teach French. Duty with the Armed Forces took him away between 1942 and 1945. He returned, garnered a Penn Ph.D., and stayed until 1962, when, to Juniata's loss, he resigned to go elsewhere.

Three other men of shorter tenure but who gave academic strength to the faculty were Pressley Crummy, Kenneth Smoke, and Herbert Zassenhaus. Dr. Crummy, a tall, handsome biologist with a Pitt doctorate, appeared in 1937 and became registrar when Russel Stambaugh left in 1942. He resigned after fourteen years to take a position at Kirksville College in Missouri, the first college of osteopathy and surgery in America.

Psychologist Kenneth Smoke, doctored at Ohio state, taught from 1938 to 1946, and then went to Gettysburg College. He was a gentle, kind man, tall and slim as a ramrod, with long, delicate fingers. His lectures were punctuated by an incessant nervous cough, the kind of habit Harvey Brumbaugh had. He met his bride, Lillian Harbaugh '31, an assistant librarian, while at Juniata.

Herbert Zassenhaus, who fled Germany with his Jewish wife, was a Swiss-trained economist. His doctor's degree was from the University of Berne, and his years at Juniata coincided with those of Dr. Smoke. A brilliant scholar, he later became a high-ranking government official in the field of international finance. It was Dr. Zassenhaus whom President C. C. stopped one day on Founders Porch and reprimanded for his strong language in class.

During C. C.'s presidency, then, the college made major gains in professional strength. This was done by a balanced infusion of both Brethren and non-Brethren blood into the faculty. Already by 1936, however, church leaders were reporting that Juniata was unique among its sister schools because it had fewer Brethren on the faculty. For the academic year 1939-40 only fourteen out of a teaching staff of forty-six belonged to the denomination.

Dr. Ellis continued the practice of opening the first faculty meeting of the year with prayer. Beginning the fall of 1936, however, weekly meetings gave way to biweekly ones, lasting no more than an hour generally. With October 1939 the faculty went on a monthly business schedule, the practice to this day. Standing committees were still appointed by the president rather than elected. The traditional trustee-faculty dinner, now a spring affair, originated as a fall mixer in 1932. That same year the faculty were given the option of being paid on a twelve-month instead of a ten-month basis.

The Ellis era, which coexisted with the great social reforms of the New Deal, marked noteworthy advances in faculty fringe benefits. A retirement plan sponsored by the Teachers Insurance and Annuity Association went into effect the fall of 1938. TIAA had formed in 1918 to provide a fully funded, fully vested, portable pension system for college and university teachers. Group health insurance followed two years later. It was worked out through the General Education Board of the Church of the Brethren in cooperation with a major insurance company.

Typical of schools like Juniata, the normal teaching load was fifteen hours a week. There was, of course, only minimal encouragement given to faculty research and publishing. Still, surprisingly, fourteen professors in 1932 claimed authorship of a total of forty-one books and articles.[11]

Because of the financial strains of the age a policy of sabbatical study was infeasible. It was possible, however, for someone with seven years of service to take a leave of absence. During this leave the regular salary went on, but the professor had to provide at his own expense a substitute acceptable to the administration. Only two persons took advantage of this provision.

Faculty salaries at Juniata during the depression were no better or no worse than those at other Brethren colleges like Elizabethtown and Manchester. Under the basic pay scale that obtained from the early Thirties on into the war years, professors got from two thousand five-hundred dollars to two thousand nine-hundred dollars; assistant professors from one thousand dollars to two thousand five-hundred dollars, and instructors from one thousand three-hundred dollars to one thousand eight-hundred dollars. This scale did not apply to the head coach and director of physical education, however. His salary was three thousand five-hundred dollars for a nine-month's contract. Beginning in 1932 the faculty (and all college employees) suffered a series of paycheck cuts to ward off excessive deficits caused by declining enrollment. By 1936 these reductions totaled fifteen percent. Even as late as 1941 salaries were still off-scale by five percent at every rank.

A NEW PHILOSOPHY OF EDUCATION

Midway through C. C.'s presidency Juniata was offering nine different programs, seven of which led to a B.S. degree. But the number of B.A. and B.S. recipients each year usually came out the same. The multiplicity of degree programs, most of which were designed for teacher training, was in large part due to state law. The majority of Juniatians were still going into education work—57.9 percent for the period 1921-31, according to one study of the vocational distribution of graduates.[12] In that same decade ten percent entered business, while 6.9 percent chose some kind of religious service, and 3.7 percent took up graduate study.

But the 1930s, as we saw earlier, set on foot a liberalizing trend in the preparation of Pennsylvania teachers. This opened the way for wholesale curriculum reform at Juniata. A committee composed of Dr. Calvert Ellis, Dr. Harold Binkley, and Dr. Homer Will devised a curriculum, introduced in 1937, that stood for a quarter of a century. The committee was not unaware of the strong vocational outlook of most college students of that day—a fact of higher education in America that would only get worse with time. But it was their desire to develop a curriculum that would give Juniatians "enough contact with a liberal discipline to guarantee that [they] will be *men* as well as *craftsmen*."[13] They reduced nine programs to one.

"What we now have," wrote Dr. Binkley about the committee's handiwork, "is the expression of what amounts to a philosophy of education with respect to this College."[14] He went on to explain: "The curriculum from which we changed was a curriculum accumulated to satisfy the demands of students upon the College; the one we have has been designed to meet the needs of a student in a liberal arts college." The inspiration for Juniata's new curriculum, which got attention in the *New York Times* for its novel features, was Dartmouth College, a pioneer in integrating liberal arts education.

Crucial to the operation of the curriculum was the alignment of departments, now grouped in three divisions:

I. *The Arts and Languages* (Art, Classical Languages, English, French, German, Music, Spanish)
II. *The Social Studies* (Biblical Studies, Economics and Business Administration, Education, History and Political Science, Home Economics, Philosophy, Physical Education, Psychology, Sociology)
III. *The Natural Sciences* (Biology, Chemistry, Drawing, Mathematics, Physics)

The freshman year was highly prescribed. In their first semester all JC neophytes were required to take three "integration" courses, one in each of the divisions: The Arts and Humanities; The Nature of Society; The Nature of Science. The first-semester program was rounded out with The Mind or a foreign language. In the second semester they followed up with introductory electives in each division chosen from a special list, plus Biblical History and continued language study.

It was further required that students take at least six semester hours — beyond the work of the first-year program — in a division other than the one in which they were majoring. The sixth — and last — course requirement was Ethics, for first-semester seniors.

But the capstone of a Juniata education from now on was to be the comprehensive examination. (Actually, "comps" had been around since 1934, when Registrar Russell Stambaugh sold the idea to the faculty.) This final-semester ordeal, the catalog explained, was "a logical continuation of the principle, begun in the Divisional introductions of the first year, of integrating courses of study into a wider understanding of their mutual relations." Students sweated through six hours of "writtens" and an hour-long "oral." Three faculty members, one from outside the student's major division, made up the grand inquisition in each case. Comp marks fell into one of three categories: "distinction"; "pass";

"failure." The last grade meant a delayed diploma, a minor tragedy that struck College Hill nearly every year, it seems. In most cases a retesting a few months later lifted the sheepskin penalty, but not always.

The 1937 curriculum boasted other innovative parts. It put a premium on "competencies" in certain academic areas, intending to prompt initiative. The two-year foreign language requirement, for example, could be met at any time through a special test. As for the "sacred cow of freshman composition," Dr. Binkley once waggishly wrote, it was "quietly and contentedly slaughtered" by the mid-Thirties curricular overhaul. Large-class instruction was replaced by a tutor plan or "conference program," in which each student would meet a half hour every two weeks with an "English adviser." Not all of these advisers came from the English department; "the responsibility for using our language effectively is not to be limited to one special department," Dr. Binkley used to say. Papers were drawn from the integration courses and other freshman offerings, allowing for more flexibility and relevance in the writing experience. Importantly, students could be exempted from writing conferences any time they attained a reasonable standard of proficiency.

Graduates majoring in Division I, of course, received the B.A. degree; those in Division III, the B.S.; Division II majors had a choice.

In 1942 the college went on a more-or-less three-term academic calendar—summer, fall, and winter—designed to allow students to accelerate and finish their work before being called into military service. It was now possible to graduate after three winters and two summers of study.

THE ALTOONA EXTENSION CENTER

Within a fifty-mile radius of Huntingdon in the 1930s were eight other colleges. Two of these were junior colleges—in Johnstown and Chambersburg. There were two teachers colleges and four liberal arts colleges within this area. But until the depression era the upper Juniata Valley, for Protestant students at least, was pretty much JC's "sphere of influence."

Almost from the start of its extension work under the directorship of Dr. Fayette McKenzie, Juniata College had been holding evening classes in the Altoona High School. The school board of that railroad city began to agitate for a junior college in 1930, and the University of Pittsburgh showed some interest in setting one up there. This scared the JC trustees, who protested that Pitt had no business interloping on another school's territory.[15] With little further delay, Hilltop officials okayed, on an experimental basis, a freshman-year college program on Blair County soil.

The Altoona Extension Center opened in September 1933, promotional literature billing the mother institution as "The College of the Juniata Valley." One tenth of the income went to the Altoona School Board for rental charges. Classes met late afternoon and in the evening. The first year sixty-eight Blair Countians entered the freshman program, extension studies claiming another fifty students. On the night of Thursday, March 20, Center Juniatians met in Altoona's 8th Avenue Methodist Church for a special service. At that time they officially adopted an honor code and, with high ceremony, took the Athenian pledge, slightly modified, to signify their loyalty to the college and its ideals.[16]

When the 1937 curriculum went into operation the freshman core courses and other basic first-year offerings took their proper place in the center's academic program. Sixteen Hilltop faculty members, most department heads, made up the teaching force by then, at meager extra pay.

Between 1933 and 1939 146 persons got started in college work at the Center. About 30 of these Altoonans went on to graduate from Juniata. An additional 354 individuals enrolled in some kind of extension study during the same six-year period.

Meanwhile, Penn State, uninvited, tried to move in on the Altoona territory and get a junior college going. But Dr. C. C. successfully fought off any inroads by the Centre County land-grant school. However, sentiment for a junior college was strong in Altoona. Thus, in late 1938 its Board of Education and Chamber of Commerce jointly petitioned Juniata to start one there. The college was offered an unused school building rent-free while the Chamber of Commerce volunteered to raise the funds to equip it.

But after a careful study of the situation the JC Board of Trustees turned the offer down. Not only was there uncertainty about the future, but such a move, it was feared, might jeopardize Juniata's drive for accreditation by the American Association of Universities. With college leave, Altoona city fathers then turned to Penn State, which began its operation of a downtown undergraduate center in the Webster Building the fall of 1939. Reported Dr. C. C. to the trustees after the decision to abandon the Altoona Center to Penn State: "While we cannot but anticipate a temporary disadvantage in our day student enrollment, I am hopeful that ultimately we will reap some advantage in our upper classes."[17] Unfortunately, his was a vain hope, the disaster of Pearl Harbor only months ahead.

OLLER HALL: DREAMS AND DISAPPOINTMENTS

Depression or no, the college was able to buy more land (athletic field addition), give some away, acquire new properties, renovate extensively, and, after a patient wait, put up a badly needed auditorium. Meanwhile, the Cloister got its name.

A flagstone walk in 1932 replaced the rotted boards laid out between the street and the "Men's Dorm," for which the trustees were still trying to think up a name. The next June they came up with the "Cloister," in recognition of M. G. Brumbaugh's interest in early Church of the Brethren history and the style of architecture. The trustees, in a patronymic gesture, then dubbed the Arch the Alexander Mack House (after the church's founder) and the Wing the Christopher Sauer House (after its most famous colonial leader). For some reason this nomenclature never caught on.

In 1932 the college got possession of the T. T. Myers place (for $8,250), across 17th from Carnegie Library, and in 1934 the Crownover corner dwelling (for nine thousand dollars) at 18th and Moore. A frame house behind Oneida Hall became the college infirmary in 1932, the asylum of the Hilltop sick for the next thirty-five years. An addition in 1937 provided two faculty apartments.

The Founders-Brumbaugh complex not only was remodeled by stages into the campus social center, but its transept gained a brick and steel fireproof stairway annex the fall of 1936. Ten o'clock most evenings would find the "fire tower," to use a student expression, a crowded mass of bodies, oblivious couples lining the walls in good-night embraces.

In 1939 the college converted the "love nest," which is what campus wags called the faculty apartment house behind the gym, into a coed dorm. Eighteen women, freshmen and juniors, moved into the building in September. The trustees named it the Geiger House in honor of Mrs. Mary Geiger of Philadelphia, Juniata's early benefactress.

Two years before, the trustees had deeded a small section of land to the borough for a playground. This patch, across Muddy Run below 16th Street, had been leased (one dollar a year) to the borough for recreational use when M. G. was president. He had promised that the college would eventually turn it over to the town, and the 1937 transaction honored that commitment. The West End public playground is still located there.

However, from a buildings-and-grounds standpoint, the one regnant dream of the C. C. Ellis years was the construction of a large music hall. Back in 1926 the college had first gone to the Presser Foundation of Philadelphia for help in such a project. Immensely impressed with the music program at Juniata, the officers finally came through with a proposal in January 1931 that seemed to assure the asked-for hall. The Foundation pledged fifty thousand dollars toward a one hundred thousand dollar structure to be called, when erected, the Presser Music Building.

Wasting no time, the trustees accepted the offer and among themselves quickly raised more than twenty thousand dollars. By midsummer a few selected contacts had accounted for an additional twenty-one thousand dollars. Before the year was out Harrisburg architects had blueprinted a steepled "T"-shaped edifice of American colonial architecture. With a seating capacity between 550 to 600, the auditorium was to stand on the present Oller Hall site.

Then came the setbacks, just when everything was falling into place. Excessive bids, which necessitated cost-cutting adjustments and many a revision in plan and specification, held up progress for another year. But the big blow fell two weeks before Christmas 1932. The Presser Foundation notified the college that the deal was off, at least until the depression bottomed out. "Postponed, not cancelled" was the way its heartbreaking communiqué read in reference to the fifty thousand dollar matching grant. As it turned out, the phrasing should have been reversed.

For beginning in August 1937 the most precipitous economic decline in American history put the finishing stroke to the Foundation's good intentions. The stock market fell by forty-three percent. In all, the economy plunged about one-half as much in nine months as it had from 1923 to 1933.

Yet the college, with Rooseveltian optimism, went boldly ahead with other plans, right in the teeth of this paralyzing mid-New Deal recession. The need for an auditorium and chapel was still there; so was studio space for the music department, which had to take over a third dwelling for that purpose, the T. T. Myers house. The fall of 1937 Pierce and Hedrick of New York City (Bayard Hedrick had a son at Juniata) directed a "national memorial campaign" to raise three hundred thousand dollars. Besides an auditorium and music hall the funds, to be collected over five years, were to go toward the M. G. Brumbaugh endowed chair in education and additional student scholarships. Huntingdon citizens contributed well over thirty-nine thousand dollars, exceeding the town's quota by four thousand. Altoonans, grateful for the Juniata Extension Center, subscribed better than five thousand dollars. By January the nationwide drive had accounted for subscriptions totaling one hundred forty-five thousand dollars. But with war on the horizon that was as close as the college would get to its three hundred thousand dollar goal.

"This is the first generation of students in ten years who will be able to see ground broken for a new college building on this campus," stated Dr. C . C. in a chapel announcement on a late October day in 1939. He then told of the recent trustee vote to construct a one hundred thirty thousand dollar colonial-brick auditorium, designed by the Altoona architect firm of Hunter and Caldwell. It was Dr. Ellis's idea to call the white-pillared structure Oller Hall in honor of the Oller family, especially Jacob, an original trustee, and his son Joseph, the late board president. The 74' x 140' architectural delight was dedicated at an impressive ceremony on Saturday, October 19, 1940. Governor Arthur James was there and spoke, introduced by alumnus William Livengood, Jr. '29, Secretary of Internal Affairs. Despite the snowstorm and cold weather nearly twelve hundred persons shivered through the service.

Oller Hall, still the main auditorium today, contains a large stage, a balconied auditorium seating nine hundred, a projection booth, and two practice-organ rooms. However, the Hall's showpiece is its Moller Organ, donated by alumna Rello Oller '20, sister of Jack, in memory of her parents. *Diapason,* the national organists' magazine, rated the Moller Organ one of the best to be built in 1940.[18] It was designed by Dr. Carl Weinrich, organist at Vassar and Wellesley colleges. The voicing was done by Richard Whitelegg, then one of the outstanding tonal architects of the country. The Moller Organ has three manuals with thirty ranks of pipes (two thousand in all) and forty-three stops, including a set of chimes. Freshman William Wagner, a brilliant musician from Altoona, won the audition held to choose Juniata's first organist.

Within a year, artists such as Rose Bampton, leading soprano of the Metropolitan Opera, and the Tyrolean Trapp Family Singers, directed by the young composer-clergyman Dr. Franz Wasner, had made Oller Hall appearances. Unfortunately, it had not been ready for an April 1940 concert by Bela Bartok, the Hungarian composer-pianist on his second tour of the United States. The music department's Dorothy Domonkos, once a student of his, induced him to come to Juniata for the only college recital given on his tour. It took place in the gymnasium.

THE BOARD OF TRUSTEES OPENS UP

Charter-trustee William Swigart, sixty-one years on the board, died November 22, 1939. Among colleagues his was a weighty voice to the day of his death. Until 1937 he had never missed a commencement on College Hill.

Other key board members were lost by death, among them Joseph Oller, John Fogelsanger, and Walter Englar. Chairman Oller's place was taken by Dr. Gaius Brumbaugh, one of the college's first students and graduates, who would wield the board sceptre until 1952. Both Englar and Fogelsanger made the college residuary legatee of substantial sums, close to fifty thousand combined.

The commencement day trustee meeting in 1939 proved to be quietly historic for the college. It opened the way for a broader representation of interests on the board. The charter was amended to increase the number of trustees to thirty, but the most drastic changes came through bylaws revision in October. The major redaction allowed for one-fifth of the board membership to be non-Brethren. This action greatly upset W. J. Swigart, a month away from dying. He had always argued that "the College was founded by members of the Church of the Brethren and that in the early years money had been contributed on the condition that the College remain affiliated with the Church."[19] But his was the lone voice of protest. However, the board made no change in the bylaws provision that, in case of dissolution, college property reverted to the Church of the Brethren for purposes of christian education.

Another significant reform provided for the election of a college trustee by each of the supporting church districts of Pennsylvania (Western, Middle, and Southeastern) as well as three more by the Alumni Association. Six trustees are still elected this way, each for three years, although as such they are not eligible for reelection.

The first non-Brethren trustee co-opted by the board was Huntingdon's Chester Langdon, an Episcopalian. Chet, who had been a close friend of M. G.'s was to serve thirty years on the board. Before long he was joined by other Protestants elected by the alumni.

As before, there were other newcomers like Chet Langdon who put in long, loyal years on the board. One of them was Samuel Hess of Huntingdon, whose green-thumb touch for forty-one years did much to beautify the campus. John Baker, then assistant dean of the Harvard Business School, came on in 1936. A future university president, he is still a JC trustee. Others included Calvin Bowman (1936-58), a Johnstown educator, and Mahlon Brougher (1930-52), a Greensburg, Pennsylvania, pastor.

"FRIENDS" AND ALUMNI

Their model the Waynesboro group, other Women's Fellowship Leagues sprang up during the depression years. The Huntingdon ladies organized in December 1932. Mrs. Clyde Mierley, their first president, piloted the local League until 1944. In those years the women raised hundreds of dollars for renovation projects and the furnishing of Oller Hall. The formation of similar leagues in Altoona and Johnstown followed in November 1936. A third, the Morrison's Cove League, took shape two months later. These organizations evidenced a like charitable vein.

Charity came from other sources, too, but for a different cause. The 1930s gave rise in many colleges and universities to groups calling themselves "Friends of the Library." Originally the purpose of these "friends" was to constitute a body of sleuths to uncover idle books in the private libraries of the community.

Juniata's librarian, Lillian Evans, the woman behind the founding of the Huntingdon County Public Library in 1935, was the chief promoter of this latest Hilltop movement. The Friends of the Juniata College Library organized at a luncheon held May 15, 1937. Pittsburgh businessman and nonalumnus John Warfel, who for a few years (1926-32) had put up an annual good-conduct prize, was elected the first president. The group, which soon began to issue its *Friends of the Library Bulletin*, adopted the custom of sponsoring commencement-time teas, often featured with a distinguished speaker.

A friendly interest in the college, however, was not much in evidence within general alumni ranks during the 1930s. Former Hilltoppers were told by Association President Harry Wagner in 1934 that only 470 ex-Juniatians out of a possible four thousand five hundred counted as dues-paying ($2.50) members. There was some slight gain the last half of the decade, but not much. Indeed, statistics in 1935 showed that of the 2,457 JC graduates since 1879 the number of contributors among them numbered no more than 771.

But the college did not want for ways of keeping in touch with former students. In 1931 it inaugurated Alumni Week in connection with summer school. This mid-July vacation of sorts, subsidized by the Alumni Association, was geared to offer graduates and others a "few days of intellectual refreshment, physical recreation, and good fellowship." There were eighty in attendance the second year, but interest began to wane after that. The last of these Alumni Weeks was held in 1938.

In 1935, the golden anniversary of the Alumni Association, Secretary Lewis Knepper compiled a special register of ex-Juniatians called the *Alumni Record*. This was a prodigious undertaking that endeavored to list every person who had attended the college from the beginning.

Today's *Alumni Bulletin* was another depression-days invention. It replaced the alumni page in the *Juniatian*, which had been introduced in 1928. Issued quarterly, the *Bulletin* made its first appearance in May 1936.

Radical changes in the organization and operation of the Alumni Association took place in 1939. Lewis Knepper, for a decade its secretary, resigned and was replaced by Harold Brumbaugh. Constitutional revisions put the association under direct college control and into its budget. Annual dues were abolished and all Juniatians now automatically gained membership. Active membership, however, belonged only to those contributing to an annual major project. Choosing projects would be the responsibility of the Juniata Development Committee, which the board of trustees created in the fall of 1938. It was this committee, a representative group charged with looking after Juniata's fund-raising needs, that originated the One Hundred Club. A Will Judy idea, the club included all one hundred dollar donors each year. In 1943 the club numbered thirty-eight contributors who gave more than a third of that year's total alumni giving of little over twenty thousand dollars.

A decade before, meanwhile, the Saturday preceding baccalaureate Sunday had been designated Alumni Day. Ever since then the association's annual meeting has taken place at that time.

11

Surviving the Depression
1930-1943
(Part 2)

PROFILE OF A DEPRESSION-PLAGUED STUDENT BODY

The early depression year 1931-32 marked Juniata's largest enrollment in its history to that time — 534. Trying as the 1930s were economcally, the student population on the Hill, however, never took a precipitous nosedive. Overall decline in numbers did occur — from 534 to 402 by 1941-42 — but the drop came in a fluctuating up-and-down curve. Actually, at the depression's very depth Juniata was faring better than most small church-related colleges in the Keystone State, even those much older. For example, JC's enrollment in 1935 was 464, which compared very favorably with Albright's 343, Geneva's 458, Haverford's 326, Lebanon Valley's 396, Muhlenberg's 294, Susquehanna's 232, Thiel's 257, Ursinus' 455 and Waynesburg's 388. Sister college Elizabethtown, twenty-four years younger, was struggling along with a full-time student body of 157.[1] Among the fifty-seven accredited colleges and universities of its home state, Juniata ranked twenty-second in enrollment in 1935. Indeed, five of the thirteen state teachers' colleges had fewer students than did Juniata that year.

Academic standards did not slip much at all in the fierce competition for students. By and large, over eighty percent of depression-era Juniatians each year came from the upper two-thirds of their high school classes (better than half from the top third). About ten percent of the freshmen brought either valedictorian or salutatorian laurels with them. Furthermore, Juniata's attrition rate was exceptionally low for a college of its type. The drop-out count for each student generation of the 1930s never exceeded sixteen percent.

The first black person to graduate from Juniata was Nancy Slaughter (Lee) in 1932. A local girl, quiet and soft-spoken, deeply spiritual, she went on to teach school. There would not be another minority grad until 1945, Raymond Day's class.

When a threesome from the church's General Education Board paid a campus visit in November 1936, two things impressed them about Juniata's student body. First, its social and economic status was manifestly highest of the Brethren colleges. Then, too, the predominance of non-Brethren students was all too obvious to them. All during C. C.'s presidency Juniata Brethren, though not outnumbered denominationally, never at any time constituted a third of the Hilltop population. Behind them in descending order numerically came the Methodists and the Presbyterians, with the Lutherans somewhat farther back. All other denominations and faiths were only minimally represented.

Alumni brood, however, well populated the campus during the Thirties. In 1938, for example, there were sixty-four students (out of 476) one or both of whose parents had attended Juniata. The student body that year even included one fourth-generation and one third-generation Juniatian.

While FDR and Congress conjured up federal and state agencies of every alphabetical label to restore jobs and prosperity, a strange thing was happening on College Hill. Suddenly, by 1935, Juniata found itself somewhat out of character; it was no longer predominantly a residential school. About half the student body had become commuters, to cut down on costs. Day students who flocked in each morning on the "Pennsy" now had to take a bus from the station to College Hill, the "Toonerville Trolley" having been untracked in 1931. The commuting phenomenon would only be temporary, of course; after the war dorm life regained its ascendancy.

Out-of-staters still made up only a small minority of the college population. Among the 432 enrolled in 1938-39, for instance, just fifty-seven—a mere thirteen percent—resided outside Pennsylvania. While eleven states and Puerto Rico were represented in this total, the bulk of non-Keystoners hailed from three neighboring territories: New Jersey (seventeen); Maryland (fourteen); and New York (ten).

Fortunately, the PRR, like most railroads, provided a "College Special" fare almost all of the depression years. This reduced the cost of a ticket by as much as one-third.

To give prospective students a glimpse into college life and a look at Juniata, Sub-Freshman Day was introduced in May 1939. Some three hundred high school seniors witnessed May Day activities, under a clear blue sky on Saturday the 7th. The spring prefrosh visits became traditional and, in those ante-World War II days, the occasion for Dr. C. C. to name the winners of the competitive scholarship awards.

For years fourteen annual trustee scholarships (eight at fifty dollars and six at one hundred dollars) had been granted on a basis of scholastic merit and financial need. But in 1933, in an all-out effort to buy quality students, the trustees created nine more, these based on a competitive examination. The testing for these scholarships was held only on campus at first, then later in certain high schools (mainly the Camden, New Jersey, and Pittsburgh areas) as well. Six scholarships were worth eight hundred dollars over four years, going to residence students; day students had a crack at the other three, valued at five hundred dollars each (reduced to two starting 1937-38).

During the academic year 1934-35 one-third of the student body was on some kind of financial aid or scholarship, an amount totaling well over fifteen thousand dollars. This was only eight thousand dollars less than that year's entire yield on its endowment, which had progressively eroded with the deepening economic crisis—by as much as fifty-seven thousand dollars since 1929. Nevertheless, some forty specific scholarships were available in the mid-1930s. In addition, all high school honor graduates got help as did all Church of the Brethren ministers and their children. There was also limited aid for children of "evangelical" clergymen.

Domestic pocketbooks got no fatter as the decade progressed, however. By 1937 only about one-fourth of the students on the Hill were there on their own. "Everyone has some sort of work to do at Juniata," observed the campus paper, its editor impressed by all the self-help everywhere evident. Many Juniatians then had part-time campus jobs under the National Youth Administration program. (The NYA, an allied agency of the WPA, would eventually aid six hundred thousand students in college and 1.5 million in high school.)

It was the practice of the NYA to assign students to projects that would not only benefit the college but be educational to them personally. Thus someone interested in becoming a librarian might be assigned to the library's picture collection or to a clerical job. For 1937-38 there were thirty-three students working in the library, seventeen on NYA assignments. The aspiring biologist might end up making charts or preparing insect life-history exhibits for the biology department. And an NYA assistant in the English department likely made signs calling attention to colloquial and ungrammatical expressions. But others were assigned to projects that were a direct change from textbook study. Among their jobs was rebuilding tennis courts and refinishing the gym floor. The NYA allotment for 1939-40 amounted to $5,940, about a third of the total student aid. This form of governmental largess finally came to an end in 1942.

In 1940 a tuition remission policy went into effect for families of full-time college employees. The college rebated half the charges. For that year the cost of a Juniata education averaged about $689, up from the 1931 figure of $511.

On the whole, the vocational picture of Juniata graduates of the 1930s changed little from that of the previous decade. Slightly fewer went into educational work. There was a notable gain in medicine, however; forty-five Juniatians hung out M.D. shingles between 1931 and 1940. They got into some of the best medical schools in the East: Harvard, Johns Hopkins, Pennsylvania, Jefferson, Temple, Hahnemann, Pittsburgh, Maryland, and George Washington. Chemistry made a big jump, too, with thirty-nine careerists for the years 1938-42.

The classes of 1938 through 1942 produced 445 alumni. Of these, 132 went on to do graduate work upon or soon after leaving the Hill. In numbers the field of education was tops, attracting twenty-five. It was followed by medicine (twenty-two), the ministry (twenty-one), chemistry (nineteen), and dietetics and home economics (sixteen).

A college degree during the depression, needless to say, was no sure passport to a good job. But Juniatians, like fellow collegians elsewhere, had a Placement Service going for them. It was set up in 1931, with Dr. Calvert Ellis the first director, at the cue of the Alumni Association. In 1934 its name was changed to Bureau of Recommendations.

STUDENT INITIATIVE AND VITALITY

The 1930s brought a major change in the form of student government. Enforcing college regulations had soon lost its glamour for the heirs of the 1922 Student Councils. The responsibility for discipline was not only time-consuming but tended to heap odium upon those councilors conscientiously performing their duties. On petition of the students themselves, disciplinary functions, except for "frosh regs," were returned to the faculty in the fall of 1935. At the same time Dr. Calvert Ellis and the two deans, Stayer and Gillard, collaborated with Student Councils in creating the Juniata Senate. Student government would now take on a more positive image.

The new plan, which would stand the test of more than three decades of change on College Hill, was an attempt to centralize all of the many campus activities under one governing body. The Senate was composed of twelve student members and three faculty advisers (the two deans and an elected third one). The student members were divided into two groups —first, the officers: President, Vice-President, Secretary, and Central Treasurer; second, eight chairpersons: Social Activities, Women's House, Men's House, Freshmen, Publications, Activities, Athletics, and Religious Activities. The officers and representatives had to be juniors and seniors who were nominated by the retiring Senate and elected by the student body.

Oddly enough, three officers of the first Senate later became Juniata trustees: President LeRoy Maxwell (1961-present); Vice-President Thomas Miller (1967-present); Treasurer Denton Emmert (1959-62; 1963-present). The fourth officer, Secretary Louise Lee, was not to be outdone. She showed her mettle by becoming the wife not only of a future trustee but also of Juniata's seventh president, John Stauffer. One other aboriginal senator would also see trustee duty: the senior who chaired Men's House, Donald Dupler (1964-67).

The first senator in charge of campus social life was Christine Rosenberger (Conners), a charmer from Philadelphia. She took over the functions of Prof. Jack Oller, who in 1931 had been named Director of Student Social Activities. Neither Prof. Oller nor Miss Rosenberger, however, condoned "streaking," which, supposedly a national phenomenon of the 1970s, was not unknown on College Hill in early New Deal years. But it was done under cover of darkness then. The challenge was to race from the Cloister to Founders and back in the buff, avoiding the darting beam of Nightwatchman Mac's flashlight.

Under senatorial auspices the social atmosphere quickened. Clubs of all kinds multiplied and flourished. Though coeds still lived under regulations limiting their frequency of dating, they enjoyed much greater freedom to keep informal company with men. Off-campus ambulation perimeters now went by the board.

But Room C in Students Hall, set aside for general after-classes social use, was a make-shift arrangement that soon proved woefully inadequate. Some relief came in 1936 when the north end of Brumbaugh Hall was thrown into a large, open lobby flanked with alcoves and featuring an exquisitely mantled fireplace. This lounge area was comfortably furnished, and here many a troth would be plighted by sofa-cuddled couples. The new parlor was stocked with table games, though banned from play on Sundays. In fact, a presidential fiat even forbade use of the social room itself during church hours.

The Brumbaugh Hall alcove became a much-trafficked place after the Senate installed an intradorm telephone system in the spring of 1942. Using the alcove phone the fellows could reach any floor of Brumbaugh and Oneida by means of a buzzer system. At the same time Cloisterites picked up a couple of dorm phones for their own use.

Then in January 1943 the rear of the old chapel was converted into a recreation room, complete with Ping-Pong tables and ceiling-high closets for storing game equipment. Movable screens separated the two sections of the room, the eight rows of benches in the front part retained for special meetings and Bible classes.

The social code even eased enough to accommodate tobacco users, though a double standard still kept coeds under a no-cigarette ban. With 1935, men could smoke in the privacy of the Cloister but not publicly on campus.

Blinked thereafter was cardplaying, too, but the antidrinking policy remained in force. Nor did the college give in to strong student pressure in favor of dancing. When the Senate forced a decision upon the trustees in 1942, the board felt obliged to stand firm, it explained, "in view of the long-time traditions of the College and its historical connection with the tradition of the Church of the Brethren."[2]

Every meal began with audible grace, student-given. The social code still bound men to wearing coats in the dining hall for the evening meal and on Sundays.

All Class Night, yet today the most riotous event of the social calendar, made its debut as a Hilltop tradition in February 1938. The sophomores took the silver cup and five-dollar prize money for its skit, "Land of Cotton." Gabriel Chiodo, the talented tenor, was the star performer. In delightful good taste, Luella Robertson (Treuhaft), as "Mammy," gave a plausible explanation to her little dark-skinned urchin, Susanna Dilling, why pickaninnies are black instead of white.

Dramatics, until Oller Hall was built, labored under the handicap of a cramped gymnasium stage and inadequate equipment. But student enthusiasm never lagged under the tutelage of Dr. Binkley, who somehow was able to combine the jobs of professor, carpenter, play coach, and stage designer into that of general utility man. Beginning in 1934 drama carried academic credit. As was the custom, Masquers gave a full-length play each semester with some of one act in between.

No extracurricular activity of the 1930s attracted a more avid following than music. The orchestra, conducted by Karl Gilbert (to 1937) and Turner Jones (1937-42), still numbered nearly half a hundred instrumentalists for its December 1941 concert, the first presented in Oller Hall. A band of thirty pieces finally took hold, after several false starts, the fall of 1935. Its members, in 1936 attired in Yale-blue sweaters, collegiate hats, and white trousers (coeds joined the ranks a year later), did more than goosestep and play at football games or pep rallies; they gave band concerts as well. In 1932 the A Cappella Choir, a consolidation of the Men's and Women's Glee Clubs, began its long reign as the Hill's touring choral group. By 1940 orchestra, band, and choir members were all getting partial academic credit for their musicianship.

By then, too, Juniatians were singing a new *Alma Mater*. It began with a search for a different, original tune for *Hail to Juniata!*, the old *Alma Mater* arranged to be sung to *Maryland, My Maryland*. The new tune contest grew out of a Camp Myler proposal the fall of 1934. But the selection committee did not think much of the attempts at rescoring and decided to throw the baby out with the bath water. It recommended another song altogether: the familiar *To Juniata*, composed by Frank Ward back in 1926. Ward, who once taught history and political science on the Hill, wrote it for the Jubilee Edition Songbook. Prof. Charles Rowland had helped him set the lyrics to music. *To Juniata*, adopted by the Alumni Association in June 1934, still stirs memories of "days within her halls."

Those JC halls, in depression America, saw debate going strong as ever. Some years as many as eighteen forensic contests were scheduled. In the early Thirties Juniata teams were among the first to use the Oregon Plan in debating, before it became popular on the intercollegiate scene. The chief feature of the Oregon plan was the cross-examination conducted by the second speakers of the respective sides. A first in the history of forensics at Juniata was the "international debate" in November 1931. This event, staged in the chapel, pitted Joseph MacCarroll and Paul Bechtel, a pair of wily veterans, against two English students on a debate tour of the United States. The Britishers—from University College, Nottingham, and St. John's College, Durham University—took the affirmative side of the query: "Resolved, That the world had more to fear from Fascism than Bolshevism." The Oregon Plan was followed, putting the Englishmen, who were unused to it, at a slight disadvantage, and the decision went in favor of the Juniata team. A second JC-British debate took place the fall of 1935. The overseas visitors this time were from Cambridge University. Neither side won, since it was a split-team match-up. Women's debate, briefly revived in 1935 after a six-year lapse, fizzled out for good the next year.

Somewhat earlier—in 1933—the college began to liberalize its policy on required attendance at various religious services. Resident students were now given an option for Sunday worship; attendance could be either in the morning or evening, at Stone Church or downtown. In 1940 chapel went on a three-day schedule—Monday, Wednesday, Friday. At the same time Sunday school attendance was made voluntary. Nevertheless, excessive absences from church or chapel could bring suspension from college.

There was no let up on "frosh regs," however. Campus ordinances kept first-semester freshmen duly servile. The year 1937 brought them further hardships when the front steps of Founders Porch and the diagonal walk from Students Hall to the street were closed to them. Bedinked at long last in 1940 were "greenie" coeds. Tribunal-harried men sometimes got a sympathetic word from their "Big Brothers," a freshman-orientation program that the YMCA borrowed from their campus counterpart in 1932.

It had been the Ys that originally sponsored the "Camp Myler" conferences each fall before college opened. With the 1930s these religious retreats began to take on a broader aspect. They became a time for student leaders and faculty consultants to grapple with campus problems, the Ys passing out of the picture. The tradition then developed for each Leadership Conference, planned by student government, to present the administration with a series of resolutions. Beginning in 1937 these pre-classes, weekend gatherings were for years held at Camp Kanesatake, the State Sunday School Association campgrounds near Spruce Creek.

Parents Day was an idea that came out of one early Leadership Conference—in 1936. Sponsored by the Senate, the first one took place on Saturday, October 17, that fall. Ned Johnston, the grand Masquer, headed the event, which attracted some 240 parents and friends to the Hill. Activities included a campus tour and a football game with Grove City in the afternoon—which the Blue and Gold won. Open-house visitation and a buffet dinner followed by a short musical skit in the chapel filled out the day's entertainment. The *Papoose*, a "J"-Club publication, for years served as the official program for the annual visit by moms and dads.

It was a Camp Myler suggestion that prompted the first junior class reception for seniors in May 1936. This springtime hosting of soon-to-be graduates survived for nearly three decades.

Another tradition born of 1936 was the annual Firelighting Ceremony in the Brumbaugh social room in October. It was held to acquaint freshmen women with the Indian heritage that is Juniata's. To the slow, steady thump of a tom-tom Indian maidens advanced down the aisle to the fireplace. There the legend of Alfarata was solemnly read. The evacuation of Brumbaugh Hall for a new women's dorm in the late 1960s put an end to this annual ritual.

Until the mid-Thirties the *Alfarata* was peddled each year on a subscription basis. This kept the cost high, since many Juniatians chose not to buy one. But with 1935, by student vote, the price of an *Alfarata* copy (reduced to five dollars) was figured into the incidental fee. Now Juniata had a "college annual," declared the campus weekly, not just a "class book." That same year *Alfarata* editorship passed from junior to senior hands. The 1938 yearbook, edited by Lynn "Corky" Corcelius, won a first-class rating from the National Scholastic Press Association—the only time ever. It was one of only thirteen annuals from colleges with a less-than-five-hundred enrollment to be so judged. "Juniata Through the Camera's Eye" was the award-winning *Alfarata*'s theme.

The year after the NSPA citation, Juniatians for the first time made the pages of *Who's Who in American Colleges and Universities*, an annual publication honoring graduating campus moguls. The biographies of eight seniors were entered in the 1939-40 edition, five men and three coeds. They were Robert Bair, Lloyd Bergstresser, Gabriel Chiodo, Charles Ellis, George Weber, Martha Brubaker (Weil), Doris Caldwell, and Mary Gaines (Friend). In the mid-1950s, however, the faculty ceased making *Who's Who* nominations. Today they are made by the Student Government.

It was often the case that *Who's Who* entrants also got elected to the Honor Society. The Honor Society took wing the spring of 1942, its constitution largely the work of Dorothy Domonkos of the music department and historian Charles Read. A special faculty committee and President Ellis made the original selections. Six 1941 graduates retroactively became charter members by constitutional provision: Eric Greenbaum, Dorothy Griffith (Meszaros), Mary Jones (Haines), Augusta O'Donald (Morgan), Helen Rankin (Harper), Perry Tyson. Eight charter inductees were seniors: Anna Acitelli, Jack Ayres, Jean Good (Ellis), Kathryn Green (Byerly), Charles Griffith, Herbert Landes, Laban Leiter, and John Saylor. Erwin Hahn and Ann Hill (Duffield) were the two juniors elected.

Honor Society members, as might be expected, were frequent winners in the Joseph F. Biddle General Information Test. John Biddle and his sister, Josephine, had, upon the death of their father in 1936, continued the popular contest in his memory, underwriting the prize money. Student interest in the test began to wane in the 1960s, though it was kept on the books until 1973.

The thirty-five contestants who sat for the Biddle prize the Saturday of March 28, 1936 had only days before watched flood waters rage through the lower end of town. The St. Patrick's Day catastrophe, with the river higher than during the great Johnstown Flood of 1889, saw houses, bridges, barns, and other property carried to destruction. All lines of communication with the outside world were broken, and for several days Huntingdon had no light, water, gas, or utility service. On College Hill candles and lanterns illuminated dorm rooms and hallways. Drinking water had to be hauled in from Cold Spring; commode tanks were filled with water pumped from Muddy Run. Afterward WPA employees and CCC boys drew the Herculean chore of cleaning up, which lasted most of a year.

Herculean, too, was a feat of Paul Walker—earlier, in 1932. Thoreau was Walker's spiritual hero, and Paul's "singular behavior" as a freshman vexed the Tribunal to no end. Not surprisingly, therefore, he has immortalized himself in Hilltop history for staging Juniata's first marathon—single-handedly. "Bunyan Derby" they called it officially.

It started at Skip's over a bottle of orange soda the first day of July, on a warm summer school afternoon. Walker, in fun, cracked that he could walk fifty miles around the track inside twelve hours. Three fellows, Alvin Leonard, Romeo Mari, and Malcolm Weiss, overheard him and threw out a challenge. On the spot they drew up a mock contract, guaranteeing Walker a five-dollar gold piece if he lived up to his boast.

The next morning, Walker, clad in running pants and heavy shoes, was down at the Athletic Field bright and early. At 8:00 A.M. he set out to hike, stopping at noon after one hundred laps, to suck on a lemon and eat a candy bar. Students came by from time to time to cheer him on. Wearily, Walker pushed on and completed his 237th—and last—circuit with twenty-one minutes and ten seconds to spare. Dr. I. Harvey presented the foot-sore schoolteacher-to-be with his gold piece at the next day's chapel.

THE SWARTZ ERA IN ATHLETICS

With the early Thirties "Hoovervilles" began to dot the American landscape in a rash of urban sores and people by the hundreds of thousands went on relief, but varsity sports did not go begging on the Hill. Athletic scholarships had for some while represented a significant financial outlay. The trustees had been a little uneasy about a Carnegie Foundation study of athletic abuses in the late 1920s. However its report, which identified derclict colleges, made no mention of Juniata.[3] There were fifty athletes, almost one-tenth of the student body, on scholarships in 1931, each grant worth $150. The big three sports—football, basketball, and baseball—got the lion's share of help, track the least.

But in December 1931 the Middle States Association came out against all athletically based aid, charging colleges and universities of the day with overemphasizing sports. An athletic scholarship interdict was set to begin September 1933, excluding those already committed. Juniata abided faithfully to the letter of MSA's law, though often there were suspicions that other colleges on its sports schedules had found loopholes. The college still attracted its share of good athletes, but the MSA ruling made it harder.

When Ronald Siersema left in 1930 to study medicine, Milford Swartz, then coaching at Dickinson Seminary in Williamsport, Pennsylvania, took over the athletic reins. "Carty," who wore a Knute Rockne-like pugnacious scowl, had been a three-sport sensation at Lebanon Valley College and later pitched three years in the International League. Coach Swartz was Juniata's man in sports a dozen years.

In that time he made men's intramural sports an important part of campus life. There were organized leagues in softball, touch football, volleyball, tennis, and track. The freshman-sophomore football game grew into a regular Homecoming Day spectacle. The full schedule of Hilltop competition was climaxed each year with the traditional interclass meet.

Over the years other recreational facilities became available. Soon after he came, Swartz, a handball devotee, somehow managed to squeeze two courts into the low-ceilinged gym basement. Then by the fall of 1941 a golf driving range and four greens beautified the former wasteland acreage on the northern edge of the campus, behind and to the east of the Cloister. This was part of a projected nine-hole golf course, thought up by Jack Oller and taken over by trustee Sam Hess, as a means of reclaiming that swampland area. The war, however, put an end to further work.

Swartz was a hard-driving but well-liked coach. In football his scholarshipless gridders gave him an overall twelve year record of thirty-five wins, forty-four losses, and five ties. His lone winning season was 1937, with a 5-3 log. Victories over arch foe Susquehanna still meant cancellation of Monday classes, a practice that began in 1929. A polio epidemic in Huntingdon forced the Indians to cut the first two games of their 1941 season. The Kiwanis Health Club at nearby Martin's Gap was the scene of Juniata's first (and only) football camp in 1946.

A plot of ground (400′ x 150′) purchased in 1931 extended the Athletic Field further toward Muddy Run. As a result, in 1939 the football field was laid out so play would run east and west. That same fall, in time for Parents Day, the college erected a press box (7′ x 18′), designed by Richard Allen, director of publicity. It provided a public address system, wire service, and on the roof space for photographers.

The 1930s also saw changes in football rules, the most radical since the turn of the century. They were designed to reduce the rising rate of gridiron injuries. Dropped was the "flying wedge" on the kickoff, the "flying tackle" and the "flying block." It became legal for the defensive team to use its hands; there was freer substitution. The ball was blown dead when any part of the ball-carrier's body hit the ground, except his hands and feet.

Swartz departed the summer of 1942 to direct a USO center in North Carolina, leaving the sport to Mike Snider. The genial Snider introduced the "T" formation, and three straight early-season wins produced a 3-2 first-year coaching record. Football was dropped the next fall; too many boys and the coach by that time were in an Uncle Sam uniform.

Swartzmen on the basketball court recorded 71 wins and 105 losses. Their best year was 1932, with a 7-5 mark. The 1934-35 Hilltop dribblers held Elizabethtown to but nine points in one game. As with the gridiron sport, the 1930s also introduced the nation to modern basketball. The fast break caught on; so did the one hand shot. The man-to-man yielded to the zone defense, and in 1938-39 the center jump after goals would be abandoned forever. The 1940 Pennsylvania coaches and Associated Press sports writers named three Juniata cagers to the honorable mention list of that year's All-State Team. They were captain George Weber, a center; guard Albert "Albie" Leopold; and the freshman high-scorer, Walter Joachim. A Leadership Conference recommendation led to use of the Huntingdon High School floor the second half of the 1939-40 season, a school board courtesy renewed each year until Memorial Gymnasium went up in 1951. Jack Oller finished out the 1942-43 hardcourt season for Mike Snider, who received a Navy commission in February. The Blue and Gold went 5-7 for the two coaches.

On the diamond Carty Swartz coached the Indians to ninety-six wins, suffered but sixty losses. Three times his Juniata teams were the Eastern Pennsylvania Intercollegiate Baseball League champions—1932, 1933, 1938. The EPIBL, dreamed up by students at Drexel Institute of Technology, organized in May 1931. Of the fourteen colleges invited to join the league, six decided to do so: Juniata, Drexel, Bucknell, Susquehanna, Ursinus, and Lebanon Valley. The 1932 baseball nine went eleven and two, sparked by senior Karl "Zeke" LaPorte, a "man of all sports" and Juniata's answer to the "King of Swat." The 1933 horsehiders were led by Captain Dick Fraker, the hurling ace, and three potent hitters: diminutive left fielder Harry Hummel (.421), second baseman Jack Nicholson (.379), and catcher Roscoe Wareham (.314). The champs of 1938 had port-sided Kalb Roher, who accounted for seven of the team's eight victories and chalked up over ninety strikeouts in his eight outings. His biggest day was against Elizabethtown one April afternoon, fanning twenty men and yielding only two hits before a happy home crowd.

The 1943 wartime nine, under interim coach Edgar Kiracofe, logged a team record of five wins and three losses. Five JC men batted over .300 and the team averaged .269.

Juniata tracksters of the 1930s proved to be crowd pleasers, too, displaying notable trophy-winning ways. Debutant Coach Mike Snider started it off in 1931. His mile relay team of Milt Fetner, Bill Jamison, Ordo and Oden Pletcher, in a strong wind and pelting rain, captured a Penn Relays' first place plaque. Bronze tablets from the Philadelphia spring classic went to Juniata again in 1932, 1934, 1935, 1938, and 1939. The relay victory in 1938, won by Chal Lesher, Jake Dick, George Weber, and Don Snider, running in that order, brought to the college temporary possession of the Rodman Wanamaker Cup, which was to go to the school that won three times. Breaking the existing JC record, the speedsters-four set a time of 3:27:9 for the event. During the spring four other college records were gathered by the 1938 thinclads—in the discus, pole vault, 440-yard dash, and two mile. In 1939 the Penn Relay combination of the year before sprinted to a repeat triumph, giving Juniata two legs on the Wanamaker Cup. Unfortunately, conquest number three forever eluded the racing Indians.

Two depression-era thinclads hold the JC record (since retired) in the 220 low hurdles. George Walton posted a time of :25.8 in that event in 1935, which Robert Mitchell tied his senior year (1941).

Track, as with football and tennis, became a casualty of the war. The college was unable to schedule even one meet in 1943, other schools showing no interest. Nevertheless, in an interclass contest that May, Bill Thorn set a JC mark that still stands. He ran the 120 high hurdles in a time of 15.1 seconds.

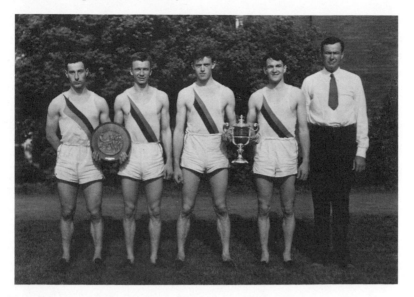

Two-Time Penn Relay Victors, 1938-39. C. Lesher, J. Dick, G. Weber, D. Snider, Coach Snider.

Tennis, though Juniata never lacked for top-notch players, had few winning seasons (two). It was temporarily dropped in 1936 and again in 1943.

The depression also killed the Hill's one coed intercollegiate sport: basketball. Overall between 1930 and 1935 JC sextettes, coached by Nancy Burke (Bloxsom) and, after 1932, Harriet "Betty" Fleck, ran up an impressive 16-6 victory margin. Olive "Ollie" Sell (Underkoffler), side center and forward, captained the 1931-32 women squad to an unblemished 5-0 season. But the sport reverted to a strictly intramural status in 1935 when the economy of hard times forced other colleges to cancel their schedules.

Betty Fleck, assistant director of physical education, did much to diversify the women's intramural athletic program on the Hill. She introduced field hockey in 1932, and the annual freshman-sophomore tilt became a big attraction the morning of Homecoming Day. A girls' athletic field, below Scott Street, got its first use in 1937, at once increasing the number of hockey enthusiasts.

In November 1938 Hilltop coeds organized the Women's Athletic Association to take the place of their "J" Club. The WAA's motto, "A sport for every girl and a girl for every sport," had a familiar ring. It paraphrased the catchword of the Women's Division of the National Amateur Athletic Association, founded by Mrs. Herbert Hoover back in the early 1920s: "A team for everyone and everyone on a team." Women athletes would now receive WAA emblems instead of "Js". Credit toward these emblems accrued not only from participation in intramurals such as hockey, basketball, softball, speedball, and volleyball, but also from individual sports such as Ping-Pong, badminton, tennis, skating, riding, hiking, shuffleboard, deck tennis, and others.

WORLD WAR II HITS THE HILL

During most of the 1930s American attention was centered on domestic problems. Yet foreign events occurring in the same period were to affect the United States even more profoundly than the New Deal. Aggressive military states threatened to dominate Europe and Asia. Through 1939 and 1940 events in Europe moved swiftly—Germany overran Poland, occupied Denmark and Norway, then blitzkrieged through the Low Country and into France, leaving Great Britain isolated. Step by step the United States became involved on the Atlantic side, isolationism and neutrality giving way to British aid. And at the same time—in the Pacific—Roosevelt imposed stiff economic sanctions against Japan, then at war with China. *Juniatian* editorials took note of all this from time to time, as "preparedness" talk grew louder, and worried.

In September 1940 Congress adopted the first peacetime conscription law in American history. The Burke -Wadsworth Act, however, deferred all draftable college men until the end of the current academic year. In all, fifty-five Juniatians, faculty and students, registered for the draft that fall. Otherwise, Juniata continued much as usual through the year, relishing to the hilt the many advantages of Oller Hall. The enrollment for the fall of 1941 showed only a slight decline.

Then Pearl Harbor—Sunday, December 7th. America at war! The Juniata campus, like the nation, was momentarily stunned. On Wednesday the 10th, two days after Congress declared war, President C. C. spoke to the students in chapel on the subject "Our Attitude in the Present Crisis." Urging duty to one's country, he hardly sounded like an absolute pacifist (which he was not—"conscience," he so often was to say, "works both ways on the question of military service"). Americans, his chapel talk stressed, have received many benefits from their government and "everyone ought to be ready to give back such help as he or she can render."

For yet a while the war touched College Hill in only minor ways. A committee on Civilian Morale, representing every segment of the campus, soon appeared, chaired by Dr. Ellis. In January some 250 professors and students began to study first aid under Red Cross instruction. War Time (FDR preferred this phrase to Daylight Saving Time) began Monday, February 9. Sugar rationing came in May and each dining room table was allotted a half-cup of sugar a day (each student one tablespoon full). All male students had to take part in a physical fitness program, at first three hours a week, later five.

But not for long could College Hill escape the sting of war's fury. The week before Thanksgiving 1942 came the sad news of Marine Lt. David Crosby's death. The handsome, wavy-haired Carlisle, Pennsylvania, English major '40 had fallen on Guadalcanal, Solomon Islands. Then during the Christmas holidays word reached the Hill that Lt. Jack Shuck '47 of Lewistown, Pennsylvania, had gone down with his Spitfire over Northwest Africa. Shuck, it was later learned, had bailed out and was alive. As a prisoner of war he eventually ended up corralled in the north compound of Stalag Luft III, the notorious German POW camp for Allied airmen at Sagan, Silesia. There, one of six hundred-odd conniving American and British air force officers, he became party to an incredible wartime story. For Stalag Luft III was the prison camp that stunned the Germans with one of the most daring mass escapes of all times, since celebrated in book and movie as *The Great Escape*.

On Monday, February 15 the college gave twenty-eight Army Reservists a special sendoff that included a chapel service and individual Testaments from the Student Volunteers. Four more men, three in the Army Air Corps Reserves and one in the Navy Reserve Corps, left the next week. And by mid-April 19 others had bade farewell to the Hill to enter various branches of the service. The early months of 1943 saw faculty members don khaki uniforms, too — Mike Snider, George Clemens, and Inez Nienow. By fall Juniata's roll of men and women in civilian and military camps approximated 350 names. Of this number seven had been reported lost or missing in action, and at least fifty were in foreign service or in active duty on the high seas.[4]

As in the First World War there was no military unit on College Hill. The War Department had approached the college as early as 1939 for permission to set up a flight school. But the trustees still felt bound by the Brethren peace position and said no to that tender and to other later ones. It cost the college dearly, of course, in terms of students and cash. Of the 249 students who enrolled for the fall of 1943, only sixty-five were men.

For the first time in untold years women invaded Founders Hall, third floor. The war year of 1943 brought Juniata's largest enrollment of resident women ever. This, said the *Alumni Bulletin*, was "attributable to the fact that Juniata is the only Pennsylvania co-educational college accredited by the Association of American Universities, with entire facilities and faculty personnel available for civilian higher education."[5]

September 1943 also marked the close of Dr. C. C.'s presidency. He had turned sixty-nine in July. Worries had piled up on his desk with every new month of the war and every added disruption of civilian economy. Someone younger, he felt, should carry the college through the dark hours ahead.

12

A Quarter Century
of Dynamic Growth
1943-1968
Part I

FINDING DR. C. C.'s SUCCESSOR

When the trustee selection committee met in the spring of 1943 to choose Juniata's sixth president, the end of the war was not in sight and the future was very uncertain. The projection of student enrollment for the fall was bleak indeed — less than 250. Among the six-man committee there were some who feared the meeting would be a stormy one. The trustees were not of one mind on a lot of issues, especially on college regulations. The decision, everyone felt, was tantamount to a "hinge of fate." The presidential transition must bring as little shock as possible to the college.

Moreover, no agreement existed as to who the next president should be. Among the names considered, however, that of Calvert Nice Ellis, board secretary since 1938, clearly stood out. As Dr. John Baker, who was one of the committee members, recalls that day in 1943, the leading nominee was "well known to all, was steeped in college tradition, [and] his educational background was ideal."[1]

But not all on the board — or on the faculty — at first jumped on the Calvert Ellis bandwagon. Across the street one colleague in particular voiced fears that the sciences would suffer neglect under the younger Ellis should, as rumor early had it, the election go his way. And a certain trustee wondered whether he could raise money, or at age thirty-nine,

Calvert Ellis in salad days of presidency.

had the "human touch" that marks the deft administrator. Said John Baker, "The trustees recognized that only the future could answer [such] questions."[2] And so on commencement weekend Calvert Ellis was unanimously elected president.

Getting him to accept was another story—he turned the offer down flat. Pressured, he asked for several days to think it over. Then on Monday, May 31, he closeted with the whole board to make a statement. He agreed to succeed his father provided he could continue on as manager of the D. Maurice Wertz Orchards in Franklin County. In 1940, upon his father-in-law's death, Dr. Ellis had taken over the management of the Wertz business, then the largest orchards (cherries, peaches, apples) in the Commonwealth. (He would be a fruit grower until 1960 when the business was sold to Knouse Foods.) The trustees raised no objections to this extramural involvement and the matter of presidential succession was settled. The transition had been effected with smoothness and large good will.

CALVERT NICE ELLIS: A NATIONAL FORCE IN HIGHER EDUCATION

Born in Zion City, Illinois, Calvert Ellis never attended public school. His father had experienced a bad reaction (paralysis of his legs for a time) to his own vaccination and so denied the vaccine needle to the two Ellis boys. They were tutored by their mother at home and by teachers at the Academy. A 1919 Academy grad with some study at Princeton Preparatory School, Ellis received his B.A. degree from Juniata (1923) the year after his call to the ministry by the Huntingdon church (eventually he was ordained an elder). Pursuing graduate studies over the next nine years, he received a Th.B. from Princeton Theological Seminary (1927), an M.A. from Princeton University (1927), and a Ph.D. from Yale (1932). His dissertation on Karl Barth made him one of the first American scholars of that Swiss theologian, destined to greatness within the decade. In 1932, turning down a position at Mt. Holyoke College, he heeded his father's invitation and joined the faculty of his alma mater to teach religion and philosophy. He made it plain, however, that he had no plans for staying, even though he built a home in 1934. But of course, that was not the way it worked out for him.

Calvert, a warmer, more outgoing person than his father, of similar build but with sharper facial features, would go on to pilot Juniata for a quarter century. His has been the longest presidential tenure in the college's history. His years in office coincided with the dynamic postwar decades and the upsurge of higher education that attended them. Dr. John Baker put Calvert Ellis's long presidency in historical focus when he wrote:

> Dr. Ellis' administration covered many of the most crucial years in the history of American education. One world war and several smaller wars; too few students, too many students; Sputnik, with the upgrading of all education; changing social mores; restlessness among faculty and students; faculty shortages; inflation with its attendant financial problems; government aid and involvement and a host of other issues beset him and all other college presidents. Those were indeed exacting times and any president who succeeded in guiding his institution through this era successfully merited high praise.[3]

The name of C. C. Ellis was a familiar one to Pennsylvania educators, but as someone said of his son, "He helped mold the fabric of higher education in America."[4] From 1944 to 1947 he was on the staff of the House Education Committee, which hammered out the guidelines for the first federal aid to private colleges and universities. He had much to do in winning the historic congressional legislation that allowed G. I. Joes to use government funds to attend whatever colleges or universities they wanted to. For twenty years Dr. Ellis was called upon to testify before Congress in behalf of higher education—not the usual role of a small college head. In Washington he was known as a "progressive conservative." Jay du Von, then director of the College Housing Branch of the Federal Housing and Home Agency, told a group of Juniatians in 1963:

> Your president has a reputation for integrity coupled with vision which goes beyond the State or Pennsylvania and has made him one of the educational leaders of the nation. His wise counsel and advice are sought by the Federal Government on every important problem affecting higher education. . . .[5]

While in office much of Dr. Ellis's off-campus time was given to the work of the Association of American Colleges. Established in 1915, the AAC represents some 870 liberal arts colleges, large and small, church-related and secular, public and private. From 1949 to 1955 he headed its Commission on the Arts, later chairing the Commission on Legislation (1961-64)—of which he was a member for eight years. In 1965 he was elected to the Board of Directors, and in 1968 became the association's national chairman. He was the fifth college president from Pennsylvania to be so honored.

He was no less active in the Middle States Association, over which he presided in 1965. He also served as director of its Commission on Institutions of Higher Education (1948-54). Seventeen times he led evaluation teams on their missions to colleges and universities of all sizes and sorts, including two great Protestant seminaries.

Nor was he without honor in his home Commonwealth. He headed the Pennsylvania Association of Colleges and Universities (1953-54) and the Foundation of Independent Colleges of Pennsylvania (1962-63). During 1965-66 Dr. Ellis was a member of the Advisory Committee on Higher Education to the State Board of Education. In 1966 he was appointed by Gov. William Scranton to the Higher Education Advisory Committee to the Education Compact of the United States.

During the academic year 1966-67 he was a consultant to the Ford Foundation, studying the question of faculty development by visiting thirty colleges that had received Ford Foundation grants.

Like his father, Dr. Calvert gave liberally of his time to the church. Not an orator of his father's class, he was nevertheless an effective preacher much appreciated as a pulpiteer whether featured at Annual Conference or filling in for a rural pastor. He preached every Juniata baccalaureate sermon but one while president. He was moderator of Annual Conference for the year 1947-48, refusing other nominations for the position later on in the belief it should be passed around. For nine years he was chairman of the General Brotherhood Board (1948-54, 1966-67), the denomination's chief policy-making agency created in 1947. Dr. Ellis was a delegate to ecumenical church meetings in Amsterdam, Netherlands, Evanston, Illinois, and Lund, Sweden. And twice he toured various parts of the world to survey Brethren missions.

At the community level Dr. Ellis, a Rotarian, somehow found energy and time to carry other responsibilities. In 1936 he became a trustee of J. C. Blair Memorial Hospital, assuming board chairmanship from 1960 to 1962. The first Grange National Bank (now the Penn Central National Bank) elected him a director in 1946.

A good banker he has been. The same has not always been said about his operation of a car. A heavy foot on the accelerator has given him the reputation of driving like someone trying to qualify for the Indy 500.

THE COMMITMENT TO A "SMALL COLLEGE"

The Calvert Ellis administration preserved the best of Juniata's past without limiting in any way the college's entry into the demanding revolutionary world of the 1950s and 1960s. Many small colleges in those decades, with the rising tide of students, burgeoned into universities with national constituencies, their church ties severed or neglected. But as far as Juniata's second Ellis was concerned, he would have been happy to preside over a college with no more than seven hundred students. He was heard to say this more than once.

Ellis believed the small college had been basic in our nation's life and history, a unique American tradition. In his inaugural address "The Purpose of the Small College," he said:

> It is my conviction that the small, denominationally related college, rooted in local tradition has a significant role in America's future—a role the college has visioned but only partially grasped—to provide a basic education in the arts and sciences in an atmosphere friendly to the Christian faith.[6]

Only reluctantly, at trustee urging, did he watch the enrollment gradually climb to over eleven hundred by the time he retired. But it was a controlled growth. Seen now in retrospect this was a wise policy, preventing the college from overexpanding during the student "boom" of the Sixties. Many colleges failed to act so deliberately and they met with financial chaos when the bottom dropped out in the early Seventies.

The success of a small college, said Dr. Calvert once in a commencement speech, is not whether it produces great persons, for that will rarely happen. "Juniata has never been a college for geniuses," he said, "although a few have survived!" He went on:

> Juniata will continue to admit students with intellectual capacity and then develop in them an appetite to know so they will accomplish more in graduate school and life than would have been expected when they entered college. I expect to live long enough to see educational institutions judged on the basis of what they do for students rather than on the college board scores of their freshmen.[7]

Like his predecessors, Calvert Ellis constantly stressed that Juniata College was "Christian in purpose." The small liberal arts college, he believed, had a responsibility to develop sound habits and attitudes. He treasured the testimony of James Shook, a Reading, Pennsylvania, principal, who said, "I learned more in the university, but I got my set of soul at Juniata." In 1967, when student unrest was beginning to peak on the nation's campuses, he said in his report that year: "Juniata College believes that its constituency wishes certain standards to be taught. . .and that God places obligations upon us."

He usually spoke of Juniata as *church related*, seldom as *independent*. (It was he, back in 1939, who pushed the idea to give the three church districts representation on the board.) The steady decline of Brethren students bothered him. Yet he felt the times dictated against registering Juniata as a "denominational college" under a special state law enacted in the early 1960s.

With time Dr. Ellis built around him an efficient administrative staff — otherwise he could not have taken on so many outside obligations. But up to the very end his presidential style continued in the paternalistic vein of those who went before him. The Middle States team that visited the campus in 1962 referred in its report to "the family spirit which provides easy access that shortcuts organizational charts."[8]

Socially, though, this paternalism took special, intimate forms. From year one of the Ellis presidency, Calvert and Elizabeth entertained the faculty each spring. First it was at their beautiful Taylor Highland home. Then, because of an overgrown faculty, at a variety of public places.

Summer term profs were not forgotten either, their treat an evening party of games and food.

In the 1950s the Ellises began taking newly doctored faculty and their spouses on a junket to Erculiani's, fabled for its multicoursed meals, near Cresson. This was his unique way of prodding Hilltop people to see their doctoral studies through. In 1967 a record crop of Ph.D.s (five) plus wives gorged themselves at presidential expense. (By 1968 forty-six percent of the full-time faculty had doctorates, not all, of course, Erculiani-induced.)

And it was Mrs. Ellis, early in her husband's administration, who brought faculty wives together for regular fellowship. "Juniata Dames" they called themselves. It was her concern that the women come to feel as though they belonged to the college, too. The Dames still exists as a sodality.

Academic paternalism, once fashionable, is passé today, even resented. But one thing was clear about Calvert Ellis: he knew his faculty and cared about them. He took a genuine interest in their families, able in many cases to call children by name.

Until his last few years it was his practice to interview every graduating senior. This was the personal touch, he felt, that made Juniata different.

THE CALVERT ELLIS FACULTY

No future JC chieftain will likely so utterly transform the campus the way Calvert Ellis did, long-time presidencies apparently now a thing of the past. Yet is is not the number of buildings he erected that fills him with pride in his retirement, but the quality of faculty Juniata was able to attract during his administration. As he told the trustees in his 1954 report to them:

> It is easy to become discouraged in the work of a college such as Juniata. There is not much that one can offer to his colleagues except hard work and modest financial remuneration. But it is thrilling to be associated with a group of committed persons devoted to the education of youth for service in tomorrow's world.

He complained in his report the next year about how hard it was to find faculty, the question of salary a prime deterrent. Yet, in those days of unparalleled mobility in academe, forty-eight Ellis appointees stayed on for ten years or more. Only three in this category afterward took positions elsewhere. Despite retirements and one death, well over half the 1975-76 faculty (forty-nine out of eighty-four) are carry-overs from the Ellis regime—seven years since its end. True, the stagnant professorial job market of late partly explains the tenacity of Ellis-appointed faculty. Juniata no longer serves as a stepping stone for ambitious young instructors as once it did. Then, too, eighteen of the forty-nine carry-overs are alumni. But, nevertheless, something there is about Juniata that makes good teachers want to stay.

Fourteen Ellisites hung on for two decades or more, with a good dozen others fast approaching that mark today.

Esther Doyle, who worked off a Ph.D. (Northwestern) when in her fifties, gave thirty years to the English department (1945-75). Drama and oral interpretation were her major interests at Juniata. She, the apostle of the pear-shaped tone, has been by all odds the college's most traveled professional. Dr. Doyle made scores of tours giving interpretive readings at United States colleges and universities.

Historian Kenneth Crosby (Ph.D., George Washington) has put in twenty-eight years, with still more to go. A good mechanic, he belies the myth that professors are all thumbs when it comes to manual work. Through the years he has been the chief adviser to prelaw students. He met his wife Jane Miller '38 on the Hill where she taught home economics. Who of their friends will forget the sabbatical trip they took the academic year 1974-75. In a specially outfitted VW bus (dubbed "Casabat"—for "Sabbatical House") they made a nine-and-a-half month trek that carried them through seventeen continental Latin American nations and over thirty-two thousand miles.

A near-tradition passed when Prof. Donald Johnson gave his twenty-seventh annual fall organ recital in 1970. It was his last one. It was also his sixty-eighth major public performance at Juniata since he joined the faculty in 1944. For fourteen years, having succeeded Charles Rowland, the mustachioed organist and department chairman directed the Juniata Concert Choir.

Eva Hartzler (Ph.D., Penn State) retired in 1976 after twenty-six years with the chemistry department. An alumna ('32), she was a stimulating teacher who more than lived up to the reputation of the man she replaced—Dr. N. J. Brumbaugh. When not in her lab or the classroom, Dr. Hartzler, an active member of the Standing Stone Garden Club, could be found, once she became a homeowner, puttering around her lawn.

Marriage, as much as anything, brought on Miriam Schlegel (Musselman's) (Ed.D., George Peabody) premature retirement—in 1975—after twenty-five years in the education department. An ex-Wave, she taught grade school for twelve years before coming to Juniata. She succeeded Edgar Kiracofe as department chairman in 1960. While on the Hill Mrs. Musselman served on important commissions for the Pennsylvania Department of Higher Education and was a member of numerous evaluating teams for the Department of Public Instruction.

Retired faculty, Calvert Ellis appointees. E. Doyle, D. Johnson, E. Hartzler, M. Musselman, H. Miller, E. Blaisdell, S. Hettinger, T. Henry.

"Hell, guys!" was a common Herbert Miller exclamation during the twenty-three years he taught business administration (1946-69). He will also be remembered for his financial forecasts given every January at local service club meetings. His M.B.A. from the Harvard Business School,

"Herbie," a man of rare instincts in coping with the mysteries of the stock market, became the board of trustee's first investment consultant. He operated a tax and investment office while teaching at Juniata.

Fellow economist Thomas Nolan is another twenty-three-year veteran, although he is far from retirement age. "Black Tom" was the label students gave him soon after his 1953 arrival. He had a fondness for pop quizzes, especially on Saturday mornings in that age of the six-days-a-week schedule. Now the registrar, he is the first Roman Catholic to call the Hill home for any length of time.

A trio have put in twenty-two years. One of them, another centennial year retiree, is Edwin Blaisdell (Ph.D., M.I.T.). After all this time his speech still betrays his New England rearing. He was a research chemist in industry before joining Juniata's chemistry department, bringing with him the college's first research grant, from duPont. Dr. Blaisdell, who probably never sat mute through any faculty meeting, in 1954 became chairman of the mathematics department. In 1963 when Juniata purchased an IBM 1620 computer, he became its first caretaker.

Mary Ruth Linton '38, daughter of O. R. Myers, needed two stints to accumulate her twenty-two years of service. A member of the faculty from 1942 to 1951, she returned to the music department in 1963. A pianist with a degree from the Eastman School of Music, she has been a steadying influence among the Hill's music masters. Mrs. Linton, as had been her father, is active in the Pennsylvania State Sunday School Association.

The third member of the twenty-two-year group is George Dolnikowski, whose association with Juniata began under story-book conditions. In 1941 he was a Russian inmate of a German prisoner of war camp, captured after being wounded by a land mine. The war over, he left Europe for America, entering as a displaced person through the help of the Church of the Brethren. Late afternoon January 7, 1950 he arrived on the Juniata campus. "That's a date I will never forget," says Prof. Dolnikowski with a smile. He was unable to read or write English. Students and professors tutored him in his new tongue while he worked as a janitor. It was Dr. Kenneth Crosby, under whom he took his first college course, who suggested that he set a long-range goal of obtaining a degree. Within three years, all the while firing a dormitory furnace, he had his B.A. diploma. Encouraged by Dr. George Clemens, he then went on to earn a master's degree in Germanic literature at the University of Pennsylvania. Prof. Dolnikowski joined the faculty in 1954. At first he taught German; now it is Russian studies.

A pair of Hilltop instructors, Bernice Engman Heller and Philbrook Smith (Ph.D., Iowa), came twenty-one years ago, both in their mid-twenties. Both found their spouses on campus, the former a math prof, the latter a recent coed. "Bernie," who fusses over house plants, teaches Spanish. Dr. Smith is a medievalist, known for his dry wit and dislike for early morning classes.

Sarah Steele Hettinger '24 spent two decades on the Hill after her appointment as assistant librarian in 1944. She took full charge in 1952 upon Miss Lillian Evans's retirement. By then space in Carnegie Library was taxed beyond a comfortable margin. Sometimes students actually sat on the floor to study. Mrs. Hettinger's tenure lasted through the move to the L. A. Beeghly Library, for her "a glorious day."

Though his teaching days fell short of twenty years by one (1946-65), Tobias Henry (Ph.D., Pitt), an alumnus ('26), cannot be passed over. He retired early because of illness. "Toby," who was a letter winner in tennis and whose hobby is collecting jokes on absent-minded professors, came to Juniata from the pastorate of Stone Church. He has served the Church of the Brethren in many important roles. Through all his years at Juniata he was the mainstay of the sociology department. In fact, during most of that time he *was* the sociology department, turning out, on the average, a dozen majors a year. A long-time counselor in family relations, Dr. Henry was a member of the advisory committee of the Huntingdon County Child Welfare Services from 1948 to his retirement, fourteen of those years as its chairman.

Only two birthright Brethren among the whole pack of them! In fact, the number of faculty reared in the denomination could easily, in Dr. Ellis's last year, be counted on both his hands. But over the years many of those from a non-Brethren background have ended up joining Stone Church.

It was the postwar development program, with its fund-raising burdens, that forced Dr. Calvert to look for an academic dean. In 1948 he chose thirty-six-year-old Morley Mays '32, his Ph.D. from the University of Virginia. Dean Mays taught philosophy in his early administrative years, winning admiration as a first-rate instructor, though a tough one. Eighteen years he was Juniata's chief academic officer, respected by the faculty as a detail man and for his expertise on curriculum development. All during his deanship he served annually on evaluation committees for the Middle States Association, chairing a number of them. Twice he was a consultant for the Maryland State Department of Education and once for the New York State Department of Education. In the spring of

1963, when the college administration was reorganized, he was named one of three vice-presidents. Thrice Mays was acting president of Juniata for brief periods. An ordained minister, he held a host of high offices in the operations of the Brethren. In 1966 he resigned to become president of Elizabethtown College.

Donald Rockwell, then chairman of the natural sciences, was made acting dean while a search went on for Mays' successor. The fall of 1967 his appointment became permanent. As dean, Don Rockwell was loved by the faculty but he was not happy in the office. He much preferred the classroom to deaning, only a sense of duty and his deep affection for Calvert Ellis compelling him to make the sacrifice.

The dean's haunt at first was what is now the office of the female associate dean of students and the room next to it. (In 1948 the rear portion of Founders Chapel, then in use as student recreation space, had been subdivided into four offices and a central lobby.) In 1965 the dean of the college took over the present location, east of the Tower hallway, where for a long time the registrar did business.

Meanwhile, over the years the problem of paying the faculty competitive salaries bedeviled the president and trustees to no end. Inflation kept driving the cost of living inexorably upward. A study of faculty income at eighteen Pennsylvania colleges with an enrollment between five-hundred and one-thousand in 1954 revealed that Juniata's average salary of forty-five hundred dollars was next to the lowest in the group.[9] Ellis pointed out to the trustees in his report that year the injustice of paying beginning instructors within a thousand dollars of the salary of those who have given their lives to the college. By 1968, though, Juniata's scale was above the median for Pennsylvania colleges, except for full professors. The top figure for them on the Hill was then $13,500. The president's own paycheck was but a few thousand dollars higher.

But expanded fringe benefits helped atone for modest annual increments. Social Security, which in 1951 was amended to include college employees among others, plus the TIAA pension plan relieved some of the anxiety about the "sunset years."[10] Updated group life, hospitalization, and surgical insurance programs followed.[11] Then came major medical coverage.[12] The Ellis-Stauffer transition year added permanent disability insurance.[13]

Faculty housing—or rather the lack of it—had become a major problem by the late 1950s. The trustees seriously thought of putting up an apartment building to ease the situation. The spring of 1958 they voted to purchase up to six lots in the "Hollywood" section east of campus where a new $2.5-million high school was under construction.[14] These lots were to be sold at cost plus curb or street assessments to faculty members who wanted to build. The trustees again, in April 1967, authorized acquiring more lots—this time on Taylor Highland—for the same purpose. Before the faculty got too big the college gladly granted first mortgages to home buyers; later only second mortgages were taken on. The trustees also began to lay hands on more houses in the vicinity of the campus to be used as low rentals for faculty.

Up to 1964 children of JC profs got only one-half off tuition costs when attending the home college. However, in the early 1950s Juniata had joined with several other institutions in a Faculty Children's Tuition Exchange Plan. The college pulled out of this consortium several years later because, as it turned out, the formula used for exchange did not balance out equitably for Juniata.

In 1964 the trustees introduced a plan staggeringly generous—unheard of at but a few schools. More than one above-par teacher has been saved for Juniata because of it. One part of the twofold plan is not unusual since other institutions have a similar tuition remission policy. It discounts for children of *any* full-time college employee—faculty, administration, office, housekeeping, food service, and maintenance—all but two-hundred dollars of tuition costs if they attend Juniata. But the unique feature of this plan—and it applies only to faculty and administrators—is this: their children can go to any college or university where, in the event tuition is different from JC's, the grant is limited to the lower tuition less one-hundred dollars. (This latter benefit was revoked in 1976 for future appointees but does not apply to those already hired.)

The trustees knew what they were getting into. Some unofficial census taker had reported a "baby boom" among the faculty and staff back in 1960. He tallied 135 future collegians of Hilltop parentage even then, the multiplying appointments and hirings of that decade still to come.

A little ego-building can often compensate for thin wallets, Calvert Ellis knew. He looked for ways to reward merit. The rank of associate professor was added in 1955. He saw to it that name professorships (most modestly endowed) did not long go unclaimed. The John Downey Benedict Professorship in English (named for a friend of the college killed in World War II) went to Harold Binkley in 1952 and to Esther Doyle in 1966. Donald Rockwell became the first Jacob H. and Rachel Brumbaugh Professor in chemistry in 1958. (It was established by the will of Dr. N. J., who left the major share of his estate to the college at his death in 1953). Miriam Schlegel (Musselman), after a three year lapse, inherited the Martin G. Brumbaugh Professorship in Education in 1963. The Mary S. Geiger religion title, last held by the president himself, went to Earl Kaylor in 1966. Two others got name professorships that year: Evelyn Guss (Ph.D., Pitt), the I. Harvey Brumbaugh one in classics (never claimed since established by the alumni as a memorial in 1938); and Wilfred Norris (Ph.D., Harvard), the recent William I. and Zella B. Book one in physics. (The donors were both alumni, the husband, a trustee, having taught physics at Penn.)

By the time of Ellis's retirement there was a sabbatical leave policy (a maximum of four annually.) The faculty was more than ready for it. There has been no change in the four-a-year quota.

In 1968 trustee Donovan Beachley, a Hagerstown, Maryland, furniture manufacturer, and his family endowed a Distinguished Professor Award. A one-thousand dollar check each year goes to an outstanding teacher who is also active in college life and community affairs. The winners have been: Kenneth Crosby (1968); Paul Heberling (1969), former dean of men turned sociology professor; Donald Rockwell (1970); Eva Hartzler (1971); Earl Kaylor (1972); Esther Doyle (1973); Klaus Kipphan (1974), a historian trained at Heidelberg, Germany; William Russey (1975), a chemist and Harvard Ph.D.; and Peter Trexler (1976), a geologist with a Michigan doctorate.

Institutional loyalty was not overlooked, either—on the part of administrators and staff as well as faculty. Hilltop longevity was first celebrated at a Founders Day tea in 1949 when twenty-five persons were honored for ten years of service or more. The 10-Year Club, with induction rites spiced by brief humorous citations of anonymous authorship, has become a new Founders Day tradition. In the twenty-seven years since its inception there have been 141 inductees.

The 25-Year Club was an invention of the Alumni Association in 1961, thanks to Dr. Paul Bechtel '32, then national president. A dozen members made up the first group at the alumni banquet that year. Among them was Mrs. Anna Groninger Smith, the practically snafu-proof secretary to four presidents over forty-four years. Her retirement in 1965 was no slight loss to Calvert Ellis. The 25-Year Club, too, has become a tradition, though obviously not an annual affair.

Moreover, superannuated profs and administrators get a special send-off into retirement at the annual trustee-faculty dinner in the spring. This practice dates back to 1960 with Edgar Kiracofe's farewell.

During the Calvert Ellis years there was no tenure system. The trustees rejected the idea in 1961 in favor of three kinds of appointments: annual, term (three years), and indefinite. Indefinite appointments were automatically granted to full professors.

Not until 1954 did the faculty begin to elect the personnel of their standing committees, putting an end to presidential decree on this matter. In 1962 they moved their monthly meetings from Room C in Students Hall to Founders Chapel, shifting again in 1965 to Alumni Hall. And until almost the very last Ellis year absences at faculty meetings did not go unnoticed; the secretary kept an attendance record.

Gone now is the Faculty Club coffee break, which lured in the teaching troops from all over the Hill each nonchapel morning between 10:00 and 10:30. Introduced in 1950, it was a happy time of fellowship and gossipry for nearly twenty years. Dropping chapel and a new class schedule did it in. But so far as bringing the faculty together in a special, relaxed way nothing has taken its place.

The so-called family spirit was breaking down among the increasingly cosmopolitan faculty by 1968. Cliques had formed—along age and interest lines. Regular all-faculty social get-togethers, once monthly events, died out by the Sixties. Only the fall picnic at Rockwells still holds any communal interest.

During all the Calvert Ellis years there was only one divorce among the faculty—in the late Forties, the first in Juniata's history. Since 1968, however, broken marriages have become less rare in the teaching ranks.

More common, too, are faculty cocktail parties, which, however, were not unknown before 1968.

And with "women's lib" came more working faculty wives.

PLAUDITS FAR AND WIDE FOR JUNIATA

When the trustees conferred a surprise honorary doctorate on Dr. Ellis in 1963, his citation made the point: "During his lifetime and largely under his leadership, Juniata has reached its eminence in the world of liberal arts colleges." And so to the question, Why Juniata? the reasons given by incoming frosh during the Ellis II era invariably fell into the following order: (1) smallness; (2) scholastic reputation; (3) ideals of the college. Juniata, whose enrollment did not climb past one-thousand until fall 1965, had by then got its share of far-flung recognition for the second category. The *Small College Annual*, first issued in 1948, included Juniata from the start as one of the "best" in the country.

(Comparative guides to colleges and universities were then practically unknown.) In 1950 JC began appearing in *Good Housekeeping Magazine*'s yearly listing of notable small independent colleges—one of but thirteen in Pennsylvania. The College and Career Department of *Mademoiselle Magazine* rated Juniata in 1955 among 137 outstanding minisized liberal arts schools.

Earlier, in 1949, the Trytten Report, a five-volume study by President Truman's Scientific Research Board, had come out with kudos for Juniata. The report noted that many small colleges had, from 1936 to 1945, "contributed scientists out of all proportions to the number of their students."[15] It said that five colleges combined—Hope, Juniata, Monmouth, St. Olaf, and Oberlin—produced more candidates for doctor's degrees in chemistry than did Johns Hopkins, Fordham, Columbia, Tulane, and Syracuse all together. Percentagewise, Juniata was rated eighth in the nation among smaller institutions.

Then in 1953 the Ford Foundation for the Advancement of Education gave the college another pat on the back. In a nationwide survey the foundation ranked Juniata among the top fifty colleges and universities with the best records for producing "young American scholars of promise."[16] Placing forty-third, Juniata was one of only four schools in its native Commonwealth to make the list, five steps above Penn.

The year 1957 yielded other statistical evidence of Juniata's academic strength. According to the National Research Council, 101 JC grads earned doctorates (not counting the M.D. degree) between 1936 and 1956.[17] (The count went to 161 for the period 1920 to 1961.) A single banner year during Calvert Ellis's presidency was 1964-65 when a total of twenty-three JCers won doctor's chevrons.[18]

To get good students the college had begun, just prior to the Second World War, to go into as many high schools as possible with a test prepared by the American Council on Education. It was the same one taken on campus by subfreshmen vying for depression-years scholarships. Melvin Rhodes '38, then field representative, was the one who came up with the high school testing idea. After the war the college was getting into no less than 250 high schools, giving the ACE exam to as many as seventeen-thousand college-minded students. Even the faculty went on the road to help administer these exams. The backbreaking chore of correcting them fell upon the college itself. Of 259 colleges and universities reporting in 1954, JC stood thirty-ninth in performance on the ACE test. In 1958 Juniata substituted the College Boards for candidates seeking admission.

Though good, the freshman Board SATs have not been superior. But the Ellis years reflected significant progress. The average verbal score of entering students rose from 476 in 1958 to 542 by 1967 and the average mathematics score from 515 to 571. This was well above the national performance. The new testing requirement, President Ellis announced in his report for 1957, would not affect Juniata's commitment to its three major constituencies, "even if they do not have the highest academic potential."

At first in the postwar years admissions was a part-time job, concerned more with selection than with promotion. Dr. Pressley Crummy was registrar and professor of biology while director of admissions (1942-47). Melvin Rhodes combined admissions work with being dean of students (1947-52). The first full-time director of admissions was Robert Newcombe (1952-57), who now was made answerable to the dean of the college instead of the president's office. Following him were two alumni, Kenneth Wenger '50, from 1957 to 1960, and Ronald Wertz '59, 1960 to 1963. The next dozen years saw Richard Kimmey bring Juniata's enrollment to its peak. From first-floor Founders, the admissions office in 1958 was moved downstairs to its present location just inside the Tower entrance.

THE CURRICULUM OF THE 1960S

Dr. Calvert's headship entertained two Middle States visits — in 1951 and 1962. These come at about ten-year intervals. On both occasions it was found that Juniata's virtues far outweighed its faults. The 1962 evaluation noted that the college's " 'family' concept is important to students and faculty alike." It warned, however, that organizational shortcuts "inevitably invite friction." Juniata, its enrollment then just under eight-hundred, "offers," said the reaccrediting report, "a program of studies that is good — not distinctive, but distinctive notes are there."[19]

Already in operation when the '62 team showed up was an overhauled curriculum, initiated the previous fall. A faculty foursome, including Dean Mays, had spent three weeks at a Danforth-sponsored workshop at Colorado Springs the summer of 1959 restructuring the general curricular requirements. Faculty meetings the next academic year were given over to debate on the proposed changes.

The new pattern of education called for two basic courses, a year-long one for freshmen and another for seniors. Frosh took Great Epochs of World Culture, at first taught by Steven Barbash (M.F.A., Yale), art instructor and the faculty's one Jew. Barbash, a flamboyant New Yorker, got his share of spoofing each year by freshmen in their All Class Night

Familiar end-of-the-semester scene in 1950s and 1960s: final exams in gym.

skit, as did the course itself and those who handled subsection discussion groups. For the seniors there was The Integration of Art, Knowledge, and Conduct, whose pompous title was later changed to Nature of Man.

General education, long one of Juniata's commitments, was provided for by the distribution strategy. Every student had to take four courses in each division outside his/her field of concentration, spread over two different departments. In 1965 the distribution requirement for Division III was changed, reducing it to three semesters of work in any two departments of which at least two semesters had to involve a natural science laboratory.

"Concentration" and "collateral" became the jargon for major and minor. Collateral courses, though, could cut across several disciplines. Dual concentration, in which a student attained a measure of depth in two different departments, became an option in 1964. It carried with it several alternatives with respect to the comprehensive examination.

Still retained was English conference. And requirements continued in foreign language, religion (upped to two courses—Biblical History plus a second—but reduced back to one in 1966), and physical education. Nor were comps given up. Applied credit also stayed on the books—up to four hours for extracurricular participation in music. But journalistic activity, debate, and drama no longer qualified, as they once did, after the 1963 spring semester.

The Dean's List, which replaced the Honor Roll after Juniata got an academic dean, turned into two in 1964, a first and a second. The next fall midterm grades became obsolete, replaced by deficiency slips. A rather liberal pass/fail system (one p/f course per semester outside the field of concentration) went into effect in 1967. By then a variety of independent study opportunities were available to students. Few, though, took advantage of them.

The 1961 curriculum, of course, maintained the three-division structure. In 1963 division chairmanships, which heretofore had been largely honorific and of indefinite tenure, now went on a three-year cycle (as did department heads), the appointments by the president. The intent was to vitalize the three posts, providing the dean of the college with closer faculty liaison in carrying out the academic life of the institution. An undesigned result was divisional envy—especially toward the well-heeled sciences, enriched by the post-Sputnik bonanza.

The humanities, with 20.9 percent of all majors in 1965, howled the loudest. The administration responded by funding a double-faceted program worked out by the division: short stay artists-in-residence and a lectureship in comparative studies. Jack Gilbert, 1962 winner of the Yale Younger Poets Award, got things underway as resident number one the spring of 1964. The first lecturer in comparative studies, beginning the fall of 1965, was Dr. Lawrence Abler, a young scholar from California who taught in the general areas of English and German.

Other gains came to the humanities during the decade of the Sixties. A modern language laboratory went into the I. Harvey Brumbaugh House in 1961. History, linked up with political science as a Division II department, split off and joined the humanities in 1964.* At that time "Clio" was second only to biology in number of majors—108. The art department, which had been revived in 1953, got quarters befitting its

---

*The religion department had already made the jump.

dignity in 1964. (Until 1953 there had been no instruction in the graphic arts since 1921). Before taking over renovated Carnegie Library the department made do in one of the Village's old barracks on Round Top. In 1966 speech and theater was given its autonomy by the English department. Russian, meanwhile, had been introduced back in 1961.

Phased out in 1968, however, was music education, a May 1965 trustee decision. Too costly for the returns, the board said. The emphasis now was to be on the cultural value of music for all students instead of teacher preparation.

At the same time Division II lost home economics. When World War II ended it had been the college's largest department. From 1947 to its demise the department occupied a white frame building, provided by the Federal Works Agency, which stood just east of Women's Gym. Its nursery was the little cottage behind Brumbaugh Hall. Limited financial resources left the trustees no choice about home ec's fate. There were twenty-one in its last graduating class.

Division II claimed the greatest number of majors the spring of 1968—35.9 percent of the college total. Education topped the heap (122), thriving on what Howard Crouch (Ph.D., Ohio State) in a 1966 *Juniatian* editorial called the "worst teacher shortage" in twenty years. Economics and business administration ran a close second (ninety-three). Sociology majors nearly doubled those of psychology (seventy-nine to forty-seven), as LBJ's "Great Society" dreams made the job market in social welfare a good bet. Political science, far down the column, got something of a boost when JCers were admitted to two off-campus programs in 1966: the United Nations Semester through Drew University and American University's Washington Semester.

In springtime 1968 nearly thirty-five percent of JC students were concentrating in some field of science. Biologists were by far the most numerous on the Hill (227). Chemists came in a distant second (sixty-one). Math and physics were tied at seventeen. However, geology—introduced in 1962—had built up a following of twenty-nine. Its lowly departmental birth under "Pete" Trexler had taken place in the basement of Students Hall. By 1968, of course, Division III was settled in the Brumbaugh Science Center, a small-college wonder, then three years old.

The division then had—and still does have—several cooperative programs going that had been negotiated in the early 1950s. They include medical technology, engineering, and forestry. In the latter two cases, under a 3-2 plan, dual degrees are involved, one from Juniata and one from the other institution.

What most quickened the envy of Divisions I and II in the early

Sixties was the way the sciences were bankrolled by Uncle Sam, running scared after Sputnik went into orbit. Thousands of dollars, some for equipment but the lion's share for training undergrads in research, flowed Juniata's way, almost for the asking. The National Science Foundation, the Atomic Energy Commission, and the National Institutes of Health played Santa Claus with grants. From 1961 to 1966 the chemistry department conducted NSF-funded summer institutes for high school chemistry teachers. Juniata's 1961 grant was one of only twenty-two held throughout the country under NSF auspices.[20]

A curricular innovation in 1962, though adivisional, has since worked most for the benefit of the humanities. This is the Brethren Colleges Abroad program. BCA, which provides study in Europe during a student's junior year, is sponsored by the six colleges associated with the Church of the Brethren. Its first year program was limited to Phillips-Universitat, more commonly known as Marburg University. Juniata's inaugural contingent was made up of Carol Barnhart (Weiss), Nancy Graybill (Becker), Betty Miller (Taffe), Ronald Smelser, and John Tobias. Junior-year study abroad was expanded in 1963 to include the University of Strasbourg, France, and in 1972 the University of Barcelona, Spain. Two JC profs have put in time as a BCA overseas director: Miriam Schlegel Musselman (1966-67) and George Dolnikowski (1970-72). Some JCers soon began going over on their own to study under other programs approved by the college.

Adivisional, too, was the Will Judy Lectureship, established in the fall of 1958. The captain's twenty-thousand dollar gift was intended to "supplement and enrich" the college's academic program by bringing to the Hill speakers of note from a wide spectrum of areas—government, education, the arts, natural science, business, and other important fields of the public sector. Today the choice of lecturers is rotated among the three divisions.

Meanwhile, the early Sixties brought a new library (1963), long awaited and urgently advised in both Middle States reviews. Mrs. Anne Catlin had come as director of libraries, a new position, the year before to take charge of preparing for the massive move to north-campus headquarters. In the spring of 1967 Juniata joined the Area College Library Cooperative, then comprised of nine other Central Pennsylvania institutions (now seventeen). Mrs. Catlin called it "a model for inter-library cooperation throughout the United States." Each college has developed an area of specialization.[21] For Juniata it is the Myers Science Library, whose first librarian was Russell Powell '65.

Registrars, no less than librarians, must cater to faculty and students if the academic process is to move along smoothly and happily. Occupants of this office during the Ellis quarter-century were: Pressley Crummy (1942-49); William Engel, Jr. (1949-56, 1958-59); James Bray (1956-58); Hans Zbinden (1959-60); Ronald Cherry (1960-63); and John Hollinger, a '58 JC grad (1963-68).

There was never a dull moment at the registrar's counter when alumnus Ronald Cherry '53 (Ph.D., Princeton), a forceful individual, held sway. It was he, however, who began to translate the data accumulated in his office into useful statistical studies. They paved the way for the first feeble efforts at institutional research, now a full-blown position, in 1966. In his day the registrar was stationed on third floor Founders where the office (previously located in what is now the academic dean's office) moved in 1962. Then in 1965 the rest of the old chapel, used as a classroom, was renovated and given over to registrar use.

Part of the renovation included a data-processing center where four IBM machines were installed. At first the equipment was used primarily by the registrar, but with time all records-keeping departments switched to automation.

A BOARD OF TRUSTEES THAT DARED

One of the most interesting aspects of his presidency, Calvert Ellis once observed, was helping businessmen to understand educators and vice versa. "Educators tend to be autocrats — there is no need to compromise," he said.[22] "Businessmen compromise constantly." Ellis had a way with men of affairs, and the rapport between him and the board of trustees remained exceptionally strong the whole of his twenty-five years as president.

He inherited more than a score of board members from his father's administration. But gradually he built a dedicated corps of his own. Some were discovered when elected by the alumni or a church district. The board between 1944 and 1968 co-opted twenty-three charter members. They represented a wide range of business and occupational interests. Two were women. In the order of their years of service they were: Donovan Beachley '21, 1945-present; Dale Detwiler, 1949-present; John Montgomery '21, 1950-present; John Swigart '30, 1950-present; George Detweiler '28, 1947-50, 1953-74; Joseph Good, 1952-present; Lester Rosenberger, 1952-present; William Flory '21, 1946-69; Chalender Lesher, 1947-68; Robert Baker, 1956-76; Edith Hartman Cutrell '27, 1957-present; C. Jewett Henry '29, 1959-present; Paul Robinson '35, 1959-75; Denton Emmert '36, 1959-62, 1963-present; Percy Blough, 1944-47, 1952-62; William Book, 1946-49, 1951-62; Robert Miller, 1957-69; Charles Ellis '40,

1966-present; Cecil Loomis, 1967-present; Thomas Miller '36, 1967-present; Charles Rice, 1967-present; Thomas Martin, 1968-present; Florence Fogelsanger Murphy '12, 1963-68. John Stauffer '36 joined the board in 1967, the year before his election to succeed Dr. Ellis.

When Calvert Ellis became president, Dr. Gaius Brumbaugh, the last personal link to the college's inception, was presiding trustee. After forty years on the board, its chairman since 1936, he resigned in 1948 at age eighty-six (he died in 1952). Elected in his place was Henry Gibbel, a Lititz, Pennsylvania, banker and insurance executive, whose father had been Juniata's third board chairman. For more than a decade, long a close Ellis friend and an ardent fan of Indian football, he gave vigorous leadership. He was felled by a heart attack in 1959, still in his fifties. That same year Dr. Clyde Mierley, a prominent Huntingdon dentist, stepped aside after twenty-two years as vice-chairman. So did Ross Murphy, a Brethren pastor, secretary since 1943. John Swigart, grandson of W. J., has kept the minutes these last seventeen years.

There followed a succession of one-year chairmanships after 1959: Newton Long (1959-60); Chalender Lesher (1960-61); Warren Hershberger (1961-62); Joseph Kline (1962-63). This practice ceased in 1963 when John Baker took the helm because, the trustees saw, he and Ellis "made such an effective team."[23] The latter has often said, jokingly, that he never had a real "boss" until the day of Dr. Baker's election.

John Baker, a tall, suave, energetic native of nearby Everett, would be "boss" for thirteen years. His M.B.A. degree from Harvard in 1923, he remained there until 1945, first in a number of Business School positions and then as associate dean of the university. From 1945 until 1961 he served as the fourteenth president of Ohio University. Said *Time Magazine* in 1951: "A Yaleman founded the school, but a Harvardman put it on its feet."[24] The college in Ohio's Hocking Valley was in "shabby shape," John Baker discovered upon his arrival. "He searched like a talent scout," acclaimed *Time*, "for the best men he could find to fill the vacancies." The Baker administration provided Ohio University, founded in 1804, with its period of greatest growth, both physically and academically. Enrollment more than quintupled — to eight-thousand — and thirty-two major buildings were added to the campus. In 1954, 1955, and 1956 Dr. Baker was appointed by Dwight Eisenhower as chief U. S. representative to UNESCO. He later conducted State Department studies of education needs in Cambodia and Colombia and in 1975 served as an adviser to the government of Iran.

No one can properly assess what his experience and vision in higher education has meant to the board. Fortunately, back in December 1944, when voted to Ohio U.'s top post, he was talked out of abdicating as a JC trustee.

Just before the Baker-Ellis team was formed the trustee bylaws underwent a significant revision. In 1959 they were altered to read: "A majority of the elected members of the Board shall be members of the Church of the Brethren." This replaced the four-fifths prescript. The rationale? Most trustees were alumni well aware of the college's religious past and many Brethren, who lived in places not churched by their denomination, had joined other faiths.

Something said by James Baxter, president of Williams College, had hit home with Calvert Ellis back when he took office. Dr. Baxter wrote, while World War II raged at full fury: "The colleges and universities cannot go unreconstructed in a world undergoing a general reconstruction."[25] On the Hill these words inspired the Planning Commission, set up in 1944. It involved over one-hundred persons—trustees, alumni, faculty—through associated committees, deliberating the aims and goals of Juniata once peace came. Out of the commission's study sprang the "Juniata Postwar Fund," approved by the trustees shortly before V-E Day. Its goal was one-million dollars—for buildings and endowment. This was the first million-dollar drive in the college's history. It delivered the goods by 1953.

Yet Calvert Ellis could say that year: "The plight of the private college continues to be precarious."[26] And John Baker was writing from Athens, Ohio: "The small college of 500 students, which idealistically I admire, is no longer an economic unit."[27] There were deficits in the early Fifties as JC's enrollment, hurt by the Korean War, dropped off sharply from a 1949 high of 710. Quoting the *New York Times*, Dr. Ellis told the trustees in October 1951 that more than half the colleges of America were operating on deficits caused by the draft and enlistments. Massive federal aid to higher education was still a decade away, but industry, at least, Juniata's president told the trustees in 1953, was beginning to awaken to its responsibilities.

He was referring to the Foundation for Independent Colleges, a movement that originated in the state of Indiana and that—in 1952—Dr. Ellis had helped organize in Pennsylvania. Juniata was one of thirty-six charter members, its president the foundation's first treasurer. The foundation still exists, heads of member institutions donating time each year to personal solicitation of commercial and industrial concerns. The money is equitably distributed among the free-standing colleges according to a formula.

The fall of 1953 the trustees came out with the two-million dollar "Build Juniata Program," projected over the next decade and calling for an enrollment of 750. It was upped to $2.5 million in 1955. The Ford Foundation that December added special cheer to the Christmas season on the Hill with the announcement of a $138,600 gift, Juniata's largest single windfall up to that time. It went into the endowment fund for faculty salaries.

Parents began to take an interest in the college's financial health. DAJUMO (first two letters of Dad, Juniata, and Mother) came into existence the spring of 1957. The first officers were: Chairman, Benn Goodrich, Ridgeway, Pennsylvania; Vice-Chairman, Horace Raffensperger, Elizabethtown, Pennsylvania; Secretary, Thomas Chase, Philadelphia. Said Mr. Goodrich, "There is a need for the support, both spiritually and financially, from the parents."

In July 1957 came the appointment of Charles Bargerstock '47, an ex-Marine and Iwo Jima hero, to the newly established position of director of development. The former Indian star athlete and insurance underwriter left in 1962. His work was taken up by Harold Brumbaugh, who was advanced to vice president for development the next year (forcing him, against his will, to lay down his first love: alumni work).

The summer of 1961, meanwhile, Juniata had received one-hundred thousand dollars from the estate of nonagenarian Allen Shaffner, a retired local banker. Designated for a scholarship loan fund in memory of his wife and sister, it was til then the biggest bequest from a Huntingdonian.

That same year, while making progress toward the $2.5-million mark, the trustees lifted their sights again, this time to a figure of $5,350,000. Board members themselves subscribed $248,830, and a "quiet campaign" netted $249,355 in Huntingdon. Foundations, business, and industry began to show interest. Parents upped their gifts to nearly four-thousand dollars in 1961. And the alumni, spurred on by a Joe Good-directed effort, responded with higher levels of giving. The fiscal year 1963-64 produced a record in Hilltop charity — the first time gifts to the college exceeded one million dollars ($1,607,635).

In November of 1964 Harold Brumbaugh gained a ball-of-fire, twenty-seven-year-old aide named Gerald Quigg, an Army Reserve 1st Lt. from Delaware. As associate director of development, Quigg, a history major and a track star in college, was assigned the Juniata Valley area.

His personality and hard work earned him a promotion to director of development in 1966.

On Founders Day 1967 the college celebrated a happy ending to the Build Juniata Program, completed sooner than expected and oversubscribed by twenty-thousand dollars. All of this with only a minimum of professional fund-raising help—from American City Bureau, early in the going.

Over the past half-dozen years the student population had risen thirty-three percent, to over one-thousand. The faculty had more than doubled. The operating budget stood at $3.2 million—as against the two-hundred-and-forty-thousand dollars on which the college was run back in 1943.

Since September 1965, however, a Long Range Planning Committee, made up of trustees, faculty, and administration, had been looking into the future—beyond 1967. Among other things it projected, as the optimum enrollment, a college of 1,250 students. This called for more buildings, facilities, and a higher endowment. The cost of educating a Juniata student in the mid-1960s meant that eighty-five cents of every dollar was paid from tuition and fees.

Thus even before the 1967 Founders Day hurrahing, the trustees had hatched another campaign. At the same time there was gathered round Dr. Ellis a President's Development Committee of thirty-three persons, all nontrustees. The council was to assist the college in coping with the increased breadth and complexity of development activities—by representing Juniata to foundations, corporations, and individuals. It was a good group. They made excellent contacts.

This latest capital expansion program, set at an unprecedented $10.1 million and to culminate in the college's centennial year, carried the name "Margin of Difference," coined by Jerry Quigg. What did it mean? In the words of President Ellis, the hoped-for funds "will provide Juniata with that margin of difference in the quality of its education without which it could not successfully meet the challenges of the future."[28] Relying solely upon volunteers, the campaign got underway in April of 1968. The trustees, pledging over three-hundred-and-seventy-thousand dollars, again showed that they were willing to carry their share of the load.

When Ellis retired the endowment had built up to $2,168,594, nearly a fourfold increase since 1943.

Who was responsible for reporting accurately the character and purposes of the development programs? For twenty years (1946-66) it was a man short of stature but long on energy—William Engel. An experienced journalist, having worked on newspaper staffs in the Harrisburg and

Pittsburgh areas, he came to the Hill as director of publicity. But other jobs were soon superadded. Besides editing all college publications and writing countless news releases, he "registrared" for seven years, kept faculty meeting minutes (1954-66), directed summer sessions (two years), announced Juniata football games for WHUN for a decade, taught journalism, advised the *Juniatian*. No wonder that paper said, when he signed "Thirty" to his press desk, it would take more than one person to fill his shoes. The *Alumni Bulletin* (Summer 1966) paid him fitting tribute when he resigned to become director of foundation appeals at Penn State. Someone wrote, ["He has been] the soul and conscience of Juniata's public relations."

Barnard Taylor, a professional designer and painter with a background in newspaper reportage, took Engel's place (1966-73). He, too, was a man of many talents and great drive. While at Juniata he painted, lectured, wrote, ran his office, and—in his mid-fifties—finished an M.F.A. degree at Penn State. His commissioned canvas of Christopher Sauer's printshop hangs in Beeghly Library. The centennial logo, a tree sprouting from an open book, was his design. His graphic skills and instincts brought a fresh look to all college publications.

A CAMPUS BEAUTIFUL

A profusion of buildings stand as a monument to Calvert Ellis's presidency, though this is not, as he has said, what he wants to be remembered for. Feverish construction was a phenomenon of the times on all campuses, he says, in brushing aside his brick-and-mortar achievements. His presidential years, however, saw the main campus enlarge from forty to fifty-five acres, beautified by planned landscaping. The physical plant multiplied to twenty-four buildings, valued at more than ten million dollars.

The campus transformation began modestly enough. There was no major reconstruction until eight years after he became president. Some of the first buildings—government surplus—are gone. Sherwood Lodge, better known as the "Green Shanty," was a 1946 addition. It was a temporary barracks-style dorm, H-shaped, that stood in the hollow north of Cloister—to house eighty-six veterans. On Easter Sunday 1955 the east wing was destroyed by fire (ignited by town children playing with matches). That summer a buyer dismantled the undamaged part. Sherwood Lodge, however, had encroached upon the unfinished golf course, which had suffered badly from wartime neglect. A campus links, it was soon evident, had no future.

The "Village"—for married vets—also went up in 1946, on the present site of Brumbaugh Science Center. It consisted of six buildings with dwelling units for twenty families. For its original occupants there must still linger nostalgic memories of diapers on washlines, baby carriages on the grass, ice cards in the windows, and coal in outside bins. Later, after the vets left, faculty occasionally made use of the Village for housing. As we saw, the art department also moved in. The once-peopled colony finally disappeared in 1964, to make way for science.

The immediate postwar years also saw: M. G. Brumbaugh's old home, fire-gutted in January of 1945, reconstructed into the Faculty Club (1946); the college take over the I. Harvey Brumbaugh House (1947), a gift of trustees Henry Gibbel and Donovan Beachley; home economics barracked, as already noted, behind Brumbaugh Hall (1947). The I. Harvey Brumbaugh House became an extension of the library until the language lab was installed. (Later on it was also converted into offices for faculty linguists, and then, in 1972, turned over to public relations.)

High on the priority list of the postwar Planning Commission had been a student center with a refectory that could seat all resident students. That never developed, but an addition to the Oneida Hall dining room did (1950). Now over 470 could be served at one time. This ended, for a while at least, the two-platoon system of eating, a necessity since 1946.

Swigart Music Hall (1950), a private home last owned by Francis McSherry, president of the J. C. Blair Co., was a godsend.[29] The 1945 fire at the corner of Moore and 17th had deprived the music department of several studios and practice rooms. The McSherry property was made possible through a gift of W. Emmert Swigart, "W. J.'s" son. The three-story structure, which still houses the music department, underwent extensive renovation in 1964 when the exterior (brown brick) was painted white and the front porch removed.

The big construction thrust lay ahead. The seventeen years after 1950 would see one building after another dot the campus—ten in all. The parade got started with the Memorial Physical Education Building (1951), erected in honor of the nearly seven-hundred Juniatians who served in World War II. Designed by John B. Hamme of York, Pennsylvania, it was the forerunner of all later Pennsylvania gyms and was the first of its kind to use an arched roof.[30] Folding bleachers, above which is laid a mezzanine indoor track, seat 1,080.

The old 1901 building now became the "Women's Gymnasium."

Meanwhile, Elizabeth Ellis fretted. Not knowing the future, she was afraid her husband's presidency would be remembered only for a gymnasium, while that of his father's for Oller Hall, a cultural center. Time would allay her fears.

Aerial shot of campus, early 1950s. Notice Hollywood area (top) is undeveloped. Geiger House is across 18th from Memorial Gymnasium.

In October 1952, while Dwight Eisenhower and Adali Stevenson were squared off for the upcoming presidential election, Dr. Ellis carried good news to the trustees. "Build Juniata" plans were then all but finalized. He announced that outgoing President Truman had at last released forty-million dollars for housing loans to colleges and universities under a law passed by Congress in 1950—a law Dr. Ellis had personally lobbied for.

Hamme-designed North Hall, on the eminence overlooking the northeast campus, became the second dormitory in the country to be partially financed by funds under the 1950 Act.[31] Erected in 1955 in two sections with a connecting lounge, it accommodates 128 men.* A structural problem (noise carried through the halls and rooms unabated) soon elicited pejorative nicknames for the dorm. "Campus Albatross" or "Wart of Huntingdon County" it was called. (The problem has been remedied for the most part.) Architecturally, North Hall set the pattern for all campus buildings to follow—contemporary colonial style of red brick in four blending shades.

That autumn the college changed architects—to an Altoona firm, Hunter, Caldwell, and Campbell (it goes by a different name today). All major buildings since have been their architectural creations.

East Hall (renamed Maude Lesher Hall in 1960), L-shaped and four floors high, reared up in 1957 where the Geiger House had stood.** Rooming 120 women, it has a dining room (for two-hundred but no longer used), a lounge, and recreation area. The college infirmary, with doctor's offices and nurses' quarters, is also in this building. Lesher Hall made media human-interest news when the late Capt. Will Judy, ever the imaginative and willing alumnus, furnished a room "to be occupied only by titian-tressed ladies in honor of my wife, Ruth."[32] Joan Greenwood (Metro), a senior elementary education major from New Jersey, was the first auburn-haired occupant of room 201 (not until 1964 did two redheads live together there).

---

*The Maintenance Building was a 1955 project, too—a two-floor concrete block structure next to the Heating Plant. Here are located the shops for carpentry, plumbing, and painting and the Central Stores where college supplies are kept.

**Three private residences were acquired during the 1950s for additional student housing, each named for a prominent person in Juniata's history. They were: the N. J. Brumbaugh House (1953), at 1808 Moore St., the chemistry professor's actual home; the Emmert House, corner of 18th and Moore, for David Emmert; and the Saylor House, 18th and Mifflin, for Joseph Saylor. The "N. J." House and the Emmert House also had faculty apartments. Only the N. J. House is still used for student housing. The Emmert House was razed in 1975 and Dr. Kenneth Crosby bought the Saylor House in 1961, remodeling it for his own use.

Sherwood Hall, a three-floor men's dorm (for 120) east of North Hall, went up in 1961. Next year came L-shaped South Hall (for 150 women), at the corner of Scott and 17th, one wing overlooking College Field. This brought about the total evacuation of Founders and parts of Oneida.

Faculty from Divisions I and II rushed in—except for art, music, and the languages. They commandeered third and fourth Founders for badly needed private offices, heretofore a denied luxury to most of them.

Now came a five-year respite in dorm-raising. But the Altoona architects were not kept idle. A library and a science complex were on the drawing boards.

Ever since 1946, on a tip from alumnus Edgar Diehm, then a high school teacher, Calvert Ellis and Harold Brumbaugh had been making regular trips to Youngstown, Ohio. There they would call on Leon A. Beeghly, a wealthy industrialist, cultivating his interest in building a library on the Hill. Mr. Beeghly's grandparents had been prominent in the history of the Church of the Brethren in Ohio.

The Beeghly Foundation, however, was for years tied up in litigation with the government. In the end, the IRS lost and in 1963 Juniata got its library—at a cost of over six-hundred-thousand dollars. Located along Moore Street but facing Memorial Gym, the L. A. Beeghly Library has space for one-hundred-and-fifty-thousand volumes and reader locations, including individual carrels, for more than four-hundred students. A decorative feature above the main entrance displays the seals of the college, the town of Huntingdon, and the founder of the Church of the Brethren in colorful ceramic tile. This was a gift of Stanley Davis of Lansdale, Pennsylvania. The second-floor William Emmert Swigart treasure room, with its rare books, incunabula, and first editions, holds great attraction for visiting scholars. Until the College Center was built, the bookstore took up most of the basement area.

The old library, renamed Carnegie Hall (1964), was imaginatively redesigned as a fine arts center. The Col. Henry W. Shoemaker Galleries now occupy the main floor for exhibitions.* Upstairs, in the rotunda, is a historical museum, Harold Brumbaugh its curator. The rest of the

---

*Col. Henry Shoemaker had been a close friend of M. G. Brumbaugh. A two-war veteran, he had been at one time or another a banker, railroader, newspaper publisher, and ambassador to Bulgaria. He wrote hundreds of books and pamphlets on Pennsylvania history and folklore. His home was at McElhattan in the eastern part of the state, but for thirty-eight years he published the *Altoona Tribune*. He had a Juniata honorary doctorate and many of his works are in the college Archives.

building is given over to the art department for studio space and general classrooms. At first ceramics, including a kiln, had space there, too, until relocated elsewhere.

The site of a projected new science building was decided in 1958 — west side of Moore Street where the Village stood. Blueprints showed a pretentious structure. The major breakthrough in funding it came in 1962 when the Longwood Foundation of Wilmington, Delaware, announced a four-hundred-thousand dollar challenge grant (then the single largest grant in JC's history, eclipsed the next year by Beeghly bounty). Brumbaugh Science Center (1965), constructed at a cost of $2.7 million, is probably one of the finest of its kind among the nation's small colleges. Making use of natural topography, it is laid out in four elevations, three wings radiating from a large hub. The multiunit complex contains a chemistry wing (south), a biology wing (west), and a geology, mathematics, and physics wing (north). The north wing is also the location of the college computer center (which started out in the basement of Carnegie Library). The two-story circular unit at the hub has a four-hundred-seat Alumni Auditorium above which are the Myers Science Library and two pie-shaped lecture halls. The Myers Science Library has space for eighty-thousand volumes and forty readers.

By November of 1966 the college was in debt to Uncle Sam some one-million dollars for loans on dorms and the Science Center.[33] On top of that applications had been made for another $1,150,000 in loans plus a federal grant of two-hundred-and-fifty-thousand dollars for additional construction.

One application was for the Tussey-Terrace Complex (1966), a two-unit, L-shaped building connected by a one-floor social center, on the northwest section of campus. It provides rooms for 176 students. Also an apartment for Harold Brumbaugh, who for years had been ensconced in the Cloister Arch.

The other application was for what at first was called the Academic Classroom Building (1967), the enlarged (wings on either side) and totally remodeled 1916 Science Hall. Air conditioned like Beeghly Library and the Science Center, it provides thirty-two classrooms, five instructional laboratories, and twenty-two faculty offices for the social science division. (The humanities now reigned supreme in Founders' upper reaches.) The language laboratories moved into the new structure (basement) from the I. Harvey Brumbaugh House.

After seventy-two years Students Hall stood empty and silent, deserted. But not for long. It was invaded the next year by children from the Alexandria-Petersburg area, whose grade school had burned to the ground. Then it fell silent again, this time for good.

The Academic Building ended the Ellis era of construction. But others were in the works, to come under the next administration.

At the tail end of the Ellis era the college came into possession of some off-campus property, donated by JC friends. A bequest from Dr. Clyde Mierley gave Juniata half-interest in the Wagner-Mierley Building, corner of Washington and 7th streets, from which the college realized an income from commercial rentals. In the mid-1960s Juniata got close to sixteen acres of land from the late State Sen. Charles Mallery. This acreage lies along the highway from Water Street to Alexandria adjacent to the Juniata River and north of Alfarata Park. The J. C. Blair Building was a gift of Westab Corporation of Dayton, Ohio [now Mead Products] in 1965 (then valued at $345,000).* In spite of rentals it became something of a "white elephant," the cost of maintenance outrunning income.**

KEEPING AN EYE ON THE BOTTOM LINE

When the Ellis switch took place in 1943 William Price, up in years, became the treasurer. But his health was failing and he died in 1949. Mrs. Rhoda Metz Rhodes, assistant treasurer, ran the office until 1952 when she left. John Fike was then hired to handle the college's financial affairs. His trustee father had led the fight for board ratification of the TIAA faculty pension plan back in the late 1930s. A Somerset, Pennsylvania, native, Fike, towering well over six feet, was an active Brethren layman and a civic leader during his nineteen years on the Hill. In 1963 he became a vice-president, along with Morley Mays and Harold Brumbaugh. As the chief budget officer, he had the rare quality of being able to say no and not make anyone mad.

Promoted to John Fike's assistant in 1952 was Hilda Nathan, German-born, who had joined the treasurer's office in 1946. In 1969 she was elevated to chief accountant. Her retirement, in the centennial year, closed out a career spanning three decades on College Hill. All that time she never knew what a forty-hour week meant, driven by her teutonic genes. Her work brought her into close contact with students, for whose names she demonstrated an amazing memory. A friendly woman of many interests, Miss Nathan has always been a sports fan, especially of Juniata teams and the Pittsburgh Pirates.

---

*Both the Wagner-Mierley Building and the Blair Building were sold in 1975.
**In 1967 trustee Joseph Good of Hollidaysburg, Pennsylvania, gave the college a warehouse in Williamsport. But it was sold the same year for sixty-five thousand dollars.

Also employed in 1946 was Paul Friend '37, as business manager. A football standout for the Indians, he rose from infantry private to captain during World War II (Pacific theater). On his shoulders fell most of the responsibility for maintenance of buildings and grounds until 1963 when he also became assistant treasurer (which made him purchaser of *all* college supplies). The care of the campus then became the worry of Eugene "Gene" Esterline (1963-73), with plenty more construction ahead.* Paul Friend gave twenty-one years to his alma mater in the business office.

CHURCH RELATIONS AND ALUMNI AFFAIRS

Annual Conference began helping out shrunken Brethren colleges, most worse off than Juniata, during World War II. For thirteen years after 1944 it made regular appropriations to each school—in Juniata's case something like fifty-thousand dollars altogether. Not much, but it was intended more to symbolize denominational support than pay bills, especially after the wartime crunch.

Early in the postwar development program the college went after more tangible backing from the three church districts represented on the board of trustees. Edgar Detwiler '12, a retired Brethren pastor from Morrison's Cove, became director of church relations on a part-time basis (1948-57). Then in 1954, the Build Juniata program in high gear, Clarence Rosenberger '36, called from a pastorate, joined Rev. Detwiler as a full-time partner.

Rosenberger, who in 1945 had helped organize the first "Heifers for Relief" shipment and served as the "Zona Gale's" crew chief, spent fifteen years in the church relations office. He expanded the college's contact with the nearly 140 churches in the three districts. He introduced Brethren Campus Day, a Saturday of visitation by pastors and college-minded high schoolers, and began publishing a news sheet, the "Builder," in 1955. He arranged for Hilltop faculty, administrators, and student deputation teams to present "Juniata College Day" services in local congregations. It was his idea to make Juniata the repository of all Middle District historical records.

For the quarter-century after 1943 contributions from the churches of the three districts increased from less than twenty-seven hundred dollars to slightly over twenty-eight thousand dollars. Ironically, however, the number of Brethren students declined from twenty-six percent of the enrollment to 12.8 percent for the same period.

---

*During 1962-63 Paul Friend had help from Donald Schaaf, who carried the title Superintendent of Buildings and Grounds inherited by Gene Esterline.

In many of the district churches, of course, there were alumni who contributed to the college independently. Back in 1919 Charles Eliot of Harvard had said that a college had no right to expect financial assistance from others if its own alumni will not rally round its alma mater. JC grads, between 1943 and 1968, gave their fair share of seed money. Twice—in 1963 and 1964—Juniata received achievement citations from the American Alumni Council. By 1968 alumni had contributed over two-million dollars in the twenty-nine years since the annual giving program originated. That year there was a 36.6 percent participation, not the highest in the country but well above the national average of 17.9 percent. Averaged out, each Juniata contributor gave $81.72 more than his/her counterpart elsewhere ($118.64 to $36.92).[34] Will Judy, the nationally known dog fancier and publisher who had thought up the One Hundred Club, scored again in 1948 with the One Thousand Club. The Five Hundred Club had a 1966 delivery. In 1967 it became the practice to call these three groups collectively "The Founders Clubs."

The spring of 1953 forty-seven seniors, their class treasury depleted and unable to do something to commemorate their days at JC, cooked up a novel plan of systematic giving to the alumni fund. At the instigation of Ronald Cherry, soon to come back to teach, and Paul Good, of Youngstown, Ohio, the forty-seven became the "53 Investors Club." Each member promised to contribute $10 a year, to be invested over the next decade by a board of directors. At its tenth reunion, held at Motel 22, the fifty-three Investors turned over their entire portfolio—worth $5,817.15 —to the college as an endowment gift (for library books).

Midsummer 1966 Harold Brumbaugh acted as host guide for the first alumni tour—to Europe. There have been nineteen subsequent tours, including an African safari, Caribbean cruises, and trips to the South Pacific and subequatorial countries of the Western Hemisphere.

At the time of the first European tour H. B. was, of course, no longer alumni secretary. William "Whitey" Martin '59, as genial as they come, was secretary from 1963 to 1966. It was Whitey who arranged the first telethon—in 1964—to raise alumni funds. Then out of the pastorate came Glenn Zug '51, a no less outgoing personality, for the next half-dozen years.

By 1968 there were over six-thousand living alumni. The local associations numbered twenty-two, ranging from California to Florida to Boston. The Alumni Office kept close track of ex-Juniatians, publishing two updated directories (1948 and 1958).*

---

* Later directories came out in 1971 and 1976.

A disproportionate number of graduates had made *Who's Who*; some were even newsworthy enough to get coverage in popular publications like *Life, Reader's Digest*, and the *New York Times*. And, of course, there was 103-year-old William Beery, a hero of Juniata's early past and in 1955 the oldest living college alumnus in the United States. Every April 8th (his birthday) since 1940 he had sung over a nationwide network from station WLS Chicago (he died January 29, 1956).

Ten years before William Beery's death the Juniata Women's League (combining the five local groups) consolidated in a central organization for "the purpose of promoting the spiritual and financial welfare of Juniata College." Its charter meeting was held October 26, 1946. For many a spring the League's "Continental Breakfast" has made replenishing the treasury for its manifold projects a painless and most pleasant experience. "White elephant" sales plus dues also provide income. Besides beautifying the campus and providing other amenities, the League helps to form a closer relationship between the college and the community of Huntingdon. About four-hundred Countians are Leaguers, some Juniatians but many not.

A Quarter Century of Dynamic Growth 1943-1968

(Part 2)

THE GI CAMPUS INVASION

The tides of battle had not yet turned when Calvert Ellis took charge on College Hill. In Europe D Day's cross-channel landing at French Normandy was still in the planning stages. In the Pacific the assaults on the Philippines—at Leyte and Luzon—were a year away. The fall of 1944 found only sixty-five men on campus, which was not the lowest male population among colleges of similar size in the state.[1]

A spirit of "carry on" pervaded the student body of 295 that autumn. Enrollment would slip no further. At Christmastime the Senate and Lamba Gamma sent special greetings to all JC men and women in the service as "a gesture of friendship and loyalty." And Alumni Secretary Harold Brumbaugh kept in touch with them through the "Jay-Ce-O-Gram," a mimeographed news sheet.

Then came fierce fighting on German and Japanese fronts: the Battle of the Bulge, crossing the Rhine, Iwo Jima, Okinawa. The awful costs of war did not spare Juniata. The total number of students and alumni in the armed forces finally reached 675, of whom twenty-four would not return home.[2] Probably fewer than half a dozen Hilltoppers served in Civilian Public Service camps as COs.

At last the fall of Nazi Germany in May 1945. In August the devastation of Hiroshima and Nagasaki. Five alumni, said N. J. Brumbaugh, had been connected with groups that did research on the developoment of the A-bomb.[3] On August 14th the 110 summer students breathed a prayer of thanks when sirens announced the surrender of Imperial Japan.

The GIs who returned to the Hill in September did not feel at home at first. They organized a Veterans Club to provide, reported the *Juniatian*, a "niche" for themselves, most of whom were "unfamiliar with present campus faces and organizations, and naturally [have] little incentive to join strange organizations."[4]

By spring veterans constituted twenty-four percent of the student body. That fall the enrollment soared to 573, doubling in one year. Of the 349 men on campus, 257 were GIs of whom fifty-seven were married.

Calvert Ellis was uneasy about what was happening. He wrote John Baker at Ohio University:

> I am. . .anxious that we accept only those veterans who will be able to do the work and be satisfactory graduates of Juniata. We find a number of men are applying for admission who actually are not fitted to carry forward college work satisfactorily. It is difficult to refuse admission and yet I feel that we must maintain our integrity as educational institutions.[5]

Faced with a housing emergency, the trustees vetoed the use of trailers. They turned to off-campus rooms and, of course, Army surplus buildings the Village and Sherwood Lodge. The "Green Shanty," however, was not ready until October, and so for nearly a month eighty-six veterans bedded down in the old gymnasium. Their married counterparts in the Village organized the next year and elected a mayor, Richard March, a Scottsdale, Pennsylvania, biology student.

The number of vets on the Hill peaked the academic year 1947-48, when over half the student body was there on the GI Bill. By 1949-50 only about one-fourth were vets, the freshman class counting but twenty-one of them. The average age of students had declined, and campus leadership was passing to those coming directly to Juniata from high school. A total of 583 ex-World War IIers had studied at JC by July 21, 1951, the cut-off date for the GI Bill.

Scholastically the veterans had more than proved equal to the task. For them a degree seemed to hold out the promise of economic security. A survey in 1949 concluded college-going vets were "curiously old before their time."

The new breed of students replacing them struck Calvert Ellis — at least at first — as lacking their motivation.

CAMPUS LIFE DURING THE POSTWAR FORTIES

The vets came back to find women pretty much running the Hilltop show. For the first time in its history the Senate drew up an all-female slate for president the spring of 1945. Frances Clemens (Nyce), a junior, was elected. ("Fran" was not the first woman president, however. Barbara Boyd, Senate veep for 1944-45, moved up to the top slot when president-elect William Maclay entered the service.)

Myron Dunlavy, today a businessman and owner of nearby Lincoln Caverns, was mildly disgusted with the campus situation on his return the fall of 1945. He wrote a letter to the *Juniatian* — "Are We Mice or Men?" — which he, the father of a daughter, must now recall with great amusement. It began: "Who dominates the activities at Juniata — the women!" And then went on:

> He [the veteran] is thankful to those courageous souls for their fine efforts in doing men's jobs during the emergency. . . .
>
> However, the war is over and the women at Juniata, as well as women all over America, must relinquish many of their war-time jobs. It must be realized that women have an entirely different attitude than men toward many things and therefore are not as qualified as men in certain offices. Further, women should remember that men dislike domineering women.
>
> Imagine if you can the lack of force and progress Juniata life would have in three or four years if the leadership were not returned to men at least in part. Remember that our American way of life is basically patriarchal — it has been this way of life which has set America where it is among nations — it has been this way of life which has set Juniata where it is among colleges![6]

Who won the next election for Senate prexy? Glenora Edwards (Rossell), Myron's letter notwithstanding.

The vets soon worked changes on the campus. They reveled in their newly gained freedom from the restraints of military life. They did not take kindly to civilian ones. After all, they were men now, not boys. With them, for one thing, came college-sponsored dances. The first one (December 17, 1946) was discreetly arranged to be off-campus — at the Huntingdon Country Club. The *Juniatian* cryptically referred to it as a Veterans Club "party," a "semi-formal event," with "music furnished by a ten piece orchestra from Altoona." Some trustees were unhappy, but sixty-four-year-old Bessie Rohrer said the board had more important things to think about and to let the president run the campus. She silenced the issue forever. Next year, two dances were held on the Hill itself, one by "J" Clubbers, the other by the vets. The *Juniatian* did not now resort to euphemisms in publicizing them. Saturday night dances in the gym after that were a regular part of the social calendar.

In other less unprecedented ways the peacetime campus came alive. In October 1945 the college bussed to Paradise Furnace for Mountain Day, last observed in 1941. Drama, a casualty of the war in 1942, was revived by Esther Doyle in December of 1945. The reorganized Masquers, under her direction, staged Kaufman and Hart's "You Can't Take It With You."

Pygmalion, Masque production (Nov. 1947). A. Saltzman, M. Roop (Mitchell), D. Belz (King), W. Fegan, D. Norris, B. May (Sacra), D. Eshbach (Muir).

The A Cappella Choir, campused during the war years 1943-45, took to the road for its fourteenth concert tour the spring of 1946, Prof. Rowland still directing. The Rowland-conducted a cappellists had heretofore sung at chapel services in Oller Hall. But the fall of '46 Donald Johnson organized a Chapel Choir, made up of non-Rowland singers. (in 1963 it was renamed Convocation Choir.)

Mary Ruth Linton kept orchestral music alive from 1943 to 1945 through small instrumental ensembles. During 1945-46 Donald Johnson conducted a rejuvenated orchestra that gave three symphonic concerts. Then he turned the baton over to Herman Scholl, back after military service.

With October 1946 the familiar strains of *Washington Post* and the marked beat of the drum were heard on the athletic field for the first time since the war. Scholl's forty-five-piece Juniata Band, however, though led by five snappy majorettes, marched without uniforms [they had gone up in flames in the "1630" fire (Faculty Club)]. Parents Day next fall, though, saw the band newly accoutered in navy blue and gold.

Move-Up Day 1946—and all thereafter—took on more hoopla as a result of Senate action that it "include a recognition service at which time awards for various contests, athletic achievements, etc., might be made." As had been the custom, everybody adjourned from Oller Hall to the front campus. The sophomores lined both sides of the "Diagonal" while the freshmen marched through ending up on Founders' front steps where they gave forth with several cheers. Everybody sang the *Alma Mater* and all frosh regs were off after that.

A poll taken by the Senate in the fall indicated strong student disapproval of compulsory church attendance. The trustee committee that consulted with Senate officers refused to rescind the requirement. They were concerned about preserving the "best traditions of the College" for the "spiritual welfare of students."[7] A year later, however, student resistance prevailed. The catalog now substituted the word *expected* for *required*.

Sadie Hawkins Day ("Ef a gal ketches you, then yo're hern") was a fall 1946 social innovation, climaxing with a square dance in the gym. But TWIRP Week, introduced two Octobers later, replaced Sadie Hawkins Day as the annual women-ask-men turnabout. Twirping went on every fall until very recently.

Some dorm rooms, when the 1946-47 school year got underway, were decorated with prints of famous paintings borrowed from the library. Art loan began in 1940 as a project of the Friends of the Library but was temporarily discontinued when Miss Lillian Evans was on leave during the war. The Juniata Women's League contributed eighteen new prints soon after its formation. The library still lends pictures—to anyone of the college community—from a collection expanded with the years.

Room judging, initiated in 1945, became a Parents Day tradition that lasted into the 1970s. For a while it included men's residences, but it started out and ended with those of women.

March of 1947 Huntingdon got a radio station: WHUN (Then "1400 on your dial"). President Ellis and the A Cappella Choir took part in the inaugural broadcast. WHUN's first program director was sophomore Cary Simpson, now head of his own radio network. Three ex-JCers made up the initial staff of announcers. Until a campus station went on the air, WHUN provided valuable experience for Hilltoppers interested in radio. A half-hour each week was set aside for college-programmed shows.

Miss Homecoming I was Betty Kiracofe (Weicht), whose coronation ushered in a new tradition when the Indians romped over Ursinus 31-14 on a November day in 1947. The contest for a Hilltop homecoming queen was conceived by the *Juniatian* staff, who conducted the election. Betty, a senior whose father chaired Juniata's education department, was guest of honor at the "J" Club dance that night in the gym.

The month of November also marked the appearance of Dr. C. C. Ellis's book, *Juniata College: The History of Seventy Years, 1876-1946.* The trustees had commissioned the president emeritus to write an official history of the college back in October 1943.

That fall's honor roll was a kind of Hilltop curiosity. For the first time there was listed a husband-wife duo: John and Rosalyn Schell, both vets. They repeated the same feat in the spring, John's last semester.

Debate, dormant since 1942, came back during 1947-48 under Dr. "Toby" Henry, himself a JC debater of years gone by. Benjamin Lavey, who had broken down and wept openly during a softball game on April 12, 1945 upon learning Franklin D. Roosevelt, a man he greatly admired, was dead, presided over the society. Others on the team, which compiled an impressive 9-1 record, were Otis Jefferson, Alfred Crease, Phyllis Baughman (Bush), David Armacost, and Elizabeth Taylor (Dexter).

AMERICANZA, the first all-student musical revue ever to reach the boards at Juniata, was staged three nights in mid-February 1948. It was directed by Jack Shaffer, a senior married to Patricia Malone, whose father, Pat, was the one-time baseball pitching great. Curtain time opening night, Jack was pacing the maternity ward of an Altoona hospital where his wife—nine hours later—gave birth to a boy. The production, a story of music from Indian days to modern times, was given as a benefit to bring a Chinese student to campus by the Juniata World Service Fund.

JWSF, the campus' own annual charity, first began in February 1944 and lasted through the Calvert Ellis era. It was an outgrowth of the Juniata Community Chest Drive, which went for the support of two Brethren missionaries. But with the outbreak of war, JC aid came to include the World Student Fund (for the relief of needy students in Europe and China)—hence the birth of JWSF. Later JWSF divided its proceeds several ways, one of which was to bring a foreign student or two to the Hill. Dean Melvin Rhodes inspired the practice—in 1948—of making the fund's goal identical to the figures of the current year. This meant a hefty increase over previous campus giving, but Sam Hastings and Bob Saylor, the key men of the 1948 drive, pulled it off with dollars to spare.

The 4th Street Transit bus in 1949 stopped off at the college every twenty minutes. Postman Frank "Beanie" Leister, who for thirty years had toted twenty-five to forty pounds of mail each day over his College Hill route, refused that year to be reassigned to a shorter business district beat. "Joe" Yoder, the Big Valley native and erstwhile Juniata recruiter, brought out his *Rosanna's Boys*, sequel to *Rosanna of the Amish* (1940).[8] The Associated Press and *Time* alerted the American people in May that Joseph Brady, Jr., who preached each Sunday at the Grier School for girls near Tyrone, had met with a dastardly deed. Someone had stolen 120 sermon outlines from his dormitory room. Anticlimactically, the sermons were recovered not long after the story broke. But "whodunit" remained a mystery. Melodic tones of electrically controlled carillon bells drifted from Founders Tower over a two-mile area to herald the Christmas season. Installed in Stone Church, the bells, still amplified from the Tower, are played from the church organ. W. Emmert Swigart donated them in memory of his parents.

On the world scene as the half-century mark approached, the communists took over China, while the Marshall Plan salvaged many European countries from the same fate, and just over the horizon was the Korean War.

On College Hill: Skip's, after twenty-four years, was popular as ever as a meet-the-gang spot—an overcrowded sanctuary for the girl who smoked; coeds could not wear slacks or shorts to classes and labs; they still had to "sign out" when leaving campus for any reason, and "lates" were prorated according to class (none for frosh until Move-Up Day); the vets drank and got away with it; clubs, social, religious, and preprofessional, were more active than ever before; baccalaureate had a Stone Church setting (until 1950, and then Oller Hall); except for weekends, dining room assignments, a Senate responsibility, dictated tablemates; senators were urging faculty to deemphasize cuts in giving grades and make use of student evaluation forms; the 1948 selective service act hung over the heads of men between nineteen and twenty-five; the average total expenses in residence at Juniata amounted to $835.

In the meantime, since June 1945, Juniata alumnae had been joining the AAUW with full membership status, a privilege still.[9]

That fall, however, the as-yet-unrelieved manpower shortage prevented football's return to the sports schedule. In 1946, after a three-year hiatus, it was back on the autumn calendar, coached by Mike Snider. But the Tower bell did not toll a single victory (one tie, five losses) that revival season. Bill Smaltz (1947-53), Penn State's prewar fullback great, then got the head coach job and led the Juniata gridders to a 12-8-1 record over the next three years. Several of his players won post season honors. Center David Croft twice (1948 and 1949) made honorable mention for Little All-America by Associated Press. In 1949 two others joined Dave, halfback Mike Dzvonar and offensive end George Smith, while sophomore tackle Cecil Jackson did somewhat better in being named to AP's third team.

The YMCA relinquished its annual fall football banquet in 1947 to Huntingdon's VFW Post 1754, which wanted to honor an ex-serviceman-studded team. The Post's fete took place each year for another quarter-century. The 1947 season will be remembered for the near-tragedy that occurred when, in a November home game against Ursinus, the bleachers collapsed and two-hundred people went spilling to the ground. Two persons were seriously hurt; others required medical attention. While Indian gridders were making Little All-America in 1949, the "J" Club went about erecting an electric scoreboard on the east end of the playing field. It lasted until the centennial year.

Basketball, winter middleman in the athletic program, was the one sport that held its own during the war years. Jack Oller's "boys" won twenty-three and lost thirty from 1942 to 1945. Away trips were made in Jack's Mercury convertible, far from air-tight on a cold winter's night, and his more comfortable Lincoln Continental. The recently opened stretch of Pennsylvania's "Super Highway" cut down the travel time eastward. Mike Snider coached from '45 to '49, his first season's 13-6 record slipping to a three-year overall mark of 10 and 46. The 1947-48 squad set a JC record for the most defeats in a season — seventeen. Huntingdon dentist Arnold Greene, a fullback on Pitt's 1937 Rose Bowl team and former baseball pro, then took over the hardcourt helm. "Doc" was to coach basketball a dozen years (1949-61), longer than anyone else on the Hill except "Carty" Swartz, who had put in the same length of time. The Greene-coached 1949-50 Indians, employing Doc's newly developed HAZ defense,* allowed the fewest points ever per game (62.7).

America's National Pastime on the Hill suffered a one-year lapse (1945) during the war. But Coach Edgar Kiracofe's 1944 team won five and lost one, and his 1946 nine went 8 and 3. Near-sighted Henry "Hank" Eisenhart, who got into the Army by memorizing the eye chart, was on the 1944 team, a recent discharge. Hank could not see very well but he could throw hard, from portside. He was given a try-out with the Cincinnati Reds that May. Things did not work out for him, but they did for a fifteen-year-old kid who pitched in the same game as Hank—Joe Nuxhall. Bill Smaltz became baseball mentor in 1947, winning twenty-two and losing eighteen through the last three seasons of the Forties.

In 1946, after a four-year layoff, the Indians resumed intercollegiate competition in track. From then through 1949 Coach Snider's thin clads broke even in dual meets (6-6) and came in last in each of three triangular contests. But there was record-breaking talent among the lettermen, like Joe Beyer and Bill Murray.

It was Jack Oller who introduced golf as an intercollegiate JC sport in 1947. The first lettermen were John Burych, Orville Dore, Jay McCardell, Blair Miller, and Harold Wagner. They split in a four-match schedule. But the second season, coached by Edgar Kiracofe (1948-53), Indian golfers putted themselves to eight wins and an undefeated season. Their record in 1949 was almost as good (8-1-0).

Tennis, however, was the "black sheep" in JC's postwar athletic rebuilding program. Dropped in 1943, it returned for one season—1947— and was then ignored the next two springs.

Since depression days athletically minded coeds were, for the most part, limited to intramural sports. But, beginning in the postwar years, the WAA did participate in occasional "playdays," both at home and away, which involved interschool competition. This was the way it would be until the return of a varsity sports program in the mid-1970s.

The Hyatt Cup, long the highest honor accorded a Juniata athlete, was discontinued in 1946. Established in its place was the Stanford Mickle Award—to recognize "that man of the graduating class who, like Stanford Mickle, loved athletics, particpated and manifested a wholesome interest in sports, and contributed to the promotion of athletics at Juniata." Stan, a high school valedictorian whose parents set up the award,

---

*An acronym (which ought best not to be spelled out) for a variation of the zone defense.

Undefeated Golf Lettermen, 1948.
Row 1:   R. Korody, B. Miller.
Row 2:   J. Burych, J. McCardell.
Row 3:   R. Rhodes, Coach Kiracofe, O. Dore.

drowned his sophomore year trying to swim across the Raystown Dam. His dream was to play big-league baseball. The first winner of the Mickle Athletic Award—in 1947—was "Chuck" Bargerstock, JC's director of development within another decade and a half.

THE "SILENT GENERATION"—THE 1950S

That was the tag put on midcentury college students by author Thorton Wilder. Others called them the "Beat Generation." The "squares," went the stereotype, were those who considered "good causes" and "excellence" worthy of their energies, time, and devotion. Excesses were expended in panty raids and hazing. The general mood on U. S. campuses was one of complacency. Said Calvert Ellis of college students in a 1955 speech at Philadelphia's Bellevue Stratford Hotel: they are "interested in preparing for a vocation"; they are "internationally minded"; young women are "interested both in marriage and a career"; they are "seeking a faith."[10] On College Hill social activism might have been absent, but Senate leadership all through the Fifties, calling for greater student responsibility, belied Wilder's label on many counts.

For Cold War-tense Americans the decade began pessimistically. In June the North Koreans suddenly struck across the 38th parallel. The United States, fighting under the blue and white United Nations flag, bore the load in what President Harry Truman called a "police action." But Lt. Ralph Harrity '47, first known JC alumnus engaged in the Korean conflict, wrote back: "It's a dirty, filthy war. The enemy takes no prisoners."[11]

For Juniatians everywhere June 1950 was mournful for other reasons. With Korea also came news of Dr. C. C. Ellis's death, a month short of his seventy-sixth birthday. Every yuletide season since his retirement he had entertained students with a reading of Dickens' *Christmas Carol.* Harold Binkley kept this custom alive til the mid-Sixties. Christmastide, beginning in 1950, was for a decade and a half the occasion for the Juniata Christian Association's party for underprivileged children of Huntingdon.

Spring semester 1950 the *Juniatian*, edited by senior Robert Smith, future Washington, D. C. newspaperman and biographer of Sen. Wayne Morse, won first-time critical acclaim from the Associated Collegiate Press. Honors came again, in that day when journalism carried academic credit, in 1955, 1957, 1958, and 1959. The "All American" rating in 1957, ACP's highest category, was based on excellence of news and sports coverage, features, headlines, style, photography, advertising, and editorial writing. That year's editor was Joan McClure (Hamm), a senior from near Harrisburg. The *Juniatian* of the 1950s produced a steady flow of insightful political commentary on world and domestic problems. It came from fellows like James Montgomery '57, Newton Taylor '57, Delbert McQuaide '58, Herbert Deuchar '59, and Alan Quackenbos '61.

Mark Van Doren was on campus in April 1951 to help the college celebrate its seventy-fifth anniversary. There were then some one-hundred JCers on the Hill who hailed from homes where either grandparents,

parents, or siblings were alumni. But the famous writer saw fewer Juniatians than he would have the previous year. The Korean War was taking its toll in enrollment, which would not bottom out (at 586) until next year. Dr. Calvert and the trustees seriously considered a ROTC unit of fifty men in science. Staff Sgt. Robert Keim, president one day of the Alumni Association and a trustee-to-be, was the first Korean vet to return — in September 1951. The Veterans Club reorganized in 1954 and in another year had sixty-four members. However, the Korean Conflict GI Bill, somewhat less generous than the World War II version, favored low-tuition public schools. The spring of Mark Van Doren's visit inaugurated the prestigious Charles C. Ellis Memorial Scholarship, established by friends and alumni and awarded to outstanding students irrespective of need. The first recipients were Lois Miller (McDowell), Miss Homecoming 1950, and Douglas Martin, both '52 grads. Spring 1951 also initiated the one-hundred dollar William Price Social Studies Prize, won by magna cum laude-grad, Gerald Hartzel.

In 1952 the college forbade boyfriends to accompany JC coeds when babysitting, and Esther Doyle was complaining that students did not attend evening public programs very well. The faculty decided to extend chapel period to fifty minutes four to six times a year to be used for special cultural events. Music major Miriam Smith (Wetzel), enthroned as Juniata's first coed radio ham (call letters — WN3TBE), became upon graduation 1952's Miss Pennsylvania. At Atlantic City in the Miss America pageant that September, she played Convention Hall's giant organ in the talent section, which no contestant had ever done before.

Both student deans, Melvin Rhodes and Edith Spencer, left in 1952.* Dr. James Penny replaced Rhodes in his Founders chamber and Mrs. Alice Dove '17 moved into the Dean of Women's office in Brumbaugh Hall. Dwight Eisenhower won over Adlai Stevenson in a landslide presidential election that November, and Korea, the "forgotten war," remained a Chinese puzzle.

The frosh, beginning in 1953, were subjected to compulsory study halls three nights weekly the first semester (extended the whole year for those not attaining the magic 1.20 average). This academic help program, Senate-approved, went on a voluntary basis in 1956. On the 1953-54 Senate, for the first time in the eighteen-year history of Hilltop student

---

*Rhodes was ill during the academic year 1949-50, and Raymond Sollenberger'25, a member of the Pennsylvania Legislature, was made acting dean.

government, were twins. They were Juanita and Lolita Carfora, language majors from Toms River, New Jersey. Involving all four classes competitively in the decoration of designated areas of the campus at Christmastime was a December 1953 innovation. The early 1970s would put an end to this form of Hilltop cheer.

The talk of the Hill in 1953, of course, was the opening of Totem Inn in the basement of the old gym. The dream of a Student Center began at Leadership Conference in 1952. Future Alumni Association President Russell Hill was appointed chairman of a Student Center Planning Committee. With help from trustees and the administration plans progressed rapidly. On March 2nd, after a lively kickoff assembly, "Operation Cooperation" got underway, supervised by John Dale. Over three-hundred students appeared for demolition work with shovels, axes, picks, and hammers. Four busy weeks later the gutted basement was ready for skilled laborers to move in. They completed the remodeling over the summer.

Totem Inn, paid for in part by a Senate-imposed student fee, contained a snack bar, lounge and recreational area, book store, post office—and a one-hundred-record juke box and television set. Robert Fisher, a local businessman, became the center's full-time manager (up to this time some member of the faculty had run the book store). In November Juniata became a U. S. Postal Sub-Station. Meanwhile, Russ Hill's plea, with coeds foremost in mind, that smoking be permitted in "Tote" got no support from President Ellis. His response was: "Many parents of students, especially girls, disapprove of their children smoking, and one of the reasons that they are in attendance at this institution is that traditionally we have been concerned in this point of view."[12] Downstreet, Skip's Inn would hang on for a while longer, mostly as a smoking den, but its days were numbered.

With spring 1954 came the "latest student brainstorm": a campus radio station, built with their own money. Physics major Eugene Hyssong of Altoona was the mastermind behind WJC. It started out in a 6' x 17' cluttered cubicle in the basement of Student's Hall, under Dr. Kiracofe's office. But a regular broadcast schedule—8:00 P.M. to midnight daily except Saturday—did not begin for the twenty-watt-power station until September. Robert Hamm was the first program director. In programming, the broadcast of football games was added to music and current news the next fall. Overradiation caused WJC to be closed down temporarily in 1956, however, but the installation of a coaxial cable put WJC on dorm radios again.

Spring 1954 also introduced a new policy for All Class Night, then sometimes held in the first semester. The types of skits were divided into four categories — history, music, drama, comedy — to rotate every fourth year as theatrical themes. This is still the policy today. Commencement-day reports in June mentioned what everyone thought was the first Fulbright Scholarship to go to a Juniatian. The recipient was Wilfred Norris, a physics summa cum laude, who would study at the University of Tuebingen, Germany.*

The school year 1954-55 began with news that finally Joseph "Trial-by-Slander" McCarthy, who in 1950 had set out on a one-man anti-communist crusade, was in trouble with his Senate colleagues. The Hill's American history students heard Ken Crosby cheer when the Red-hunter from Wisconsin was spanked with an official censure. Except for the excitement over the second consecutive undefeated football season and all the victory bell ringing, it was a relatively quiet Juniata campus both semesters.

Coeds clad in Bermuda shorts *and* knee socks could be seen — by fall 1955 — at a few restricted places, which did not include the social rooms or front campus on Sunday. Also, at Senate instigation and on trial, women had the privilege of visiting North Hall's lounge during designated hours over the weekend. That winter the dean of men set up quarters in the basement of Students Hall, taking over the area where the book store had once been. January 1956 marked the last January commencement, traditionally held heretofore at the midyear convocation. For some reason, perhaps because of the 1954 Supreme Court decision on school segregation and the more recent Montgomery, Alabama, bus boycott, wondering students were writing the *Juniatian* about the "conspicuous absence" of blacks in the dorms.[13] Comps were under attack, a growing unrest with them becoming more evident. In the hottest Senate race in years James Stayer won on the third ballot in the March elections. And in an article titled "Grab for Grads," the *Alumni Bulletin* said that American industries during 1955-56 had sent more "talent scouts" than ever before on recruiting missions to college campuses.[14] Like most institutions, Juniata discovered that the demand exceeded the supply in many fields.

---

*It so happened that Fulbrights went to two other Juniatians — both from another era — that year. Dr. Glenn Gray '36, author and college professor, and Dr. Wendall McMillan '48, agricultural economist, were the pair. Three other JCers subsequently studied abroad as Fulbright scholars: Galen Frysinger '53 in 1956-57, and James Martin '57 and Richard Quinn '60, both upon graduation. The Fulbright-defrayed postgraduate study abroad program was enacted by Congress in 1947.

1956 was a presidential election year and all the evidence that fall (mock student balloting and faculty poll) showed the campus three to one for "Ike," going for term two. Two campaign whistle stops in Huntingdon brought Hilltoppers down to the raildroad station in droves. Adlai Stevenson, the second-time Democratic hopeful, made an early October appearance. He was greeted by a pack of Hilltoppers and a banner: "Juniata College Chapter, Youth for Eisenhower-Nixon." Stevenson did not lack for a repartee: "I, for one, believe in the redemption of sins. . . .And I believe the longer you are educated in college the more you'll vote Democratic."[15] Several weeks later it was Richard Nixon's turn. Sophomore Sandra Cohick of Whittier, California, the vice-presidential candidate's hometown, boarded the train to present him with flowers. This time there were hecklers with signs representing the Stevenson-Kefauver ticket. The stir they caused, overplayed by the media, made newspapers all over the East and several radio broadcasts. The *New York Times*, which was supporting Eisenhower, devoted eleven column inches to a criticism of the incident.[16]

One of the Nixon baiters had been Jim Stayer, his hair short-cropped and the Senate's dynamic president. The highlight of his twelvemonth tenure was the debut of a Campus Judiciary. Work toward this goal had started four years earlier as a step toward an honor system. The 1955-56 Senate, Jim Hunt-led, should be credited with working out the proposal for student self-discipline, which in a next-year October referendum won the approval of eighty-one percent of those voting. The jubilant Stayer, today a history professor in Canada, had this to say about the "courageous" stand his fellow students took:

> Happily the Juniata student body has voted to make Juniata its community rather than its cage. If the ideals of this college are to become more concrete and its traditions nobler in our community, it is up to us to start thinking about honor and how real it can be in our personal lives.[17]

The purpose of the Judiciary, its constitution read, was "to implement the rules of college life in non-academic matters, to give the student body an explicit means toward self-discipline, and a greater opportunity for self-government, and to improve cooperation among our respective groups." The original judges were seniors Joan McClure (Hamm), Henry Gibbel, Eloise Holsinger (Douds), and juniors Marbrie Goodrich (Beefelt), Ray Ono, and Del McQuaide. The Senate president and the two student deans were automatically members. Donald Rockwell was elected faculty representative. Hilltop history had run full cycle on the matter of disciplinary control since the 1920s, and the ultimate outcome, as we shall see, would be the same.

The same fall, JC's Senate became a member of the National Student Association. And to stress how times had changed, George Fattman, *Juniatian* editor (and today an alumni elected trustee), wrote that senators of ten to fifteen years ago were preoccupied with coordinating club activities and carrying out simple projects. Recent Senates, he said, are "concerned with such projects as student self-discipline, the rising tide of young people seeking a college education, and the curriculum and how it is being presented."[18]

Even so, life on the Hill went on pretty much as usual in the post-referendum months. Supervised by Del McQuaide, the freshmen carried "Operation Recreation," a skating pond project on the eastern edge of the campus, to near completion. "Snowflake Lake" the frosh named it, their privilege for being hard-working peons. And the first of many-to-follow "Ugliest Man" contests took place, the Senate president himself a candidate. A social calendar called the "Pow Wow" could be picked up each week in Totem Inn, giving the low-down on what, where, and when things were taking place. Men forced to live off campus enjoyed free bus rides — on the college — to and from their downtown rooms. That was the last year of public transit service in Huntingdon, except for a cut-short experiment in another few years. In March students lined up in Memorial Gym for free Salk polio vaccine shots. Hilltoppers unhappy of late with the *Alma Mater* encouraged a special committee to come up with a better one. The new composition, Senate approved, was "railroaded out of existence," many felt, by the music department's blunt verdict: "No better than barbershop music." Not consulted by the *Alma Mater* committee was Johnstown, Pennsylvania's Richard Livingston, a 1958 English graduate (summa cum laude) and talented organist. He was one-hundred dollars richer that spring, the winner of the new Emma G. Wald Arts and Languages Prize.*

---

*In 1965 it became the John R. and Emma Wald Humanities Prize, established by the Wald Foundation, Inc., of Huntingdon, Pennsylvania. Until 1964 the Wald, Brumbaugh and Price awards stood as the premier academic cash meeds for the three divisions. In that year they were joined by the Wilbur W. Oaks Prize in biology and in 1965 by the Alice G. Blaisdell Prizes in geology and mathematics, each worth one hundred dollars. Other cash awards were set up during the Calvert Ellis period. Among them was one of fifty dollars by Charles Rice in accounting (extant) and the twenty five dollar Women's Work Council Award (since dropped).

At mid year Dr. James Penny left for a professorship at Boston University, and Charles Godlasky, sociologist and line coach in football, deaned the men second semester. Paul Heberling, Penn State letterman in hockey and an experienced penologist, became dean of men in August. Barbara Bechtell (1956-60), her favorite hobby fishing, had replaced Mrs. Dove the previous fall.

By the academic year 1957-58 students were issued ID cards with "Mug shots" of the bearer. But one of the big stories of that fall was the Asian flu epidemic. It all began Sunday, October 6, when seven JCers were admitted to the Lesher Hall infirmary. By Wednesday over forty students had the "bug," and before long beds overflowed into Lesher's dining hall and recreation area. Hi-fi sets and record collections made their appearance and supplied, the sick joked, "music to cough by." A temperature of 102° was the admission ticket to medical care in the just-opened women's domicile. In all, 194 ended up in the make-shift infirmary, most staying three to five days. Many more were treated in their dorm rooms. The college did not close, but the epidemic caused the cancellation of Mountain Day, two football games (although one was made up), and the postponement of Homecoming until Parents Day.

But sore throats, hacking coughs, headaches, and sneezes were forgotten on Monday night the 21st—a date also memorable. A "mob" of men rushed Lesher Hall intent on a panty raid, the Hilltop's first. They gained entrance, leaving some damage along their trail. More than a little displeased, President Ellis told the Senate: "I do not know of a single raid on a women's dormitory in a coeducational college which did not result in the suspension of those involved, and the administration cannot countenance the action of last Monday evening."[19] At an open hearing of the Judiciary, its first one, 150 students crowded into Founders chapel and heard the accused pair of "ring leaders" offer unshakable alibis. They were found not guilty. The October 21st *coup de main* would not be the last, but those of the future did not take on a storming-of-the-Bastille character. The fellows would simply stand outside shouting while obliging coeds dropped lingerie out the window.

That panty-raid fall there were some three million collegians on the nation's campuses, up a startling forty-five percent over six years ago.

On the Hill, where cafeteria-style breakfasts became the vogue upon Lesher Hall's opening, the Senate, now McQuaide-steered, promoted innovations of its own. Student proctors stood in for profs, upon request, at testing time—which included final exams. Periodic Sunday morning all-college worship services—to give resident students a "church on campus"

—began in January. A Hilltop referendum added a thirteenth Senate post—chairman of educational activities. And President Ellis gave the green light for a formal midwinter dance, big band and all, to be an annual event beginning the next year.

JC Senator Del McQuaide, a history major from Western Pennsylvania, became the first of four Hilltoppers—three of them in the Ellis age—to win Root-Tilden Scholarships. Highly competitive and in 1958 valued at seventy-two hundred dollars, they are good for study at New York University's Law School. Only two a year are awarded in each of the ten federal judicial circuits.*

With Frances Mathias's resignation as college dietition, Crotty Brothers of Boston took over food service in September. There followed, to the Senate's satisfaction, weekend suppers via the cafeteria line, further eroding the sit-down tradition.

Halloween month 1958 marked the passing of the President's Sunday morning Bible class, which had been a familiar Founders chapel experience for generations of JCers. But now too many of them were sleeping in on the Lord's Day.

Senate prexy "Chuck" Brown, like his predecessors, pushed for an honor code, egged on by Dr. Crosby, student government adviser. Both men had hoped the Judiciary and the proctoring system would pave the way. But cheating was too rampant, books related to the integration courses kept disappearing from the library, copying of lab reports was widespread, and nobody wanted to be tagged a "stool pigeon." Campus resistance to an honor code was for senators of the 1950s a great disappointment.

But the Senate in 1959, turned down by Dr. Ellis in a bid for control of the student activities fee, found itself in a new position. Heretofore, campus organizations dealt directly with the administration on financial matters. Now the Senate was empowered to draw up a budget, in consultation with Hilltop groups, which the administration would act upon. A lump sum would be set aside and the Senate had the responsibility of dispersing the funds to individual organizations. The position of Senate treasurer now became a time-consuming job.

The orchestra, in decline since Prof. Jack Brammer left in 1957, had played its last note for a long time to come.

---

*The other two Ellis-days R-Ts were Charles Brown '59, McQuaide's successor on the Senate and in 1974 president of the Alumni Association, and Robert Rose '61, like the pair before, a history major. There was a hiatus of over a dozen years and then Karl Kindig, a political scientist, made the grade in 1972.

Juniatians in 1959, under an inclusive fee system introduced the previous year, were paying $1,525 for their education. A quarter of the student body received aid of some kind. But the National Defense Student Loan Fund, a Sputnik spin-off, was now available and hundreds of JCers would take advantage of its liberal terms in the years ahead.

In May 1959 Clyde "Mac" McCracken, a campus legend, died at age seventy-two. The day of a lone night watchman had passed; the times required a security force.

Mac died before the "Glory Years" (1953-59) of Indian gridiron history came to an end.* Under three head coaches, Bill Smaltz, Robert Hicks (1954-55), and Kenneth Bunn (1956-59), Juniata enjoyed football success that even Notre Dame or Ohio State could envy. In that span of seasons the Blue and Gold won fifty games, losing two and tying two. Those seven teams accounted for the Tribe's only undefeated seasons— five of them: 1953, 1954, 1955, 1957, 1958. Hick's 1955 gridders earned a Tangerine Bowl bid in Orlando, Florida, the college's first postseason appearance in any sport. On January 2 the Indians, outweighed twelve pounds per man, played the favored Missouri Valley Vikings (Marshall, Missouri to a 6-6 tie before ten thousand fans. The Glory Years put Juniata on radio waves, play-by-play broadcasts carried first by WJC and then by WHUN perennially ever since.

All kinds of team records were set, but fullback Bill Berrier, now associate dean of student services at JC, was one of many individual standouts emerging throughout those years. Seven of his marks still stand on the school's record rolls, four of which are tops in the MAC. Thrice he was Little All-America— 1957 (honorable mention), 1958 (third team), 1959 (second team). Other Little All-Americans of those years were: end Barry Drexler (third team, 1955); halfback Pat Tarquinio (honorable mention, 1955); guard William Haushalter (honorable mention, 1955); tackle Charles "Moon" Mullen (honorable mention, 1956); center John Staley (honorable mention, 1956); tackle Bernie McQuown (honorable mention, 1957); tackle Al Dungan (honorable mention, 1959); tackle Robert "Bo" Solomon (honorable mention, 1959). Only Joe "The Toe" Veto, a tackle and kicker, was the Tribe's first-team choice ever, in 1954.

---

*The fall before Mac's death, the Goal Post Trophy, symbolizing football rivalry between Susquehanna University and Juniata, came into existence. JCers, in a frenzy of victory in 1952, tore down SU's goal posts and brought a seven-foot section back. After some controversy, school authorities wisely converted the splinter of wood into a trophy, which still goes to the winning team each year.

In addition, many of these players won All-Pennsylvania, Eastern Collegiate Athletic Association, and Williamson Little All-America honors.*

Starting Eleven, Tangerine Bowl, 1956.
Line: K. Birmingham, W. Waryck, W. Schott, J. Staley, W. Haushalter, C. Mullen, B. Drexler.
Backs: P. Tarquinio, R. Bechtel, R. Sill, D. Pheasant.

* By 1953 Juniata belonged to the National Collegiate Athletic Association, the ECAC, and the MAC. The Middle Atlantic Conference, organized as a loose confederation in 1912, unified in 1952 as an actual playing league. Ever since Juniata has been a member of its northern division in all varsity sports. In 1976 the college dropped out of the ECAC.

Co-captaining, in 1953, the college's first unbeaten, untied team was Chuck Knox, a 180-pound tackle. Twenty years later Knox, son of an Irish steel worker from Sewickley, Pennsylvania, became head coach of the Los Angeles Rams. Earlier, as an assistant on the New York Jets staff, he played a key role in the signing of Joe Namath, also a Western Pennsylvanian, to a four-hundred thousand dollar package, then the biggest sports payment in history. Knox is the only Juniata graduate (in history) to be associated with a professional football team. A "jewel of a college" was *Esquire Magazine*'s description of Knox's alma mater in a biographical sketch of the Rams' coach.

Head football coaches on the Hill, until recently, also looked after baseball.* During the 1950s Juniata's overall horsehide record was seventy-six wins and fifty-four losses. The best seasons were 1952 (10-4), 1954 (10-4), 1957 (11-3), and 1958 (9-2). On Saturday, May 26, 1951 Earl Detrick, a radiologist today, pitched the only no-hitter thrown by a JC moundsman — against Lycoming. It was the junior right-hander's first season out for baseball. Until 1954 there was an admission charge to watch the home team. Two sparkling freshmen on the 1957 nine, which garnered the most diamond wins in twenty-five years, were Don Ross and Bill Berrier, both destined to sign pro contracts upon graduating. Ross, a strong-armed third baseman, hit .543 and .418 his last two years respectively.

Basketballers of the 1950s gave Doc Greene a ninety-two and eighty-eight log in the won-loss charts. The winningest teams were those of 1953-54 (15-6) and 1955-56 (14-7). The mid-Fifties may not have been Glory Years for basketball per se, but they certainly were for Jacob "Jake" Handzelek. The sharpshooting guard in jersey #40, also a four-year letterman in baseball, set eight standing records. Among the more important ones are: most points, career (1,950); most points, season (553); career average (23.8); season average (26.3). He is the only Indian player to score over 400 points in four separate campaigns. But there was also Walter Vanderbush, a Ph.Ded Michigan high school principal today. The 6'6" center played all four years with Handzelek and holds two records: most rebounds, career (884) and most rebounds, games (33).

Track in the 1950s, under Athletic Director Mike Snider, won ten dual meets and lost 31. Snidermen did not cop first place in any of ten triangular meets. The one bright spot of that decade was provided

---

* In 1954 Doc Greene filled in for Bill Smaltz who left during the winter.

by Gene Rothenberger, a four-year star. His leap of 23' 1" in the long jump (1954) is still extant. Three times he took first place in this event at the Middle Atlantics.

Record-Setting 1955-56 Basketball Team.
Row 11: L. Hallman, M. Armstrong, T. Froisland, W. Vanderbush, B. McLaughlin, B. Oriss, J. Handzelek.
Row 2: T. Quarantillo, W. Burchfield, W. Biehl, R. Ewald, M. Miller, A. Kramer, J. DeNicola, R. Kimble.
Row 3: Coach Greene, Manager, S. Ulsh, G. Ewers, N. Roth, W. Wise, R. Wertz, A. Custer, R. Scialabba.

It was Coach Snider who, in April 1956, planned the first invitational scholastic relay meet for high schools of Central Pennsylvania. It became an every-spring event, although today it is limited to the Mountain League. The original purpose of the invitational was to stimulate interest in track and field sports.

Back in 1936 Mike Snider had mapped out a cross-country course around the "little loop road," a distance of about 2.5 miles. Over the years the track team used it for fall workouts, timing themselves for the fun of it. Then in 1955 Juniata held three practice meets. By then the course consisted of 4.3 miles of hilly Huntingdon terrain. It began behind Memorial Gym and finished in Sherwood Forest. The route covered Taylor Highland, the woods along the ridge, Petersburg Pike, Cold Spring Road, and Warm Springs Avenue. From 1956 to 1959 JC harriers, paced by Don Layman, Herb Deuchar, and Frank Hrach, hied themselves to a victory edge of twenty-one to one for Coach Snider.

Hilltoppers had reason to glorify golf in the 1950s, too, since JC linksmen swept to three MAC titles—in 1951, 1952, and 1954. Two titles and forty-five wins went with Ed Kiracofe-coaching (with only seven losses and one tie). Led by Co-captains Raymond Korody '51 and Robert Rhodes '51, the JC teemen in 1951 swept to a 10-1-0 record, the best ever. William Germann '49, college trainer since 1947 (a service he still performs) and general manager of WHUN (as he is today), accepted the reins of the golf team in 1954. Besides the MAC title that year, the squad won the fifteenth annual Western Maryland Invitational. Frank Arasin, playing number one position, took medalist honors in both tournaments (the fifth and last time since 1949). The aggregate log of the Fifties was fifty-five and thirty-seven.

Tennis at midcentury ran through five coaches, although the results in the won/lost column were not bad at all—thirty-one and forty-nine.* The netmen of 1954 had one of the best seasons in the sport's history at JC, winning seven and losing one. Phil Lankford played number one man and lost only one match. The tennis courts behind Women's Gym and at the foot of Round Top were clay and not in good shape. But in 1958 Horace Raffensperger of Elizabethtown, Pennsylvania, an officer of DAJUMO and father of two Hilltoppers, made possible the eventual construction of seven all-weather, hard-surface courts.[20]

Meanwhile, beginning the spring of 1950, sports-minded alumni furnished loving cups to go each year to top-ranking athletes in each

---

*The coaches were Mike Snider, Dean James Penny (1952-53), Dr. Theodore Lockwood (1954-55), Rev. Robert McFadden (1956—58), and Prof. James Thomas (1959-60).

varsity activity. The original six trophies and their winners were: Dr. J. Harold Engle '23, football back—Mike Dzvonar; George L. Weber '40, football line—Aldo Bonomi; Jack E. Oller '23, basketball—Holmes Ulsh; J. Foster Gehrett '16, track—Joseph Beyer; C. Blair Miller '49, golf—Ray Korody; Charles F. Goodale, Jr. '39, baseball—Julius "Squeeze" Long, who also got the Mickle Award. Two other trophies came later in the 1950s. Tennis was added anonymously (by Calvert Ellis) in 1954—Richard Fusco, and cross-country by C. Clifford Brown '29, in 1958—Herbert Deuchar.

1960S: THE MAKING OF THE "NOW GENERATION"

Students of the 1960s had no personal recollection of the Great Depression or World War II. They accepted the radio, television, jet travel, automobile, atomic energy, antibiotics, new medicine, and the wonders of science quite casually as though they had always existed. But American youth on most campuses during the Sixties decade were a different "breed o'cat" from the goldfish-swallowing, panty-raiding collegians of the Fifties. Students became involved in many causes such as sit-ins, write-ins, drive-ins, lay-downs, etc.

There was the fear colleges and universities, growing in leaps and bounds, were becoming soulless educational factories. A preview of the disruptive struggles that were to break out in full fury in 1968 took place at the University of California four years earlier. Angry students staged sit-down strikes in university buildings, organized a "filthy speech" campaign, and generally disorganized the institution over a period of weeks. The crisis led to the eventual resignation of the university's president, Clark Kerr.

The war in Vietnam exacerbated the situation. Many students considered the war immoral. Since college men were deferred from the draft, large numbers of young men without much interest in furthering their education enrolled merely to avoid military service. These tended to find the experience meaningless. By 1968 Lyndon Johnson and members of his administration were virtually barred from speaking on most campuses for fear of violent disruptions their presence might inspire. A nationwide left-wing group, Students for a Democratic Society, took the lead in organizing harrassing tactics against government leaders in their speech-making.

Knotty social problems turned students into intransigent absolutists. Racial prejudice was evil; it must be totally eradicated. To them, starvation and economic inequalities in the Land of Plenty were a serious reproach to the American Way.

But campus discontent was symptomatic of something else, particularly for residential colleges like Juniata. Reared-by-Dr. Spock's-book-students, accustomed to lack of parental discipline, rankled at parietal rules affecting their lives and life-styles. Said one Juniata spokesman of Hilltoppers in 1967: "The historical concept of *in loco parentis* is being challenged."[21] JCers were beginning to protest administrative policies that appeared unfair and that threatened their concept of freedom.

In the area of civil rights and politics, this spokesman noted, JC students are "extremely conservative" for the most part. He detected little or "no concern" about Vietnam or the draft—they are "not like the students you read about in newspapers." But, he went on to stress, they

do not lack enthusiasm for the sexual revolution which is sweeping across the country. Juniata students are in the middle of it. The past patterns of behavior are considered "old fashioned" or "prudish." A new code for sexual conduct is being established. Students display their affections openly and talk more fully about sex. . . .For some the free love movement has an appeal. We do not have an organized free love group on campus, but the undertone is there.[22]

In loco parentis, however, remained the college policy to the end of the Ellis administration. The women continued to "sign in" and "sign out." Lesher, South, and Brumbaugh-Oneida Halls had residence directors who became "mother confessors" to many a troubled coed. Mrs. Mary Horoschak (1957-67), Mrs. Dorothy Spillers (1960-70), Mrs. Maude Butler (1962-63), Mrs. Rebecca Brownlee (1963-68) and Mrs. Anna Neely (1967-69) were always ready to lend a sympathetic ear.* Smoking outdoors on the central campus did not become a right of any member of the Hilltop community, no matter of what status, until fall 1967. The dress code went out at the same time regulations on the use of tobacco were relaxed. Not only Bermudas and slacks were legit anywhere, but so were mini-skirts and tight fitting tapered trousers. But drinking alcoholic beverages anywhere on campus, at any college function, or on any college-sponsored trip still carried enforced penalties. One Senate president missed out on a June diploma when caught tippling just before commencement (he got his sheepskin in August).

---

*The men's dorms did not each have a live-in director. North Hall had single faculty members in residence for a while. Later, there was a central director, married, who lived in one of the dorms. They were Ralph Ebersole (1961-65), Richard Frankhauser (1965-66), and David Lee (1966-71).

Student-registered automobiles began to proliferate like Al Capp's schmoos, and parking space was at a premium. Table assignments at mealtime went out with the new decade.

The fellows had a hard time for a while in the early 1960s keeping track of where the dean of men's office was located. From the basement of Students Hall it went back to Founders in 1962 — to the original domain of the registrar. Then in 1965 Dean Heberling made an exchange with Vice-President Mays and jumped across the hall into the old conference room and the adjoining complex of rooms, there to stay.

For coeds it was the names of their deans that taxed memory, not office location, so rapid was the turn over. After Dean Bechtell came Christine Yohe (1960-64), Clare Low (1964-67) and Frances Helms (1967-68), who were followed by two more before the decade's end.*

Student personnel services were reorganized in 1966. To fill a new position, dean of student affairs, President Ellis chose Dr. Charles Schoenherr (Ed.D., Columbia) from Wheaton College, Illinois. Under his charge fell the dean of women, coordinator of student activities, campus minister, director of financial aid and placement, director of student health services, and the various residence directors (men and women). Dr. Schoenherr's mother-in-law, Mrs. Margaret Landon, wife of a Presbyterian missionary to Thailand, was the author of *Anna and the King of Siam*. Hollywood had a go at her book as did Rodgers and Hammerstein in the Broadway musical *Anna and I*. Ironically, this filmed hit was one of the last movies shown at the Grand Theater before it closed down the spring of 1962, leaving Huntingdon with just the Clifton for cinema buffs.

Paul Heberling, who as dean had been known for his "quiet effectiveness" in governing JC men, now joined the sociology department. His specialty has been anthropology and he has conducted a number of "digs" at prehistoric Indian sites in Huntingdon County and out West. His stature as a teacher was soon attested by the fact he was selected for the second Beachley Distinguished Professor Award.

As for excellence among the student body, the *Juniatian* had in 1960 got an A-1 rating for the spring semester from the National Newspaper Service. This was the paper's last such recognition. Kay Gillies (Dixon), who became editor-in-chief in early February, was the first sophomore to tackle the job. At the time the *Juniatian* had a circulation of over sixteen-

---

*This list does not give the last names of those who married after leaving Juniata.

hundred. No Hilltopper before or since that spring shared the good academic fortune of Richard Quinn, Senate president. He won three prestigious scholarships: a Fulbright, a Danforth, and a Knapp (University of Wisconsin), making use of the first and the last ones. Meantime, sponsored by such Congressional luminaries as Joseph Martin, Wilbur Mills, Barry Goldwater, Harry Byrd, and Hugh Scott, the Richard M. Simpson Memorial Scholarship Fund (one-hundred-and-fifty-thousand dollars) was established in February. Huntingdonian Richard Simpson was twenty-three years a member of the United States House of Representatives. Robert Rose, the later Root-Tilden grantee, was the first to benefit from this "living memorial to [a] great American."

That was the spring the women voted into existence a smoking room in South Hall. It was also the birthday of Juniata's first literary magazine since Juniata's nascent years, thanks to Ben Rose, Carol Baish (Brann), Ed Jones — all seniors — and Senate backing. It became the *Voice* under editor Nancy Fitch, and in 1964-65, when edited by Dale Evans, *Kvasir*, named after what is best described as the poetic muse of Norse mythology. That is the title it kept.

Late March of 1960 Dr. John Stauffer, then dean of Wittenberg University in Ohio, spoke with campus leaders about an honor system. Wittenberg had had such a code for four years.

In the fall the *Scout*, a companion of frosh for thirty-six years, became the *Student Handbook* and in 1961, more poetically, *The Pathfinder.** The old run-down tennis courts behind Women's Gym disappeared and the area leveled and seeded, an improvement the Senate had lately been calling for. State Police made Memorial Gym homebase for driving tests on certain days of the month. For over a decade Hilltoppers wended their way around cars of would-be licencees lining 18th Street. A camera was put to use in taking chapel attendance. Students sat in keen anticipation until they saw the lens sneakily emerge from near the top of the closed stage curtains. The audience reaction produced comic pictorial results, not to mention the bewilderment upon the part of the speakers who had no idea what was going on. (Other methods of taking a head-count soon replaced the camera.) Homecoming floats made their initial appearance in October when College Field was the scene of a football game with the Western Maryland Green Terrors and the crowning of Miss

---

*Published cooperatively by the Senate and the administration the first year, it was taken out of student hands after that.

Homecoming XIV, senior Jean Davies (Ewers). WJC, with its forty announcers, moved into the basement of Brumbaugh Hall.

Late October Vice-President Nixon, now after the White House himself, enjoyed an uneventful whistle stop in Huntingdon. He had won handily over John Kennedy in a mock campus election, and Rich Caulk led a campus delegation carrying "Nixon-Lodge" banners to the station, emceeing prearrival ceremonies for a crowd that included two high school bands and some Penn Staters. Wife Pat accepted the bouquet of roses when the train pulled in, snow flurries filling the air.

But it was John F. Kennedy and his New Frontiersmen who rode into power in January 1961. Early in the game, by executive order, JFK created the Peace Corps, Congress putting it on a permanent basis later on. *Juniatian* editorials were for it — all the way. On College Hill the first Children's Theater filled Ollér Hall with one-thousand youngsters from surrounding schools in February. They saw *Rumpelstiltskin*, starring freshman Nancy Roop (Davis) in the title role.

The honor code was not a dead issue for the Senate, and under Richard Quinn one was drawn up. It was the job of Ronald Vinson's senators to drum up Hilltop support. The faculty was behind the principle "wholeheartedly." "Honor Week," a time of acquainting students with the code, ended on Tuesday, May 11 with a student referendum. The Senate set seventy-five percent as a minimum vote for acceptance. But the Quinn plan failed when only 57.1 percent on the Hill favored it. At the same time the balloting on a second question indicated Hilltoppers would like to see some type of academic honor system instituted at Juniata College. And so the new Senate, John Rummel's, went to work on a revised system.

Come June, commencement, since 1921 a Monday affair, was shifted ahead to Sunday afternoon, sharing honors with baccalaureate.*

A profile of entering freshmen for fall 1961 showed the sexes all but equal on combined SAT scores: women, 1,067; men, 1,056. The rigors of gym initiation that Senate President Jim Hunt, back in 1955-56, had tried to outlaw, went out with the Class of '65. No more mud, no more syrup. No more jeers, "Pray for rain, Frosh!" But other regulations remained in force, as did the "frosh-soph" Homecoming games to determine if dinks came off or stayed on another week. And "storming the Arch" continued to embroil freshmen in a fall donnybrook.

Calendar year 1962 started out with the student body rejecting a

---

*From 1879 to 1921 commencement always took place on Thursday.

second revision of the honor code on January 9th. That vote buried for good the whole idea.

The Senate was now in the bike rental business, and on a Saturday in late March twenty-seven Hilltoppers headed for Harrisburg in a bicycle marathon. It was to be a test of endurance. Sophomore Richard O'Connell, averaging fifteen miles per hour, reached the Capitol steps first, at 12:55 P.M., after a ride of six hours and twenty-five minutes. All was deserted. His first act was to hunt for a water fountain. Twenty-four out of the twenty-seven contestants, all males, made the ninety-eight-mile trip. O'Connell had done some winter training, and it paid off.

Two Masque plays, *Liliom* and *The Man Who Came to Dinner*, both directed by Prof. Bruce Spencer, caused a flurry of excitement over the question of censorship. Dr. Ellis thought the former "out of line," as did many of the college constituents. Not wanting to be a "censor" he nevertheless made it plain when the latter production took place: "We must be careful not to have profanity or drinking on the stage."[23]

Individual faculty members entertained in their homes nearly 450 students over the year, their hospitality partially reimbursed by the college under a policy dating back to 1955 (still in effect today).

Innovations seemed to be the order of the day all of 1962-63. Homecoming Day featured a pregame parade through Huntingdon that included the JC and Huntingdon High School bands, Queen Lynnea Knavel (Detwiler), an elementary ed senior who would reign again in May, her rivals, floats, and the football team. Seniors Judy Carleton (Barnett) and Judy Fairweather (Young) started a kind of journalistic fad on the Hill—they were the first of three successive duos to co-edit the *Juniatian*. In April students, clamoring for "big name" entertainment, brought to Oller Hall on their own the Lettermen, popular recording artists. Ron Smelser, in Germany for his junior year abroad, won the Senate presidency in an unprecedented write-in campaign. Tom Paxton, a philosophy major, wondered why "there is no active student peace movement" on the Hill and urged the formation of one. A request from class president Lou Browdy, Indian mascot of the football team, set the tradition of seniors wearing white (B.A.) and yellow (B.S.) tassels on their mortarboards at commencement.

The academic year 1963-64 had some new twists, too. For the first time in Juniata's history the faculty reception was minus a receiving line—a concession to the size of the student body. Chapel, or convocation as now it was being called, was scheduled once a week (Wednesday) and extended to forty-five minutes. The emphasis was to be religious rather than a combination of worship services and cultural programs. Periodic public lectures and performances, by the same token, went under the rubric Focus Series. Juniata that fall was the first of the Brethren schools to appoint a campus minister, the suggestion of a student Religious Convocation Study Committee. He was Robert Faus, a young Pennsylvania Dutchman with an endless repertory of jokes. The jolly reverend and his musically gifted wife, Nancy, soon won their way into the hearts of all on the Hill. The house at 410 Seventeenth Street became the College Manse.[24]

Hardly had the Fauses moved in when, on September 19th, "Book Switch" took place. Early morning of that day nine-hundred students and faculty members began to move books, President Ellis leading the first group, from the old to the new library. Over sixty-thousand volumes were moved by yellow, blue, and red teams under the direction of traffic cops headed by Dr. Cherry, wearing a big, black, broad-brimmed hat. The band provided peppy music and halfway through the morning there was a break for coffee and donuts. The operation took less than six hours, counting the midmorning break and an hour-long lunch period. At 2:45 P.M. Morley Mays placed the last book, a biography of Zwingli, on the shelf. The tolling Tower bell officially signaled the end of library moving day. Over forty students had won assorted prizes.

Then, on November 22, a concealed rifleman, Lee Oswald, killed President John Kennedy in downtown Dallas, Texas. The assassination shocked the Hill, as it did all America. Oller Hall had standing room only on the 25th, a national day of mourning, for a Juniata memorial service. Hilltoppers listened in sober silence as Morley Mays paid tribute to the first Catholic to occupy the White House. For many of them the tragic and senseless murder opened their eyes to the enormous capacity for evil in this country. Dean Mays articulated their sentiments when he said, "May our rededication be not only a renewal of confidence in our American idealism, but also an act of contrition before God."[25]

Already the Senate of write-in bugleman Ron Smelser was hard at work trying to set up a system for evaluating courses offered at JC. And Simpson scholar Rodney Jones, son of missionary parents, had in September authored for the *Juniatian* an exceptionally perceptive two-part serial on Vietnam titled "Southeastern Sickness."

Senator John Fike, Jr.'s religious activities committee sponsored a three-day symposium on racial tensions in February. The committee made use of outside speakers and faculty. Then in March, Elmer Maas, a philosophy prof and social activist, arranged for the Freedom Singers, a vocal group representing the Student Nonviolent Coordinating Committee, to make two campus appearances. SNCC was a recent integration and civil rights organization that grew out of the 1960 sit-down movement in the South. This was not the last contact the Hill would have with this largely college-based movement.

Judson Kimmel, a tall, friendly descendant of the Kimmel clan linked with Juniata's founding years, received the first Wilbur W. Oaks Prize in biology.* Tragically, his promising medical career ended as the result of an automobile accident three years after he earned his M.D. His widow established a memorial scholarship in his name.

It was some of Judson's classmates who one football season swiped Mike Snider's privy from his Raystown Dam cottage. They piled it on a roaring pep rally bonfire before Mike's very eyes. Too late, he cried out: "Say, that looks like mine!" It was also a member of the Class of '64 who drove off in a steamroller being used to pave College Avenue, which bounds the east campus. The Cloisterite, learning how to control the machine by watching the operator through binoculars, one night rumbled in toward town, thirty or more fellows draped all over the behemoth, which turned left on 18th Street, and with borough police in pursuit, came to rest against a tree beside Lesher Hall. It was a state trooper, however, who made the arrest.

A member of the Class of '64 but not involved in the steamroller incident was the first of a tetrad of Juniatians to be chosen a Woodrow Wilson Fellow: Ron Smelser.** In those days that meant practically a full boat ride through a doctoral program. Now it is a fundless honor, to be parlayed into whatever shekels the recipient can at the graduate school of his/her choice.

Mountain Day had undergone a slight change by 1964, as the one at Colerain State Park on October 14 illustrated. The student-faculty softball game, a rivalry that came after World War II, had now been replaced by touch football. Moreover, the competition, involving some rough play, would hereafter pit seniors-only against the profs. The latter, after these encounters, limp into class on the morrow, bruises and abrasions all too evident. A new winter recreation made its appearance in December: skiing at Blue Knob, promoted by the Outing Club.

---

*This prize was established by Mrs. Jane B. Swigart of Huntingdon in memory of her cousin, a physician and surgeon.
**The other three were Janet Kauffman (Borland) and Mary Harsanyi (Miller), both 1967 graduates, and William Phillips '70.

The Goldwater-Johnson race for the White House was a dead issue on the Hill for some reason. A few Republicans did turn out when Goldwater's train made a Huntingdon pause. The candidate looked tired; his remarks certainly were not the rabble-rousing kind.

Until the fall of 1964 the financial aid program was administered by a faculty committee chaired by the college treasurer. Historically, with the exception of a few honor scholarships, aid had been based on need. The number of scholarship funds had grown over the years to forty-one in 1964. There were also a number of loan funds, and many students received outright grants. And, of course, Hilltop jobs were available for earning part of school expenses. Approximately 80 JCers were then in the college's employ in some capacity. An Anti-Poverty Bill passed by Congress in the summer further made possible work-study grants, which would involve students in certain kinds of community activity. The aid program was now too much of a burden for the faculty and in September Robert Doyle '60, an assistant in admissions, became director of financial aid and placement.*

Meanwhile, Southern resistance to legal and legislative gains in race relations aroused idealistic indignation on northern college and university campuses. And March 1965 witnessed the baptism of Hilltoppers into civil rights protest action — and violence. A group of students and faculty, inspired by Harriet Richardson (Michel), a beautiful black woman, and Galway Kinnell, poet-in-residence, decided to join in demonstrations for voter registration in Alabama the week of the 15th. This was in response to a plea for help from SNCC. Plans called for a four-day, fifty-mile Selma-to-Montgomery pilgrimage. Supporters nominated by acclamation four leaders to organize the movement on campus: Miss Richardson, James Lehman, recently elected student body president, Mike Marzio, and Gary Rowe, both underclassmen.

Twenty-one persons, forewarned of the dangers that lay ahead, made the trip. Three Huntingdon pastors were in the group. A Hilltop company numbering more than one-hundred marched from the college through

---

*In 1972 the 1958 NSDL fund was reenacted as the National Student Loan Program. Pennsylvania and neighboring states established Guaranteed Loan Programs to help finance the higher education of youth from middle- or upper-income families in the mid-1960s. For residents of the Keystone State a major source of funds became the Pennsylvania Higher Education Assistance Agency beginning in the early 1970s. After that came the federal Basic Educational Opportunity Grants Program.

downtown Huntingdon and bade farewell to those "Alabamy" bound. There the Juniata people joined with hundreds of colleges throughout the nation at Montgomery, the state capitol. Meanwhile in Selma, Martin Luther King and Ralph Bunche, two black Nobel Peace Prize winners, told the crowd that "no tide of racism can stop us." But the police tried. Mounted troopers and possemen assaulted demonstrators in Montgomery with cattle prods, clubs, and whips, tossing cannisters of tear gas into their ranks. "Every white person in Montgomery would have killed us, with no questions on their part," railed Chuck Lytle on his return.[26]

Several persons from the Juniata contingent were physically hurt. English professor Donald Hope received head injuries, was hospitalized, and released. The *New York Times* carried a front page picture of Elmer Maas administering first aid to Hope after he was struck down. Galway Kinnell and the Rev. Gerald Witt, one of the pastors (First Evangelical United Brethren Church), also took beatings. In *Life* that week there was a half-page shot of Harriet Richardson, her brow furrowed from strain, tenderly wiping at Galway Kinnell's bloodied face. It was a photograph that angered many unsympathetic JC alumni and parents. On the way back the motor of one car was ruined after someone put sugar in the gas tank. Its riders had to call home for money to buy another car. A highly emotional debriefing took place in Oller Hall on an evening soon after the Alabama demonstrators returned.

Another Hill group—sixty-four in all—traveled to Washington, D. C. on Sunday the 14th to participate in civil rights demonstrations there. Juniata students carried signs proclaiming such slogans as "Freedom takes time—and time is running out," "United we stand, divided we fall," "All men are created equal." They also carried placards bearing the equality emblem. Some fifteen-thousand protesters rallied at Lafayette Square. Nothing happened to mar the peaceful rally. Strains of *We Shall Overcome*, the "national anthem" of civil righters, filled the air the whole day.

Out of these experiences sprang SCORE, the Student Committee on Racial Equality, a campus organization that took in faculty and administrators. Some of its projects included collecting clothing for the South and tutoring blacks in Huntingdon and Mt. Union. It also worked with the Tri-County Anti-Poverty Program. Gary Rowe, a philosophy major, was the prime mover behind SCORE, his department professors, Fred Brouwer and Elmer Maas, working closely with him.

The civil rights movement on campus, besides raising everybody's consciousness on race, said Mike Marzio, was "valuable for secondary reasons." It was "prolonging an aggressive turn" for change on the Hill. He had in mind the Senate-drafted "Suggestions to Faculty" concerning better communications between them and students and improvements in course structure and teaching methods. He also was referring to the unrest over Totem Inn. Students had returned the fall of 1963 to find the snack bar ousted and replaced by vending machines. Grumbling and Senate pressure never ceased over the next year and a half. By April the snack bar was back.

That was the month the Focus Series featured Arthur Schlesinger, Jr., noted historian and a former special assistant to a presidential pair: JFK and LBJ. He advocated "honorable negotiation" in Vietnam over the alternative of pulling out or escalating the war. At that time Dale Evans, editor of *Kvasir*, was fighting a skirmish of his own over censorship. The Student Relations Committee, made up of faculty and undergrads, considered two proposed contributions to *Kvasir* in "bad taste" for a publication bearing the name of the college. The editor made certain concessions but he declared that the magazine, a creative outlet for Hilltoppers, should not become a "tool of the administration's image-makers."[27]

A winner all the way, though, was the Class of '65. Three straight years—since they were sophomores—they walked off with the All Class Night trophy. They were the first to do this, earning them the right to retire the cup. They were also the last seniors for whom the junior class gave a reception.

Those '65ers in the touring choir got a special thrill on Sunday afternoon, May 16. That was the day the choral peregrinators sang at the New York World's Fair (the Tiparillo Pavilion). Their appearance climaxed a year of forty-two concerts. It was Director Donald Johnson's on-the-road swan song. Next season the Lincolnesque Bruce Hirsch directed the choir, as he does today.

Thirty-one percent of the 152 graduating seniors planned to further their education, up eleven percent over the previous year's graduates.

When the Class of '69 entered Juniata in September they pushed the enrollment over one-thousand. The faculty reception departed the gym and encompassed the whole campus. Knots of faculty hosted big and little brothers and sisters in the women's dormitory lounges, Carnegie Hall (the station of the Ellises), and Tote.

New on the scene was Robert Holmes (1965-68), an administrative addition as Coordinator of Student Activities. Holmes, nowadays principal of the Huntingdon Area High School, was the man through whom students had to schedule student events: date, time, location, nature, and size. His job was intended to prepare Hilltoppers for the kinds of responsibility that would befall the director of the College Center, a building then in the planning stages. Holmes began putting out a weekly *Calendar* each Monday.

The mid-Sixties seemed to reflect campus indifference toward student government. Said outgoing president Jim Lehman in 1966, "The biggest problem the Senate faced this year was proving to the Juniata College Community that the Senate is a responsible, committed body worth existing."[28] Yet the voting on new officers in February was unprecedented in nearly all phases. The lack of a voter quorum (sixty percent according to Senate bylaws) forced an extension of the election. Then, too, only one of the four offices was opposed. Things went better, however, in the chair elections. The Judiciary was in even worse shape. From 1957 to 1962 students almost always chose to be tried by their peers. But, in the years since, the Judiciary had lost the confidence of Hilltoppers. During 1965-66, for example, 68 out of 70 cases were reviewed by the deans — an option to those accused of an offense. The *Juniatian* assessed the Judiciary's future as "dubious."

As the decade passed the halfway point, debate and the General Information Test made their permanent departure from the Hill.

This loss was of little importance to most students compared to what was happening at 1621 Mifflin Street. There, on February 11th, Salut, Juniata's off-campus coffee house, opened to a more-than-capacity crowd. The place had once been Lee Coffman's little grocery store, which the college bought and turned over to the students. With Senate funds a ten-member committee headed by the basketball team's towering co-captain, Will Brandau, Juniata's folk-style Mitch Miller, began in September to renovate the frame structure. On opening night there were tables and chairs to accommodate fifty to seventy-five people, who paid a cover charge of twenty-five cents to get in. Murals, candles, and curtains were added extras promoting atmosphere. Waitresses took orders for tea, coffee, cider, and doughnuts. In the months ahead entertainment would include music, live and recorded, and poetry readings.

The musicians for the Grand Opening were the New Century Singers, Steve Engle's campus group. The Hill first met them at an Oller Hall lawn folksing for May Day weekend 1964. They cut three records, all original compositions, and traveled throughout the East and Midwest performing for colleges, high schools, conventions, service clubs, benefits, and other organizations. The New Century Singers won second place in an Inter-Collegiate Musical Competition at Lycoming College. Their final campus show was in May 1966. When the Oller Hall concert ended the student body presented Engle, still "doing his thing" today, with a scroll recognizing his talents as a singer, composer, and director. Steve's singers included, during their Hilltop existence, Sue Judy (Wright), Bob McDowell, Bill Brubaker, Paul Morse, Patricia Dove, Dave Gould, Kirsten Miller (Gould), Don Armstrong, and John Russell.

That same May students and faculty bussed to Shade Gap to help comb the woods for the "Mountain Man," who had kidnapped Peggy Ann Bradnick walking the lane to her home after school. It was a week-long search. The National Guard was called out. The media kept the nation informed on the latest developments. There was bloodshed, the kidnapper and an FBI agent left dead from gunshot wounds. But Peggy Ann was rescued, unharmed.

At senior convocation on the 18th the first awardee of the Alice G. Blaisdell Prize, established by Dr. Blaisdell in memory of his first wife, a cancer victim, was Peggy Hockensmith (Kwadrat), a Johnstown math major.*

Coeds greeted newcomer Dean Schoenherr in the fall with a hullabaloo over a spot check for improper weekend sign-outs. The *Juniatian* editorialized that the administration had no "legal, moral and ethical right" to determine students' personal moral codes. Pressure was building against what one letter to the editor called the "bulk of our Puritan and archaic conduct rules." The immediate result was the formation of SCOPE (Student Committee on Policy Evaluation) to deal generally with the question of *in loco parentis* and to recommend policy changes where necessary. Dave Gould and Paul Morse were the organizers of SCOPE.

At halftime on Parents Day skydiving Jeff Dunkle made a free-fall jump onto the middle of College Field. While the plane, which took off from Mt. Union, circled two-thousand feet overhead in a clear blue sky, Jeff's father, the late Dr. Donald Dunkle '49, communicated by radio with the pilot. It was the sophomore's ninety-third jump, and he landed within six feet of his marked goal on the fifty-yard line. When he took off his jumping suit at midfield he was in full coat-and-tie dress, looking as if he had just come from a dance.

A couple of weeks after this aerial show, in mid-November, came the

---

*For a number of years Alice Blaisdell was director of dance and choreographer for the all-college musical shows. She also taught classes in dance at the elementary schools.

annual JWSF drive. Among the many money-raising gimmicks the charity had resorted to was one in which several profs competed in a tricycle race. No longer was the goal determined by the numerals of the year. And in 1966 — in an effort to bring their projects "closer to home" — the Senate reduced the four long-standing charities to two: the World Service Fund and the Disadvantaged Student Fund (begun by SCORE).

In February Hilltoppers went to the polls in Tote to vote on a completely new type of student government. Seventy-five percent of them said "yes" in ratifying the proposed constitution drafted during James Donaldson's Senate presidency. This constitution divided the governing body into four groups: executive, legislature, cabinet, and dormitory government. Only juniors and seniors served on the old Senate but now the sixteen-person legislature would consist of four students from each class. The legislature was to deal with campus problems. Another big change was in the position of treasurer and his/her assistant. They were to be hired and salaried, not elected. The cabinet and dormitory government embraced the former chairs, and their responsibilities would now be purely administrative, not combined, as before, with legislation.

The Spring Carnival, held outdoors on an April Saturday night, had become something of a tradition by the late Sixties. The lawn between Totem Inn and Students Hall became the location of all sorts of booths. Carnival-goers had a choice from a variety of skill or "try your luck" games at five cents a turn. The Dunk-the-Prof booth was always one of the most popular. So was the Car Smash. The body of an old wreck was hauled in and decorated with names of the campus professoriate. Students could avenge themselves on particular ones with a twelve-pound sledge hammer. Afterward there was a drawing for door prizes donated by Huntingdon merchants and a dance.

William "Toby" Dills, Senate veep, was a senior now. Toby will be remembered as a *rara avis* for thinking up outlandish stunts. Jeff Dunkle's parachute jump was his idea. Some say Lee Harvey Samseil, the fictitious character whose name was carved — immortally — on many a desk top, was the creation of Toby's fertile imagination. Dills was Lee's campaign manager for president in the former's senior year. The *Juniatian* (May 17, 1967) even printed a diploma for Lee.

But the name of Dills was part of the same breath with "marathon" once the lanky chem major from Wilmington, Delaware, arrived on the Hill. A Dills-directed football marathon (sixty-three consecutive hours) received national attention in 1964 as did a Dills-conducted headlining softball marathon (fifty hours, five minutes) in 1965.

William "Toby" Dills, smiling senate veep, 1966-67. He is standing between bespectacled prexy Jim Donaldson on his right and secretary Judith Hershey (Herr). Others in picture are T. Pheasant, W. Marham, R. Vanyo, L. Bieber, F. Boyer.

And it was Toby who got up his last year what is called "Mammoth Monopoly" in the blurb booklet of that still-famous parlor game. It began on the sunny afternoon of Saturday, April 29, ingeniously using an entire block of campus sidewalks whitewashed to resemble the playing board. Four oversized markers were used by each class. There was also giant money, real estate and property deeds. The dice were large foam rubber cubes that Toby rolled-dropped from atop Students Hall fire escape. Below a sign read: "Beware of falling dice." Walkie-talkies and messengers on bicycles were used to inform players of their moves. Big-time news media had great fun with the story.

Toby's and Lee's commencement exercises took place outside in front of Oller Hall on a blue-skied and very hot day. It was the first out-of-doors graduation in ages—and the last to date. The speaker, Dr. Vera Micheles Dean, a New York University professor, became only the third woman to receive an honorary degree at Juniata.

Students returned in the fall to be greeted by news of Calvert Ellis's resignation. No more after 1967 would freshmen be received by the college president in his home during orientation days, an Ellis tradition.

By campus vote two big-name entertainment groups came to College Hill the last Ellis year, one each semester. The Association, recording rock 'n roll artists, appeared in concert for Parents Day. The spring semester — March 16 — it was Motown Sound: Martha and the Vandellas, "Grammy" nominees and "one of the hottest recording acts in the nation," who belted out for two hours in Memorial Gym.

Meanwhile, Leadership Conference at Blue Diamond Camp called for student representation on faculty standing committees (which was already true for the Student Activities Council). The SG, backed by its adviser, Earl Kaylor, and Deans Schoenherr and Helms, carried this petition to the faculty. The matter was settled in February when profs, with little opposition, okayed their charges as voting members on all key committees except Faculty Council. The Council, SG agreed, dealt with professional business of no concern to students.* Thus, in this quiet way Juniata gave a strong voice to JC undergrads in most areas of academic policy making and the administration of their college experience. These were privileges that would only later come to the majority of colleges and universities — and then with headlining national attention.

Vietnam was striking strident chords, however, on campus. Prof. Maas, who helped form what was called the Vietnam Summer Committee, led a small band of JCers to a Washington, D. C. rally of war protestors in October. Then in November Sotirios Nicolopoulos surprised Capt. John Brennan, a Marine recruiter, by presenting him with a petition of 503 signatures in support of the war. Nicolopoulos, a Vietnam veteran, said the petition was evidence that the students who participated in the October Peace March on the Pentagon did not truly represent the majority feeling on the campus. Yet a survey by math major Linda Hartman (Bianchi) for an independent study in her minor, political science, indicated sixty-three percent of JC students disapproved of the government's handling of the situation in Vietnam.[29] But sixty-five percent opposed a withdrawal. Linda concluded that although a majority were unhappy about the present policy, they remained open to a negotiated settlement as long as it did not appear as a "victory" for the Viet Cong.

However, the antiwar faction on campus was at work in other ways then just marching around Foggy Bottom. They had become fans of

---

*Before long students had a vote on *all* faculty committees.

"dovish" Sen. Eugene McCarthy of Minnesota, an idealistic and quiet-spoken ex-professor. His candidacy, taken seriously by few people, aroused college students who flooded New Hampshire ("The Children's Crusade") for its early March presidential primary. "Clean Gene" won, to the surprise of most politicos. Pro-McCarthy Juniatians and townspeople made a door-to-door canvass of Huntingdon alerting the local electorate that McCarthy was on the Pennsylvania primary ballot. Their watchword was: "Make Pennsylvania Another New Hampshire." Among the Hilltop leaders were Profs. Maas and Sara Clemson, and students Chris Moore, Marta Daniels, Mike Marzio, and Jeff Cawley. To "Be Clean for Gene" the campaigners, both students and faculty alike, ruefully gave up encroaching hair and beards. The Keystone State, to their dismay, did not turn out to be another New Hampshire.

With 1967 sit-down table service became a Monday through Thursday evening only and Sunday noon affair, tables still Senate assigned. The Class of 1968 was the last one to observe the candlelighting and mantle ceremonies.

In August, at an informal commencement for summer graduates, Dr. Ellis conferred his 3,304th and final bachelor's diploma. It was the last official act of his twenty-five-year presidential career.

INDIANS OF THE 1960s

Bill Engel wore more than one hat while looking after his office of public information. Technically he was not a Sports Information Director, but over the years he prepared an annual guide on all varsity athletic programs that became a model for small colleges. It was he who initiated the *J-Fan Letter*, a news coverage of each sports event that was sent to all alumni of the "J" Club. Juniata's first bona fide SID was Lillian Junas (1964-67), an assistant in the public information office. She was followed by David Leonard (1967-68).

And, of course, since 1960—over in Memorial Gym—there has been James Harbaugh, Juniata's first full-time equipment manager. It is hard to imagine how the varsity program could get along without him, an orderly and cheerful person whose hair has now turned white. Indians of every sport soon learn to treat him with respect.

Jim was not in the sweat-fumed equipment room during football's "Glory Years." But he saw Ken Bunn and Fred Prender (1962-68), with their aides, coach winning football from 1960 to 1967 (39-25-0). One of the most outstanding players of those years was Patton, Pennsylvania's Bill Crowell, guard and captain. In 1963, his senior year, he was All-State,

All-Conference, second-time All-East (ECAC), and All-America (second team). Another star was Don Weiss, record-shattering QB (eleven still on JC's books), Little All America (honorable mention) as a junior (1967), as well as All-East. There was also Little All-American Mario "Bo" Berlanda, a fullback (honorable mention, 1966). Others of the 1960s can boast standing record-making feats: like quarterback Gary Sheppard, punter Grey Berrier, field-goal kicker Don Corle, end Jeff Barnes, defensive backs Joel Delewski, Pete Straup, Randy Oeffner, Barry Broadwater (for interceptions and punt or kickoff returns), and extra point kicker Dave Fleck.

All the while, Mike Snider's hill and dalers were racking up an aggregate log of 61-31-1 before his coaching career ended in 1968. Between 1957 and 1963 the Snider harriers enjoyed five consecutive unbeaten seasons and ran up a thirty-eight-meet winning streak. From time to time, however, the cross-country course has been lengthened. Earl Samuel (1961-65) retired the record for the original 4.3-mile circuit (22:58:5), which began and ended in front of the press box on College Field. He was one of only two Indian athletes to win a pair of alumni awards (track and cross-country) and get a Mickle cup in the same year.* Another pack-pacer of the Sixties was Rick Beard, Student Government president and thrice a Brown-trophy runner, who in his junior year (1966) laid lasting claim to the 4.6-mile time (24:26:6). From 1967 to 1973 the course was 4.8 miles long, but the best time for it eluded a Juniatian.

Basketball had a harder time of it, three coaches posting forty-five wins against ninety-nine losses. Arnold Greene resigned after the 1960-61 season with a 103-131 won-loss total for a dozen years. High school teacher Ralph Harden (1961-66), whose Hollidaysburg, Pennsylvania, teams had dominated the Mountain League for sixteen years, took over the Greenemen and relieved Mike Snider as athletic director. A crack administrator as AD, he was bitterly disappointed with his five-year coaching mark of 27-61. His last season he termed a "personal nightmare" (2-15). Returning to high school teaching, he has not coached again. Fred Prender took his place in the AD's office but remained as head football coach. Keystoner Russell Trimmer, who led Middletown Area High School to 120 wins, twenty-one losses, and five championships in the Capitol Area Conference over nine seasons, became Hilltop cage mentor. Trimmer, a truly great coach, had an exciting Jekyll-Hyde aspect to his personality. Off-court he was relaxed and easy going, a soft-spoken,

---

*Lance Shomo did it in 1969, his two sports being football and basketball.

likeable man. But after the opening center jump of a game he became a towel-throwing, chair-kicking, red-faced, hollering near maniac for the next forty minutes of play. But within two years he had Juniata back on the winning track, and to visiting teams packed Memorial Gym, the din of cheering deafening, was commonly known as the "snake pit." There were stars on those losing quintets of the Sixties, such as 6' 4" center Leroy Mock, eighth in all-time career scoring and fourth in rebounding, and dazzling guard Clair Kenyon, ninth among the top career point-making leaders.

Wrestling won varsity status in 1960, but unlike basketball just about broke even in wins and losses over eight seasons (36-38-0). Outsiders coached JC matmen until 1962 when Bill Berrier stepped in. Under him the Blue and Gold went 33-28. The second best season in grappling history on the Hill was 1964-65 (7-3-0). Senior Duane Ruble, strongman of the unlimited weight class, won nine matches by falls. When a sophomore, Ruble won the first David L. Helsel '61 Wrestling Award. He copped it each of the next two years. Dr. Ellis's last year, Chris Sherk, the 145 pounder himself among the Helsel elite (twice), posted an undefeated dual meet record of 9-0-1, the only JC wrestler to do so. He capped that with a second-place performance in the MAC championship meet, another College Hill first.

Golfers of the 1960s had good and bad seasons that evened out at 46-46-0. The first year of the decade was their best. They won nine and lost two and finished second in the NCAA Coast Regional championships. Smooth-swinging Jack Vernocy, to be thrice the C. Blair Miller cup awardee, won ten of eleven in fairway duels.

The tennis team that year won two and lost six. Then historian Ernest Post, a college letterman in football and tennis, tried to turn things around in 1961 (he did and he has been coach ever since). Six of the next eight squads were winners, taking forty-five matches and dropping thirty-one. The 1967 season (8-1-0) was all-time second best on the Hill. Stan Conner and Larry Bieber each got the Ellis tennis trophy twice in those years. A premed student, Bieber also won the John E. Blood Memorial Award instituted in 1967, Larry's last year. It goes to the senior athlete, who has earned four letters in any sport, with the highest academic average.*

---

*John Blood, food director at Juniata, 1964-66, was a baseball fan while on the Hill, the unofficial "batting coach." He had written a book on Ted Williams.

Tracksters fell short of tennis' upsurge and from 1960 to 1968 won only twenty-six dual meets while losing forty-two and tying one. In triangulars, Snidermen took four firsts. Three of these came in 1963, JC's best overall track season ever, when the squad piled up ten wins to one loss. The season climaxed with a third place finish in the MAC's, the highest showing until 1973. The Tribe of the 1960s, paced by the likes of Don Layman, Bob Berthold, Rob Gardner, Earl Samuel, Bill Williams, and John Stultz, shattered their share of records. But these all fell in the early 1970s.

Track and cross-country coach Mike Snider, once a star athlete on the Hill, retired in 1968. Ever since 1930, except for his three-year World War II Navy hitch, he had been a part of the athletic department— instructor, coach, athletic director. Said Fred Prender at a testimonial dinner in Snider's honor: "Losing Mike is losing a great part of Juniata's tradition."[30]

Of all the Hilltop sports during the 1960s only baseball turned up professional talent. 1960 was the year of the "bonus babies," stirring memories of the early Twenties when Joe Shaute went with Cleveland. Don Ross, the Tribe's thirdbaseman and leading hitter, signed with the Baltimore Orioles for a bonus in excess of twenty-five thousand dollars after getting offers from twelve major league clubs.* "Golden Boy" Bill Berrier, who shared the Mickle Award with twin-brother Jim, a classy athlete in his own right, inked a pro contract with the Los Angeles Dodgers as an outfielder and received ten-thousand dollars for doing it. Both Ross and Berrier hailed from Harrisburg. The big surprise was Ed Hoffman, a junior from nearby Saltillo, playing his first full season for the Indians. Hoffman, a left-hand hitting outfielder, signed with Cincinnati. Only Bill Berrier stuck it out. He enjoyed a six-year playing career that included Triple-A ball. Since then he has spent his summers managing in in Dodger system.**

Under coaches Bunn, Kaylor (1963),*** and Prender diamond victories outnumbered defeats sixty-seven to forty-eight (one tie). In 1962 Tony Faber captured the MAC crown "going away," hitting at a phenomenal clip in seven games. Only two other Hilltoppers—Gary Sheppard (1964) and Tom Streightiff (1973)—have swung their way to the MAC batting title. Grey Berrier, younger brother of lookalike Bill and Jim, signed with the Chicago Cubs in 1964 and played one season in the minors.

---

*Ross was traded to the Los Angeles Dodgers right after signing his contract.
**Since 1961 Berrier has combined his playing and then his managing career with responsibilities in Juniata's Office of Student Services during the off-season.
***Kaylor subbed as coach when Ken Bunn left in midwinter for another position.

For Chet Langdon and the athletic department, the spring of 1963 marked the realization of a twenty-five-year dream—separate baseball and football fields. Langdon Field (baseball), east of the old playing area, was ready first, in early May. But College Field (football and track) took longer, and the fall 1963 home gridiron games were played on Huntingdon's War Veterans Memorial Field. Gone now were familiar landmarks to JC athletes and fans for years—the old grandstand and the green, rickety fence that cordoned off the scene of action.

Ellis-era athletics ended in a show of respect for a president who enjoyed sports and appreciated their place in the college's life. Bob Richards, former Olympic pole-vaulting champion, spoke to over 350 Juniata fans on Saturday night, May 25th, at a banquet honoring Dr. Ellis upon his retirement.

14

Girded For The Second Century
1968-1976

JOHN N. STAUFFER: JUNIATA'S FIRST LAY PRESIDENT
The college, for most of its history, had been run by a Brumbaugh or an
Ellis, all preachers. This men-of-the-cloth presidential dynasty ended in
1968. Earlier, Calvert Ellis, sixty-three, made known to the trustees his
decision to retire not later than June 1969. In his statement he said:
"Juniata needs vigorous leadership and new ideas for the years ahead which
will be critical ones for the independent, church related, college."[1]

John Baker responded for the board: "We respect his decision, but
without him Juniata will hardly be the same." Chairman Baker knew that
in the previous year three-hundred college and university presidencies
had gone begging.[2] But that was not what he had in mind when he
acknowledged that Calvert Ellis would be a hard person to replace. He
was talking about the man's rare qualities.

But the search, involving a faculty committee (an Ellis idea), was
over before spring. In early March the Hilltop community got the word.
Among the trustees themselves was found a worthy successor in John
Stauffer (Ed. D., Penn State). The strapping big alumnus brought to the
office an impressive set of credentials. At age fifty-two, he was a tested
administrator and hardly a gray hair to show for it. He had spent twenty-one
years in administration at Ohio's Wittenberg University — as dean of students
(1947-57), dean of the college (1957-63), and president (1963-68). A

359

John N. Stauffer.

Lutheran layman, he was the first Wittenberg president selected from within the faculty in sixty years.

To Dr. Baker, accepting Juniata's presidential call, the Palmyra, Pennsylvania, native wrote: "I have a deep sense of debt to Juniata as alma mater, a debt I have acknowledged but that I never expected to be able to attempt to repay."[3] And in an open letter to Wittenberg faculty and students, he said: "Those who do not understand the language of love for Alma Mater — who do not sense the respect and gratitude for Juniata that I have felt deeply since my student days — will not understand my decision. . . ."[4] Such were the sentiments of the man whom the JC alumni once (1959-60) elected their national vizier.

Coming back to the Hill held added attraction, said Stauffer, because of Juniata's "academic reputation," the "size and character" of its student body, its "commitment to liberal arts education." There was another persuasive factor:

The structure and function of Juniata's board of trustees are, in my opinion, most desirable and defensible. While committed to the Christian tradition, the college and its board stand free from control by a church body. Juniata's tradition and present posture are favorable to the pluralism and the ecumenism appropriate to the needs of students.[5]

John Stauffer left behind a solid reputation in his adopted state. During his five years as Wittenberg's ninth president, the university, double the size of Juniata, made major advances on all fronts. Among Ohioans his name was known and respected everywhere in the field of higher education. At one time or another he had been a member or officer of every key educational agency in the Buckeye State.

Active in church and civic affairs and a YMCA leader at the national level, JC's president-elect was also interested in the business community. He was (and still is) on the board of directors of the Columbia Gas System, Incorporated as was he of the Cincinnati branch of the Federal Reserve Bank of Cleveland.

Trustee Baker shook his head in disbelief the day Stauffer's election was made public. He said to Earl Kaylor, chairman of the faculty search committee: "I never imagined it possible to talk John into leaving Wittenberg."

With no pomp or circumstance Juniata's seventh president was installed the following October. He purposely dispensed with the more elaborate type of inauguration, the Installation Convocation involving just Juniata people. "Simplicity" was his desire — to save "time and funds which can well be used elsewhere," he told the trustees.

The former residence of Morley Mays, a modest white frame structure on 18th Street west of Moore, became the President's Home.

Calvert Ellis, of course, was still around. But he discreetly minded his own business. He was given use of an office in Beeghly Library.

THE BEAT OF A DIFFERENT DRUMMER

The Stauffer years on College Hill began when the "student power" movement was reaching a strident pitch in the academic world. The so-called now generation had lost patience with the glacial pace of campus adjustments. Riots were beginning to convulse the best of schools, even Harvard and Columbia. They ruined many a presidential career.

It was against this background of alienation, which seemed to be tearing at academe's very innards everywhere, that John Stauffer pledged on Installation Day to create "a climate of mutual trust and respect" on campus. Quietly he began to work a major change in college governance. By Homecoming Day 1970 his goal of an "open" campus was a reality. That weekend students and faculty were sitting (as observers) for the first time on all trustee committees. Hilltop undergrads, already yoked with the faculty, were now involved at every level of the decision-making process.

There were other things he wanted to do at Juniata. He was disturbed at how few blacks and members of other minority races were to be seen among the student body. He set out to correct this racial imbalance. But he had little success in what he viewed as our "society's most urgent domestic need" — educating disadvantaged youth.[6]

Blacks, though welcome and recruited, have found little at Juniata to interest them. Its rural setting turns off the ghetto-reared, more at home in the "asphalt jungle." Small-city and suburban nonwhites, however, have taken more kindly to the Hill. What few of them have made their way to Juniata have been mostly athletes — and males.

Not only was John Stauffer anxious to guarantee an open and more heterogeneous campus, but also, as he once wrote, to assure that "henceforth Juniata College shall be in practice, as well as in fact, an independent institution."[7] Upon his ascension as chief executive, the trustees began to rework the bylaws with this in mind. On May 10, 1969 the totally revised document was unanimously adopted.

Deleted was the proviso that a majority of the trustees had to be Brethren. To further establish the college's independence, the trustees in 1975 took legal action to amend the Charter. Unlike before, the Church of the Brethren no longer stood to inherit Juniata should it ever fold. In such an eventuality what was to be done with the college rested solely in the hands of the trustees. "The institution's assets shall be assigned to non-profit educational purposes as determined by the Board and as further approved by the appropriate court."[8]

Stauffer's "new dream of what Juniata can become" included a recast curriculum, one relevant to the student of the Seventies. In the spring of 1969 he established a Task Force "to study the whole spectrum of the educational program of the College." But that story will be told later.

NEW ADMINISTRATIVE BLOOD

"Youth" was an accent often heard in John Stauffer's speeches when he referred to his administrative team. Gradually, as openings occurred or new positions were created, he brought in his own people, most unfledged.

This was to guarantee "vitality" and "continuity" of leadership he explained.

When the search for an outside academic dean proved unproductive after Don Rockwell resigned in 1970, the president decided the next one should come from within the Task Force. Ultimately the choice fell on Wilfred Norris, a 1958 Hilltop returnee and Task Force chairman. Later, in 1972, the young physicist was made provost, a new office of larger authority.* This was done to allow the president to concentrate his efforts on providing "general leadership." But it also released him to give more attention to the financial development of the college, which included increased political action in behalf of independent higher education both at state and federal levels. The dean-provost's immediate challenge, at the same time, was to whip up faculty favor for the Task Force package and put it into operation.

Wilfred Norris is a man of some reserve, though not unfriendly. He smiles easily. Lanky and baldish, he plays his recorder to relax. As an administrator Norris leans over backwards to be fair. Despite burdens of office he has not abandoned the classroom, teaching a course or two every year.

Youth was evident elsewhere in the Hilltop hierarchy. Thomas Robinson '66, administrative assistant to the president, replaced Charles Schoenherr as dean of student affairs in 1972. Floyd Roller became business manager and controller in 1969, taking over John Fike's responsibilities (but not his vice-presidential title) when the latter left three years later. Foster Ulrich, Jr. took Gerald Quigg's place as executive director of development in January 1970. (Harold Brumbaugh had been out of development since 1968.)**

The average age of these men, in charge of the college's four primary administrative areas, was—in 1972—just thirty-five.

Robinson, handsome and lavish of wardrobe, a long line of Juniatians on both sides of his family, resigned in 1975 to work on his doctorate.*** His position went to Donald "Terry" Hartman (Ph.D., Michigan), a bright philosopher-hunter-angler in his early thirties. Hartman had come to Juniata in 1968. A Task Force member, he became the official espositer of the curriculum it spawned. His interests inclining toward administration rather than teaching (which he does well), he was made

---

*The title was abolished in 1975 in favor of the old one, dean of academic affairs.
**In 1968 he was given the title vice-president for college relations.
***Dean of women at Juniata became a vanished breed in 1968 when Delores Maxwell arrived as associate dean of students. After her there have been Janet Cumming (1970-72), Karen Gabriel Stanley (1972-75), and Elizabeth O'Connell (1975-present).

associate academic dean in 1971. He emerged as a likely candidate for Robinson's job because of his committee work in studying the quality of life on campus. His duties as dean of student services, a new title, include supervision of the director of admissions. This is a change in the organizational chart.

Roller, who watched over balance sheets like a hawk, instituted new budgeting and financial control procedures. Sometimes his negative on a request when the ledger verged on red was less than affable. There were inevitable clashes. Some Hilltoppers took longer to adjust to hardnosed accounting brought on by the economic realities of the times. The lush Sixties had passed; the skimpy Seventies were at hand. Out of one area of tension came unionization of maintenance and housekeeping personnel. Roller left at the end of the centennial year.

By then fellow administrator Foster Ulrich was a vice-president. From Lancaster, a graduate of Franklin and Marshall (1966), his master's degree from Temple, Ulrich is in the Marine Corps Reserves. He got the silver leaves of a Lt. Col. after coming to Juniata. "Fuzz," as he is best known on the Hill, has a soft-sell approach to development quite in contrast to the Quigg way. But the pleasant, quiet-mannered Taylor Highlander is terribly efficient, close to his staff, a decision-maker, and gets equally good results. Under his guidance the Margin of Difference Campaign has moved steadily toward its goal as December 1976, the target date, approaches. His promotion in Juniata's one-hundredth year indicates how the trustees feel about him.

There was not only an infusion of new blood high up in the command; virtually all second-level administrative positions were restaffed, too.

MATTERS PROFESSORIAL

Socially the faculty found John and Louise Stauffer to be more private than Calvert and Elizabeth Ellis had been. The Stauffers, of course, were not in a position to entertain in the grand style of the Ellises. The Norrises, Wilfred and Lona, looked after the official partying of Juniata dons. They hosted small groups from time to time in their own home.

John Stauffer early won the utter trust of the faculty despite their limited social contacts with the Hill's first family. It was he — in 1970 — who marshaled the trustees into line on the matter of tenure. As a result, the board adopted the AAUP's Statement of Principles on Academic

Freedom.* "The free search for truth and its free exposition" was axiomatic with Juniata's first non-Brethren president. Now, after a six-year trial period, those below the rank of full professor had a crack at permanent appointment.

The academic program, though Stauffer did push for revision, he left solely in the faculty's lap. Ordinarily the curricular "buck," in Harry Truman's slang, did in fact stop on the desk of Wilfred Norris. There was no meddling from down the hall. Upon becoming provost Norris presided over faculty meetings, and the president ceased to attend.

No sooner had Stauffer set foot on campus than he began talking about the need to do more to recognize superior teaching. An opportunity for this came in the form of a two-hundred-and-fifty-thousand dollar challenge gift from the Charles A. Dana Foundation in 1970. The half-million dollar endowment was to go toward establishing several supported professorships. Juniata, thanks to Gerald Quigg's alertness and persistence, became the fifteenth educational institution in the nation to benefit in this way from the philanthropy of Charles Dana, a Connecticut industrialist. Other Pennsylvania colleges already favored were Dickinson, Franklin and Marshall, and Lafayette.

The original four Juniata Danas were Esther Doyle, Ronald Cherry, Eva Hartzler, and Earl Kaylor. Subsequently, after Drs. Doyle and Hartzler retired, their professorships went to Philbrook Smith and Robert Zimmerer (Ph.D., Penn State), a biologist. Chemistry's William Russey (Ph.D., Harvard) will become the fifth one in 1977. Dana salaries are determined by a certain formula based on the median emolument of full professors. But Dana money is only supplemental, hence the term *supported*.

For the last couple of years Juniata's six name professorships — in classics, religion, education, English, physics, chemistry — have had no claimants. That will be partially corrected the fall of 1976. Howard Crouch will get the Martin G. Brumbaugh Professorship in Education and the Jacob H. and Rachel Brumbaugh Professorship will go to chemist Paul Schettler (Ph.D., Yale).

Also in autumn of 1976 a major gift from a family foundation will

---

*The American Association of University Professors was founded in 1915 to advance the standards, ideals, and welfare of the academic profession. Recently the trustees have modified the tenure system. The number of tenured faculty has been frozen, but outstanding teachers can be retained beyond the magic six-year probation period on term contracts. As tenure openings occur they will become eligible candidates.

add a seventh name professorship. It honors the late W. Newton Long, for more than 40 years a trustee, and his wife Hazel. It is in history and will go to Kenneth Crosby.

Meantime, the previous fall had given rise to what is today Juniata's only fully endowed chair, the J. Omar Good Visiting Distinguished Professor of Evangelical Christianity. Omar Good, a "jovial" student on the Hill in the mid-1890s, was a Philadelphia printing executive who died in 1969 at the age of ninety-two. He willed one-million dollars to Juniata, the largest gift ever made to the college. (The Academic Building, erected in 1967, promptly got a memorial name: Good Hall.) In addition, the nonagenarian's will left substantial residual funds, the use of which was to be determined by trustees of the estate, Mr. and Mrs. Lester Rosenberger of Narberth, Pennsylvania. There was a testamentary stipulation, however, that these funds be used for "the perpetuation of the Historical Triune Faith of Protestant Christianity."

Lester Rosenberger (right) and John Baker standing next to plaque honoring J. Omar Good, for whom Academic Building is named.

Mr. Rosenberger, a soap manufacturer and a trustee since 1952, got the inspiration for a religion chair one morning while driving through the New England countryside. He envisioned "recognized authorities in the field of evangelical theology" as residents of College Hill teaching, writing, and available for off-campus lectures and preaching. There was to be a frequent turnover of scholars (no one staying longer than five years). The first incumbent is Dr. C. Samuel Calian (Ph.D., Basel), internationally known theologian and author, now on a second year contract. Dr. Calian is an ordained minister of the United Presbyterian Church and teaches at the University of Dubuque Theological Seminary in Iowa.

Stauffer did not stop at rewarding a special few. At Wittenberg he had improved overall faculty salaries and benefits by an appreciable amount. He set out to do the same at Juniata. The results speak for themselves. The latest AAUP report on small-college faculty compensation shows Juniata just a hair shy of the top category for full and associate professors. At the other ranks, on a one to four scale, the college rates a "two."

The faculty today do their business in Good Hall. They have a set of bylaws for self-governance, a Stauffer suggestion. These bylaws expelled certain administrators accustomed to voice and vote on academic matters. The faculty have reorganized their committee structure twice, coordinating it with curricular changes. The first time they created a monster, and committee work became all-consuming. That has recently been changed. Through the Personnel Committee they have a say in decisions about promotions, tenure, term contracts, dismissals. But it has meant learning to live with constant evaluation from all quarters.

Juniata's is a young faculty. Their average age is just forty-one. Altogether (part- and full-time) they number ninety-three. About half hold doctorates, credentially a standstill in the last eight years.

Of late more are making a stab at writing, not only articles and reviews but books. Especially the humanists and social scientists. For example, Esther Doyle, Klaus Kipphan, theologian Jose Nieto (Ph.D., Princeton), sociologist Duane Stroman (Ph.D., Boston U.), and political scientist William Vocke have recently authored or edited scholarly volumes. More are in the offing. Productive and jealous use of sabbaticals have opened the press gates at a teaching-above-all-else college.

The paintings of Alexander McBride and the pottery of Jack Troy, himself at work on a book entitled *Salt-Glazed Ceramics*, have done honor to the art department at more than one juried show.

Habitants of Brumbaugh Science Center always have something going, especially the chemistry department. A trio of chemists, Paul Schettler, William Russey, and Donald Mitchell (Ph.D., Vanderbilt), are tackling one of the day's biggest problems: energy. Federal funding has enabled them to carry out research — on coal and on hydrocarbon shale interaction — both on the Hill and overseas.

On a sadder note, biologist and JC-grad John Comerford '50 died in September 1972, a heart victim at age forty-two. Down through the decades the Grim Reaper had frequently reached into the student body. But Comerford's was the first younger-than-sixty-five faculty death since the 1920s and the sixth in Juniata's one-hundred-year history. He had succeeded Homer Will as department chairman.

A CURRICULUM IN FLUX

Academicians used to say in jest: "It is easier to move a cemetery than to change a curriculum." But that was before the time of student demands for "relevance" in their studies, before their opposition to "stulti-fying" required courses. This academic fidgets did some violence to that old cemetery-curriculum saw. Things began to loosen up with the onset of the Seventies. Curricular experimentation became the vogue almost everywhere in response to what many educators thought were legitimate criticisms. Juniata followed the parade. But it was John Stauffer who goaded the faculty into doing so, letting them march in whatever direction they thought best.

At one of their first meetings after his arrival, he called for a "redesign of the academic program."[9] The following May he took steps to form a Task Force for that purpose.

By then he had conceded to faculty-student pressure for a five-day class schedule, which Earl Kaylor had slipped into summer school during Calvert Ellis's presidency. The shortened week was to take effect in the fall, ending a ninety-three-year tradition.

As for the Task Force, it sweated for most of fifteen months puzzling out what might constitute an educational program that would "meet the needs of the '70s." From the faculty there were Elizabeth Cherry (chairperson after Wilfred Norris became dean), Sara Clemson, Donald Hartman, Esther Doyle, Robert Faus, Thomas Nolan, and William Russey. Student members were Karl Kindig '73, Michael Long '71 (both Central Pennsylvanians), and Donna Roppelt '71, from Abington, Pennsylvania.

The Task Force drew the whole campus into the study. Ad hoc committees abounded. Two "D-Days," with no classes, converted the Hill into a forum-of-the-whole.* Debate seemed to go on endlessly—in homes, classrooms, offices, on the Hilltop lawns. At last a final report was ready, in September 1970. It reflected a basic, fundamental change in educational philosophy. Five months the faculty joined issue over the document. Then they voted its adoption (63-31-1), not exactly a mandate. The guinea-pig class was to be the incoming one. Sophs through seniors would continue under the old curriculum.

Some thought this was rushing things too much. The summer was given over to crash sessions for devising core offerings in the program. That initial year was hectic. It was nine months of blood, sweat, and tears. The college operated on a two-track calendar, semesters and terms (the three-term calendar became standard the fall of 1972).

What had the Task Force wrought? In their words: to be human is to be "reflective," "interpretive," "decision-making." A very flexible program sought to develop these traits. Students, with closer faculty guidance, could tailor their studies to individual needs and educational goals. There was to be an emphasis upon interdisciplinary study and team teaching. General education would no longer consist of a distribution pattern but of core units (courses). Hopefully, the new approach would make the transition from high school to college less traumatic. Thus much of the freshman year, the most innovative aspect of the curriculum, was to be ungraded. Modes of Thought and Methods of Inquiry replaced Great Epochs of World Culture as the academic rite of passage for fresh-on-the scene JCers.

"Values—"those criteria by which intellectual, aesthetic, and moral judgments are made": *that* became the shibboleth of teaching. "Value-centered liberal education": the words had a magic sound. A new cliché had been coined.

With the new program came a shift in grading practices, for *all* students, not just for freshmen. Beginning with the era of student unrest, there was a general trend in American higher education, now reversing itself, to grade easier. Many schools, like Juniata in 1971, dropped the D and did not enter failures on transcripts. This resulted in a certain degree of grade inflation. The C was cheapened and no longer held respectable. Juniata has not been as bad as many institutions. Nevertheless, it is inter-

---

*D-Day meant discussion day.

esting to observe that over the last twenty years, making allowance for an enrollment gain of three hundred, there were four honor graduates in 1956 on the Hill, nineteen in 1964, and twenty-nine in 1976. (Contrast this with one Ivy League school where more than two-thirds of the graduating class got honors in the nation's bicentennial year.)

The expectation was that the 1971 curriculum would enjoy a healthy life span of at least a decade. But, as of the centennial year, the scalpel has been put to many parts thought ailing. The present program is hardly the one the Class of '75 pioneered. The swing is clearly to the right among the faculty, as it is generally at other schools. Many professors feel that Juniata designed a curriculum for the wrong student generation. The prevailing campus spirit in the country is drastically different from a few years ago. It is conformist and docile.

It is pointless, therefore, to spell out a curriculum in such an apparent unstable state. Certainly the flexibility is there. Team teaching will be around for a long time. Values will not be deemphasized.

But there is more muscle to the academic program now. Probation is back. The freshman year is stiffer. There are fewer ungraded units, and the D will reappear in 1977. Recent curricular changes seem to indicate a return on the faculty's part to the old distribution philosophy of general education.

With the centennial class, however, went the Program Review, a compslike experience. Unlike the old-fashioned comprehensive, the PR, which just about any format served, was not a last-ditch stand by seniors. It could not be failed, examiners simply submitting a written evaluation to be filed with a student's transcript. The faculty came to feel no one was taking the PR seriously, that it was a waste of time, and voted it out of existence.

Gone, too, come September 1977, will be the old English conference approach, which assumed a certain degree of writing competence by freshmen. It will be replaced by something like a bonehead English unit that is graded.

Whatever the future holds curricularly for the Hill, the five years since 1971 have been far from routine ones for its dwellers. Thick-thatched and graying Tom Nolan, registrar since 1969, can say "Amen!" to that. From the faculty there has been a great outpouring of new units fitted to the Task Force philosophy. And, of course, there has been all that monstrous committee work that is necessary if the faculty is to run the academic show. John Stauffer put it rightly: "Clearly the Juniata campus is a more exhilarating place than it was prior to the new program."[10]

That was rather how a delegation of three from the National Endowment for the Humanities felt on a Hilltop visit in April 1972. They spent two days on campus, impressed by what they saw. In time, Juniata received a NEH basic grant of $240,145. Supplemental amounts ultimately put the total at close to $340,000. Only eleven other colleges received NEH funds the same year. Juniata's grant, of course, was a vote of confidence in the curriculum, to be used to retool faculty, strengthen the library, and provide equipment needed in special units.

Autumn 1972 was the time for the regular ten-year review by Middle States. All went well, as expected. The eight-member team was intrigued by the attitude of JC students, who expressed "a belief in the future." This, they said, was in contrast to the outlook on many campuses.[11]

The evaluators' report suggested a rather novel administrative setup for a college of Juniata's size. However, it was one that made sense to Provost Norris. And so in 1973 divisional chairmen were promoted to assistant deans — to decentralize the decision power and improve internal communications. "Mini-deans," the faculty irreverently spoke of them at first. Their authority, however, has grown with time. They form the Deans Council.

Robert Wagoner (Ph.D., Harvard), an ex-Chicagoan and, typical of philosophers, articulate, is Division I's dean. He deserves much of the credit for charming the NEH people into their good deed for the college.

Duane Stroman, whom coeds find easy to look at, was dean of Division II one year. Today he is in charge of the continuing education program.* James Lakso (Ph.D., Maryland), a laconic economist, deans the division now and runs summer school.

Tall, mild-mannered, RV-camper Dale Wampler (Ph.D., Wisconsin) of the chemistry department keeps Division III happy.

The times, however, find the humanities less cheerful. Enrollments are down in all departments. There is little consolation in the fact that this is a national trend. Rampant vocationalism is sweeping higher education, intensifying pressure for "career-oriented" courses and preprofessional training. Tarrel H. Bell, United States Commissioner of Education, said in early 1976: "The college that devotes itself totally and unequivocally to liberal arts today is kidding itself. Today, we in education must recognize that it is our duty to provide students with salable skills."[12] President Gerald Ford himself has called for a closer relationship between the life of the mind and the world of work.

---

*It is similar to the one that existed for a few years in the early 1950s. The appeal is to industrial workers, although not exclusively.

Small private colleges, traditionally oriented toward the liberal arts, have always had to contend — especially during economic recessions — with the problem of job-hungry students. But the debate over occupational preparation vs. liberal education has never been more heated. Stronger schools like Juniata, less worried about survival, hope to be able to develop new relationships between the two approaches.

The humanities, without a language or religious requirement for graduation since 1971, is far from moribund, however. Certain recent revisions in the present curriculum are designed to strengthen it. Ernest Post (Ph.D., Michigan State) of the history department has aroused considerable interest in urban studies. Juniatians participate in Urban Semester Programs — a period of time in one of the nation's major metropolitan centers — sponsored by other schools. Clayton Briggs and Bruce Davis have introduced units on films. Purchase of a complex of buildings behind North Dorm on College Avenue provides a quonset-hut Pot Shop for Jack Troy's ceramics students. The Folgelsanger-Murphy Lectureship in the Humanities (an endowment of more than eighty-five thousand dollars by a family of late trustees) keeps Ralph Church, head of the English department, busy scheduling visiting speakers, scholars, and artists for the division.*

Division II's department of economics and business administration, as might be expected in light of latter-day vocationalism, is king of the Hill in 1976. Its centennial year total enrollment was 1,096 (compared to once-regnant biology's 739). Spring 1969, the department began its intern program, which puts students out into the working world for eight weeks. In 1971 the Herbert A. and Marjorie F. Miller Endowment provided a benefaction of one hundred thousand dollars to support teaching in economics and business administration. Sociology, meanwhile, has held up well, too, its internships continuing to provide practical experience in a variety of social service agencies. The education department, historically a college pillar, has enjoyed phenomenal success in placing its graduates. Percentagewise, its results are two and a half times better than the average record of all Pennsylvania colleges and universities. The G. Graybill Diehm Lectureship in Political Science, honoring a man who gave thirty-five years of public service as a Pennsylvania lawmaker and State GOP leader, brings distinguished speakers in that field to the Juniata campus.

*Similar funds, the Calvert N. Ellis Humanities Series and the Edith B. Wertz Endowment for Support of Cultural Events, go toward the Focus programs that are of a broader, nonacademic nature open to the Hilltop-Huntingdon communities.

Curricularly, Division III's latest development has been the Frank Peirce Biological Station on Lake Raystown, Central Pennsylvania's newest impoundment and recreational site. The 385-acre station is on a point of land not far from where the "Forge Refugees" shivered through their founding days ordeal. It is leased from the United States Corps of Engineers, and Robert Fisher (Ph.D., Cornell), the college's principal ecologist, is in charge of it. Environmental biologists number half of the six department members, a response to modern ecological worries.

World peace, a deep concern for which has been a part of Juniata's heritage, is a contemporary worry, too. Yet on the Hill there never were any specific offerings in peace, except for one taught by Robert McFadden, religion instructor from 1955 to 1958. In recent years, however, some members of the Juniata community felt it was time to make a curricular commitment to peace study. John and Elizabeth Baker provided financial support.

And so in 1974 a Peace and Conflict Studies program was introduced, plans for which had been developed by a student-faculty committee headed by Klaus Kipphan. Says the catalog: these studies embrace "a core of units exploring causes, morphology and consequences of conflicts as well as methods of conflict resolution." It is interdisciplinary, unit work in 1975-76 involving two hundred students and ten professors. One-hundredth anniversary celebrations included the publication of a journal, *Juniata Studies: Peace, Justice and Conflict*, edited by Ralph Church and Klaus Kipphan. All contributors were from the College Hill professoriate.

With all these curricular gains, the libraries, of which Robert Sabin, JC's science librarian, became director in 1972, were not ignored. NEH money went toward general education materials and basic humanities collections. Of much importance, too, was, in the spring of 1969, the revival of the Friends of the Library, defunct for over a decade. The library's greatest friend during the Stauffer years was the late Aaron Rabinowitz, a wealthy New York real estate executive. He was an admirer of Lillian Wald, the famous settlement house worker in Manhattan's poverty-stricken East Side, who had taken the philanthropist in tow in his boyhood. In 1974 the college dedicated a seminar room on the second floor of the Beeghly Library in memory of these two illustrious people.

MARGIN OF DIFFERENCE PROGRESS AND NEW PHYSICAL RESOURCES

The alumni and church districts continued to elect strong people to the board of trustees. However, the death or resignation of trustees on regular appointment created several vacancies. These were filled with the co-optation of able and dedicated men like corporation executive Thomas Martin (1968), investment banker Edwin Kennedy (1969), attorney LeRoy Maxwell, Sr. '36 (1970), auto dealer Klare Sunderland '56 (1970), coal mine operator/banker Earl Croner '38 (1974), and Jack Oller '23 (1975). Calvert Ellis, of course, remained on the board after his presidency. Edward Kennedy of New York City, a director of numerous oil companies, succeeded retired Herbert Miller as the specialist on the college portfolio.

All the while, the Margin of Difference Campaign moved successfully through Phases I and II, achieving its $5.3-million-dollar goal by 1973. The third and last phase took the name "Juniata Centennial Fund." The year John Stauffer resigned (1974-75), total support from all sources exceeded the two million dollar mark for the first time in the college's history.

Mid-1976 the college had seven hundred thousand dollars to go to close out the drive. The trustees themselves had come through with $1,850,105 since 1968, a princely sum. Yet at Homecoming 1975 they flung out "Challenge '76." This will bind them to matching dollar for dollar—up to five hundred thousand dollars—all gifts from individual alumni and friends through 1976. Quite a challenge and quite an eight-year achievement! All in the face of the fact that for 1974-75 voluntary support of the country's colleges and universities dropped about eighty million dollars.

It was Stauffer who added a new wrinkle to Juniata's development program: the Annual Support Fund. This was quite apart from the major campaign and was directed primarily at the alumni. No longer would they have specific yearly projects as had been their custom. Said the president in 1969: "In the face of inflation the College is trying to fill a substantial gap between the cost of providing quality education and the dollars supplied by student fees and by income from the endowment."[13] At that time Juniata's endowment yielded a return of only one hundred twenty four thousand dollars a year. William Swigart '37, prominent Huntingdon insurance executive and grandson of "W.J.," was general chairman of the initital (1969-70) annual support drive—for one hundred thousand dollars. He set a good example: all seven since have gone over the top.

Some of the Margin of Difference funds, meanwhile, had been earmarked for further Hilltop construction. A college center came first, completed the fall of 1969. The two million dollar center, with its great columned portico, is named for Charles and Calvert Ellis, Juniata's presidential family. To students, who pledged two thousand dollars toward it, the name "Super Tote" sufficed at first. The fifth campus building constructed by Paul Hickes of nearby Alexandria, Ellis College Center is located at the foot of 18th Street.* Among the ever-so-many facilities in the three-floored structure is the Baker Refectory, seating seven hundred students and now the college's only operating dining room.

Ellis Center is more than a building; it is an organization and program that plans year-round cultural, recreational, and social co-curricular activities. There is a College Center Board composed of nine students, a faculty member, an alumnus and the center director. The board is responsible for all general policy relating to the use of Ellis Hall and its programs.

The latest construction work, Hickes again the contractor, was the dormitory complex along Warm Springs Avenue. These residence halls, built at a cost of over $1.6 million, are known as East Houses because of their location on the campus. There are two buildings, each four floors, with a pair of apartmentlike units on each story.** The entire complex, which accommodates 208 students, has been dedicated to four trustees, all now deceased: William Flory, Joseph Kline, Newton Long, Sr., and Robert Miller. At present more than ninety percent of Juniata's student body is residential.

Razed, though, in 1970, because of unsafe structural conditions, were three early-years buildings. Crane and swinging ball made rubble of Students, Brumbaugh, and Oneida Halls that fall. Only the Oneida Annex was spared demolition. Into it moved the business and accounting offices. The ground floor was converted into the print shop (formerly in a Founders basement nook) under portly Irvin Thomas's supervision.

The Emmert House, where students used to sit with legs dangling over a porch-roof balustrade, disappeared in 1975.

As buildings went up and came down the college added substantial off-the-Hill acreage to its inventory of deeds (not counting the leased biology field station). In 1969 the college acquired the Metz Poultry Farm in Oneida Township. The 170 acres of fields and wooded terrain are located on a ridge along Warm Springs Avenue not far from East Houses.

---

*Earlier Hickes-erected buildings were Sherwood Hall, South Hall, L. A. Beeghly Library, and Tussey-Terrace Complex.
**This was a practical consideration as much as an attempt at innovative dormitory living. The complex can easily be converted into apartment buildings in the event enrollment ever drops permanently.

The trustees named the tract the John C. and Elizabeth Baker Nature Preserve. It is designed for educational and recreational use. Then in 1972 the college purchased a fifty-five-acre parcel of land on Piney Ridge in Penn Township close to the Seven Points Recreation Center of Lake Raystown. This ground replaced the prime timberland (36.31 acres) near

Aerial photo of current campus. Ellis Hall is in center of picture. In distance, near Warm Springs Ave., are East Houses. Baker Nature Preserve is beyond view (upper left-hand corner).

the old Raystown Branch of the Juniata River donated by the late Emory Zook '06. Given up for the new dam via eminent domain, the Zook property had contained a cabin built by the Outing Club in 1951, a popular retreat the rest of that decade. The Piney Ridge plot will be known as the Emory Zook Campground.

Closer home, the college—for protection—went about plucking up properties on adjacent blocks as they became available. Included was the apartment building known to latter-day Juniatians as the "Pink Palace" or "Pink Elephant." Today one hundred acres and twenty-seven buildings make up the Hilltop campus.

Caretaker of Juniata's fifteen million dollar physical plant is Kenneth Rabenstein, superintendent of buildings and grounds since 1973. Calvert and Elizabeth Ellis, with funding from the Edith Wertz bequest, engaged a landscape architect in 1974 to prepare a campus master plan. This plan, projected over the next quarter century (it closes off Moore and other streets), has been endorsed "in principle" by the trustees.

"TO JUNIATA, COLLEGE DEAR": ALUMNI MEAN IT

The *Alma Mater* has for some time been ridiculed as maudlin twattle. But if dollars and cents are any indication, a good many Juniatians must be sincere when they sing about "the College that we love." There are 6,491 living alumni with known addresses in 1976, to be found in every state and in twenty-seven foreign countries. And almost half of them contribute to their school. In John Stauffer's first year thirty-five percent of the alumni gave. In his last year forty-nine percent of them did. The Stauffer administration brought two more awards from the American Alumni Association—in 1969 and 1970. The one for 1970 was a first-place citation (a trophy and one thousand dollars)), besting 367 other small, private coeducational colleges in the United States. To date, alumni have contributed $1,753,000 toward the Margin of Difference Campaign. At the same time, their giving to the Annual Support Fund since 1969 totals $922,180.

An impressive record like this represents the efforts of hundreds of volunteer workers. But applaud, too, the director of alumni affairs who looks after the twenty-three area clubs, selects class agents, and guides the thirty-five-member National Council. Nor should his office help be slighted, two of whom have been with the college twenty years or more. They keep meticulous records and collect materials published in the

Bulletin. Since 1973 Clayton Pheasant '65, who sports a cookie duster mustache, has had the job.* Extremely capable, he moved up in the chain of command in 1976. He was succeeded by David Kreider '71, a three-time letterman in football and on the college's administrative staff since graduation.

In 1971 the college began to honor alumni in two areas: achievement in career and service to Juniata. The late Ralph Leiter '27, a metallurgist with the Budd Co. of Philadelphia, his doctorate from Harvard and in 1957 president of the National Association, was the first winner in the former category. Cyrus and Isabelle Caulton, both Class of '29, co-won the first service award, a surprise to no one. Their Bryn Mawr home is unlocked to all Juniatians and any college function, their time and energy freely at alma mater's beck. "Cy," now a retired RCA executive, was national alumni president in 1960.

The Caultons are members in good standing of the Juniata College Passport Club, started by Harold Brumbaugh in 1974. This group is open to all graduates, parents, and friends who have taken one or more alumni tours. So far there have been 291 tourists. The Passport Club hopes to begin a new tradition with its annual reunion at commencement time.

But no more that weekend — not since the early 1960s — is there an alumni-varsity baseball game, once a big event. Now returning grads take to the links, competing against each other to get their name inscribed on a trophy kept at the college.

Harold Brumbaugh, not much of a golfer, will never get his name on this trophy. But the Alumni Association will honor "H.B." by renaming John B. Brumbaugh's original home at 1700 Mifflin Street the Harold Bennett Brumbaugh Alumni House. The Association has also commissioned an artist to paint an oil portrait of "Mr. Juniata." The to-be-restored and -refurbished Mifflin St. house will serve as a meeting place and provide accommodations for visitors to the campus.

KEEPING BRETHREN TIES FROM UNRAVELING

The centennial year opened with Brethren constituting a mere 4.93 percent of the student body. Roman Catholics made up 18.81 percent of the enrollment, followed by United Methodist (11.45), United Presbyterian (10.43), and Lutheran (7.64). There were twelve Jewish students. Out-of-country Hilltoppers, at the same time, added up to less than a dozen.

---

*After Glenn Zug resigned, Thomas Robinson (1971), Thomas Snyder (1971-72), and David Kreider (1972-73) put in brief stints as alumni director.

The sparce Brethren population on the Hill, in steady decline since World War II, has bothered many people close to the college and the church. The disappearance of a once-major constituency can create an institutional identity crisis. But of the Dunker-founded Eastern schools Juniata is not unique in its low Brethren enrollment; Elizabethtown College is in exactly the same predicament. Youth of the church seek out the less expensive state schools.

But Juniata's suzerains have not stood around wringing their hands anxiously. They have worked at the problem. When Clarence Rosenberger left in 1969 his duties were taken over by Harold Brumbaugh as vice-president for college relations. At the same time President Stauffer created the Church Relations Council, a large representative group, to strengthen bonds with the three supporting districts of Pennsylvania. 1969 also gave rise to the Alexander Mack Scholarship Fund (now at one hundred thousand dollars) under the slogan "Help Send Brethren Students to Juniata College." Recent trustee action promises even more scholarship help for youth of the denomination. Part of this will come from the congregational giving of the three districts which for 1975-76 amounted to over twenty-five thousand dollars.

With Harold Brumbaugh's centennial year retirement, Clayton Pheasant, lately promoted to director of development and church relations, will be the official liaison between Juniata and the Brethren.

The Deputation Club and the touring Concert Choir provide other contacts with Brethren at the congregational level.

Ties with the church have certainly been helped by Andrew Murray, campus minister since 1971. He is well known and active in the denomination. "Andy," as everybody calls him, is a tall, slouchy Virginian whose baccalaureate sermons delight hard-to-please faculty. The guitar-strumming chaplain has cut a record of his own, aided by wife Teresa, herself a masterly organist.

JUNIATIANS OF THE 1970s

With the early 1970s the quarter-century-long academic boom appeared to be at an end. Federal support had been curtailed. Enrollments began leveling off, even falling at many institutions.

At the same time the mood among collegians everywhere began to change. The Vietnam War was deescalating; the draft was ending; the black protest was dying down; the 26th Amendment gave eighteen year olds the vote; most states were lowering the legal age of majority in many other ways.

With respect to "student power" or activism, therefore, the temper of the times on the nation's campuses is conservative. There is little interest in social or ecological problems. Surveys show that few would use their influence to change the political structure.

But last-decade radicals have left their mark on current collegers, Juniatians included. There is still a casual attitude toward dress. Blue jeans and decorated T-shirts dominate the wardrobe of both sexes. Some students attend class barefooted. Coeds go braless. Shoulder-length hair on men is a common sight.

On College Hill, however, the 1970s have witnessed the passing of many traditions, some institutionally ancient. Gone is the weekly convocation, the faculty reception, a May Day queen (but not the breakfast), the dink and "frosh regs," sit-down meals and table assignments, Move-Up Day, the recital of Leadership Conference resolutions to faculty and administration. There is no more JWSF drive, no more Christmas party for children, no more midwinter formal, no more decorating the campus at Christmastime, no more TWIRP Week, no more room judging at Homecoming and Parents Day, no more finals in the gym.

Of late, Senior Convocation is preceded by an Oller Hall-lawn picnic. The idea is to lure students into an empty auditorium (with little success). "Academic Festival" or "Celebration for Seniors" are ways the custom is now referred to. It it not only an occasion for honoring prize winners, but a time for seniors to make their own zany awards.

There are still clubs—professional, interest, and honorary. Those associated with a discipline are the most active.

The Masque no longer exists, although Doris Goehring of the speech and theater department is trying to keep drama alive. It is a struggle.

The Concert Choir, on the other hand, is robust. Moreover, Bruce Hirsch, its director, has made musicals a popular form of entertainment in recent years. And Ibrook Tower, just appointed in 1974, has worked an overnight miracle in resurrecting an orchestra and a band.

Religious organizations, which once included various denominational clubs, have been reduced to two: Juniata Inter-Varsity Christian Fellowship and the Deputation Club. All-College Worship Services are rarer— once or twice a year.

The College Center continues to bring big-name entertainers to the campus (mimic David Frye, singers like John Denver and Bonnie Raitt, groups like Seatrain). There are Center-sponsored coffeehouse dances and weekly movies. The Raft Regatta, a race down the Juniata River from the Smithfield Bridge to Mill Creek, has become a major Center event. It was conceived by fun-loving Will Brandau, Ellis Hall's first director, who, not surprisingly, is now the owner of an amusement park.*

Concert Choir on steps of Rotunda, State Capitol (1974). Only choir ever to sing in House Chamber. Director Bruce Hirsch (bearded) is front center, with Rep. Samuel Hayes, Jr. of Tyrone at his right.

*Post-Brandau directors have been Bruce Bader (1972-74), Sally Pennington Johnston (1974-76), and, as of summer 1976, Wayne Justham.

From the "J" Club the Center inherited Casino night, a takeoff on Las Vegas.

MARK TWAIN! Rafting down the Juniata.

These special occasions possibly have the stuff out of which traditions come. The same is true for Slave Day, when freshmen, male and coed, are auctioned off to upperclassmen to perform various "domestic" duties in the dorms. Not to be overlooked, either, is the Madrigal Dinner, a Bruce Hirsch idea that tries to capture the Yuletide spirit of the sixteenth century.

Social activities are hurt, however, by the weekend exodus of students. This situation tends to confirm the fear expressed originally by many people that a five-day class schedule would transform Juniata into a "suitcase college."

Students, of course, depart the Hill by car. Huntingdon is practically devoid of public transportation service. Two Conrail passenger tains stop daily, one in each direction. No bus passes through town.

If keeping students on campus is a problem, rounding up volunteer talent for Hilltop media is no less an enigma. Doing away with applied credit in journalism crippled communications. WJC is the one exception. The mike and turntable always seem to attract a full staff. In 1970 the "Voice of Juniata" began transmitting on cable TV, one of the first college radio stations to do so. Conrad "Terry" Wickham '68, Larry "Oz" Osborne '70, and Stephen Suplicki '71, worked to make this possible. Not all the dorms, however, are hooked up for FM (catv). Beginning the fall of 1976 WJC became an FM carrier station, with a broadcasting radius of twelve miles. Since 1970 it has been ensconced in the old print shop in Founders basement.

Publications have had a harder time of it. True, the *Alfarata*, the editor-in-chief of which no longer is necessarily a senior, has never missed an issue. But not so the weekly tabloid. "The Last Juniatian"—thus was headlined the issue for April 17, 1970 so desperate had the situation become for the campus paper. No one wanted to write for it. For a year its place was taken by the *Renaissance*, which appeared on no regular schedule. One alumnus savaged it as "the most inarticulate, infantile, illiterate, and ineptly named journal to come off the campus in many a moon."[14] Then Scott Leedy '72 of Duncannon, Pennsylvania, came to the rescue the fall of 1971. He took it upon himself "to get the College newspaper back on its feet and functioning again." He succeeded, although the reincarnated *Juniatian*, in quality, has not been its former self. *Kvasir*, meanwhile, has had its ups and downs. Right now it is kind of up. The latest printing, though unbound and iteked, reflected more interest in graphics.

While Scott Leedy went about calling the *Juniatian* to life, junior Sammy Kum Buo was giving birth to a different kind of publication. Buo, a Cameroon, had been steered to Juniata by fellow African Andy Adede '65 of Kenya. In 1972 he, as editor-in-chief, brought out the first issue of the *Journal of Cameroon Affairs*. The magazine was to be the organ of the Cameroon Students Association of Arts and Sciences, its membership worldwide. Since graduating Buo has followed in the footsteps of Dr. Adede—both with degrees from the Fletcher School of Diplomacy at Tufts University and both on current assignments at the United Nations.

Summer school students in 1972 will not soon forget Hurricane Agnes. That tropical storm, while moving northward over the Atlantic, dropped 10.15 inches of rainfall over much of Central Pennsylvania in three days (June 22-24). Highwater marks in Huntingdon reached those of '36, and at Mt. Union overall damages totalled one million dollars. Juniatians, relieved of classes, helped out in rescue work throughout the emergency.

The year preceding the Flood of '72 Juniatians ratified a new Student Government Constitution. Formerly, of course, all social events fell under the purview of the SG. But the College Center Board had moved in on this territory. Hence the need for constitutional revamping.

SG presidents got along famously with John Stauffer. They appreciated the way he had opened up the campus. Twice they expressed their esteem for him with a gift related to his interest in Eskimo culture. One of those times was a surprise presentation at the last Juniata commencement he presided over.

But openness encourages people to speak out, generates an atmosphere of dynamic tension as compromises are sought. The SG, therefore, kept the pressure on. It rode hard on food service, causing the departure of two companies. The Hill's leaders lobbied successfully for nonacademic leaves of absences. And for a time campus life-styles and residence hall rules were a big bone of contention. The college ultimately made major concessions in this area, as we shall see. SG agitation to abolish comps, or at least not make graduation contingent upon passing them, also paid off. In 1973 came unit evaluations, published in booklet form—a kind of Baedeker on what goes on in Juniata's classrooms.* Students elsewhere had been doing this for some time.

The campus Judiciary, meanwhile, has disappeared in its original form. There is such a committee still on the books, called the Judicial Board. But its members are appointed, not elected. Juniatians, as we saw in the last chapter, simply refuse to snitch on schoolfellows or initiate proceedings. Almost exclusively hearings by the Judicial Board are the results of referrals from the deans or resident assistants.

The Stauffer era, then, not only gave students a voice but listened to them more often than not. Actually the most vocal element on the Hill when John Stauffer moved into Founders was not the SG but a loosely-organized group calling themselves the Student Action Group. They had already raised the battle cry of "relevance" in a confrontation with the trustees at the time of the board's dinner for retiring Calvert Ellis in May.

The leading lights of the SAG were an interesting foursome: Marta Daniels, Kathleen Snyder (Johnson), Donna Roppelt, and Kenneth Smith. They were the best-known gadflies of their day, all gifted with plenty of

---

*There was none in the centennial year—maybe a birthday reprieve! Or confirmation of alleged current student passivism.

gray matter. They never held any elective office yet their influence was plenary. They worked behind the scenes, manipulating faculty perhaps moreso than their peers in the cause of student power. So sobersided were they that not one of them deigned to have a senior-year photograph in the *Alfarata* — "kid stuff" to them. They worked hard locally for Eugene Mc-Carthy in the fall of 1968, his dovish stand on Vietnam to their liking. They were sincere idealists, advocates of personal freedom. Today at least two of them are involved in social work that includes a peace testimony.

It was for their kind, some say, that the 1971 curriculum was devised. In fact, they had a prolocutor on the Task Force for their point of view in the person of Donna Roppelt.

The SAG, with Ken Smith the engineer, carried out Juniata's first real student protest. On February 25, 1969 Beeghly Library was the scene of a "study-in." Some two hundred Hilltoppers refused to leave at closing time (10 P.M.). Their demand was for an extension of hours til midnight during class days. Deans Rockwell and Schoenherr showed up to represent the administration. The protesters made their point — and won.

SAG, said Smith later, sprang up as a reproach to a "do nothing" student government. He believed: "A tremendous gap exists between the ideals of individuality taught in the classroom and the actual road of conformity students are forced to take in everyday actions."[15]

It was the Daniels-Snyder-Roppelt-Smith cartel that organized "Encounter '70," a colloquy during which the campus played host to approximately forty professional people. They "rapped" with students on a battery of subjects: air and water pollution, poverty, overpopulation, education, racial conflict, Vietnam, sex, the hippie scene, and more. Encounter '70 went over big with Juniatians. The gadfly-four were also the moving spirits behind Division IV, a kind of "Free University," offering self-taught, noncredit work. But the new curriculum stole a lot of its thunder and it soon fell by the way.

While the "relevance" issue was quieting down, unrest over Vietnam began to build. Students, faculty, and administrators cooperated in a demonstration called "Juniata Mobilization for Peace" on Thursday, May 15, 1969. Beginning at 10:00 A.M. Oller Lawn was alive with action for most of the day. Speakers ranged from Juniatians, including the president, to active members of national organizations. Between speeches there was musical entertainment. One speaker-entertainer was John Sollenberger '71, who sang Arlo Guthrie's satire on the draft, *Alice's Restaurant*. The crowd, hundreds strong, gave him a standing ovation when he revealed his intention to turn in his draft card.

The "Hawks," who had a good turn-out, did not let the day pass without getting in their word.

That fall (October 15) Juniatians joined in observing "Vietnam Moratorium Day," a massive nationwide student antiwar display. Starting with a Round Top morning rally, Hilltoppers rang doorbells all over Huntingdon, passing out peace literature and talking about the "madness" of the war. Afterward some two hundred of them attended a memorial service, conducted by Campus Minister Faus in Stone Church, for all who had died in the Southeast Asian conflict. It was outpourings like this all over the country that produced Vice-President Spiro Agnew's most notorious blast of adjectival invective. He said the moratorium was led by "an effete corps of impudent snobs who characterize themselves as intellectuals."

A month later a second moratorium day brought a crowd estimated at two hundred and fifty thousand (Juniatians among them) to Washington to march past the White House.

Then in late April 1970 Nixon ordered American "boys" into Cambodia. The North Vietnamese and Viet Cong had been using that "neutral" country for years as a springboard for troops, weapons, and supplies. The previous spring the president had promised in a televised address to withdraw our forces over a period of time. To collegians the Cambodian invasion seemed to spell deeper involvement rather than withdrawal. It sparked dissent, immediate and red-hot, on the nation's campuses. The coincidental killing of demonstrators at Kent State University in Ohio by National Guardsmen on May 4th added to their indignation.

A wave of faculty-student strikes closed down hundreds of colleges. Many Juniatians, too, were shocked by the rapid turn of events. Wild talk spread over the Hill about proposed life-endangering demonstrations (picket the local Armory. . .form a human blockade of Route 22). Rumors had outsiders coming in to agitate. Stauffer and his staff debated what to do to forestall possible injury to JC students. Jerry Eisenhour '71, SG president, was consulted and certain faculty. Who could know or guess what might happen?

But Stauffer's mind was made up: suspend classes until the danger had passed. Early morning May 7th students found notices slipped under their doors telling them to leave campus before the day was over. After breakfast the Hilltop community gathered in Alumni Hall for an explanation. Some faculty and students thought the president was overreacting.

He readily agreed that might be the case. But he was not going to take any chances.

Some alumni and parents at first mistook the May 7th decision as a political statement. Nothing was further from the truth.

Students were called back on Friday, May 15. This allowed a week of classes before finals. But the faculty gave the returnees four options on grades and finals. Most of them took Option #4: credit with no grade or final.

While the Vietnam War kept the country's campuses stirred up, the early 1970s also brought revolutionary changes in student living patterns. Lowering the legal age of majority to eighteen in most states rang the death knell for *in loco parentis*. Juniata changed with the times, too. There are alumni and friends who grieve that the college has deserted its earlier Brethren pietistic legalism. But the students have the law on their side.

Only a few years ago marriage automatically terminated a Juniatian's enrollment. It was necessary to petition for readmission. Now a wedding band merely requires notifying the Registrar's office of a change of status or name.

Women's hours and visitation restrictions had SG and SAG all upset Stauffer's first year. But by 1971 they were no longer an issue. Dean Charles Schoenherr, now a college president in Kansas, had abolished the former and adopted a flexible policy on the latter. The Schoenherr scheme is still in effect. Present-day Juniatians can choose from among three life-styles — A, B, C. A is the most liberal, interdorm visitation permitted twenty-four hours a day. The other life-styles are more conservative. Some dorms house *both* men and women, a not uncommon arrangement at other colleges.

Dr. C. C. Ellis, were he alive, would never be able to understand what had happened to his college.

Nor could he comprehend today's drug-and-drink culture among American youth. On the Hill the *Pathfinder* contained no policy statement on drugs until 1968, though they were in use before that. Apparently few Juniatians ever got into mind-warping LSD. But "speed" (amphetamines), tranquilizers, and "pot" (marijuana) have been common narcotics on the Hill. And JC has not lacked for resident "pushers" — often from medical families — in the vending of drugs. Sociologists would point out that this almost universal appetite of college-age youth for some kind of chemical crutch for the mind is but an extension of a "pill-popping" society at large. Nevertheless, the *Pathfinder* warns that the possession and misuse of drugs can bring serious disciplinary action, including suspension.

Alcohol was the drug, however, that kept the Hill in a tizzy. Juniatians of the Seventies predominantly came from homes, a Duane Stroman survey revealed, where alcoholic beverages were used. Yet the results of a questionnaire sent to parents in 1971 indicated that seventy percent of them opposed any change in the college's on-campus drinking policy. Student government and the *Juniatian* took the opposite side. The administration was forced into an agonizing dilemma. A trustee committee wrestled with the problem but recommended no change in rules against drinking in the dorms. For some of them it was a matter of strong moral conviction.

That did not change the situation; Juniata was a "wet campus." Said one student, "You have to work to get caught."[16] But there was a certain group who became abusive after a few drinks. They showed a disregard for college property and the rights of others. Things seemed to be getting out of hand. There were those who felt that this was only symptomatic of a deeper problem. Perhaps the new curriculum was at fault, some speculated — too much freedom, especially for freshmen. Maybe leisure time weighed too heavily on their hands.

It was this concern that lay behind Quality of Life Day, sponsored by the administration and SG on February 11, 1975. Thus was born START (Students-Teachers-Administrators Reaching Together). START organized mixed teams to visit each dorm and college house, classes canceled that Tuesday, for "rap" sessions. One purpose of the day, said SG president Carl Glaeser, was "to define a concept of wholeness of community, to seek a better relationship among segments of the college community." It was also to get at the root of what the provost had called the "at times cynical, at times hedonistic, and on occasion even barbaric" student attitude toward education and life. In the afternoon a panel reported at a jam-packed Town Meeting in Oller Hall on the "gripes" uncovered by the teams. John Stauffer presided.

A second Town Meeting was held on the evening of March 26. It provided answers to and information about issues raised at the first one. But between the two all-campus assemblies the faculty had reinstated academic probation. When that was reported on the 26th, Oller Hall range with applause by approving students. Professors sat nonplussed at this unexpected response.

The Town Meetings were cathartic. Much that was positive came out of them. A startling revelation, however, was made by Hallmark Management Services of Columbus, Ohio, which operates the dining room. Its local director reported that Juniatians were pilfering chinaware and utensils to the tune of nearly five thousand dollars a year.

As for tippling, it no longer is frowned upon on the Hill. There has been some rethinking on the use of strong drink. The policy since fall 1975 has been to permit its consumption in the privacy of dorm rooms. Also, there are certain places in residence halls where alcoholic beverages can be served at parties that have been properly cleared and scheduled. Otherwise, all campus events must be "dry." And drink-induced disorderly conduct will bring disciplinary action.

Meanwhile, the last seven years have brought two more student prizes. One honors William Schlichter, killed driving back from a choir picnic in September 1969. Now worth two hundred dollars, it went first to Glenn Billingsley '71, like Schlichter a music-lover. The other is a social science award established by Raymond Day '45, whose hometown is Huntingdon. Dr. Day, a Wooster College professor, is Juniata's first black male graduate who later won national attention for his settlement house work in Chicago. His one hundred dollar prize's initial winner was Robert Mitchum in 1976.

As we have noted from time to time, friends and alumni have been no less benevolent in providing endowed scholarships. By this centennial time these number sixty-eight separate ones, many aiding more than one student. They alone yield some sixty thousand dollars to worthy Juniatians.

INDIANS OF THE 1970s

The 1971 curriculum did away with required physical education but not the department. Since then greater emphasis has been placed on intramural sports. Spring 1976 found sixty-eight percent of the student body athletically involved in some way.[1]

At the varsity level, for the most part, Juniata continued its magnificent record without apology. Not since the 1930s have there been athletic scholarships. Walter Nadzak, an All-Ohio Conference lineman and MVP while playing at Denison University with a couple of pro years under his belt afterward, became AD and head football coach in 1969. He replaced Fred Prender, who went to Bucknell. Prender left Juniata with a gridiron tally of 30-19-0 for six seasons. His last year was also Donald Weiss', quarterback from Athens, Pennsylvania. The Two-time All-American (honorable mention) played for a short time in the Canadian Football League.

Ex-Marine Nadzak, through fall 1976, has logged a mark of 45-26-3. That makes him #1 in wins among JC gridiron coaches. Since 1972 he has had the help of two superb assistants, Dean Rossi and Richard Reilly. In 1973 the three of them coached Juniata into the first NCAA Division III national championship game. It was played in the Amos Alonzo Stagg Bowl, Phenix City, Alabama in early December. By strange fate the title game, given television coverage by ABC, matched the Indians against Wittenberg University. The score of 41-0 was not in Juniata's favor. Despite the goose egg, Nadzak was named NCAA Division III's Coach of the Year, the greatest honor to befall a member of the athletic department.

Walt Nadzak, JC's winningest football coach, with Dean Rossi and Richard Reilly on his left.

Since 1970 forty Juniatians have been voted MAC Northern Division All Stars. Three—fullback Louis Eckerl '74, his junior year, Pete Lentini (1974), and junior defensive tackle Stuart Jackson (1975)—earned MVP laurels. Three have made first team ECAC All-East. Pete Lentini '74, tight end, was Juniata's latest Little All-American (honorable mention), when a senior.*

Stagg Bowl Team, led by Captains L. Eckerl (#9) and M. McNeal (#44).

*Two juniors broke records during the 1976 campaign: Robert Devine, career interceptions (twenty); Stanley Nosal, career (twenty) and season (seven) field goals.

In 1972 College Field was enclosed by a Cyclone Fence and for fall 1975 there was a new scoreboard with an easier-to-read clock.

Overall, the Seventies have not been as kind to basketball. Before Russ Trimmer left in 1970 (44-38) he took the Blue and Gold into its first MAC playoff tourney in 1968-69. He did it again the next year. Juniata finished fourth both times. Trimmer stressed "pressure defense," but four of the players he recruited—John Smith '71, Charles Harvey '71, James McCarthy '71, Leroy Wentz '71—rank among the college's top scorers. John Smith, a 6'3" center, holds the individual scoring record for a single game. He poured in forty-six points against Lycoming in Memorial Gym one February night his senior year.

Jack Swinderman was coach then. He stayed through the 1973-74 season, leaving with a mark of 28-61. Dynamic Carl Meditch, his system a throwback to Russ Trimmer's brand of ball, has won twenty-one and lost twenty-seven in a pair of seasons. His squad's 13-12 campaign in 1974-75 was good enough for another berth in the MAC championship tournament and another fourth place finish.

Nor have the Seventies been any kinder to baseball, despite the coaching of Bill Berrier since 1969. The "Bear's" men have taken fifty-one games, dropped ninety-three. Centerfielder Thomas Streightiff '75 made first team MAC in 1973 and upon graduation decided against a pro contract.* Langdon Field, equipped with dugouts in 1975, has seemed to carry a curse.

The mats of Memorial Gym have a hex, too, on Berrier's wrestlers. They have gone 16-75-2 since 1968-69, their 8-3 season tally that year the best ever for Tribe grapplers. Heavyweight Peter Schuyler '70, 11-1 as a senior co-captain, reigns as Juniata's only MAC champ in any weight class.

Golf has done somewhat better (39-47-0). Its best season in recent times was 1972 (9-0-1) when the team came in second in the MAC tourney. The whole team was named recipient of the C. Blair Miller trophy that year.

Post-coached tennisy Indians, however, have been consistent winners the last eight years (46-33). The Tribe's winningest season ever was 1969 (10-1-0). The Raffensperger Tennis Courts next to Ellis College Center got "club-caliber" lighting in spring 1976 for night play. College and town racket fanciers can go at it into the wee hours if they want, the system controlled by coin-operated meters.

---

*Juniata's latest major league player was Thomas Dettore of Canonsburg, Pennsylvania, who spent two years on the Hill (1965-67). He won a letter in basketball, but academic probation kept him from going out for his first love in sports. He pitched three years in the National League, with Pittsburgh (1973) and Chicago (1974-75).

1968-69 basketball team, picturing four Juniata top scorers.
Kneeling: R. Chandler, Coach Trimmer, Lee Wentz.
Standing: T. Griffin, J. McCarthy, G. Galbraith, A. Barnhart, C. Harvey, A. Englesbe, K. Bowers, J. Smith, B. Bader, D. Crunkleton, R. Straley, A. Rafferty, Larry Wentz.

Track has compiled an almost identical record to tennis (46-30). But since Dean Rossi has taken over (1973), assisted by Dick Reilly and Don Mitchell, JC thinclads have performed at a 27-8 pace.* Rossi's first squad won the MAC Championship, the only time ever. What is even more remarkable about Blue and Gold cindermen of the 1970s is that they have smashed fourteen school records in the seventeen track and field events

*There was a rapid turnover in track coaches after Mike Snider retired, until Rossi, who lettered at Penn State in the sport, came along.

Juniata's only two mat finalists, Pete Schuyler (1st) and Chris Sherk (2nd) along with starting teammates, 1967 season.
Row 1:　C. Sherk, T. Light, J. Hopper, J. Biggs.
Row 2:　J. Pyle, R. Hoover, R. Feigles, Coach Berrier, P. Schuyler, D. Hoover, W. Scott.

held. Too many, unfortunately, for individual recognition here. Only the 220, the 120 high hurdles, and the long jump have survived the onslaught of the Seventies.

Herd runners, coached by the JC basketball mentor since the Snider days, broke about even (45-59). In 1974 the cross-country course was lengthened to 5.6 miles, and that November, against Gettysburg, junior Jack McCullough set the still-standing best time (32:09) for it. Dennis Weidler '72, the only Juniatian to run the 4.8 circuit faster than Rick Beard (in 1969) was, like Rick, thrice a C. Clifford Brown trophyite. Cross-country history was made in the centennial year when Evagelia "Teddy" Lyras, a freshman, ran at all Indian home meets. She is a 5'5" brunette from Merchantville, New Jersey, who runs to "take out my frustrations."

Tennis squad (1969) with best court record in Hilltop history (10-1).
Row 1: Coach Post, P. Solis-Cohen, D. Newcomer, G. Berryhill, **B. Draper**, A. White, R. Biel, T. McAulay, W. Shoaf.
Row 2: R. Hoffman, R. Cochran, D. Sell, W. Phillips, D. Buckwalter, P. Gross, D. Beahm, G. Mihalick.

Club sports have taken hold on the Hill, too. Biology's Robert Fisher, himself a blackbelter, organized a Judo Club in 1964. The JC•judoists have participated in numerous tournaments, winning a good share of them. Ice hockey, instructed by Paul Heberling, started up in February 1974. Rugby was introduced by chemist Charles Lerman (Ph.D., Harvard) the next fall.

And back on the Hill, after a four-decade respite, are women's varsity sports. Equal rights laws passed in the early Seventies forced colleges and universities to give coeds their fair share of athletic funds. At Juniata there is presently intercollegiate competition in three sports for miladies.

One is field hockey, coached the first year (1973) by JoAnne Reilly and since then by Alexa Fultz, wife of Huntingdon's mayor. JC "stickgals" have a cumulative regular season won-lost mark of 7-13-1. Vernne Wetzel '74 received the first Thomas B. Robinson Alumni Award (1974) in field hockey.

She also got the first David and Gayle Kreider Award (1974) in basketball. This sport, played according to men's rules, was inaugurated at the varsity level in 1973 by alumnus Patrick Frazier '63, now head hardcourtman at Huntingdon Area High School. He and successor Edmund Gargula have compiled a record of twenty-one wins and fourteen losses. Upcoming senior Mardi Frye, a 5'9" dead shot from Delmont, Pennsylvania, is the leading scorer to date (349). Junior-to-be Janet Edgar of Royersford, Pennsylvania, is in hot pursuit. Her twenty-six points in a game against Bucknell is the best one-night performance yet.

Tennis, just two years old, is the baby of women's varsity sports. Alumnus-physicist Ray Pfrogner (Ph.D., Delaware), a tennis MVP on the Hill in his student days, got it going. Elizabeth Herritt, a graduate student at Penn State, debuted in 1976 as coach. Pfrogner-Herritt netters are 5-8. The first Jack M. Haskell '65 Tennis Award (1975) went to Alice Herritt, undefeated as a sophomore and sister of the next year's coach.

Indian athletics, male or female, continue to get excellent coverage despite the absence of a Sports Information Director. That job for a time was done by assistants in the public relations office. But of late, like in Bill Engel's time, the director of public information personally handles sports publicity. Today that is tall, versatile, red-headed Charles Pollock, as good as they come at turning a neat phrase.

Also close to JC athletics has been Mailand McIlroy, twenty-three years sports editor of the *Daily News*. One of the best around, "Mac" is as much confidante to Hilltop coaches as reporter.

FREDERICK M. BINDER: LEADS JUNIATA INTO ITS SECOND CENTURY

John Stauffer's letter of resignation in March 1975 hit the campus with the impact of a bombshell. There was no hint of its coming. Over coffee faculty expressed concern, both for what provoked the letter and about his stepping down. But due to a life-long heart condition he had

Women's Varsity Basketball Team, 1974-75 (8 wins, 5 losses).
Row 1: J. Prentiss, L. Apple, N. Reinhold, C. Dickey, S. Rosshirt, J. Bechtel.
Row 2: B. Woodworth, K. Norris, L. Whittaker, M. Frye, D. Madey, J. Edgar, K. Weed, Coach Gargula.

Women's Varsity Field Hockey Team, 1973.
Row 1: J. Snyder, H. Harmon, M. Morgan, L. Hollyday, M. Prentiss, J. Gilford, A. Kustanbauter, S. Wiser, R. Bepler.
Row 2: Coach Reilly, P. Weaver, L. Steiner, L. Whittaker, E. Becker, K. Norris, K. Messick, K. Middleton, N. O'Connell, V. Wetzel, B. Martin, J. Prentiss, P. Theodos, D. Lingafelt.

been advised by his cardiologist that "the work of a college president is no longer compatible with [your] health."

Stauffer's seven-year presidency had put Juniata in sound fiscal condition. The college's endowment and annuity funding increased by seventy percent, to $7.6 million. Total assets in the same period advanced from $15.7 to $24.7 million, a rise of more than sixty percent. The current operations budget grew from $3.6 to $5.8 million.

The college was able to maintain a stable enrollment of between eleven and twelve hundred full-time students against national trends.

Stauffer will be remembered as one of Juniata's most progressive presidents, certainly the most student-oriented. Naturally, not everybody saw eye to eye on his approach, including some trustees. He was designated president emeritus, given responsibilities in the field of long-range financial development, and an office in the I. Harvey Brumbaugh House. He thought it prudent, for the best interests of his successor, not to continue as a trustee.

The centennial year was almost upon the college when he resigned. Plans for its celebration were well underway. The Margin of Difference Campaign was building to a climax. The reins of leadership needed to be picked up quickly and surely.

By federal laws the opening had to be publicized. Over seventy applicants responded, the selecting process involving all elements of the Juniata community. The name of one man, his qualifications extraordinary, moved topmost on the list fast. He got the job.

Frederick M. Binder, fifty-five, is not a Juniata alumnus (he graduated from Ursinus) or Brethren (he is Episcopalian). He has been head of two colleges: Hartwick (1959-69) in Oneonta, New York, and Whittier (1970-75) in California. For the year 1969-70 he was Associate Commissioner for Higher Education of New York State.

A native of New Jersey, Binder earned his master's degree and Ph.D. in American economic history at Penn. His doctoral dissertation won the Newcomen Prize. In 1967-68, while on leave from Hartwick, he was the first Fulbright Lecturer in American History appointed to Yugoslavia. He has published two books, *Coal Age Empire* and *The Serbian Assignment*, a spy novel. Recently he finished the manuscript of another cloak-and-dagger yarn. He has also written numerous scholarly articles and reviews.

Juniata's eighth president is an earthy man, friendly and built like an athlete (which he was), who wants to be called "Fred." He speaks in a deep, booming voice. His "hero," when he was a young dean at Thiel

Frederick M. Binder

College in the 1950s, was Calvert Ellis. Juniata's traditions and historical background, therefore, are not unfamiliar to him.

His past presidential achievements and his experienced leadership promise a bright future for Juniata. The Binder presidency at Hartwick saw students and faculty each more than treble. In ten years twelve new buildings were constructed. His five years at Whittier, Richard Nixon's alma mater and an independent liberal arts college with a Quaker heritage, were equally distinguished. There, it was said, he was "not the ivory-tower type of administrator."[17]

All the while, he has held high office in national and regional academic organizations, not to mention his membership on numerous independent college commissions.

Why Juniata for him? He was attracted to the college, he says, because of "its outstanding reputation in the sciences and in all the pre-professional areas of liberal arts education, and the strength of both its faculty and its board of trustees."[18] Indeed, Binder will bring quality of his own to the Hill's professorial ranks. It has been his practice as a president to teach at least one course each year.

The presidential family lives on Taylor Highland in a home formerly owned by Dr. H. Ford Clark and donated to the college by Owens-Corning Fiberglas Corporation.

Administratively, the centennial year has not been merely one of "getting the feel" for Fred Binder. He took hold at once. The combined problem of admissions and retention got immediate attention. He brought "no-need scholarships" back to Juniata, last used as a major recruiting tool in the depression years. In January 1976 he announced two new programs of academic merit awards: Brumbaugh-Ellis Presidential Scholarships (ten) and Alumni Annual Support Fund Scholarships (twenty). These programs will provide thirty-five thousand dollars each year in new grants to entering freshmen of superior ability regardless of financial need.

Already for fall 1976 this has produced an incoming freshman crop of much higher quality.* Moreover, the Class of 1980 promises to be one of the largest in the college's history. Juniata's second century dawns with students paying $4,290 for a Hilltop education.

In fall 1975 Binder introduced the "Fifty-Fifty Club." It is an effort to involve more people in continuing education. Anyone age fifty or older can enroll in College units for fifty percent of the regular fee.

Then the next May Juniatians learned of a major advance for the humanities division. Enterprising Foster Ulrich opened the door for a one hundred thousand dollar challenge grant from the Charles A. Dana Foundation. When matched (it has to be done within a year), the funds will be used to develop the Charles A. Dana Humanities Cluster. The Cluster will include six renovated McKinley-era buildings along 17th Street between Moore and Mifflin, housing the departments of art, history, foreign languages, philosophy, and English.

---

*A great deal of credit properly belongs to William Asendorf '65, acting director of admissions (1975-76), and his staff for this bright picture.

Summer 1976 the administrative staff underwent a number of changes, some of which have already been noted. In the Oneida Annex, William Alexander, director of institutional research (since 1972) and economics instructor, became business manager. William Rutter, director of accounting, was named controller, and Dorothy Leffard took Hilda Nathan's place as chief accountant.

In Founders, Thomas Snyder '66, thrice a football "J'" man and formerly an assistant in admissions (1966-71), has returned to old stamping grounds, this time as associate dean in charge of the admissions office. Cynthia Gilbert Clarke is director of institutional research, and Kenneth Grugel replaces Ronald Shunk in financial aid.*

William Martin, another returnee, comes back as director of placement and career counseling. His office is in Ellis College Center. As in the depression decade, Juniata not only seeks to attract students in these financially trying times by more scholarships, but also by better career counseling that will give graduates a competitive edge in a glutted job market.

The centennial year, however, was to be a time of celebrating. Homecoming weekend, October 10-11, set festivities in motion. The highlight for homecomers was the public debut of the Centennial Needlepoint Project at the anniversary dinner Saturday evening. More than five hundred alumni and friends viewed the unveiling.

Elizabeth Ellis was behind the project and enlisted the help of twenty women skilled in needlepoint. Constructed with approximately six thousand stitches, the $5' \times 4'$ fourteen-mesh canvas depicts in Persian wool thread some of the most memorable buildings, scenes, and activities connected with Juniata's one hundred years. The memorial hanging is displayed in a special glass-fronted case in the main lobby of Ellis College Center.

In February *A Season of Good Favor*, a multimedia portrayal of College Hill history, began its tour of alumni meetings, civic groups, and churches. This delightful work in sight and sound was developed by James Lehman '66, a free-lance writer and media consultant. While a senior at Juniata the now bushy-bearded Lehman was president of Student Government. A philosophy major, he graduated *cum laude*. *Season* caught the fancy of Juniatians every bit as much as the needlepoint project.

---

*David Lee '64 was director of financial aid 1968-71, succeeding Robert Doyle and preceding Shunk.

Centennial needlepoint project. "Book on the Tree", centennial development program logo, is featured in center.

Sensitive, fast-moving, its script superbly written, the 280-slide showing sent people away deeply moved.

On Arbor Day, April 5, students, faculty, and administrators began to plant a tree for each of Juniata's one hundred years. The eight thousand dollar tree project—involving ten varieties—is part of the master landscaping plan. In addition to beautifying the campus, the planting helps replace 101 trees lost by Dutch elm disease since 1973.

Centenary activities peaked in the month of May. Close to four thousand friends of Juniata made their way to College Hill for the two culminating events: The Centennial Convocation (May 1) and Commencement/Reunion Weekend (May 30-31). Rainy weather on both occasions failed to dampen spirits.

The Centennial Convocation (it was not held on Founders Day, which fell during spring vacation) included the investiture of Fred Binder as president. It was quiet and simple. "I've already been married twice before," he quipped when planning the program, attended by fifty-five delegates from colleges, universities, churches, and associations.

Struck as an added observance of the anniversary was the bronze Presidential Medallion featuring the college seal. It will be worn by the president for all special college ceremonies. Calvert Ellis and John Stauffer were also honored with personal strikings.

The day's ceremonies also included presentation by the National Alumni Association of a college mace. Heretofore faculty marshals had carried a billy-club length of wood with a blue and gold ribbon attached. The yard-long centennial mace was designed by Barnard Taylor, former college editor, and made by the E. B. Endres Lumber Company. It was hewn from a beam from the now-razed James Creek Church, home congregation of the three Brumbaugh founders. The head of the mace bears four medals: the college seal, Founders Tower, the Church of the Brethren's 250th Anniversary Seal, and Huntingdon's Standing Stone. When not in use for processions the mace is displayed in the Ellis College Center.

A large number of direct descendants of the founders and early faculty members were in attendance and recognized at the convocation.

Main speaker for the May 1 celebration was Dr. James B. Rhoads, archivist of the United States. Honorary degrees went to him, Dr. Warren Groff '49, newly elected president of Bethany Theological Seminary, and John Swigart, "a most energetic and favorite son" of Juniata.*

Dr. Blair Helman, president of Manchester College and moderator of the Church of the Brethren, addressed the 212 graduating seniors on Sunday, May 31. He received an honorary degree along with Elizabeth Wertz Ellis, once Queen of May (1926), who married her college beau and Juniata president-to-be. She and John Baker the previous day had shared the Alumni Association's annual Service Award. (Dr. Baker also got the Achievement Award.) Said the late Melvin Rhodes, former dean of students and director of admissions in assessing the "First Lady Emerita's" importance to the college: "Mrs. Ellis has had an impact on

*Dr. Groff was elected a trustee to fill the board position vacated by another Juniatian, Dr. Paul Robinson, president emeritus of Bethany.

the character and the future personality of Juniata no less than that of her distinguished husband."[19]

Two students, David Mingle and Janice Diehl Raub, both of Roaring Spring, were centennial year summa cum laudes. Mingle, a premedicine major, graduated with a perfect A academic average.

But concluding centennial year celebrations carried word that Dr. John Baker, after thirteen years as board chairman, had asked to be relieved. He will continue on as a trustee, however. The board, in recognizing his many generous benefactions and past forty years of service, has commissioned a portrait of him to be hung in the Baker Refectory of Ellis College Center. Jewett Henry, a leading Huntingdon attorney, was elected to lead the board into the second century.

*   *   *   *   *   *   *   *

Fivescore years is young so far as the life of collegiate instutitions go in this country. Still living in this centennial year are not a few Juniatians who have known their alma mater longer than the half-life of its history. They have seen vast changes — as the college has repeatedly tried to redefine its relation to the Brethren, to redefine its educational philosophy and fit this into a curriculum, to reevaluate student life and activities as mores shifted among the youth and in the nation. Juniata has moved with the times. College Hill, in contrast to its parochial beginnings, has been transformed into a microcosm of American society. America's strengths, its problems, its enabling dreams and aspirations. . .all are reflected on the Hilltop.

Said James Lehman in his fascinating slide presentation: "The Normal School that began in the imagination of the three Brumbaughs has become more than anyone expected." He concluded:

> The College has enjoyed a hundred years of good favor. It has been blessed with strong leaders, human fellowship, and academic excellence. Juniata has enjoyed the fruits of a rich heritage. It has traditions to cherish, students to do interesting things, and alumni to remember those things fondly. *Its difficulties have strengthened it; its disasters have not overwhelmed it; and its achievements have graced it.*

Lehman has admirably put into words the spirit of "Juniata Past." The pages of this centennial history, however, end with the story of a living institution still in progress. What about the future?

Fred Binder answered that question in his brief investiture remarks. He said: "We have been, we are, and we shall continue to be a strong, undergraduate liberal arts college, interested in the individual student, concerned with moral and cultural values, and committed to learning."

"With roots in the tradition of the church," he concluded, "Juniata can do no more in its second century than remain faithful to its motto: *Veritas Liberat*, 'Truth Sets Free.'"

Centennial Year Trustee Board.
Row 1: T. Martin, E. Kennedy, E. Cutrell, F. Binder, J. Swigart, L. Rosenberger, J. Baker, C. N. Ellis, J. Henry, L. Raycroft, D. Beachley, L. Waltz.
Row 2: L. Maxwell, F. Zimmerman, K. Sunderland, W. Kimmel, H. Gibbel, T. Miller, E. Croner, D. Detwiler, C. Ellis, S. Glass, C. Loomis, J. Oller, G. Fattman, J. Montgomery, J. Good, C. Rice.

Humanities Faculty, 1976-77.
Row 1: E. Cherry, I. Tower, M. Linton.
Row 2: P. Smith, R. Wagoner, M. Hochberg, J. Nieto, E. Post.
Row 3: G. Dolnikowski, B. Heller, E. Church, E. Kaylor, C. Frijters.
Row 4: K. Crosby, J. Lewis, B. Hirsch, D. Goehring, C. Whipple.
Missing: C. Briggs, S. Calian, R. Church, B. Davis, W. Hofelt, R. Hunter, K. Jaeger, K. Kipphan, A. McBride, A. Murray, J. Troy.

Social Sciences Faculty, 1976-77.
Row 1: H. Masters, J. Dortch, W. Vocke.
Row 2: M. Da Silva, D. Stroman, R. Reilly, D. Drews, D. Wright.
Row 3: H. Crouch, S. Seider, M. Clark, L. Goodstein, P. Heberling.
Row 4: R. Cherry, J. Lakso, T. Nolan, A. Bargerstock, L. Nollau.
Missing: G. Giebel, H. Klug, M. Miller, S. Ondrejcak, C. Wise, T. Woodrow.

Natural Sciences Faculty: 1976—77.
Row 1: J. Senft, D. Sally.
Row 2: K. Rockwell, R. Washburn, T. Gustafson, W. Fagot, D. Wampler.
Row 3: J. Bowser, S. Esch, P. Schettler, W. Russey, M. Heller.
Row 4: I. Engle, P. Trexler, R. Reed, T. Fisher, P. Sipling.
Missing: J. Cauffman, R. Fisher, J. Gooch, Don Mitchell, R. Pfrogner, R. Zimmerer.

Administration, 1976-77.
Row 1: F. Ulrich, D. Hartman, F. Binder, W. Norris, W. Alexander, W. Martin.
Row 2: K. Grugel, C. Clarke, R. Sabin, I. Jackson, W. Berrier, J. Ruby.
Row 3: D. Kreider, B. Kenyon, R. Fisher, H. Salter, D. Leffard, W. Rutter.
Row 4: H. Weaver, B. Rowe, D. Peterson, C. Pheasant, I. Thomas, T. Snyder, W. Nadzak.
Missing: N. Davis, D. Diercksen, S. Himes, W. Justham, G. Kreider, E. O'Connell, J. Park, T. Peters, C. Pollock, E. Straub.

Supporting Staff, 1976-77.
Row 1: S. Stoianoff, M. Lloyd, B. Reck, R. Heaton, P. McMahon, M. Snyder, S. Martin,
Row 2: D. McClain, J. Cook, M. Reynolds, B. Hartman, P. Kann, M. Heaps, R. Walker, P. McGinnis.
Row 3: J. Itinger, T. Stoner, D. Lynn, M. Johnson, M. Litzenberger, T. Copenhaver, D. Henney, D. Herzberg, L. Conley, H. Crouch.
Row 4: V. Horne, N. Yocum, J. Furry, H. Keena, L. Speck, S. Brechbiel, J. Parks, L. Fluke, L. Payne, V. Hamilton.
Missing: D. Blaisdell, J. Brown, M. Brown, M. Christopher, Dr. J. Daly, D. Grinnell, S. Hochberg, D. Kurtz, S. LaVere, P. Masters, M. Layton, Dr. F. Wawrose.

Service and Grounds Workers, 1976-77.
Row 1: E. Putt, S. Miller, M. Rogers, N. Suba, L. Fink.
Row 2: W. Bratton, W. Ross, W. Ebersole, M. Isenberg, G. DeLine, G. Rickeard.
Row 3: E. Parks, R. Jones, D. Rupert, R. Cassatt, J. Hardy, J. Tedeschi.
Row 4: F. Isenberg, L. Shoop, C. Cassatt, L. Dell, H. Long, D. Baker, K. Rabenstein.
Missing: W. Baker, D. Bennett, H. Clark, K. Coons, J. Day, D. Dick, B. Frantz, D. Harker, M. Holland, W. Hood, A. Jenkins, G. Johnston, R. Klippert, M. Lightner, L. Morningstar, A. Nabozny, M. Richards, R. Ross, F. Scott, C. Streightiff, E. Turnbaugh, V. Yablonski, A. Yocum.

Notes

Key to Abbreviations

AB — *Alumni Bulletin*
FM — *Faculty Minutes*
MAM — *Minutes of Annual Meeting*
SM — *Stockholders' Minutes*
TM — *Trustee Minutes*
TTM — *Temporary Trustee Minutes*

CHAPTER 1

1. *MAM* (1853), Art. 28.
2. *Gospel Visitor* (March 1856), p. 76.
3. Ibid. (Sept. 1856), p. 249.
4. Ibid.
5. Ibid. (June 1857), p. 189.
6. *MAM* (1857), Art. 19.
7. *Gospel Visitor* (June 1857), p. 190.
8. Ibid. (April 1857), p. 110.
9. *MAM* (1858), Art. 51.
10. *A History of the Church of the Brethren in the Middle District of Pennsylvania* (Prepared and published by the District Home Mission Board, 1925), p. 497.
11. W. Arthur Cable and Homer F. Sanger, eds., *Educational Blue Book and Directory of the Church of the Brethren, 1708-1923* (Elgin, Ill.: Published by the General Education Board of the Church of the Brethren, 1923), p. 37.
12. *Two Centuries of the Church of the Brethren: Bicentennial Address* (Elgin, Ill.: Brethren Publishing House, 1908), p. 347.

13. For a biographical sketch of Henry Brumbaugh, see Earl C. Kaylor, Jr., *Henry Boyer Brumbaugh: Dunker with a Cause* (Juniata College Keepsake, 1970).
14. *Pilgrim* (March 7, 1871), p. 106.
15. Gaius M. Brumbaugh, *Genealogy of the Brumbaugh Families* (New York: Frederick H. Hitchcock, 1923), p. 524.
16. Ibid., p. 522.
17. Ibid., p. 531; see also the *Juniata Echo* (Jan. 1908), p. 4.
18. *Christian Family Companion* (Nov. 5, 1872), p. 696.
19. *Pilgrim* (Jan. 3, 1873), p. 6.
20. John H. Moore, *Some Brethren Pathfinders* (Elgin, Ill.: Brethren Publishing House, 1929), p. 252.
21. *Pilgrim* (April 1, 1873), p. 103.
22. See also Ibid. (Sept. 1, 1874), p. 276.
23. David Emmert, *Reminiscences of Juniata College* (Harrisburg, Pa.: J. Horace McFarland Co., 1901), p. 115.
24. *Pilgrim* (July 28, 1874), p. 236.
25. Ibid. (Oct. 6, 1874), p. 316.
26. *Gospel Messenger* (May 16, 1908), p. 317.
27. Henry R. Holsinger, *History of the Tunkers and the Brethren Church* (Oakland, Cal.: Pacific Press Publishing Co., 1901), p. 271.
28. This account is taken from a Founder's Day speech by John Brumbaugh, printed in the *Gospel Messenger* (May 16, 1908), pp. 317 f.
29. I have taken the liberty to insert the sentence, "Do it on a small scale," from another account of this conversation supplied by John Brumbaugh and recounted in Solomon Z. Sharp, *The Educational History of the Church of the Brethren* (Elgin, Ill.: Brethren Publishing House, 1923), p. 72.
30. D. L. Miller and Galen B. Royer, *Some Who Led* (Elgin, Ill.: Brethren Publishing House, 1912), p. 195.
31. Brumbaugh, *Genealogy*, p. 531.

CHAPTER 2

1. Henry R. Holsinger, *History of the Tunkers and the Brethren Church* (Oakland, Cal.: Pacific Press Publishing Co., 1901), p. 411.
2. This incident was told by John Brumbaugh in an article, "History of the Life of Prof. Zuck," written for the *Juniata Echo* (April 1896), p. 50.
3. This journal, along with his diary for the same year, is deposited in the Archives of the Beeghly Library.
4. Wayne G. Broehl, Jr., *The Molly Maguires* (Cambridge, Mass.: Harvard University Press, 1964), p. 83.
5. David Emmert, *Reminiscences of Juniata College* (Harrisburg, Pa.: J. Horace McFarland Co., 1901), p. 5.
6. *Gospel Messenger* (May 16, 1908), p. 317.
7. Holsinger, *History of Tunkers,* p. 412, seems to provide the most accurate account (though extremely sketchy) of this period of his life. Much of the extant biographical data on Zuck is erroneous and contradictory. I have tried to reconstruct the main outline of his life by seeking to reconcile this conflicting body of data with material I have turned up.
8. *Christian Family Companion* (Oct. 17, 1873), p. 632.
9. *Pilgrim* (Sept. 8, 1874), p. 282.
10. *Primitive Christian* (July 31, 1877), p. 471. Italics are mine.
11. *Gospel Messenger* (May 16, 1908), p. 317. John Brumbaugh was confused about the year and circumstances of this letter, dating it 1872 and connecting it with the Waynesboro position. They did not know each other unitl 1873, which was after Zuck taught there. I have taken the position that the letter was written in 1875 after Zuck was elected principal at Mt. Pleasant.
12. Undated excerpt in Zuck's scrapbook.

13. Emmert, *Reminiscences*, p. 12.
14. Ibid., pp. 16 f.
15. Quoted in Charles C. Ellis, *Juniata College: The History of Seventy Years, 1876-1946* (Elgin, Ill.: Brethren Publishing House, 1947), pp. 238 f.
16. *Gospel Messenger* (May 16, 1908), p. 318.
17. Ibid.
18. *Pilgrim* (May 23, 1876), p. 321.
19. *Gospel Messenger* (May 16, 1908), p. 318. See also *Juniata Echo* (April 1896), pp. 56 f.
20. *Pilgrim* (Oct. 10, 1876), p. 642.
21. *Primitive Christian* (Nov. 7, 1876), p. 710.
22. The minute book for the society's earliest meetings are deposited in the college Archives.
23. *Primitive Christian* (Feb. 6, 1877), pp. 90 f.

CHAPTER 3
1. *TTM* (Jan. 27, 1877).
2. John Brumbaugh wrote of this incident in the *Juniata Echo* (April 1896), pp. 51 f.
3. *TTM* (Jan. 27, 1877).
4. *Primitive Christian* (May 29, 1877), p. 330.
5. David Emmert, *Reminiscences of Juniata College* (Harrisburg, Pa.: J. Horace McFarland Co., 1901), p. 38.
6. Ibid., pp. 40 f.
7. Ibid., p. 20.
8. *Primitive Christian* (Nov. 20, 1877), p. 719.
9. Emmert, *Reminiscences*, p. 27.
10. *Primitive Christian* (July 31, 1877), p. 471. Italics are mine.
11. Emmert, *Reminiscences*, p. 27.
12. Ibid., p. 28.
13. *Primitive Christian* (May 29, 1877), p. 330.
14. J. Linwood Eisenberg, ed., *A History of the Church of the Brethren in Southern District of Pennsylvania* (Quincy, Pa.: Quincy Orphanage Press, 1941), p. 383.
15. Emmert, *Reminiscences*, p. 43.
16. Ibid., p. 44.
17. Ibid., pp. 45 f.
18. *Gospel Messenger* (May 15, 1908), p. 318. See also Emmert, *Reminiscences,* pp. 96 f.
19. Emmert, *Reminiscences*, p. 48.
20. Ibid.
21. "Story About the Boys at Orphans' Retreat, by One of Them." College Archives.
22. Ibid.
23. Emmert, *Reminiscences,* p. 92.
24. Ibid., p. 130. See also *Primitive Christian* (Feb. 19, 1878).
25. See *Primitive Christian* (April 30, 1878), p. 263, where Zuck writes of having rented a "new brick dwelling-house," which was "well adapted to the purpose and is quite convenient to the school building." Zuck's account book in the Archives identifies the house's owner and its address.
26. Ibid. (May 28, 1878), p. 327.
27. The data on contractors and construction costs were pieced together from trustee minutes and early financial records.
28. *Primitive Christian* (Nov. 19, 1878), p. 736.
29. Ibid. (Jan. 7, 1879), p. 6.
30. Quoted from an undated excerpt in Zuck's scrapbook.
31. Emmert, *Reminiscences*, p. 77.
32. *Juniata Echo* (April 1896), p. 51.
33. Emmert, *Reminiscences*, pp. 73 f.
34. Quoted in Charles C. Ellis, *Juniata College: The History of Seventy Years, 1876-1946* (Elgin, Ill.: Brethren Publishing House, 1947), p. 239.
35. Emmert, *Reminiscences*, p. 80.
36. Not May 10, as Emmert and Ellis say.

37. *Juniata Echo* (July 1911), p. 114.
38. Emmert, *Reminiscences*, p. 88.
39. Ibid., pp. 84 f.
40. Ibid., p. 85.

CHAPTER 4

1. *Primitive Christian* (June 24, 1879), p. 386.
2. See a letter from E. D. Kendig in Ibid. (July 15, 1879), p. 445.
3. David Emmert, *Reminiscences of Juniata College* (Harrisburg, Pa.: J. Horace McFarland Co., 1901), p. 38.
4. *Primitive Christian* (July 22, 1879), p. 457.
5. Mt. Morris College was scheduled to open on August 20. The Illinois Brethren had purchased the defunct plant of the Rock River Seminary, consisting of two buildings and a seven-acre campus.
6. Emmert, *Reminiscences*, p. 120.
7. *Primitive Christian* (July 22, 1897), p. 456.
8. Emmert, *Reminscences*, pp. 122 f.
9. Huntingdon *Daily News* (Nov. 19, 1934).
10. *Juniata Echo* (June 1897), pp. 83 f.
11. Emmert, *Reminiscences*, p. 125.
12. *Golden Dawn* (Dec. 1885), p. 242.
13. She is not listed in the college catalog for 1887 and 1888, but the biographical sketch of her in Gaius M. Brumbaugh, *Genealogy of the Brumbaugh Families* (New York: Frederick Hitchcock, 1923), pp. 614f, states that she taught the fall and spring terms of both those years.
14. Emmert, *Reminiscences*, p. 137.
15. *TM* (March 9, 1880).
16. Ibid. (September 11, 1880).
17. *Advance* (March, 1885), p. 75.
18. Ibid. (Nov. 1884), p. 59.
19. Ibid. (Feb. 1884), p. 32.
20. Circular for 1881, in Jacob Zuck's scrapbook.
21. See *Juniata Echo* (May 1907), pp. 63 f, an article in which Joseph Saylor reminisces about his years as librarian.
22. *Golden Dawn* (Dec. 1885), p. 241
23. *Advance* (March 1884), p. 31.
24. *Golden Dawn* (March 1886), p. 80.
25. *Advance* (May 1884), p. 44.
26. *Golden Dawn* (Nov. 1885), p. 208.
27. See the manuscript biographical sketch of Dr. A. B. Brumbaugh, presumably written by his son, Gaius, in the college Archives.
28. Letter among the *Trustee Minutes.*
29. *Golden Dawn* (Nov. 1885), p. 208.
30. *Advance* (Aug. 1884), p. 54.
31. *TM* (Oct. 13, 1882).
32. Emmert has a very short chapter, "Some Good Work," on the orphanage in his *Reminiscences.*
33. *Golden Dawn* (March 1886), p. 80. See also *Advance* (Aug. 1884), p. 52.
34. See the chapter in Emmert's book, "Beginning Life on the Hill."
35. J. Simpson Africa, *History of Huntingdon and Blair Counties, Pennsylvania* (Philadelphia: J. B. Lippincott & Co., 1883), p. 481.
36. *Golden Dawn* (June 1885), p. 62.
37. *Gospel Messenger* (March 9, 1886), p. 155.
38. *Advance* (March 1885), pp. 72 f. See letter from a stockholder, dated Dec. 14, 1884, and filed with the *Trustee Minutes* for that year.
39. *Golden Dawn* (May 1885), p. 11.
40. Ibid. (May 1887), p. 158.

41. The incomplete manuscript minutes of the early years of the Alumni Association and its original constitution are preserved in the college Archives.
42. This entire episode is reconstructed from several funeral speeches in Mary N. Quinter, *Life and Sermons of Elder James Quinter* (Elgin, Ill.: Brethren Publishing House, 1909).
43. Ibid., p. 55.
44. Ibid., p. 61.

CHAPTER 5

1. *A History of the Church of the Brethren in the Middle District of Pennsylvania* (prepared and published by Home Mission Board, 1925), p. 408.
2. Ibid., p. 407.
3. *TM* (June 16, 1890); (July 16, 1891).
4. Ibid. (June 27, 1890).
5. Charles C. Ellis, *Juniata College: The History of Seventy Years, 1876-1946* (Elgin, Ill.: Brethren Publishing House, 1947), p. 43.
6. *Advance* (Aug. 1890), p. 102.
7. *Juniata Echo* (Nov. 1890), p. 5.
8. Ibid.
9. "Juniata College During the First Decade of the Twentieth Century." Written in October 1967, it is preserved in the college Archives.
10. Anonymous letter dated April 8, 1887, among the papers of Dr. Gaius Brumbaugh in the college museum.
11. *Advance* (Aug. 1884), p. 56.
12. *Juniata Echo* (Aug. 1891), p. 25.
13. See David Emmert, *Reminiscences of Juniata College* (Harrisburg, Pa.: J. Horace McFarland Co., 1901), p. 149. Emmert was gone during this period but he does mention such drills when the gymnasium was moved to Students Hall.
14. *Juniata Echo* (Aug. 1891), p. 27.
15. *TM* (Sept. 11, 1890).
16. Ibid. (March 21, 1892). Court records show he purchased the lots in his name. But I have not been able to trace out how and when the transfer to the college was made.
17. *Juniata Echo* (July 1895), p. 26.
18. *MAM* (1890), Art. 14.
19. Ibid. (1893), Report of School Visiting Elders.
20. *Juniata Echo* (June 1894), p. 3.
21. *MAM* (1897), Report of the Publishing Department.

CHAPTER 6

1. There is need for a thorough and scholarly biographical study of Martin G. Brumbaugh. The only full-length treatment of his life and career is Valentino Anthony Ciampa, "Martin Grove Brumbaugh, Educator" (unpublished Master of Arts thesis, The Pennsylvania State College, 1937). This thesis, however, concentrates on his contributions to the public school system and does little with his governorship, while completely ignoring his two presidential stints at Juniata.
2. *Juniatian* (March 19, 1930).
3. Ciampa, "Martin G. Brumbaugh," p. 27.
4. Henry Brumbaugh Diary.
5. Edward Potts Cheyney, *History of the University of Pennsylvania, 1740-1940* (Philadelphia: University of Pennsylvania Press, 1940), p. 401.
6. *Juniata Echo* (June 1896), p. 94.
7. Ibid. (May 1898), p. 71.
8. Ibid., (Nov. 1897), p. 130.
9. For a look at Brumbaugh's achievements as commissioner see Ciampa, "Martin S. Brumbaugh,", pp. 32-49.
10. Ibid., p. 23.

11. There is a chapter in Ciampa, "Martin G. Brumbaugh," on his superintendency, pp. 50-67. I have drawn heavily upon the data it provides.
12. M. G. Brumbaugh to Trustees of Juniata College, in Brumbaughiania, Beeghly Library Archives.
13. M. G. Brumbaugh to Dr. A. B. Brumbaugh, Ibid.
14. David Emmert, *Reminiscences of Juniata College* (Harrisburg, Pa.: J. Horace McFarland Co., 1901), p. 158.
15. *TM* (June 26, 1899).
16. *Juniata Echo* (June 1894), p. 5.
17. Ibid. (May 1900), p. 75.
18. Huntingdon *Semi-Weekly News* (Sept. 11, 1902).
19. Ibid.
20. This ruling was made in 1881, but the trustees took no immediate action because the college had just been chartered in 1878. See *MAM* (1881), Art. 26.
21. *Gospel Messenger* (April 10, 1894), p. 225.
22. *Juniata Echo* (July 1896), p. 111.
23. *TM* (Feb. 12, 1901).
24. *SM* (FEb. 1, 1904).
25. *TM* (Feb. 2, 1906).
26. Martin G. Brumbaugh to I. Harvey Brumbaugh, Feb. 1, 1907, a letter in the Archives of Beeghly Library.
27. There are several letters in the Archives between college officials and George Henderson, the Philadelphia attorney who gave legal counsel in calling the stock, dealing with this matter. On the matter of paying off the family, see George Henderson to I. Harvey Brumbaugh, July 24, 1908.
28. I Harvey Brumbaugh to Martin G. Brumbaugh, May 17, 1907, in the Archives of Beeghly Library.
29. A typewritten copy of these bylaws are in the Archives of Beeghly Library.
30. *Gospel Messenger* (Feb. 15, 1908), p. 100.
31. *Juniata Echo* (July 1907), p. 112.
32. Ibid. (Dec. 1900), p. 164.
33. Ibid (Jan. 1901), p. 15.
34. Ibid. (Nov. 1900), p. 148.
35. Ibid. (Feb. 1905), p. 25.
36. *TM* (Jan. 17, 1910).
37. Annual Meeting declared: "We also declare distinctly that our loyal and faithful brotherhood should neither fellowship, countenance nor tolerate those who should undertake to establish, under any pretence or color whatever, theological schools, or theological departments of schools or colleges, having in contemplation or purpose the training or graduation of any youth specially for the ministry of the Brotherhood or elsewhere. . . ." *MAM* (1882), Art. 10.
38. W. Arthur Cable and Homer F. Sanger, eds., *Educational Blue Book and Directory of the Church of the Brethren, 1708-1923* (Elgin, Ill.: Published by the General Education Board of the Church of the Brethren, 1923), p. 227.
39. Ibid., pp. 317 f.
40. *AB* (Oct. 1906), p. 3.
41. *TM* (Nov. 15, 1904).
42. Ibid. (March 6, 1905).
43. *Juniata Echo* (Jan. 1899), p. 2.
44. *AB* (Oct. 1909), p. 2; also *TM* (July 9, 1908).
45. *TM* (Nov. 25, 1902).
46. *Juniata Echo* (May 1905), p. 80.
47. Ibid., (Nov. 1894), pp. 10 f.
48. Ibid., pp. 12 f.
49. Henry Brumbaugh Diary.
50. Emmert, *Reminiscences*, p. 106.
51. *Juniata Echo* (April 1898), p. 59.

52. Ibid. (March 1901), p. 50.
53. Emmert, *Reminiscences*, p. 150.
54. *Juniata Echo* (Jan. 1897), p. 9. The student prank involved in getting the stone from Mrs. Summers is found in the March issue, pp. 44 f. M. G.'s letter of request to her is among the college's Brumbaughiania.
55. Cassel also sold portions of his library to Mt. Morris College and the Pennsylvania Historical Association. When Mt. Morris merged with Manchester College in 1932, most of its Cassel books went to Bethany Theological Seminary. For a biographical sketch of Cassel, in manuscript, see Donald Durnbaugh, "The Great Antiquarian: Abraham Cassel and His Collection at Juniata College." It is in the Archives.
56. These letters are among the Brumbaughiania in the college Archives.
57. *Juniata Echo* (April 1900), p. 60.
58. See the article on "The Library of Juniata College," Ibid. (Oct. 1904), pp. 114-17.
59. *TM* (March 22, 1905). President M. G. had received Carnegie's affirmative answer on March 12.
60. A copy of this cablegram is among Brumbaugh's papers in the Archives.
61. *TM* (July 9, 1908).
62. *Juniata Echo* (May 1909), p. 81.
63. Ibid. (July 1907), p. 114.
64. *Juniatian* (Sept. 26, 1929).
65. His college-days diary was found among old papers in the college Archives.

CHAPTER 7

1. In 1903 the college urged parents to prosecute the Washington House proprietor for illegal liquor sales and even inquired into initiating action itself.
2. Huntingdon *Semi-Weekly News* (Sept. 17, 1908).
3. *Juniata Echo* (June 1896), p. 93.
4. Ibid. (Nov. 1902), p. 137.
5. The manuscript minutes of this organization from 1893-1911 are in the college Archives.
6. The Volunteer Board was only unofficially connected with SVM. Then, between 1906 and 1911 for some reason, the Board was defunct. Revived the later year, it affiliated officially with SVM in 1916.
7. At first it was simply called Mission Band but its name was changed the next November. Its manuscript minutes to Feb. 28, 1900 are in the college Archives.
8. Quoted in Winthrop S. Hudson, *Religion in America* (New York: Charles Scribner's Sons, 1965), p. 322.
9. *SM* (Feb. 19, 1900).
10. This portion of the vow is taken from the first minutes of the Girl's Christian Band, which presumably was modeled after the Boys'. These manuscript minutes are in the college Archives.
11. This petition is in the college Archives.
12. See *Juniata Echo* (Oct. 1900), p. 127. The constitution of the JAA, in manuscript, is in the college Archives, as are its minutes for 1908-10.
13. The Lyceum's early minutes are in the college Archives.
14. See the manuscript account of these debates in the Archives as part of the Lyceum records.
15. A copy is in the Archives.
16. This pamphlet is in the library vault. Some of Dassdorf's later correspondence with Cassel is in the college Archives.
17. *Juniata Echo* (April 1905), pp. 62 f.
18. Letter dated Dec. 12, 1906, Brumbaughiania, college Archives.

CHAPTER 8

1. *Juniata Echo* (Oct. 1911), p. 119.
2. *TM* (June 14, 1917).

3. Charles C. Ellis, *Juniata College: The History of Seventy Years, 1876-1946* (Elgin, Ill.: Brethren Publishing House, 1947), p. 192.
4. *Juniata Echo* (Jan. 1913), p. 11.
5. Ibid. (June 1921), p. 128.
6. This letter is filed with the *Trustee Minutes* in the vault.
7. *TM* (April 15, 1918).
8. Ibid. (Nov. 13, 1918).
9. Ibid. (Dec. 4, 1922).
10. *Juniata Echo* (July 1911), pp. 103 f.
11. This treatment of Holsopple was told the author by his daughter, Mrs. Naomi Adams, in a telephone conversation, June 6, 1975.
12. *TM* (April 25, 1924).
13. Ibid., (Jan. 13, 1916).
14. *Juniata Echo* (May 1912), p. 71.
15. *TM* (Feb. 8, 1922).
16. *Juniata Echo* (June 1922), pp. 116 f.
17. Ibid. (Oct. 1923), p. 152.
18. See a summary statement on this subject in Herbert Hogan, "Fundamentalism in the Church of the Brethren, 1900-1931," *Brethren Life and Thought,* 5: (Winter 1960), 32.
19. *Gospel Messenger* (March 25, 1922), p. 180.
20. Ibid. (Sept. 11, 1920), p. 542.
21. *TM* (April 17, 1919).
22. Letter dated August 7, 1919, in the college Archives.
23. *AB* (Oct. 1916), p. 4.
24. *Juniata Echo* (April 1919), p. 62. The college Archives has the minutes of the Council from Dec. 7, 1921 to May 3, 1922.
25. For a brief period in the fall of 1913 Earl Speicher, a Somerset County senior, was editor-in-chief of the *Echo*, but Alphaeus Dupler took over in January 1914.
26. *Juniata Echo* (Jan. 1920), p. 73.
27. Ibid. (Aug. 1922), p. 145.
28. W. Arthur Cable and Homer F. Sanger, eds., *Educational Blue Book and Directory of the Church of the Brethren, 1708-1923* (Elgin, Ill.: Published by the General Education Board of the Church of the Brethren, 1923), p. 622.
29. See *TM* (April 26, 1920); (April 17, 1922).

CHAPTER 9
1. Jennie Newcomer to *MGB* (undated letter), Brumbaughiania, college Archives.
2. Frank Foster to *MGB* (May 26, 1924), Brumbaughiania.
3. C. C. Ellis to *MGB* (May 22, 1924), Brumbaughiania.
4. See the manuscript biographical sketch by Harold B. Statler, Brumbaughiania.
5. See the basic work, Wayland F. Dunaway, *A History of Pennsylvania* (New York: Prentice-Hall, Inc., 1935), p. 577. Also Robert Fortenbaugh and H. James Tarman, *Pennsylvania: The Story of a Commonwealth* (Harrisburg, Pa.: The Pennsylvania Book Service Publishers, 1940), pp. 314, 315.
6. J. T. Salter, *The People's Choice* (New York: The Exposition Press, 1971), pp. 27-28. See also William S. Vare, *My Forty Years in Politics* (Philadelphia: Roland Swain Co., 1933), pp. 63-64, 125-26.
7. Salter, *People's Choice*, p. 28.
8. Ibid., p. 29.
9. Statler, "M. G. Brumbaugh," p. 20.
10. *Lancaster Daily New Era* (March 2, 1914).
11. *Philadelphia Inquirer* (Oct. 3, 1914).
12. *Lancaster Daily New Era* (March 15, 1914).
13. Fortenbaugh and Tarman, *Story of a Commonwealth*, p. 315.
14. Letter from Hiram W. Johnson to *MGB* (April 14, 1917), Brumbaughiania.
15. *Juniatian* (Feb. 3, 1925.).

16. *MGB* to J. S. Noffsinger (April 3, 1929), Brumbaughiania.
17. From a manuscript titled "M.G. Wants Me for a Sunbeam."
18. William Faust to *MGB* (April 21, 1928), Brumbaughiania.
19. *Juniatian* (Dec. 13, 1928).
20. Ibid. (Jan. 12, 1928), p. 1.
21. *Juniata Echo* (Oct. 1910), p. 122.
22. *TM* (Oct. 24, 1925).
23. Among N. J.'s papers, preserved in the museum.
24. *Juniatian* (March 12, 1930).
25. *AB* (Oct. 1925), p. 4.
26. Ibid. (Oct. 1927), p. 4.
27. *TM* (Dec. 2, 1924).
28. *Juniatian* (April 21, 1927).
29. See Claude Flory's "M. G. Wants Me for a Sunbeam."

CHAPTER 10
1. Letter to the Board of Trustees, dated April 17, 1930, among Dr. Ellis's papers.
2. *AB* (Oct. 1931), p. 2.
3. In a paper read to the faculty, Sept. 1946.
4. *AB* (Feb. 1931), p. 6.
5. In a paper read to the faculty, Sept. 1946.
6. Quoted by Dean Clyde Stayer in an undated mimeographed script of a mock radio program honoring Dr. Ellis.
7. *Sunday School Times* (July 15, 1950), p. 601.
8. Charles C. Ellis, *Juniata College: The History of Seventy Years, 1976-1946* (Elgin, Ill.: Brethren Publishing House, 1947), p. 198.
9. *Juniatian* (Dec. 4, 1940).
10. Ellis, *Juniata College*, p. 196.
11. Robert Kelly, *A Survey of the Colleges of the Church of the Brethren* (Association of American Colleges, 1933), p. 14.
12. Ibid., p. 23.
13. *AB* (Oct. 1938), p. 2.
14. Ibid. (Oct. 1939), p. 3.
15. *TM* (April 17, 1930).
16. *Juniatian* (April 11, 1934).
17. *AB* (Oct. 1939), p. 3. President's Report.
18. *Juniatian* (Feb. 5, 1941).
19. *TM* (Oct. 20, 1938).

CHAPTER 11
1. *The Pennsylvania Manual, 1935-36* (Harrisburg: Bureau of Publications, 1936), pp. 196f.
2. *TM* (Oct. 15, 1942).
3. Ibid. (Nov. 6, 1929).
4. *AB* (Fall 1943), p. 5.
5. Ibid.

CHAPTER 12
1. *AB* (Spring 1968), p. 4.
2. Ibid.
3. Ibid., p. 2.
4. Ibid., p. 11.
5. *AB* (Spring 1963), p. 7.
6. Huntingdon *Daily News* (Oct. 25, 1943).
7. *AB* (Spring 1963), p. 7.

8. Ibid. (Fall 1962), p. 8.
9. Report of the President to the Board of Trustees, June 7, 1954.
10. *FM* (Oct. 9, 1950); *TM* (Oct. 20, 1950; April 16, 1951).
11. Treasurer's Report to the Board of Trustees, June 4, 1956.
12. *TM* (Sept. 8, 1967).
13. Ibid. (March 2, 1968).
14. Ibid. (April 21, 1958).
15. *AB* (Spring 1949), p. 3.
16. Ibid. (Summer 1953), p. 3.
17. Ibid. (Fall 1957), p. 10.
18. *Juniatian* (Sept. 17, 1966).
19. Report of the team which visited the campus, Feb. 25-28, 1962.
20. *AB* (Spring 1961), p. 9; *Juniatian* (Jan. 10, 1961).
21. *Juniatian* (April 7, 1967).
22. Taped personal interview with Calvert Ellis.
23. *TM* (May 15, 1965).
24. *AB* (Winter 1951), p. 10.
25. Ibid. (Spring 1944), p. 10.
26. Calvert N. Ellis, *Ten Years as President*. A pamphlet in the Archives.
27. John Baker to Calvert Ellis, Jan. 4, 1952. Presidential papers.
28. *AB* (Spring 1968), p. 1.
29. Built by John Cassady in 1921, the house was later sold to the Orphans' Home after the Cloister was erected. Later it was purchased by Francis McSherry, five of whose children either graduated from or attended Juniata.
30. Huntingdon *Daily News* (March 8, 1976). Obituary of Philip Snider.
31. Interview with Calvert N. Ellis, June 16, 1976.
32. *TM* (June 3, 1957).
33. *Juniatian* (Nov. 4, 1966).
34. *AB* (Summer 1968), p. 8.

CHAPTER 13

1. *TM* (Oct. 21, 1944).
2. *AB* (Fall 1946), p. 3.
3. Ibid., (Fall 1945), p. 5.
4. *Juniatian* (Oct. 10, 1945).
5. Calvert Ellis to John Baker, March 26, 1946. Presidential Papers.
6. *Juniatian* (Nov. 7, 1945).
7. *TM* (Oct. 25, 1946).
8. The Yoder papers are deposited in the L. A. Beeghly Library.
9. Janet Howell Clark to Calvert N. Ellis, June 19, 1945. Presidential Papers.
10. *Juniatian* (April 1, 1955).
11. *AB* (Fall 1950), p. 9.
12. *Juniatian* (March 2, 1953).
13. Ibid. (April 29, 1955; March 2, 1956).
14. *AB* (Spring 1956) p. 6.
15. Ibid. (Fall 1956), p. 2.
16. *Juniatian* (Nov. 9, 1956).
17. Ibid. (Oct. 12, 1956).
18. *AB* (Summer 1957) p. 13.
19. *Juniatian* (Nov. 1, 1957).
20. *TM* (Aug. 15, 1958).
21. Ibid., (May 12, 1967), Dean of Student Affairs Report.
22. Ibid.
23. *Juniatian* (May 11, 1962).
24. The trustees bought the house from the I. Harvey Brumbaugh daughters, whose mother had lived there after selling her corner residence.
25. *AB* (Winter 1964), p. 11.

26. *Juniatian* (March 19, 1965).
27. Ibid. (April 23, 1965).
28. Ibid. (Feb. 18, 1966).
29. Ibid. (March 8, 1967).
30. Ibid. (May 3, 1968).

CHAPTER 14
1. *AB* (Feb. 1968).
2. *Juniatian* (Oct. 13, 1967).
3. *AB* (March 1968).
4. Ibid.
5. Ibid.
6. *AB* (Fall 1969), p. 5.
7. Ibid. (Feb. 1972), p. 2.
8. Ibid. (Dec. 1975), p. 37.
9. *FM* (Oct. 1968).
10. *AB* (Dec. 1975), p. 35.
11. *Juniatian* (Nov. 1, 1972).
12. *The Chronicle of Higher Education* (Feb. 9, 1976), p. 3.
13. *AB* (Fall 1969), p. 2.
14. *Renaissance* (Dec. 15, 1970).
15. *Juniatian* (April 25, 1969).
16. Ibid. (Oct. 13, 1971).
17. *AB* (Sept. 1975), p. 6.
18. Ibid., p. 1.
19. Quoted in the centennial year commencement program.

Index of Personal Names

Alumnae are listed by their maiden names, followed, where known by their married names in parentheses.